China Hand

China Hand

An Autobiography

John Paton Davies, Jr.

PENN

UNIVERSITY OF PENNSYLVANIA PRESS

PHILADELPHIA

A volume in the Haney Foundation Series, established in 1961 with the generous support of Dr. John Louis Haney.

Published by
University of Pennsylvania Press
Philadelphia, Pennsylvania 19104-4112

Printed in the United States of America on acid-free paper
10 9 8 7 6 5 4 3 2 1

Library of Congress Cataloging-in-Publication Data
Davies, John Paton, 1908–1999.
    China Hand, an autobiography / John Paton Davies, Jr. — 1st ed.
        p.   cm.
    Includes bibliographical references and index.
    ISBN 978-0-8122-4401-4 (hardcover : alk. paper)
    1. Davies, John Paton, 1908–1999.   2. Diplomats—United
States—Biography.   3. Diplomatic and consular service, American—
China.   4. United States—Foreign relations—China.   5. China—Foreign
relations—United States.   6. China—History—20th century.   I. Title.
E748.D214A3   2012
327.2092¡dc23   2011033181
[B]

CONTENTS

I never had the good fortune to meet John Paton Davies, Jr. But I made his inspiring acquaintance, all the same, in the summer of 1979, thanks to a pair of remarkable books. The first was Eric Sevareid's then recently reissued 1946 memoir, *Not So Wild a Dream*, which recounted the harrowing story of his and Davies's forced bail-out from a crippled American transport plane into the welcoming arms of a jungle tribe of headhunters along the Burma-India border in World War II. And the second was *The China Hands: America's Foreign Service Officers and What Befell Them*, a gripping account by E. J. Kahn, Jr., a veteran staff writer for the *New Yorker*, of the perverse way Davies and his diplomatic colleagues in China in the 1940s were punished for being right: by predicting the eventual victory of Mao Zedong's Communists over Chiang Kai-shek's tired and corrupt Nationalist regime.

I thought, then, as an undergraduate, that Davies's story was a boy's adventure come-to-life—especially if the boy in question happened to be a sensitive soul from a solid family, a straight-arrow good student, a keen observer of human nature, and a very good writer. I think all that, still (and Steven Spielberg and George Lucas would do well to take note of the tale that unfolds in the following pages). What I now also know—after a close reading of this elegant, if tantalizingly reticent and incomplete memoir—is that Davies was one of the indispensable Americans of the "Greatest Generation," and his story is all the more compelling because he was largely (though not entirely) deprived of adequate public recognition in his long, rich lifetime.

His memoir is a whirlwind, globe-girdling "Who's Who" of the middle fifty years of the twentieth century. He was born to American Baptist missionary parents in Szechuan, China, in the last months of Theodore Roosevelt's presidency, and he died in Asheville, North Carolina, in the aftermath of Bill Clinton's acquittal on impeachment charges. In between, he worked with, tangled with, or merely brushed up against, a dizzying array of the most fascinating figures of his time. He was educated at the University of Wisconsin, at Yenching University near Beijing, and, finally, at Columbia University in New York, where, if he had been slightly more athletic (or more interested in beetles), he might well have become personal tutor to the teenage David Rockefeller. Instead, he took a job as a dishwasher and decided to apply for the Foreign Service.

In his first postings, in China, in the early 1930s, he experienced the sleepy, seat-of-the-pants diplomacy that prevailed in the age before the American Imperium, then witnessed the steadily gathering storm of World War II, from the Japanese invasion of Manchuria on through Pearl Harbor and his service as special diplomatic attaché to General Joseph W. Stilwell, commander of the Allied China-Burma-India theater, and frustrated chief of staff to Generalissimo Chiang Kai-shek. From this perch, Davies met, and took the measure of, legendary figures, from Gandhi to Nehru, Franklin D. Roosevelt, General George C. Marshall, Wendell Willkie, Lord Mountbatten—even Noel Coward and Frank Capra. At the height of World War II, Davies learned, from no less an authoritative source than the American spymaster William "Wild Bill" Donovan himself, the shocking news that FBI Director J. Edgar Hoover was gay. When Davies's plane crashed over the jungle as he was bound from India for China in 1943, he was carrying a rare bottle of cognac and some special brown ink as a gift for Madame Sun-Yat-sen, widow of the father of Nationalist China. Later, on the staff of Ambassador W. Averell Harriman at the American Embassy in Moscow, he would have cause to observe Joseph Stalin at close range. George F. Kennan, the titan of postwar American diplomacy, was Davies's close colleague and friend, and besides Sevareid he numbered among his journalist friends the giants of the age, including Theodore H. White and David Halberstam, who wrote at length about Davies's contributions and ordeal in *The Best and the Brightest*.

That was the kind of A-list life Davies led. But in this memoir, drawn heavily from his voluminous personal letters and journals, as well as from the formal "white papers" and reports he prepared for his State Department and military superiors, he is never the hero of his own life, however heroic

his deeds sometimes are. Rather, he is the perpetually detached, wry, knowing observer, with an elegant turn of phrase or a touch of whimsy seemingly
always at his fingertips. On a hair-raising ride in the engineer's cab of an
Indian mail train, he marvels that the front of the engine "wasn't plastered
with sirloins and spareribs," so prevalent were wandering sacred cows along
the track. He decides that "dignified friendliness" is the only proper approach
to the Naga headhunters who welcome his and Sevareid's party. He sums up
Chiang Kai-shek as an "aloofly gracious soldier-statesman-Methodist-sage of
the East." He writes, discreetly, but with unbounded love, of the "matchless
young woman," Patricia Grady, with whom he would make a happy marriage of fifty-seven years, and raise seven children.

Again and again, Davies's judgments in these pages are uncannily prescient. He foresaw the difficulties for the Allied war effort of Britain's linger-
ing imperialist posture. He understood, as he put it at one point before the
end of the war, that "the Communists are in China to stay, and China's
destiny is not Chiang's, but theirs." He realized, as early as 1943, assessing
the volatile prospects for postwar international relations, "that we can now
be assured of further war and revolution in our time," thereby envisioning
what John F. Kennedy would later call "the long, twilight struggle" of the
Cold War.

It was the great tragedy of Davies's life—and the searing cautionary
crux of this book—that in the most parlous of those times, John Paton
Davies's country was deprived of his services, not because he was ever determined to be disloyal, but because after nine successive internal security
reviews prompted by the McCarthy-era hysteria that swept the country
beginning in 1950, a State Department Loyalty Security Board at last concluded that he lacked "judgment, discretion and reliability," the very three
characteristics he possessed in full measure. What he really lacked, of
course, was timorous conformity with the prevailing demands of domestic
American politics in an age of fear. He was informed of this indictment in
November 1954 by Secretary of State John Foster Dulles, who promptly
undermined the credibility of the findings by offering to provide a character
reference should Davies ever need one. It is the bitterest of ironies that
Davies's dismissal came less than a month before the downfall and censure
by his Senate peers of Joseph McCarthy himself, and just six months after
the defeat of French colonial forces at Dien Bien Phu—thus robbing the
State Department of one of its most distinguished Asia experts in the very

years when his presence might have mattered most to the wise conduct of foreign policy in Vietnam.

Davies writes tersely of these developments in this manuscript, which he began in Spain in 1972 and labored over reluctantly for more than twenty years before putting it aside, still unfinished. Though he had published two other books in his post-Foreign Service years—*Foreign and Other Affairs* in 1964, a collection of essays, and, in 1972, *Dragon by the Tail,* a history of Chinese-American relations in the 1930s and 1940s—he put off telling his own story. "As he got closer and closer to the unpleasantness," his daughter Tiki told me, "he slowed down and slowed down and slowed down." How lucky for us that he did not stop completely. Our own moment in history is different from Davies's, but similarly tumultuous. We hear the mayor of New York declare that among some members of Congress, "nobody knows what China is," and the Senate Republican leader seems determined to prove him right, when asked for his view of U.S. policy toward China, by replying, "I don't really have any observation about that." In such times, Davies's gentle but bracing erudition—on China and so many other subjects—arrives as a tonic.

Like so many great figures under-appreciated in their own times, Davies came to grief at the hands of smaller men than he. But he lived long enough to see his views vindicated and his reputation restored, and long enough, too, to hear his old friend Sevareid, that most unsentimental of Norsemen, declare that while he had "known a great number of men," he had never known one "who seemed more the whole man . . . in all that a man should be, in modesty and thoughtfulness, in resourcefulness and steady strength of character" than Davies. What a gift that a new generation can now come to know this rare man all over again, here, in his own words.

PART I

LEAVING AND RETURNING

CHAPTER I

THE FIRING

At 2:30 p.m. on November 5, 1954, I walked into the lofty office of the Secretary of State and there, waiting for me, stood John Foster Dulles. Alongside the tall, stooped Secretary was Herman Phleger, his Legal Adviser.

The last time I had seen Dulles was in Moscow. As a gesture of bipartisanship, the Truman administration had included him as a Republican in the American delegation to the 1947 Foreign Ministers' conference there. I was then a First Secretary of the American Embassy. He dined affably with my wife and me, she took him shopping for souvenirs, and he had us to dinner at one of Moscow's less awful restaurants. Now he was presiding over the Department of State in the administration of Dwight D. Eisenhower.

On orders from the Department, I had arrived in Washington on November 3 from Lima, Peru, where I was Deputy Chief of Mission at the American Embassy. The change was not simply hemispheric, nor from spring to autumn, nor from one culture to another. It was also from an atmosphere of placidity to one of anxiety, rancid with suspicion.

What I sensed was not a new development. The American people's post-World War II disillusionments and their fears of the Russians, the Chinese, the bomb, and an eerie new phenomenon in American life—Communist subversion—had been inflated and exploited by a relatively few politicians, publicists and military men for nearly nine years. In the late 1940s the party out of power—the Republican—discovered that accusing the Democrats of losing China and tolerating a Communist conspiracy in the government was their best chance of winning public support and taking over the government.

The demagogues and political vigilantes directed their assault primarily at the State Department, and most viciously against some of those Foreign Service officers who were China specialists and had dealt with Chinese Communists. These diplomats, of whom I was one, were made out to be part of a ramified plot that had delivered China to Communism. Senator Joseph McCarthy went so far as to accuse the then Secretary of State Dean Acheson and General George C. Marshall of heading this conspiracy.

The demagoguery had its effect on a befuddled public and contributed to the election of Eisenhower and Richard M. Nixon to "clean up the mess in Washington." This included widening the criteria for firing civil servants from reasonable doubt of loyalty or security or anything tending to indicate that a man was not reliable, a remarkably pliant measure of character. A man pronounced as deficient in reliability was categorized, not as disloyal, but with the scarcely less sinister designation of "security risk." My colleague John Carter Vincent had been forced into disgraced retirement by Dulles on the grounds that Vincent's professional performance had not been up to an undefined standard—notwithstanding the contrary judgment of preceding Secretaries of State.

The coming to power of the Republicans and the broadening of the purge did not placate all of the agitators. For example, McCarthy on November 24, 1953 declared that in my case the Eisenhower administration's "batting average is zero," "struck out," for I was still on the government rolls. The White House staff regarded this as an attack on the President, but the beloved and mighty Ike remained mute. So did Dulles, who, for a man of prominent principles, was less than dauntless in his relations with the political vigilantes.

In June 1954, I was summoned from Lima to the Department to appear at a hearing before a specially selected Loyalty Security Board. This was the ninth formal scrutiny of my loyalty and security; the first was in 1949. In July I returned to Lima, where I awaited word of the Board's findings. Then in October, with no word from the Board, I received orders to proceed to Washington.

Meanwhile, the time was approaching for the selection of those Foreign Service officers to be promoted. The efficiency reports on me were such that I was qualified for promotion to chief of mission. So when I arrived in

Washington on November 3, I did not know whether I would be fired or asked which vacant Embassy I would like to preside over.

As I approached Dulles and Phleger on that afternoon in 1954, I observed that they were solemn, almost mournful of countenance. It was as if I were being met by two ushers waiting to conduct the bereaved to his pew. Their stance, however, suggested something less accommodating. They had planted themselves only a short distance inside the office and it immediately became evident that while I might receive condolences, I was not going to be invited to proceed further and sit down.

Dulles and Phleger began by invoking their acquaintance with and esteem for my parents-in-law, Henry and Lucretia Grady. The Secretary added that he also knew and held in high regard my cousin, Richard L. Davies, a fellow Presbyterian layman. Having established a rapport of sorts, Dulles turned to the matter at hand. It was a hard thing for him to do, he said, but he had to do it. The Loyalty Security Board had concluded that I was not a Communist or otherwise disloyal, but that I was lacking in judgment, discretion, and reliability. I must therefore be, in government genteelism, "separated" from the Service, i.e., fired.

Obviously, this was neither the time nor the place to argue subjective appraisals of intangible qualities in my personality, but I did want clarification on two points. I asked if my indiscretion, as Dulles had put it, referred to the period of my service in China. Yes. Any indiscretions later? He said that he could not think of any. Did he agree with the Board's finding, I asked Dulles. Without ring of conviction he said yes.

Well, that was that. So I bade the two men goodbye and went directly to the Department's press room. There newsmen were milling about querying Lincoln White, the Department's spokesman, about a release he had just handed them announcing my dismissal. The correspondents, with some of whom I was acquainted, clamored to know what I had to say. From my pocket I drew several copies of a statement and passed them out. Having thus distracted attention from myself, I walked briskly out of the building.

My statement read:

Naturally, I cannot say that I am happy about the Secretary's decision. Nor can I say that I feel that there are adequate grounds for such a judgment. But the Secretary of State has more important problems on his hands than the reputation and future of one civil servant.

As a professional diplomat of some 33 years' standing, I am perhaps more aware than most of the magnitude of his problems. And with this awareness comes a determination not to add to them.

There has been enough recrimination. I am not prepared to add to it and thereby detract from the strength of my country and its mortal struggle with the Communist enemy.

So I shall not contest the Secretary's decision or seek to compare my record with those of others. I must be content to let history be my judge. And to that end I have informed the Secretary that I would, personally, welcome the release to the public of the whole record of my case, including my 1950 recommendation that we seek a preventive showdown with the Soviet Union.

I can hope that my departure from its ranks will add to the American people's confidence in their Foreign Service, which has been so unjustly undermined. If this is the practical result of my separation, I can have no real regrets over what is for me, personally, a melancholy outcome.

I had prepared this statement in Lima, with the help of my wife, Patricia, to have ready should the decision go against me. It was clear that I would have to yield to an adverse decision by the Secretary, as his ruling was final and there was no feasible way to fight it. Furthermore, I was confident that when the aberrations then seizing the country had passed, I would be vindicated.

My wife and I had also discussed what I should do were I to be given the choice of resigning rather than being fired. Resignation would have meant less public and categoric disgrace, and less dismal prospects of getting a job. But I decided against resigning. The issues should not be fuzzed and evaded. If Dulles and company wanted to be rid of me, it was for them to act and give their reasons. I should not, in a vain and desperate effort to escape disgrace, flee through the back door of resignation, thus giving Dulles what he wanted—riddance of me—without having to take responsibility for my departure.

It was not until a few hours before Dulles fired me that I knew what the decision would be. Robert Murphy, Deputy Under Secretary of State, and the senior career officer in the Department, had asked me to come to his office. He was a careful, conciliatory and warm-hearted man who had been Eisenhower's Political Adviser in World War II. Murphy had tears in his eyes as he told me that the Board's decision was negative, and was upheld by the Secretary.

"Bob, who was not informed until last evening," I wrote Patricia in Lima,

said that I had the opportunity to resign if I wished. I said I preferred to face the music. So there we are. I am now waiting to be called, possibly by the Secretary—if he wishes to talk to me. And of course there will be the press boys. I am quite calm and shall endeavor to continue so. You will read about it in the papers.

Now what we do. You sit tight. And I shall take this business step by step, day by day until the hullabaloo dies down. Then I'll think about job hunting. One thing at a time.

Keep your chin up, darling. I know how hard this is for you. But we're beginning a new and, I trust, happier and freer life. That is the side I look on.

CHAPTER II

FROM CHINA TO AMERICA

Caleb Davies came to the United States from Wales, at the age of 23, in the 1870s. He was a merchant clerk intent on improving his lot in life, which he proceeded to do. Through diligence and frugality he became a shopkeeper— drygoods—in Chicago, until burned out by The Fire. Thereupon he moved to Cleveland, began over again, and married Rebecca French, a devout and sober Quakeress. The rugged little Welshman and the lean, gentle Ohioan, conscious of her 1776 ancestral connections, were bonded together by three consuming interests: "the store" which was their livelihood, their religious beliefs and practices, and their family, eventually embracing five children. The middle of these was John Paton Davies, my father.

Caleb and Rebecca brought up their children in fear-and-love of God, with prayers and scripture readings at the beginning and end of each day. Although Rebecca had joined her husband's fundamentalist church, the Disciples of Christ, she retained Quaker characteristics. She addressed me as thee. But more, she listened for the still small voice and waited for the spirit to move her. No temporal power had for her an authority equal to that of her conscience: and the same was true of Caleb.

By 1920 Caleb Davies was well established as a prosperous and respected merchant. Six years later, writing to congratulate me on graduating from high school, he said, "I am moved as I note a clan bearing my father's good name. I am filled with gratitude and humility for the satisfying way his grandchildren wear it and observing that the great grandchildren thus far give every assurance of keeping the Davies name unsullied . . . The goal worth striving for is just simple goodness without the remotest personal reference. To say of one 'He is a good man' or 'She is a good woman' is the greatest and best that can be said of any person . . . I wish you much happiness and many friends selected with not too great haste."

These two positive personalities, Caleb and Rebecca, were a dominant, loving force in the lives of their children. My father was particularly receptive to the Bible study and worship in which he was nurtured. So it was not surprising that, after finishing Oberlin College, he went on to the theological seminary and to a Bible institute in New York. His calling was made clear to him. It was, quite simply, to go overseas where there was the greatest concentration of heathen and save their souls.

In New York, he met Helen MacNeill, a comely, mettlesome young woman from Manitoba. She had left the farm on the Canadian prairies, near Treherne, where her father, Ephraim, toiled against the elements for barely enough to sustain his family. Possessed by an ambition to become an opera star, she traveled by day coach to New York. But her naturally full and vibrant mezzo-soprano was scarcely trained. Postponing, therefore, her debut at the Met, she obtained engagements as a soloist in church choirs. Then, in touring Georgia as one of a revival troupe and released from the formality of conventional church music, she discovered that her singing of gospel hymns could rouse sinners to repent and give themselves to the Lord. She herself underwent what she later described as a religious experience in which she emerged from shallow faith to find Christ.

John Davies, the idealistic yet matter-of-fact young preacher, committed above all else to his evangelical mission, married this emotional, aspiring frontierswoman. The American Baptists sent them as missionaries to China. In 1906 they crossed the Pacific by steamship and then proceeded up the Yangtze, halfway by river steamer, the remainder on a series of junks towed by trackers. It was some 1700 miles from Shanghai to Kiating, their destination, and the journey took about two months. Upon arrival, both of the young missionaries plunged into studying the Chinese language. John also began long hours of church work, guided by a colleague who had been in Kiating several years. John felt fulfilled, for this was what he had dedicated himself to do. Helen was miserable. She found the poverty, filth and disease of this essentially medieval town loathsome; and she felt neglected by her husband.

Two years after their arrival in China I was born. And then a year later my mother was stricken with typhoid, from which she nearly died. In 1911 she bore my brother, Donald. Five days after his birth we boarded a house-boat to flee the revolution that overthrew imperial rule and resulted in the creation of a nominal republic in China.

After a year in the United States, we returned to China and moved to the provincial capital, Chengtu. There my father was in charge of the Baptist evangelical and educational work. We lived some distance from other missionaries, and as travel by sedan chair was slow, we tended to spend most of our time at home among ourselves and with Chinese. Our occasional contacts with other foreigners were for the most part with Canadians, for the Canadian Methodist mission was much the biggest Protestant group in Chengtu. Playing with the Canadian children heightened my nascent nationalism, growing out of a natural feeling of separateness from the Chinese. The small Canadians and I traded puerile boasts over whose country was bigger and better. Being greatly outnumbered, I worked harder than they at these undiplomatic exchanges and became quite a chauvinist.

We also got together at times with an American family. Robert Service was in charge of YMCA activities, and his son, Jack, was my contemporary and good friend. My parents regarded YMCA people as a little "worldly." They were not, of course, "wicked" like Catholic missionaries, especially the nuns in a nearby convent, who were not only Catholic but also French and therefore probably immoral in addition to being idolatrous. Anyway, we all liked and enjoyed the Services, however deficient they might have been in sanctity.

Mrs. Service taught Jack and his brothers with correspondence courses sent out by the Calvert School in Baltimore. My mother was impressed by the curriculum and subscribed to a Calvert education for Don and me. This, at the age of nine or ten, was my first formal schooling. The arrival of the textbooks, after months in transit, was a great event. After the limp Chinese books that I knew, how elegant the American ones looked in their crisp, hardback covers, how thick and sleek the paper, and how exciting the pictures and maps.

Secular education, however, was not in my parents' eyes as important as Donald's and my religious education. This took the form of selected reading and interpretation of the Bible and memorizing certain Psalms and passages from the New Testament. But such indoctrination was not as compelling for me as it had been for my father. I did not then rebel against it intellectually; I was only uninterested and unmoved. When I reached 12 and we were at Oberlin, Ohio on furlough, my parents made it clear that, having attained the age of reason and therefore being competent to make a conscious, rational choice, I should declare my decision to be a Christian and be baptized. Because they were Baptists my parents considered sprinkling of infants, practiced by such as Episcopalians, to be at best an evasion of Jesus' injunction on baptism. For me it was to be total immersion, and before the whole congregation of the church.

Although I felt no elation over the decision confronting me, it was unthinkable that I should decline to go through with what was so earnestly expected of me. Yet I had no sense of original or even more recent sin needing to be washed away. I also cringed at the prospect of appearing so conspicuously before a host of strangers, proclaiming a belief in saving grace, descending into the baptistery to be submerged backwards by the preacher and then, with all eyes focused on me, sloshing off with my drenched white shirt and pants clinging to me and water from my matted hair dribbling down my face. I went through with the ritual and it was about as I had feared. But it made my parents happy.

Henry L. Mencken and *The American Mercury* came into my life three or four years after my baptism. We had moved to Shanghai where I was enrolled in the American high school there. Among the periodicals in the library was *The American Mercury*. The subject matter of the magazine and Mr. Mencken's use of the English language were quite a departure from what I was accustomed to. Much taken by the debunking, satire, and Mencken's lambasting prose, I made no attempt to conceal my newly found enthusiasm from my parents. Rather than being angered by my irreverence, they were troubled and hurt. My father, who was fundamentally more a man of reason than of temperament, tried to be open-minded and understand the Menckenian outlook. It strained his Christian charity; clearly he could not approve of it.

The Experimental College at the University of Wisconsin, which I attended in 1927–29, widened my intellectual interests. It was created and presided over by Alexander Meiklejohn as a two-year school, the first year of which was devoted to the study of classic Athenian civilization, and the second to nineteenth-century United States. Meiklejohn was one of those rare human beings—Père Teilhard de Chardin was another—who radiated warmth, composure and wisdom. His approach was Socratic: we students had to come up with our own answers. And we were encouraged to explore and discover ideas without fear of ridicule or censure.

My fellow students were disparate personalities, many of them new kinds of people to me. Victor Wolfson from New York, bursting with creative talent and enthusiasm, produced *Electra* in the Agricultural School's cattle-show pavilion, a production in which I unpersuasively acted the role of Orestes. Then there was Carroll Blair, a gnarled and bitter little native of Wisconsin who later became a Communist Party functionary. Sidney Hertzberg from New York was a Norman Thomas socialist, deliberate, orderly and temperate. There was also the fellow from one of the more prestigious military academies for boys who had done everything by bugle, could not adjust to the independent study and therefore spent most of his time looking for bridge and poker partners.

What I got out of the two years at the Experimental College was, I suppose, the development of a fairly open and, at the same time, skeptical outlook. Unlike some of my schoolmates, I did not, unhappily, store up a fund of knowledge. But the philosophical and aesthetic values to which I was exposed did make an impression on me. They did not, however, bring me closer to the theological beliefs of my parents.

While at college I wrote to my father suggesting that he read a magazine article extolling the cultivation of beauty as a substitute for religion. He replied:

> *I suppose it is true that the present student generation does not ascribe as much authority to the Bible and the Church as mine did . . . they are at best but means for bringing us to God. Some people are more loyal to them than to God himself. What is needed is devotion to the Heavenly Father— through the Bible and the Church if possible—but through aesthetics rather than not at all. If you were spurning all thought of God I should feel grieved because it would seem that we were parting company in the most meaningful sphere of life. But as long as you are making an honest earnest search for God, I feel that we are all the more drawn together for that is what I have been doing. Personally, I am convinced that we have revealed to us through Christ and the Bible a definite Plan of Salvation. It is confessedly a straight and narrow way, and the only way . . . I must obey the light I have, and not only walk in this way but also try to induce others to do the same . . . I have a hunch that God will somehow accept many who are not on my particular road. But hunches are not proper criteria, so I must hew to the line, and also remember than I am not to judge others but to bear my testimony by words and by life.*

My father was right in assuming that I had not spurned all thought of God. I was open to persuasion, but I did not find his theology persuasive. I did, however, respect his fidelity to belief and conscience.

One morning in June 1928, Alexander Meiklejohn read to us a passage that moved me more than anything else I heard or read at Madison. It was from Epictetus.

This Priscus Helvidius, too saw, and acted accordingly. For when Vespasian had sent to forbid his going to the senate, he answered: "It is in your power to prevent my remaining a senator, but as long as I am one, I must go."

"Well then, at least be silent there," said the Emperor.

"Do not ask my opinion," he replied, "and I will be silent."

"But I must ask it."

"And I must speak what appears to me to be right."

"But if you do, I will put you to death."

"Did I ever tell you that I was immortal? You will do your part, and I mine. It is yours to kill, and mine to die intrepid; yours to banish, mine to depart untroubled."

What good then did Priscus do, who was but a single person? Why, what good does the purple do to the garment. What else but to be beautiful in itself, and to give example of beauty to others.

CHAPTER III

MY ITINERANT EDUCATION

A native restlessness propelled me from Madison at the end of my two years at the Experimental College. I decided to take my junior year of college at Yenching University, near Peking, and then return to the United States for my senior year. Gordon Meiklejohn, my classmate and Alexander Meiklejohn's son, joined me in the adventure. As a first step, I drew on Gordon's and my slight resources and ignorantly bought in Gary, Indiana a second-hand Stutz. It had three bullet holes in the back. Because of these blemishes and, as we later discovered, incomplete documentation, the price was appropriately and conveniently low.

In this scarred vehicle we drove to Kansas where we briefly labored at harvesting wheat. When we had earned barely enough to fuel us to California, we resumed our journey and arrived in San Francisco nearly penniless. There we were befriended by a diminutive and effervescent Irishman named Albert Bender, friend of the elder Meiklejohns, and patron of Golden Gate arts. He put us up and induced the Dollar Line to sign us on as ordinary seamen aboard the *President Pierce*. After squeegeeing our way across the Pacific, we jumped ship in Japan and proceeded to Peking.

Yenching University, to which Gordon and I were admitted, was supported mainly by American missionary institutions, although Harvard and, to a lesser degree, Princeton had connections with it. The faculty was Chinese, American and European, and instruction was in Chinese and English. Because Yenching was regarded as one of the best universities in China, it drew students from all over the country. Foreign students were a rarity, so

Gordon and I were looked upon as minor curiosities. Gordon concentrated on the physical sciences in preparation for medical school and I majored in journalism, in anticipation of a glamorous career as a foreign correspondent, traveling about the world (first class), darting in and out of wars, mingling easily with the high and the mighty, and reporting it all in crunchy cables to an appreciative public.

My course of studies was unexacting. This left ample time for basketball, track, and convivial association with other male undergraduates. I was cautiously reserved with the women students lest, in a still strait-laced society, offense be taken, or jealousies and ill feeling aroused. I made frequent visits to nearby Peking and once met there a diplomat, O. Edmund Clubb, then a junior official in the American Legation. I regarded this as something of an event because, never having met one, I held diplomatists in some awe and was consequently relieved to find Clubb unassuming and friendly.

Political activism had periodically swept Chinese campuses, usually in the form of demonstrations against some act of foreign aggression, but the academic year 1929–30 was relatively quiet. The exhilarating National Revolution of 1926–27 had subsided, far short of its goal of unifying the country. And the Japanese invasion of Manchuria, beginning Tokyo's attempt to conquer China, was more than a year away. The Communist movement did not have the broad appeal that it came to exert during World War II; it was riven by doctrinal squabbles and rivalry between those underground in the cities and those, including Mao Tse-tung, with a fledgling "Red Army" holed up in the mountains of Central China. I was told that there were Communist students at Yenching, but I do not recall having met any. Certainly, they were inconspicuous. The majority of the students at this conservative school were then preoccupied with preparing for careers.

Following final examinations in June 1930, I journeyed to Inner Mongolia where I visited construction of an irrigation project on the Yellow River, north of the Ordos Desert. This was frontierland—steppes, horsemen, and camel caravans.

Later in the summer, Gordon and I returned to the United States by way of Manchuria (much of which was still a land for pioneers), the interminable trans-Siberian railway, and western Europe. We traveled in the company of Maxwell S. Stewart and his wife. A recent member of the Yenching faculty, Stewart had five years earlier taught me mathematics at the Shanghai American School. He was now embarked upon a journalistic career. We crossed the bleak Manchurian-Mongolian-Siberian borderland

and at the frontier encountered our first specimens of Soviet Man, the border guards. They were large, forbidding fellows who did not radiate goodwill. The smaller, scruffier functionaries and attendants on the train were no more genial. At first I thought that their sullen attitude toward me was because I was regarded as a member of the capitalist class. But then it became evident that they treated their proletarian compatriots in much the same or worse fashion—in such contrast to the outgoing, demonstrative behavior of the émigré Russians I had known and observed in China.

The Stewarts, Gordon and I traveled in the cheapest category, "hard class," on bare wooden benches. We bettered our sleeping conditions by renting bedding rolls. Food tickets for sparse, badly cooked meals in the dining room were exorbitantly expensive. I subsisted therefore on several large bars of chocolate that I had brought along as emergency rations and loaves of sour black bread bought from wizened peasant women at stops along the way. The staff of life fermented in the belly, so when I arrived in Moscow after of week of this diet I was in a state of bloat.

There was little else but black bread—and only occasionally that—at stations. 1930 was a hunger year, for Stalin was collectivizing Soviet agriculture. Consequently, food production and distribution were in deep decline. The people along the railway were shabbily dressed, much of the housing was old log cabins, and most of the roads visible from the train were mud. The Soviet Union seemed more backward than feudalistic China.

Through his journalistic contacts, Stewart arranged for Gordon and me to stay at the Moscow apartment of Anna Louise Strong, who was out of town. I regretted not being able to meet Miss Strong, as she was a celebrity—an American author of pro-Soviet articles and books and a firsthand reporter of revolutionary events in China during 1927. Her apartment was a gratifyingly economical and convenient base from which to explore Moscow, which, aside from Red Square and the inaccessible Kremlin, was either dilapidated or being excavated for new construction. After a day or two of wandering about, mostly looking for a restaurant or food shop where we could get something to eat, Gordon and I were ready to move on to western Europe.

The travel authorities, however, wanted to know when we had arrived in Moscow and where had we been since that time. There was no record of our presence in the city. Very suspicious. It took a couple of days to get from an acquaintance of Miss Strong an acceptable written statement that we had lodged in the Strong apartment. Only then were we permitted to leave.

Crossing the border, from the socialist paradise to Pilsudski's Poland, was a move from the grim and leaden, where the only decorative color was red, to good cheer and kaleidoscopic colors. In a spick and span little station restaurant I celebrated with a double order of ham and eggs.

Columbia University was next in my itinerant education. Gordon went on to McGill and a distinguished career in medicine. My credentials were so unorthodox that I was accepted as a university, not Columbia College, undergraduate. This meant that I had a wide range of studies to choose from and that most of my classes were at night. I had abandoned my superficial decision to be a newsman because my free-lance efforts out of Yenching were discouraging and I doubted my ability to become a successful reporter. I decided to try for the Foreign Service. To that end I took a course of international law under Philip Jessup.

My most pressing problem was money. From their meager income my parents contributed some. So did my aunt, Florence Davies. I had to earn what I could. Through the good offices of International House, my name was placed before Mrs. John D. Rockefeller Jr. as a candidate for tutoring her son David. She received me graciously and drew me out on my life accomplishments. A few days later I received a telegram: AS IT SEEMS IMPORTANT THAT OUR SON SHOULD BE ENTHUSED OVER ATHLETICS WE HAVE DECIDED TO ENGAGE THE MAN WHO NOT ONLY IS STRONG IN ATHLETICS BUT SHARES DAVIDS INTEREST IN ENTOMOLOGY I THANK YOU FOR COMING TO SEE ME AND REGRET NOT TO OFFER YOU THIS POSITION MRS JOHN D ROCKEFELLER JR

So I took the next available job. It was as a dishwasher in a Dixie-style restaurant on Amsterdam Avenue run by a genteel Southern woman whose staff, aside from me, was entirely Japanese, up to their elbows in corn pone and succotash.

After graduation from Columbia in 1931, I took the Foreign Service examinations. While awaiting word of the results, I stayed with my maiden aunt Flossie in her little house near the Art Institute in Detroit. She offered shelter to Donald and me any time we needed it because our parents were in China and we had no home in the United States. Aunt Flossie was then art editor of the *Detroit News*, a woman of abounding emotion, at once warmly outgoing and vulnerable. But she prided herself on being a true newspaperwoman, frightfully hardboiled. In practice this meant no more than that she was a woman of considerable common sense.

Aunt Flossie's friends were varied and entertaining—newspaper people, artists, museum curators, automotive engineers. Through her I met at one time or another Diego Rivera, hard at work on a turgid mural; the calmly droll Swedish sculptor Carl Milles; and Eero Saarinen, the architect, gingery and taciturn, both of whom lived near Detroit. Similarly, at Dearborn I participated in an evening of sycophantic square dancing at which the host was the original Henry Ford, spare and aloof in this one of his several ineffectual efforts to retrieve the lost simplicity of American life.

The Department of State notified me in November that I had passed the Foreign Service examination. In January 1932 I went abroad—a dime ferry ride across the river to the American Consulate at Windsor, Ontario— for probationary duty as a Foreign Service Officer, Unclassified (c) with a princely stipend of $2,500 a year. A year of in-job training and I was transferred during the last days of the Hoover administration to Washington for three months of tutelage in the Department.

We were fifteen novices, lectured to by Foreign Service and departmental officials on the various categories of consular work. At the end of the three-month course the instructors graded us. I received mixed appraisals. The immigration law and practice instructor wrote that I showed very little interest in the course, that my "manners left much to be desired," and that I was "the least promising of the officers in the class." I lacked "a desire to show off to the best advantage." He concluded, "I would not entrust him with visa work."

The international law instructor described me as "mature and mentally keen. He should develop in the Service, if his initiative is challenged with responsibility." The lecturer in foreign commerce considered that my "English in some respects leaves something to be desired." And the consul general who drilled us in "documentation of merchandise and shipping and seamen," C. E. Gauss, whom I would later encounter, granted me good appearance, courtesy, pleasing manners, "but not particularly energetic, inquiring, attentive or accurate. Thirteenth in a class of fifteen officers."

"Appears to have judgment and common sense," the passport and citizenship instructor conceded, and "to be older acting than his years, to be industrious, and to have a sense of responsibility. Has the qualifications of a good officer. Very serious disposition, courteous."

With these spotty, contradictory credentials I was assigned as Vice Consul to my first permanent post—Kunming, in the far southwestern mountains of China.

Created as a career organization in 1924 by amalgamation of separate diplomatic and consular services, the Foreign Service was in the early 1930s still a personalized institution. It numbered some 700 officers (11,500 in 2010), and so one could come to know, at least by name and position, a high proportion of one's colleagues. While the system operated impartially and primarily on merit, with assignments and transfers made in accordance with the needs of the government and promotion in accordance with performance, favoritism was not unknown. But it was no more, and perhaps even less prevalent than in large business enterprises, and certainly far less than in state and municipal governments.

Those who belonged to the Foreign Service tended to regard it as an elite corps. This was partly due to their status as representatives of the American government. As an apprentice Vice Consul at Windsor, I had received from the Canadian government an exequatur, engraved on vellum, authorizing me to exercise my meager consular powers, and issued over what purported to be the signature of George V, Rex Imperator. This autographed license from the King Emperor put me, in my own estimation, a notch above the boys across the river at Detroit city hall.

Another superficial factor contributing to a sense of elitism was the public conviction, fostered in novels and films, that Foreign Service life was glamorous—fraught with royal levees, deadly intrigue, and upper crust philandering. For a few it may have been somewhat so; for most it was not. A very small minority gratified a need for feeling superior by dressing the part. The workaday costume of one of these diplomats, whom I later encountered at the Peking legation, was wing collar, striped trousers, black chancery jacket, and pince nez, so that he looked like a reception clerk at a five star hotel. Along with the costuming there usually went a preoccupation with the social swim. In Washington I had impressed upon me by one of these colleagues the importance to one's career of attending debutante balls and titillating dowagers at the Sulgrave Club.

But occasional petty vanities were not the real reason for regarding the Foreign Service as an elite corps. It had inherited from the best of the old diplomatic service a compelling sense of public duty. The roots of this commitment, I suppose, reached back to a nineteenth-century assumption that with privileged status went an obligation to serve the commonweal, an attitude exemplified by the Massachusetts Adams family. This tradition was maintained on into the 1930s, and beyond, by several diplomats of the old school, notably William Phillips and Norman Armour. These men and others like them were looked up to by junior officers as models of high-minded devotion to duty. The Secretary of State at the time that I entered the service, Henry L. Stimson, was of the same character—an upright, public-spirited gentleman.

In such an atmosphere it was assumed that a Foreign Service officer was a man of honor and that in his relations with the public and his colleagues he would so conduct himself. On this assumption, the Foreign Service went about its business untormented by anxious preoccupation with security and discipline. The rare breaches of honor were usually dealt with quietly but firmly, as in a gentleman's club. The practice was that the senior officer at the mission or consulate, knowing personally everyone on his staff, dealt directly with the offender and, in accordance with his judgment, would let the incident pass with a warning, enter a black mark on the offender's record, offer him an opportunity to resign, or recommend to the department his discharge.

At the time I entered the Foreign Service, fingerprinting an officer was unheard of. When this precaution was some years later routinely put into effect, I felt a twinge of sadness, as if trust between friends had been spoiled. Bugging an officer's telephone and home or testing his veracity by lie detectors were unknown and would have been considered an outrage. The greatest security of the early Foreign Service may well have lain in, along with the tradition of honor, the close association and familiarity of its members with one another due to the small size of the staffs at posts abroad and, relatively speaking, of the Foreign Service in its entirety. A man's character and point of view became well, and with time, widely known within the service. With this understanding of one another often went a wholesome tolerance of considerable nonconformity and even eccentricity.

*   *   *

The American Consulate at Kunming was small—a Vice Consul slightly senior to me and I. American interests in this highlands corner of China, bordered by Tibet, Burma, Thailand, and Indochina, were slight. The province of Yunnan, of which Kunming was the capital, was then a French sphere of influence and the only access to it, save for ancient foot roads and trails, was a narrow-gauge railway from Hanoi. I lived, then, in a picturesque, uneventful, and placid environment. I traveled about town in a sedan chair, enjoyed the gardenias, wisteria, and jasmine that flourished in the Consulate's courtyards, and played tennis at the tiny Cercle Sportif Français.

Shortly after my arrival at Kunming a circular came from the Legation at Peking asking if any officers wished to apply for the two-year course in Chinese studies at the Legation. Graduates in this course were considered as specialists, serving most of their career in China. I applied, believing that as a China specialist my opportunities for advancement would be improved. My replacement at the Consulate was my boyhood friend Jack Service.

Most of my time during the two years (1933–35) at the Legation was spent with Chinese tutors, ceremonious gentlemen after the style of classical scholars, and in prescribed readings about ancient and modern China. Then there were diverse associations. Among them were a number of writers and scholars who were to influence foreign attitudes toward China: an unknown reporter named Edgar Snow, before he made his way into Communist territory and wrote *Red Star over China*; John K. Fairbank, then a graduate student and destined to become the dean of Chinese studies in the United States; Harold Isaacs, who was soon to produce his scathing *Tragedy of the Chinese Revolution*; Allan Priest, the curator of Chinese art at the Metropolitan Museum acquiring Chinese antiquities; and Owen Lattimore, writing about Mongols and Manchuria.

It was in Peking at this time that I also met the Jesuit paleontologist and theologian Père Teilhard de Chardin, a man of craggy radiance. Likewise, in 1933–35 I first encountered Chiang Monlin, the urbane and gentle chancellor of Peking National University, and Hu Shih, the eminent scholar who had led the revolt against the archaic cast of Chinese literature, and the movement to use the vernacular in writing.

The American Minister to China was a gregarious, roly-poly Oklahoman named Nelson Trusler Johnson. His instincts and behavior were those of a folksy, shrewd, small-town politician. But being a China specialist, he had acquired a repertoire of Chinese ritualistic platitudes that he took pleasure in rendering as the occasion required. As he had, at a mature age, recently married and promptly sired a son, he was occupied with the novelty of family life. He left the administration of the Legation to the Counselor, Clarence E. Gauss, who in Washington had been so faintly impressed with my qualities.

Round-shouldered from a life spent bending over a desk, with an underexposed complexion, a thin-lipped mouth down-turned at the corners, and pale eyes refracted through thick lenses, Gauss was a chilling spectacle at first encounter. He had begun his career as a clerk in the old Consular Service and through outstanding ability advanced close to the top of the Foreign Service. His subordinates respected his professional competence, his wary, analytical mind, and his stern integrity. Behind his defensive shyness, Gauss was a complicated personality, ready to castigate what he considered to be error, and at the same time yearning for appreciation and awkwardly warm-hearted with those who he thought did not depreciate him.

In Peking I came to know American military officers, especially those who were my counterparts in Chinese studies. One of them was Captain Frank Dorn, called Pinky, a nickname given him as a cadet because of his complexion. The Military Attaché at the end of my Peking tour was Colonel Joseph W. Stilwell. Dorn and Stilwell would later play an important part in my life. In command of the Marine Corps detachment assigned to protect the Legation was Colonel A. A. Vandegrift, who later was Commandant of the Marine Corps. One of the lieutenants of the guard was [Lewis Burwell] "Chesty" Puller, now a legendary hero of the Marine Corps. A phenomenally high proportion of the Army and Marine Corps officers stationed at Peking became generals in World War II and the Korean War. This was in part because of their special knowledge of northeast Asia. Also, it seemed to me, they were more talented than the average military officer.

Peking was blessed with many beautiful and bright young women, from the Turgout princess, Nirjidma, to bevies of visiting American and English maidens whose mamas or aunties were exposing them to the glories of old Peking. My three bachelor colleagues and I were consequently fortunate in the range of companionship available. While we gratefully embraced these opportunities, none of us married during our Peking tour of duty. In my case, I felt insufficiently established in my profession to take on so considerable a responsibility.

I left Peking with regret, not only because of fond associations, but also because this ancient, mellow, and noble city was a delight to live in. The symmetries of the great gates and walls, the squares and long vistas, the vermilion, emerald, cobalt, and imperial yellow of gates, pillars. and tiles, but most of all the casual, tranquil cadence of the old capital created an atmosphere of comfortable, well-worn elegance.

Mukden was my next post. It was the economic and transportation center of Manchuria, a coarse and important city. Manchuria was occupied by the Japanese Army, which had set up a puppet government over the region. The American government did not recognize the legitimacy of the Japanese conquest or the puppet regime of Manchukuo. Although the Japanese Army did not overtly treat us as enemies, it was evident that it so regarded us. Our position in the American Consulate General was therefore a delicate one.

Mukden was primarily a political reporting post, informing Washington of developments inside Manchuria, Chinese guerrilla movements along the Korean border, and recurrent clashes between Japanese and Soviet forces along the Mongolian and Soviet frontiers. I found this work much to my taste and at times exciting. It and a handful of American and British friends compensated for the harsh environment.

American journalists occasionally visited Manchuria. Frustrated in their efforts to get the truth from secretive Japanese officials, they called at the Consulate General for information. J. P. McEvoy of the *Reader's Digest* was one. William Henry Chamberlin of the *Christian Science Monitor* and John Gunther were others. The Consul General, Joseph W. Ballantine, made a practice of briefing the visiting journalist orally. Then, if he judged the writer to be reputable and discreet, Ballantine would pile on a conference table a collection of our reports to Washington about Manchuria and invite the visitor to draw on their contents for the enlightenment of the American public. Ballantine cautioned the journalists not to reveal where they got this information and, if asked, to say that they found it in the gutter. John Gunther spent two days with our files; much of his *Inside Asia* section on Manchukuo was a rewrite of material he had gotten from us.

Most of the documents that Ballantine and I showed to journalists were classified. There were only two grades in those days: "Confidential" and, rather sweetly, "Strictly Confidential." The latter was then regarded as "Eyes Only" in the subsequent runaway inflation of security. At any rate, we "violated security," on our own initiative and for reasons that we considered to be in the national interest. We suffered no pangs of conscience over what we did. Quite to the contrary, we felt rather virtuous over making available, through journalists, classified information that we thought the American people had a right and need to know.

Home leave came during the spring of 1937. I traveled in the company of Colonel and Mrs. Vandegrift across the trans-Siberian, this time "soft" class. I stopped off for a couple of days in Moscow where I met several members of the American Embassy staff, including George F. Kennan. Stalin's great purge was in mid-passage and the atmosphere of Moscow was tense and withdrawn. Kennan had attended the contrived "trials" as an observer and recounted to me in detail the incredible accusations against and self-incrimination of the old revolutionaries. It was a chilling story, one which stayed with me.

CHAPTER IV

HANKOW, THE FAR EAST DESK,
AND PEARL HARBOR

On my way from the United States back to Mukden in 1937 word came of
the July 7 encounter between Japanese and Chinese troops near Peking that
sparked the beginning of Japan's attempt to conquer China south of the
Great Wall. As Manchuria was already under Japanese control, I had no
difficulty in returning to my post through Japan and Korea. But I was not
to remain long. In less than a year I was transferred to Hankow, doomed
to be overrun and captured by the invading armies. I assumed that I had
been so favored because Mukden had conditioned me to living under the
heel of the Japanese Army, and because, were misfortune to befall me, as a
bachelor, my demise would be less extensively mourned than in the case of
a man with wife and children. The dear old Department was considerate in
such matters.

I was not so much as scratched, although we were bombed a bit. This
was something of a novelty in 1938, unless one were an Ethiopian or a
Spaniard. Air raids, troop movements, wounded soldiers arriving from the
front, Soviet "volunteer" airmen and German military advisers in the
streets, hordes of dazed refugees fleeing before the oncoming enemy, students rushing about the city pasting patriotic posters on walls and calling
on everyone to resist the foe, and finally the Communists planting dynamite in key buildings to greet the invaders with a scorched earth—all of
these made for a lively scene.

In Hankow I picked up strands of previous acquaintanceships: Colonel Stilwell, who, as Military Attaché, was observing the course of hostilities; Pinky Dorn, serving with him as Assistant Military Attaché; and Edgar Snow, reporting the war and less overtly violent forms of politics. His *Red Star over China* had recently been published and he had suddenly risen from journalistic obscurity to international acclaim without having been spoiled.

Because of the constricted wartime living at Hankow, with the American and British correspondents and officials concentrated in offices, apartments, hotels, and bars in a short strip along the bank of the Yangtze, and because of a mounting sense of crisis and doom from the approaching Japanese armies, the twenty or thirty Anglo-American newsmen and officials shared a feeling of camaraderie. My apartment in the Hong Kong and Shanghai Bank building became one of the eating, drinking, debating, and recreational centers for the "last ditchers," as we called ourselves.

A Marine Corps captain, Evans Carlson, whom I had known in Peking, came to Hankow from North China, where he had been observing firsthand the Chinese Communist Eight Route Army. Carlson was forty-ish, a lanky, rawboned fellow, less homely than Abraham Lincoln, less handsome than Gary Cooper. He was unpretentious and direct; also a bit wanting in skepticism. Although at President Roosevelt's request he wrote personally to FDR regarding the situation in China, I do not recall his ever mentioning this unusual relationship. It had begun in 1935 when Carlson commanded the President's Marine guard at Warm Springs and Roosevelt took a liking to the rugged, idealistic officer, who had already served two stints in China.

Carlson was the first American military man to visit Communist-held areas. He came to Hankow greatly impressed by what he had seen of Communist troops and guerrillas, their exceptional esprit de corps, discipline, and solicitude for the civilian population. The Eagle Scout behavior of the Communist soldiers contrasted with the often dispirited, disreputable life style of other Chinese troops. Carlson reported his enthusiastic admiration of the Communist forces. This raised senior American military eyebrows. When he voiced his views to the press, the Navy attempted to muzzle him. Inspired to bear witness, Carlson resigned and in the United States publicly praised the Chinese Communists and prophesied a harmonious, unified, democratic China victorious over Japan, if only Americans would stop selling war materiel to Japan.

This did not happen. Carlson found himself back in the Marines in time for World War II. He was given a battalion, popularly called Carlson's Raiders, in training which he incorporated lessons learned from the Chinese Communist regulars and irregulars. Perhaps Carlson's most lasting contribution to the art of war and to American history and culture was lexicographical. By adopting the Chinese Communist slogan "gung ho"—work together—as a motto for the Raiders, he introduced the phrase into the American vulgate where it is now defined in a sense less reflective of the original Chinese meaning than of Carlson himself—"wholeheartedly, often ingenuously, loyal and enthusiastic."

*   *   *

Here at Hankow in the summer of 1938 I also formed new acquaintanceships, some of which were renewed elsewhere or otherwise affected my life, particularly in the McCarthy era. One of these new acquaintances was Chou En-lai, then acting as the principal Communist representative with Chiang Kai-shek's National Government. This was under the wartime arrangement of a so-called united front between the two mutually hostile regimes.

Fine featured, animated, quick-witted and magnetic, Chou was well equipped for another and more productive function—public relations with foreign journalists and officials. For a Communist oligarch he was remarkably catholic in his interests and vivacious in his manner. This was for Chou the beginning of 37 years of dealing with foreigners, continuing even into the period when he was Prime Minister.

Close to the Communist delegation was a middle-aged woman named Agnes Smedley. Agnes was indelibly American—not Booth Tarkington American, rather Upton Sinclair American, with a touch of Calamity Jane and the Wobblies. She had been born into the squalor of a turn of the century Colorado mining camp and grown up in poverty, bitterness, and anger. A rebel by temperament and a writer by vocation, she championed the poor and downtrodden; initially, of all things, the cause of Indian independence from British rule during World War I. In the 1930s she was in China and appalled by the poverty and oppression that she encountered. She associated herself with the Chinese Communists and left-wing organizations, visited the Communist headquarters at Yenan, and, with the 1937

Japanese invasion of China, joined Communist guerrilla units in the countryside.

Garbed in the shapeless gray cotton uniform of the Communist Eight Route Army, complete with puttees, cloth shoes and a limp cap on her lank brown bob, Miss Smedley arrived in Hankow from guerrilla country. She was in straitened circumstances, so the American Episcopalian Bishop, Logan Roots, a practicing Christian, took her in and gave her bed and board. They were spoken of as the Moscow-Heaven Axis. And Agnes entertained herself—and the Right Reverend Roots—by addressing him as Comrade Bishop. The *Manchester Guardian* employed her as a correspondent, which ameliorated her financial plight and made her a member of the international press corps.

Agnes also solicited medical supplies for the guerrillas and money with which to buy such supplies. The British Ambassador, Sir Archibald Clark-Kerr (later Lord Inverchapel) was one of the more forthcoming donors to her wounded and sick guerrillas. Sir Archie respected this ill-favored, fervent woman and learned from her about a China and Chinese to whom very few foreigners had access. So did most of the foreign correspondents.

Although she maintained that she was not a Communist, Agnes was generally regarded as one and was certainly closely associated with them. Because she was unruly, nonconformist, and at once cynical and pitying, I doubted that she was a Communist Party member—and that the Party would accept her for membership if she applied. It did not seem to me that a Party member would have said to me, as Agnes did, that while she respected and was fond of Chu Teh (whose biography she was writing) and other Communist fighting men, she disliked the principal political figures in Yenan: "They're too slick." I wondered if Agnes might not, given the opportunity, forsake fellow-traveling.

Shortly before the press corps left Hankow in the face of the Japanese advance—the embassies had gone earlier—I had a casual dinner for some of those who were about to depart, among them Agnes. After dinner she was momentarily sitting by herself so I went over to make conversation. Where was she going, I asked. Back to the guerrillas, "That's where I belong." I then delivered some thoughts on the degenerative course of revolutionary movements, that if the cause with which she identified herself came to power she would be disillusioned, her faith in the revolution betrayed. Why didn't she give up the kind of life she was leading and function like other correspondents? "I can't," she said with tears in her eyes, "There is no other way for me."

I regretted what I had said. She did not need my lecturing. She was already aware of what I warned. And I had not suggested any acceptable alternative. Indeed, there probably was no other way for her.

For several months after she left I received brief letters from Agnes reporting what was transpiring in the guerrilla areas. She was our only source of firsthand information from that amorphous zone. And then I lost all contact.

Jack Belden, the young, bright, moody United Press correspondent, groused to me about how shabbily UP treated him and then asked what I was being paid as a Vice Consul. I told him something in the neighborhood of $3,500 a year, as I now recall it. Jack flared up, "I'm as good as you are." So he wired UP that unless it raised his salary to whatever it was that I was paid, he would quit.

He quit. As he was then without income, I invited him to stay at my apartment. One night on the way back from a restaurant dinner with friends Jack disappeared. For days thereafter we checked with the police, hospitals, and military intelligence—no Jack. We gave him up as probably dead, fallen into the Yangtze or victim of foul play.

Some ten days later he casually walked into my apartment. He had on impulse gone to the railroad station and boarded a northbound troops train. It delivered him to the front. There for about a week he was caught in a battle and Chinese retreat—days of swirling confusion and terror. Stilwell was delighted to receive Belden's account of the engagements and rout. Although the Military Attaché had gotten to other fronts, notwithstanding obstacles placed in his way by the Chinese High Command, which was ashamed of the condition and performance of its forces, he had not at that time been able to visit the front north of Hankow. Jack had brought him eyewitness, participant reports of action, to which the official communiqués bore scarcely any resemblance.

Belden slipped out of Hankow ahead of the Japanese. I did not see him again until 1942, in Burma, again with Stilwell.

Hankow, summer 1938, changed for a time the outlook for Freda Utley—a middle-aged woman of versatile convictions, each successively proclaimed with passion. Born in England, Miss Utley began life as a British subject. But while at university she joined in 1928 the Communist Party, thereby adopting an allegiance above that to King and country.

She married a Soviet citizen, went to the Soviet Union in 1930 where she worked in the Comintern, and soon became disillusioned with at least Soviet Communism. She later claimed that she did not transfer her British

CP membership to the Soviet Party and that she let her British membership lapse. The detention of her husband by the Soviet authorities further alienated Miss Utley. She was able to leave the Soviet Union in 1936, and headed to China.

At Hankow, she met the Chinese Communist delegation, also Snow, Carlson, Smedley and others having firsthand acquaintanceship with the Chinese Communists. With exhilaration she found a new faith, one in the Chinese Communists, whom she described in her book *China at War* (1939), as having abandoned the goal of dictatorship, adopted a policy of reform along capitalist and democratic lines and become, in sum, like radicals in the English Nineteenth Century sense of the word. At the same time, as she testified before a Senate subcommittee in 1950, she decided to expose the Soviet Union for what it was, "even if my husband was still alive and it led to his death." Such was Miss Utley's sense of civic duty.

Her attachment to her Chinese Victorian radicals did not last long. I would later learn that because of their approval of the Soviet-Nazi pact, she had turned against them with fury.

By early 1938 the Japanese had practically wiped out the small, Italian-trained, incompetent, corrupt Chinese Air Force. Claire Chennault, an American Army Air Corps (AAC) captain in his late forties, retired for deafness and insistence on (contrary to AAC doctrine) the vulnerability of bombers to pursuit aircraft, was retained by Generalissimo Chiang Kai-shek and Mme. Chiang as air adviser. Chennault looked like the warrior that he was—pitted face, cold straight-on gaze, thin lips, aggressive jaw. As Stilwell was the epitome of the foot soldier, Chennault was that of the open cockpit fighter pilot. These two warriors, both in Hankow during the summer of 1938, would be teamed together four years later in rancorous association.

The Chinese offered no resistance to the Japanese capture of Hankow. In contrast to its savage behavior following the seizure of Nanking, the Japanese army occupied Hankow in a relatively orderly fashion. Life for those of us who stayed behind—thousands of terrified Chinese and several scores of uneasy foreigners—meant virtual captivity; checkpoints within the city and no leaving it without a tightly controlled pass.

My work was political reporting and drafting notes advising the Japanese of the location of American properties in Central China and placing on the invading forces responsibility for damage to any of these properties or harm to any Americans by bombing or other military action. I also made, with reluctant Japanese permission, extended trips into Japanese occupied areas to check on the welfare of isolated Americans. On one of these assignments, involving the evacuation of Americans from a mountain resort held by Chinese Communist guerrillas and besieged by the Japanese, I underwent the stimulating experience of being shot at by the Communists.

*   *   *

The State Department transferred me in the autumn of 1940 to its Far Eastern (FE) Division, where I was put to work as the junior of two China desk officers. As our windows in the old State-War-Navy building, later housing presidential executive offices, faced the west wing of the White House, one of my duties was to keep at a fixed level all window shades in FE visible from the Executive Mansion, lest President Roosevelt's eye be affronted by a spectacle of irregularity across the street in the cathedral of American diplomacy. In addition, I moved about the Department prodding other divisions to do things that my superiors wanted done and collecting concurring initials on FE's draft telegrams. These menial activities were a valuable introduction to the way things were done.

My education in this respect was furthered by acquaintance, originating from Georgetown socializing, with Lauchlin Currie. He was a brisk, little, rimless-bespectacled Harvard economist who had been acquired by Roosevelt as a special assistant. Currie was developing, when I met him, an interest in Chinese affairs and after several social meetings took to phoning me at FE to ask for information or my comments on Chinese events. I thought it odd that he should occupy himself with matters so evidently outside of his expertise. But then this spontaneous straying into other jurisdictions to dabble therein was characteristic of the helter-skelter Roosevelt administration.

Naturally, I was flattered by the attention from a presidential aide. At the same time, this contact made me uneasy because Currie was clearly out of channels. By orderly governmental procedure he should have dealt with an Assistant Secretary or certainly no one lower than chief of division. I let my immediate superiors know of Currie's queries. They expressed no opinion, but I sensed they did not approve of the connection. In the absence of orders forbidding me to respond to requests from the White House, I felt that it would be priggish of me—or at least awkward—to tell a special assistant to the President to take his questions elsewhere.

The President set an example for Currie in operating out of channels and undercutting the man in charge. Roosevelt frequently bypassed his Secretary of State, Cordell Hull, to deal directly with the Under Secretary, Sumner Welles. This was, of course, the President's prerogative, and in a sense it was understandable because, while Hull was useful in coping with Congress regarding foreign policy, his knowledge of foreign affairs was limited and his approach simplistic and moralistic. In contrast, Welles was a highly competent professional diplomat.

Good management practice, however, dictated that if Roosevelt had not, for whatever reason, wished to deal with the man he had put in charge of foreign affairs, he should have replaced the Secretary with someone in whom he had full confidence. But FDR did not work that way. He was a politician, not an executive. The confusion that he, his White House staff, and his special emissaries sowed in the conduct of American foreign relations was to grow with passage of time and the emboldenment of Roosevelt's virtuosos.

Dr. Stanley K. Hornbeck, PhD exercised with some pomposity his mandate as political adviser to the Secretary in Far Eastern matters. Having been promoted from chief of FE, he regarded the division as a fiefdom obligated to serve him. Substantive papers were accordingly submitted to him for approval, or simply for information. An inveterate memo-writer, Hornbeck reacted in pedantic writing to almost anything that came to his clutter-piled-high desk. These indiscriminate memoranda on matters trivial as well as weighty fluttered back to FE throughout the day.

Hornbeck had some academic background in China, but little grounding in Japan. He was morally indignant over Japan's invasion of China and sympathized with the Chinese. But in that he was no different from most of us in the China service.

As assistant to Hornbeck, a studious young man named Alger Hiss read and screened stacks of papers coming to Hornbeck's office. I did not envy him his job, working exclusively with the ponderous fussbudget. Alger was amiable, but as he was not in the channel of communication between Hornbeck and the FE, those of us who were junior officers in FE had relatively little contact with him.

Roosevelt had delegated to Hull the tedious and, in terms of domestic American politics, risky business of negotiating with Japan for a lessening of tension between the two countries. The Secretary's principal adviser in this crucial endeavor was Hornbeck. Also participating in the negotiations, but subordinate to Hornbeck, was the man who had been my chief at Mukden, Joseph Ballantine, a rumpled, nervous and rather engaging Japan specialist.

The May to December 7, 1941 negotiations with the Japanese Ambassador took place at the State Department in strict secrecy. My fellow junior officers and I were in uneasy ignorance of what was transpiring. We drew up a statement expressing our opposition to any deal with Japan at the expense of China. This we presented to the Chief of FE, Maxwell M. Hamilton. In considerable agitation he told us, in effect, not to meddle in matters beyond our province and intimated that the Army and Navy (both urgently trying to strengthen themselves) wanted the State Department to play for time, at least to delay if we could not avoid hostilities with Japan.

My colleagues and I had acted on a misapprehension. The risk was not a sell-out of China. Rather, the risk was cornering Japan so that it had no alternative but to fight. Hull and Hornbeck were rigidly pro-Chinese and, both temperamentally and as a matter of principle, incapable of making a compromise deal with Japan for a modus vivendi, or what is now called peaceful co-existence. While I doubt that such a deal was then possible, given the rising antagonism in the American public toward Japan in 1941, the Hull-Hornbeck combination ensured that no compromise could be negotiated. And so the United States and Japan moved inflexibly, almost as if they were predestined to do so, toward war. And the American Armed Forces did not get the time that they wanted for preparation.

I was off on a blithe fortnight's vacation when the Japanese attached Pearl Harbor. From Texas eastward was unknown territory to me. So I had eagerly embarked on a scanning tour through the south. Roark Bradford introduced me to the unique charm of his New Orleans, to pleasant but vapid bayous (lacking the redolence of similar Asian waterways), and to the improbable settlement of Chinese and Slovak shrimpers on the Grand Isle of the Cajuns.

By comparison, the Gulf coast eastward was bland. And then Charleston, South Carolina, more coherent and sedate than New Orleans, architecturally harmonious, a graceful city on a personal scale. It was in this agreeable setting, on a placid Sunday midday, from excited conversations on the street and turned-up radios, that I heard the news of Pearl Harbor.

I was surprised, but not astounded, and reproached myself for not having anticipated something like this—at least as to timing. For the previous year in Hankow at a Sunday luncheon at my apartment for three American and two Japanese naval officers, a Japanese captain, exhilarated by gin and beer, had knotted a table-napkin around his head and proclaimed to the hung-over American gunboateers, "When we attack you, it will be on a Sunday morning." And of course they would, I thought at the time.

Back at FE I encountered a hushed, frantic search of records—had we passed to the military all of the messages from the Embassy at Tokyo that might have warned us of the attack? Two were of importance. One in mid-November was a general reminder that the Japanese were accustomed to strike first and then declare war. The other, earlier, relayed a report from the Peruvian Ambassador in Tokyo that an inebriated Japanese naval officer had told a member of his staff that should war come, it would begin with a Japanese attack on Pearl Harbor. FE had not been remiss, as I recall, in keeping the military informed.

Responsibility for the United States being caught napping went, of course, beyond slighting unverifiable warnings from the American Embassy in Tokyo. The disaster of Pearl Harbor occurred because American officials, civilian and military, and the American people did not sense the desperate daring of the Japanese, underestimated Japanese power, assumed near-invulnerability, and thought that if Japan expanded its China war into a Pacific war, it would strike only southward to Malaysia and the Dutch Indies.

Stimson, then Secretary of War, and Frank Knox, Secretary of the Navy, belittled the danger from Japan. And ten days before Pearl Harbor, Hornbeck offered five to one odds that Japan would not be at war with the United States by December 15. General Douglas MacArthur in the Philippines earlier in 1941 had assured Washington that he could defend the islands. The Army persuaded itself that the newly developed B-17 bombers could not only rout any attack on the Philippines but even interdict an attempt by the Japanese to advance southward toward the Indies.

Although American deciphering of Japanese cables revealed to the very few at the pinnacle of American authority that after November 29 Tokyo would abandon attempts to find peaceful accommodations, the President and his high command did not interpret this ominous intelligence as indicating that the powerful American military complex in mid-Pacific was under threat of imminent attack. To suggest that a Japanese task force might venture undetected halfway across the Pacific, with a surprise attack cripple the American fleet and air units in the Hawaiian bastion, and then get away with slight losses—such a scenario, if presented before December 7, would have been dismissed as preposterous.

PART II

"THIS ASSIGNMENT IS NOT MADE AT YOUR REQUEST NOR FOR YOUR CONVENIENCE"

CHAPTER V

TO ASIA WITH STILWELL

Almost a year before Pearl Harbor, Stilwell wrote to me on New Year's Eve wishing me a happy 1941, and passed on a message from Pinky Dorn: "if you can get us sent to China you can come along."

Well, things did not work out quite that way. Stilwell, a Major General in command of the Seventh Division at Fort Ord, California, when he wrote to me, and seven months later Commander of the III Corps, was called to Washington a fortnight after the Japanese attack. Pinky accompanied him as aide de camp. At the War Department Stilwell learned that he was to lead what was then planned as the first American offensive, a landing somewhere in French West Africa, code-named GYMNAST.

I was unaware of this when the General, Pinky, and I dined together shortly after Christmas. They intimated that they would be going overseas, but not to China. After dinner I asked Dorn if, even though they were not sent to China, I could come along.

Pinky said that he thought this could be arranged. I had suggested that my role might be something like a diplomatic attaché to the General, a mirror role to that of a military attaché to an Ambassador.

Early in January the American high command began to doubt the timing and feasibility of GYMNAST and frantically conceived alternatives to it. Meanwhile Roosevelt and Stimson, now Secretary of War, felt a pressing need to exhibit American military support of China. In impotent disarray from Hawaii to the Philippines to the Java Sea, the United States was not in a position to dispatch either troops or significant quantities of materiel to China. The best that could be done was to present Chiang Kai-shek with a high-ranking American military officer as adviser, representative of the American high command, and an earnest of large support to come.

General George C. Marshall, Chief of Staff of the Army, with whom Stilwell had served in China in 1926, asked Stilwell on January 1, 1942 to recommend someone for the China assignment. Although Stilwell himself was an obvious possible choice, he was then immersed in evaluating GYM-NAST and, in any event, was rated as one of the best combat commanders in the Army. Lieutenant General Hugh A. Drum was Stilwell's recommendation because, as he observed in his diary, Drum was pompous and of high rank. As for himself in the China role, "No thank you." The Chinese "remember me as a small-fry colonel . . . Drum by all means." Stilwell's predilection of course, was for a fighting rather than a representational and administrative command.

Drum regarded the China assignment as vague and not worthy of a general of his pretensions. And he made a poor impression on Stimson and Marshall. They turned to Stilwell. Would he take the China mission? "I'll go where I'm sent," Stilwell characteristically replied.

Stilwell viewed the plum proffered him not without misgivings. From his considerable experience in China he had few illusions about the quality of the Chinese military leadership. And the current reports from China of an American military mission headed by the urbane and discerning Brigadier General John Magruder supported what he knew—that the Chinese Army lacked aggressive fighting spirit and that the materiel demanded by the Chinese National Government was not for fighting the Japanese but for ensuring Chiang's domestic ascendancy against internal rivals after the defeat of Japan.

At the same time, China had an insidious lure for Stilwell, as it did for many China hands. And Stimson, who had been emotionally involved as Secretary of State in trying to defend China in the early 1930s against Japan in Manchuria, envisioned the command offered to Stilwell as charged with keeping China in the war and securing it as a base, initially for limited operations and eventually for a counteroffensive, possibly by Chinese forces. By mid-January the concept of the China assignment had expanded to embrace a nebulous position as chief of the Generalissimo's nonexistent allied staff. In addition to controlling the distribution of lend-lease supplies, Stilwell was told he would train Chinese troops and even command them.

How many, where and under what circumstances was undefined—until the Japanese surged out of Thailand into Burma, intent on cutting China's only remaining line of surface communications with the West, stretching from the port of Rangoon half the length of Burma to the Yunnan border. Thereupon the Chinese indicated that an American lieutenant general, but not Magruder (who knew them so well), would be granted "executive control" of Chinese forces dispatched to Burma. Whether the Generalissimo would permit an American to command Chinese troops was, Stilwell thought, a test of Chiang's willingness to allow him to function effectively.

The exchange between Washington and Chungking regarding the appointment of an American commander in China passed through T. V. Soong, Madame Chiang Kai-shek's Americanized, clever, brazen, and ambitious brother. He was Chinese Foreign Minister and resident in Washington, where he acted as the Generalissimo's alter ego, interpreting and editing communications between the American Government and Chiang.

Through one or more of his many highly placed sources of information in Washington, Soong learned that Stilwell was the probable choice for China. So he made inquiries about the General and was satisfied with what he had learned. Subsequently, the Generalissimo declared that Stilwell would be "most welcome."

With "executive control" promised Stilwell and a welcome to him from Chiang and Soong, Marshall asked Stilwell on January 23, "Will you go?" Again, "I'll go where I'm sent." But with feelings far from undiluted elation—"the blow fell," he wrote that night in his diary.

The War Department orders to Stilwell, dated February 2, designated him as Chief of Staff of the Supreme Commander of the Chinese Theater (Chiang Kai-shek) and Commanding General of the American forces (initially headquarters staff, liaison officers and technicians) in China-Burma-India. Soong confirmed that Stilwell was to act as Chief of Staff for the Generalissimo, to supervise and control all American defense aid for China and, under the Generalissimo, to command such Chinese forces as were assigned to him. To emphasize the purpose of military assistance, Marshall directed Stilwell "to increase the effectiveness of United States assistance to the Chinese Government for the prosecution of the war and to assist in improving the combat efficiency of the Chinese army."

And so a general who had been appraised as one of the best fighting commanders in the American army was dispatched on a ceremonial, negotiatory, administrative mission in which he was also to command Chinese troops at the pleasure of the Generalissimo, whom Stilwell regarded as disastrously incompetent in military matters. Why, when given the opportunity to decline, did Stilwell accept the assignment? He did because as a thoroughgoing professional soldier he took the wish of his commanding officer, George Marshall (who was one of the few men he really respected), as tantamount to an order. Then too, Stilwell believed what became something of an American military creed: that, properly fed, trained, equipped and led, the Chinese soldier would be the equal of any. This just might be the chance for him to prove this belief.

Nevertheless he already longed for the reassuring presence of American combat troops under his command. To Marshall he described the Southwest Pacific as a defensive theater, whereas China was the area from which to launch the offensive against Japan—employing at least one American army corps. This was to be a reoccurring plea throughout Stilwell's China assignment; not granted until the last year of his ordeal, and then with but one regiment.

The American high command, however, looked upon China as of relatively slight military significance. The American grand strategy assigned priority to the defeat of the German-Italian Axis over the defeat of Japan. In the secondary effort against Japan, four possible avenues of attack existed. One was the northern Pacific and the Aleutians. Weather and terrain severely limited the practicability of this route. A second was westward from the Central Pacific, a flank assault, which proved to be the main road to victory. A third, starting from Australia, was northward island hopping in arduous frontal assaults against the maximum extension of enemy strength, but enabling MacArthur to fulfill his promise to return to the Philippines.

And finally, China. Effectively blockaded from its allies for most of the war, it was a logistical monstrosity, with a line of communications stretching from the United States across the Atlantic, around Africa, through the Indian Ocean, and then either across or around the Indian subcontinent, up the Brahmaputra valley to the foothills of the Himalayas and thence, by airlift, across Burma and the high ranges to the east and so into the southwest mountain-girt corner of China. China was indeed, as often said during the war, "at the end of the line." In retrospective military logic, commitment of American men and materiel to the China-Burma-India Theater was a diversion from theaters where they could be more effectively used against the enemy.

Who was this Chiang Kai-shek to whom Stilwell was assigned? He was a slight, sleek, alternately impassive and overwrought, obstinate and vacillating, fifty-six-year-old native of the lower Yangtze valley. As a student at military academy in Japan he joined Sun Yat-sen's republican movement plotting the overthrow of imperial rule over China. Chiang had a minor part in the ensuing 1911 revolution, following which he cultivated Shanghai financial contacts, became a broker and established connections with the powerful and sometimes benevolent Shanghai underworld.

The new republic was soon fragmented by warlordism. Chiang maintained his ties with Sun, joining in at least one of that erratic leader's military campaigns to capture a base for his Kuomintang (national people's party). This paid off for Chiang. When Sun made a deal with the Soviet Union for assistance, he sent Chiang on a visit to Moscow in 1923 as his military representative. Having established a base at Canton, Sun appointed Chiang head of a new military academy there, complete with Soviet military advisers, headed by the ascendant General Vasily Blyukher.

With Sun's death in 1925, Chiang slickly disposed of his competitors, took over as Sun's successor, and showed that he knew how to handle foreign advisers. He called a Soviet bluff to terminate aid, put his Soviet military tutors briefly under house arrest, and forced the recall of several for attempted reforms of his army and one for allegedly making fun of him. Against the advice of his Soviet mentors, he launched in 1926 a northward drive to subdue warlords and unify China.

Chiang undertook the campaign in collaboration with the puny new Chinese Communist Party, which the Soviet representatives had persuaded Sun to accept in a united front with the Kuomintang. Although Chiang had continued with the united front, when the successful offensive approached his own turf, particularly Shanghai, he turned on his Communist collaborators and caused the killing of all that his men could lay hands on. Using the right wing of the Kuomintang, he established at Nanking a conservative government claiming to be the national administration, even though it controlled—and that imperfectly—only the southeastern portion of the country.

In search of respectability Chiang courted Shanghai's most powerful banking and commercial community. And late in 1927 he disembarrassed himself of his old-fashioned marital entanglements (two wives) and embraced Christianity so as to quality for marriage to Soong Mei-ling. In marrying Miss Soong, Chiang acquired a pretty, temperamental wife of inclinations with rich historical precedents—the empress or imperial favorite who usurps the throne. He also acquired a spirited assortment of in-laws.

The Soongs were a wealthy Christian family. The father, Charlie, was brought up in the United States and his progeny were educated there. He was a friend of Sun Yat-sen's and his second daughter, Soong Ching-ling, became Sun's second wife. She was the gentle, idealistic member of the family and disapproved of her brother-in-law's dictatorial nature. The oldest daughter, Ai-ling, shrewd and self-controlled, married H. H. Kung, who claimed lineal descent from Confucius and was from time to time Chiang's Finance Minister. The dominant son, T. V. Soong, a Harvard product, aggressively rose to become Foreign Minister and, like his sister, Madame Chiang, acted during World War II as a broker between the Generalissimo and the Americans.

Chiang failed in his attempt to unify China. Warlords continued to control large portions of western China and all of Manchuria, until the Japanese took over that northeastern region in 1931. Rather than going to war against Japan over Manchuria, Chiang attempted to eradicate his former allies, the Communists. They had established themselves in a small rural area in Central China where they held out against repeated government offensives. The Generalissimo's fifth campaign in 1934 finally forced them into a circuitous 6,000-mile retreat, known as the Long March, to Northwest China. His persistent harrying of the Communists resulted in a bizarre incident in 1936 wherein he was kidnapped by regional forces, released through Communist intercession, and agreed with the Communists to form again a united front, this time directed against Japan.

The Generalissimo's successful 1934 campaign had been planned by his German advisers, headed by General Hans von Seeckt. General Alexander von Falkenhausen succeeded von Seeckt and was training Chinese troops when Japan launched its full-scale invasion of China in 1937. He was largely responsible for planning the only important victory of the Chinese, Taierchuang, and was infuriated when they held back and would not press on to achieve a major success.

Early in the war the Soviet Union began military aid to Chiang—but not to the Communists—and made available to the Generalissimo Soviet military advisers. Among them were Generals G. K. Zhukov and V. I. Chuikov, both of whom, on the basis of their subsequent performances in the war against Germany, could be considered as competent to give advice to

Chiang. But the Generalissimo did not make use of them and so they returned to the Soviet Union.

To Chiang the assignment of Stilwell was not a totally new kind of experience. For some eighteen years, off and on, he had dealt with foreigners intent on telling him how to be a soldier. He had not suffered as a consequence any apparent decline of confidence in his own superior judgment in military matters. At times he accepted—and always adapted—advice; more often he did not act on it. There was no convincing reason to believe that Chiang would be more responsive to Stilwell than he had been to Blyukher or von Falkenhausen.

*   *   *

The approach of the American public to China, especially during the three years after Pearl Harbor, was largely subjective. It was a product of one hundred years of missionary compulsions and involvement, spiritual and emotional, of a sense of guilt that the United States had not gone to the rescue of China under attack from Japan and had sold war materiel to Japan, and of propaganda portraying the Chinese as heroically fighting on our behalf and wanting only American arms and know-how to drive the enemy into the sea. Central figures in this vision of China were Chiang and Mei-ling—he the unflinching Christian commander of four hundred million tillers of Pearl Buck's good earth, and she, a Wellesley girl, fragile as a peach blossom sheathed in brocade, faithful helpmeet to the devout Generalissimo (*Time*'s 1937 Man and Wife of the Year), and an eloquent pleader of China's cause (moving assembled members of Congress to penitence, high resolve, and other manly emotions).

The widespread mythology about China meant that more than facts and logic went into the making of American wartime policy toward China. The surcharged sentimental attachment to the Chinese raised the importance of China in strategic planning all out of proportion to its real military and immediate political worth. The significance of China was further inflated by a geopolitical assumption of Roosevelt's that China would become a great power after the war and therefore during hostilities it should be treated as one, and Chiang as co-equal with Churchill, and Stalin.

This caused Washington civil and military officials, notwithstanding reports to the contrary from their representatives in Chungking, to think wishfully that Chiang and his National Government might want to prosecute the war with all vigor. Washington was also anxious to keep China in the war, not fully recognizing that while Chiang was loath to expend strength against the common enemy, he would not withdraw from the war. Assuming an American victory, there was much for him to gain from remaining nominally an ally: all kinds of assistance and, after the war, territorial acquisitions.

Thanks to Pinky and the General, I received in February 1942 State Department orders assigning me as Consul at Kunming, designating me as Second Secretary of Embassy at Chungking, and detailing me to "the China Military Mission headed by Major General Joseph W. Stilwell." This was followed by the standard formula: "This assignment is not made at your request nor for your convenience."

The orders specified that my detail to Stilwell was for "liaison between the Mission and American and foreign civil officials." Three days later, on February 13, as an afterthought the Department admonished me to conduct my liaison duties "at the direction and under the supervision of General Stilwell." The Department also desired that, as practicable and appropriate, I keep the Ambassador and, through him, the Department informed of "the activities of the military mission."

My superiors in the Far Eastern Division did not favor my detail to the General, feeling that it was irregular and bordering on the frivolous. I should stick to the Foreign Service. Currie, who was administering lend-lease to China, welcomed the arrangement. I assumed he thought I could be a useful point of contact with Stilwell's headquarters.

Currie and Owen Lattimore, recently returned from serving as a personal adviser to the Generalissimo, emphasized to me the logistic importance of India in view of the impending Japanese capture of Rangoon. Lattimore referred with approval to what he said was the opinion of Chiang and Chennault, then heading a small pursuit aircraft contingent manned by American mercenaries and called the American Volunteer Group. That opinion was that the United States should direct its then limited strength against the Japanese flank from China. They asked that I assure Chennault that he was appreciated, but that he must play ball with General Henry H. (Hap) Arnold, head of the Army Air Corps. Otherwise he would get no equipment. Arnold was extremely influential, Chennault should be advised, and had to be humored.

About a fortnight after Stilwell's departure for China-Burma-India, I left Washington, on February 25. Also bound for Stilwell's theater were six officers and a sergeant. We flew by one of Pan American's original clippers, a flying boat, to Belém at the mouth of the Amazon—moist, mossed, suffocating, hyper-tropical—then Natal, and across the Atlantic to somnolent Fisherman's Lake in Liberia. The remainder of the trip was by two-engine C-47 transport planes to Kano and then Maidugiri, both in Nigeria, across the scrubby wilderness of Chad to Khartoum dominated by the Nile, up to Cairo, swarming with handsome British staff officers whom the troops called the gabardine swine, over to Tel Aviv, down to the Shatt-al-Arab, carrying the mingled waters of the Tigris and the Euphrates, out above the azure-emerald Persian Gulf to Sharjah's desert airstrip manned by an RAF ground crew of a forlorn half dozen and a gazelle, along the desolate, jagged coasts of Iran and Baluchistan to Karachi, and finally trans-subcontinentally to teeming, beholy-cowed Calcutta.

The flight from New York to Calcutta, stopping at night and encountering delays, took thirteen days. Because of bottlenecks in air transport to Burma, I remained in the effete luxury of Calcutta's Indo-Anglo-American society for some ten days waiting for my turn to join Stilwell. During this time I encountered C. J. Pao, the shrewd and engaging Chinese Consul General whom I had met in Peking and who, in my adversity twenty years later at the foot of the Andes, proved to be a staunch friend.

Meanwhile Chiang Kai-shek had given Stilwell, now a Lieutenant General, the benefit of a great deal of faint-hearted advice and orally told the American he was to command two Chinese armies (each of three understrength divisions) on their way to the front in Burma. The Japanese were north of Rangoon, which they had occupied on March 6. The mixed force of British, Burmese, Indian, and Gurkha units under General Sir Harold Alexander had been badly shaken by the swift ferocity of the Japanese onslaught. On what may be euphemistically called a line, east-west in lower Burma, the British Empire units occupied the western sector and the Chinese, with a toe-in-the-water disposition, moved tentatively into the eastern. Allied air support was from the British Royal Air Force (RAF), whose obsolescent aircraft were being rapidly destroyed, and from Chennault's American Volunteer Group. The AVG, with new P-40 pursuit planes and aggressive tactics, outperformed the enemy, but nevertheless were being ground down by sheer superiority of Japanese numbers and AVG lack of aircraft, parts and personnel replacements.

Soon after assuming command of the Chinese expeditionary force in Burma, Stilwell discovered that his assumption was indeed no more than that. His orders were secretly referred back to the Generalissimo for final decision. Chiang also issued behind Stilwell's back a babble of vacillating orders to his distracted officers in the field, even down to the regimental level.

The Generalissimo was morbidly defensive-minded, and in its most fatal manifestation: static defense, yielding the initiative to the enemy. Furthermore, in his obsessive hoarding of materiel and troops he only reluctantly committed his units to battle, and then piecemeal. For he believed that to concentrate force was to risk greater loss than committing it in minimal increments. Which was, up to a point, true. But it was not the way either battles or wars are won.

Stilwell's headquarters were at Maymyo, the prettily landscaped summer capital to which the Government of Burma had retreated. Stilwell was not at his headquarters but at the front when I arrived on March 22. And Pinky was with him.

The next day the General and Dorn returned to headquarters, a big red brick rest house belonging to the American Baptists. Stilwell was tired, but still exuded his characteristic nervous energy. On March 24, the following day, I noted in my diary,

> *General Stilwell in his bare room off the bare upstairs porch said, "Sit down." Each in a wicker chair, he said "There's nothing I can tell you about how to run your job. You're a free agent. All you have to do is keep things running smoothly between the civil authorities here and us." So much for functioning, as the Department of State had enjoined me, "at the direction and under the supervision of General Stilwell."*

Civil authority in Burma was collapsing on all sides. The Burmese, including officials and lesser government employees, felt no loyalty to their British masters. And with the Japanese trampling all under foot, most Burmese, including those who were servants to the King-Emperor, were in panic looking to their own safety and for ways in which they might ingratiate themselves with the new conquerors. The more enterprising took to sabotage, ambush, arson, and otherwise acting as collaborators of the invaders. There was precious little civil authority left for me to deal with. Any authority that existed was military—and that only when immediately enforceable by a bullet in the head.

In establishing relations with the Government of Burma, I called first on the Governor's military aide, who seemed to be not at all put out that at 4:40 p.m. I had roused him from a siesta. At tea and cakes with him and his pet gibbon, Miss Gibb, I took up with him my first piece of business— the misuse of jeeps by Chinese soldiers for private enterprise. Ah yes, the police in Mandalay had complained to the offending Chinese military on this score, only to have abuse heaped upon them. So the problem was a military one, not a civilian one.

The Governor, Sir Reginald Hugh Dorman-Smith, hospitably received me a few days later with pink gins and wide-ranging discourse. We concluded that Americans and Britons should be on guard against rumors designed to create rifts between us. The Governor made mild fun of the confused command structure in Burma, a matter on which his principal secretary, a Mr. Binns, had the day before spoken out more plainly to me. Binns had observed that General Stilwell had introduced himself as commander of the Chinese Fifth and Sixth Armies, the Chinese expeditionary force in Burma. Then General Tu, the commander of the Fifth Army, represented himself in much the same way. General Alexander, the senior British commander in Burma, of course regarded himself as in command of all the allied forces in this British colony. And finally, Binns pointed out, by the constitution of Burma only the Governor is in charge of the defense of Burma, no one else. What Binns did not know was that the Generalissimo was also in the act, regularly undercutting the authority he had conferred upon Stilwell.

By the end of March Stilwell was so wroth over the Generalissimo's bad faith and deceptions that he flew to Chungking to seek a showdown with Chiang. He took me with him, for there was nothing constructive that I could do with the Government of Burma in a condition of rigor mortis. In any event, it was time that I reported to the Ambassador from whose embassy in Chungking I was detailed to Stilwell. En route to Chungking, Stilwell picked up Chennault at Kunming, to which place Chennault had withdrawn his badly battered AVG leaving the enemy in uncontested control of the Burmese skies.

When Stilwell was having it out with the Generalissimo, I was paying my respects to the Ambassador, my tepid admirer from days at the Department and Peking, Clarence E. Gauss. Although I respected his utter rectitude, his Puritan sense of duty, and his inquiring, precise mind, I sensed that the depressing, ingrown atmosphere of Chungking, rancid with spite and intrigue, had soured Gauss. I thought that he needed a change. The Ambassador, for his part, did not think much of my detail to the General. With a wry smile he said that I belonged behind a desk, at work in his embassy, not gallivanting around China-Burma-India.

To Chennault I passed on Currie's advice about playing ball with General Arnold. Chennault said that his volunteers, among whom discontent and indiscipline had become rife, would willingly accept induction into the Army Air Corps provided they were first returned home to see their families, as promised in their contracts. Although he did not explicitly say so, it was evident from his presentation that he agreed with his fliers that it would be unfair to induct them—and himself—forthwith. Chennault, after all, had no desire to be subordinate to Stilwell, an old foot soldier. The airman enjoyed having, as a favorite of the Chiangs, direct access to the Generalissimo and Madame Chiang. They found most congenial his doctrine that Japan could be defeated by air power with minimal ground effort. And there was little doubt in Chennault's mind that he was the one uniquely qualified to accomplish this feat. As he said to me, the Army Air Corps would need one thousand men to do what he could do with one hundred and fifty.

Gauss, Stilwell, and Chennault were the three dominant American personalities in China from early 1942 until late in 1944. They were, all three, strong-willed, each highly competent in his own profession, dedicated to and tireless in what he was doing, quick to take offense, and given to righteous (each according to his own interpretation) wrath. Chennault's pretension to omnipotence and his persistent scheming to usurp Stilwell's position created and kept going a Chennault-Stilwell feud that involved the Chiangs and the White House. Gauss felt snubbed by both generals, who rarely consulted with him. And he was too unbending to take the initiative in trying to create a collaborative relationship with at least the theater commander. As for Stilwell, his disregard of the Ambassador was not because he disliked Gauss. Rather, Stilwell was not inclined to seek counsel from others—although he would welcome practical advice when proffered. In fact, Vinegar Joe Stilwell liked the Ambassador even though he looked upon Gauss as something of a sourpuss.

*   *   *

With every step that the Allies retreated in Burma, India's importance to them grew. India was a fallback position, and in depth, thanks to its size. It was the base for a vital air bridge into China, a base in which to grow and manufacture war supplies, and to prepare for and then mount a counteroffensive.

India was an area about which Stilwell and his staff were far less informed than they were about China. Not only was Stilwell a China specialist, he had then on his staff more than half a dozen exceptionally able China and Japan specialists. But he had no expert on India, an area of study that had been neglected in the American Government and academe.

I could be most useful to the General, it seemed to me, if I investigated and surveyed for him the Indian political and economic scene. I put this idea to Stilwell. He accepted my suggestion and on April 5 I left Chungking for India.

On the same day the Generalissimo and Madame Chiang flew to Burma with Stilwell. Chiang assured his American commander that he would instruct his generals to obey Stilwell's orders. Whatever the Generalissimo may have told his principal officers, it did not halt the continuing retreat nor instill in them obedience to the foreigner. The sudden and utter disintegration of a Chinese division at the eastern end of the "line" when a much smaller Japanese force out-maneuvered and struck it, meant that the allies were outflanked. The final debacle was not long in coming. By the end of April the Chinese and British Empire forces were in demoralized flight. The remnants of the Chinese armies straggled back into China, excepting two decimated divisions, which, like Alexander's surviving troops, staggered out over jungle trails into India.

It had taken four Japanese divisions four months to rout the larger, motley allied forces of Burmese, Chinese, Indian and British units. The climax was galling for Stilwell. Cut off from vehicular and air transportation, he, Dorn, and about one hundred others slogged over jungled mountains to India. There he snorted to newsmen, "I claim we got a hell of a licking. We got run out of Burma and it is humiliating as hell. I think we ought to find out what caused it, go back and retake it."

What caused the humiliating licking so far as China was concerned, Stilwell told the Generalissimo in early June, was the structure and the character of the Chinese Army. It was weak for more reasons than shortage of equipment. The three hundred Chinese divisions were understrength; if they were consolidated to full strength divisions and all available materiel redistributed, the number of units would reduced, but the overall effectiveness would be greatly increased. Furthermore, only a few of the general officers were competent. They should be retrained and the others gotten rid of, "otherwise the army will continue to go downhill, no matter how much materiel is supplied for it." Also, the Generalissimo should designate one man whose "absolute control of the troops must not be infringed upon." And awards and punishments should be promptly administered.

Madame Chiang Kai-shek, who often participated in the Generalissimo's conferences with foreigners, told Stilwell that his critique was similar to that received by Chiang several years earlier from his German military advisers. So the comments made by the American General were not new to the Generalissimo.

At a subsequent Stilwell meeting on military reform Madame Chiang was again present and again elucidating and expanding upon her husband's aloof pronouncement. In sum, she told Stilwell that his recommendations could not be put into effect and that it was necessary to be "realistic." Five years earlier, Chennault, while serving the Chiangs as military aviation adviser, had pressed the Generalissimo to take drastic action against the incompetence and corruption in the Chinese Air Force. Madame Chiang told him that her husband said that "the Chinese are the only people he has to work with, and if we get rid of all those people who are at fault, who would be left?"

The fact of the matter was that had Chiang undertaken such a sweeping purge, "all those people who are at fault" would have liquidated him before he had gotten started. While he was despotically inclined, the Generalissimo did not have the dictatorial power to purge at will, as did Hitler and Stalin. Nor could he houseclean a manifestly corrupt and inefficient arm of the government as could a strong leader in a democracy. He was a captive of the sorry forces he manipulated.

The military establishment, like the rest of the state structure, suffered from the fact that China was in transition from the traditional society, which had endured for millennia, to an undefined modern society. The Chinese Army was made up of congeries of soldiery. Some divisions, created by Chiang's central government, were regarded as modern and were usually responsive to Chiang's wishes. Many other units belonged to neo-warlords, and were regionally levied and maintained and therefore in a negotiatory relationship with the Generalissimo—he had to bargain for compliance. Finally, in 1942 relatively small Chinese Communist forces, although designated as a nominal part of the national army, were really in a state of suspended insurgency, blockaded by several hundred thousand of Chiang's less unreliable troops, while both sides awaited the end of hostilities with Japan to resume their civil war.

The warlord mentality flourished in the commanders of provincial units, lingered in the national government office corps, but did not exist with the Communists. It assumed that a military formation was the private property of its commander, a capital holding from which he derived his income. The commander of a provincial division, for example, received revenue from the people whose area his division occupied. If he associated himself with the national government he also received subsidies for troop pay, rations and other expenses. The general with a keen business sense— and most of them had that—therefore padded his statement of troop strength and kept his expenses, the number of men he actually retained, at a lesser level.

For example, the commander of the Chinese Fifth Army in Burma informed the British, who supplied the Chinese rice, salt, and a supplementary cash payment for other food, that he had 45,000 men. Although the British believed that the correct figure was under 28,000, they nevertheless accepted and paid out on the basis of General Tu's claim. After advancing 240,000 rupees, the British checked Tu's divisions, the commanders of which declared that they had not received any of the payments. So the British discontinued the subsidies pending evidence that the troops received the money due them. Tu did not produce any such proof.

As his unit was his capital, the commander-entrepreneur was not keen to engage it in any enterprise that reduced its profitability or risked its loss. It was all very well to take the offensive in the good old days when warlordism was in flower and the chances of loot and expanded territory were good speculative risks. But in this war against an aggressive, implacable foreign enemy, caution was essential. Conserve materiel and manpower by falling back and do not jeopardize your own unit if the one next to you finds itself in trouble—retreat before he does, lest he leave you exposed and vulnerable.

The defensive, negative attitude of most Chinese generals was reinforced by Chiang Kai-shek's strategy. From the beginning of the Japanese invasion in 1937 it had been based on the assumption that China could not defeat Japan, the hope that the United States or the Soviet Union would eventually become embroiled in war with Japan and thereby cause its withdrawal from China, and the conviction that he must husband his resources for the civil war against the Chinese Communists that would follow the end of the war against Japan. The Japanese attack on Pearl Harbor therefore came as a godsend to Chiang and his Kuomintang regime. His hope was well on the way to fulfillment. The Americans could now be depended upon to finish off the Japanese. And, as an ally, he could demand quantities of arms from Washington, which he would hoard against the coming showdown with the Communists.

Chiang's strategy may not have been heroic, but it was realistic and practical. And it fitted not only the outlook of the generals and the Kuomintang but also the sentiment of Chinese people who were genuinely war-weary. But to the outside world, Chiang's propagandists represented China as militant and heroic.

Stilwell believed that by bargaining, engaging in a quid pro quo exchange of American military equipment for Chinese offensive action, he might be able to activate the Chiang regime. I was of the same opinion. The General's control over lend-lease supplies entering China seemingly gave him a strong bargaining counter. But the White House—Roosevelt and his assistants Harry Hopkins and Lauchlin Currie—was early in the war sentimental about China and disinclined to place any conditions on aid to that country. Materiel assistance to China was in any event only a trickle in 1942 and 1943 because of limited production, the competing requests from our fighting allies, the British and the Russians, and after the loss of Burma, the tonnage limitations of what could be airlifted into China.

Unable at this stage to bargain, Stilwell offered inducements to action—he would train, organize, and, as American materiel became available, equip a modern army for the Generalissimo. He persuaded Chiang to let him begin with the Chinese troops which retreated from Burma into India. He also offered a program to bring up to strength, train, and equip 30 reorganized divisions. This was accepted and gotten under way. Whereupon Stilwell presented plans for another 30 divisions, followed late in 1943 by an offer for a third 30 divisions. With 90 such divisions Chiang should be able not only to expel the Japanese but also secure his domestic supremacy after the war.

CHAPTER VI

A MOMENT WITH MR. GANDHI

Writing from New Delhi to the young woman in Washington whom I would later marry, I reported in April 1942 that

> *Since leaving Chungking I have had trouble with my eyes—infection. So yesterday night after I arrived I went to a specialist recommended by the hotel, Dr. T. K. Uttam Singh, D.O.M.S. (London). First he wanted to sell me spectacles. Then he turned back both my eyelids and announced with profound spiritual detachment that I had trachoma. So I sat down in a rattan chair, tilted my head back and he painted my eyes with 2% silver nitrate caustic solution. That was about 4:40. At 5:30 my eyes ceased to feel as if hot cinders were in them, and I could see.*
>
> *But in the interim we had a most profitable conversation. It started, of course, on the Cripps-Congress negotiations and ended with the identification of oneself with God through casting out, in the order of increasing difficulty, desire, hate, greed and the sense of personal identity—the ego. En route, we touched upon the cycle through which India has passed and is passing: six thousand years in which she was the most advanced and the dominant nation in the world, then the past two thousand in which she had slept through an evil epoch, and now coming up to a golden age in which India will lead the rest of the world.*
>
> *Tomorrow morning I'm going to a plain, unimaginative, wicked, whiskey-drinking doctor to find out whether I really have trachoma. In any event, what if I do. We Americans have a health fetish. Disease is like war—it's*

normal. It's a nuisance and uncomfortable and requires a lot of fussing,
but it's good for your character, mellows you. That is, if you get over it.

I got over mine, which was no more than acute conjunctivitis.

India was to me a vast unknown when I had first passed through it a month earlier on my way to Burma and China. To be sure I was acquainted with Mowgli and Gunga Din and had even read E. M. Forster's *A Passage to India*. But beyond that I was ignorant of this manifold land.

Most Americans were uninterested in India, except as they imagined it—a freakish place inhabited by snake-charmers, practitioners of the rope trick, starving untouchables, bejeweled maharajahs, and widows flinging themselves in suttee on the funeral pyres of their husbands. Even in places where one might expect to encounter a fund of solid information there were some gaps. I remember Dean Rusk saying later that shortly after Pearl Harbor, as an earnest reserve officer at the War Department, he endeavored to learn about India. He asked for the military intelligence files on that country. He was handed a single folder in which reposed one old newspaper clipping and a *National Geographic* map of that part of the world on which someone had stamped SECRET.

The American high command, however slightly informed about India, came to regard that country as an important factor in the war against Japan. In the spring of 1942, with the defense of Burma collapsing and a powerful Japanese naval task force scudding into the Bay of Bengal, fears arose that the enemy might invade India and turn that base area for the supply of China and reconquest of Burma into a battlefield.

How would the Indian people react to a Japanese invasion? The Burmese people, we were discovering, were so anti-British that, when they did not actively collaborate with the Japanese, they passively accepted the invaders as new conquerors replacing the old. Would this happen in India? And even if the enemy did not invade, how would the anti-British feeling prevalent among Indians develop and affect us Americans? Would we, as allies and guests of the British in India, be enveloped in the hostility of a population hating its waning colonial rulers more than the new imperialism surging out of the east? We did not have the answers.

The salient facts about the India of 1942 were imposing. It was big, including what are now Pakistan and Bangladesh. Larger than Western Europe, it was referred to as a subcontinent. India was also populous, some 350 million inhabitants.

They were remarkably diverse—australoid peoples, such as the Dravidians, mainly in the south; Aryans, mostly in the north; and Mongoloids (my Naga friends, for example, whom we will learn more about later) along the northern frontiers. The diversity was most striking in the language differences, even within ethnic groups. About 1,500 languages and dialects were spoken in India.

Two of the great religions of the world, Hinduism and Buddhism, had originated in India. Islam was introduced by conquerors from the northwest and displaced Buddhism as the second most popular religion. Hindus and Muslims became inter-mingled, although the principal Muslim communities were in the northwest and northeast, while the Hindus were in the majority in the center and heavily so in the south. Other religious communities were much smaller. Among them were Sikhs, Christians, Jains, Zoroastrians, and, on the southern coast, the remnants of a Jewish colony.

It was evident in 1942 that the two major communities did not enjoy an unruffled relationship. Religious animosities sometimes flared into bloody communal rioting. Furthermore, Muslims, who were generally poorer than Hindus, resented what they believed was Hindu economic discrimination against them.

Cleavages also existed within the Hindu community. They were the rigid, hereditary differences among the four principal castes and also between those within the caste system and those outside of it—the untouchables, pariahs.

The paramount authority in India was the Viceroy, representing George VI, who, while only King of England, etc., was Emperor of India. The British wisely had not tried to impose their administration over all of India. They directly governed the 17 provinces of British India. But they allowed a constellation of native states, from tiny to big, varying degrees of autonomy so long as the rajahs, maharajahs, and other princelings, however called, acknowledged the British raj.

The instrument of British rule was the Government of India. It administered British India and supervised, usually lightly, the states. The GOI was run by several hundred Britons who occupied the controlling positions. Nearly all were members of the ICS, the Indian Civil Service, regarded by many Britons as one of the most desirable of careers. The vast majority of officials, from members of the Viceroy's Council, a pseudo-cabinet, to the village postman, were Indian. A select few were members of the ICS.

The British tolerated Indian political organizations, the most influential of which was a party called the Indian National Congress. It stood for

Indian independence and claimed to represent all Indians irrespective of creed or class. In reality its following was predominantly Hindu. Mohandas K. Gandhi, the Mahatma or Great Soul, and originator of nonviolent resistance, dominated the Congress party. Jawaharlal Nehru and Mrs. Sarojini Naidu, known abroad for their literary attainments as well as their political activities, were among the secondary figures in the party.

The Muslim League, headed by Mohammed Ali Jinnah, advocated the creation on the subcontinent of an Islamic state to be called Pakistan, in which the Muslims would be free of what they regarded as oppression by both the British and the Hindus. Militant Hindus, for their part, belonged to the Hindu Mahasabha, which called for the uncompromising supremacy of the Hindu community. Other parties and factions, including rival communist parties, sought attention and support. But none approached the strength of the Congress, the League or the Mahasaba.

My initial instructors on India were colleagues in the American diplomatic mission at New Delhi and the consulate general at Calcutta. They were well informed, generously shared what they had learned with me, and introduced me to their British and Indian contacts. This was most helpful, but I wanted to go further afield, to other parts of India, and to meet influential Indians outside the diplomatic circuit, especially the troublemakers.

Had I been on the staff of the American Mission, it would have been awkward or even improper for me to associate with those hostile to the government to which I would have been accredited, the Government of India. But I was assigned to the American Embassy in China and detailed to General Stilwell. My legitimacy in India derived from my detail to the general who, as Commanding General of American Forces China-Burma-India, enjoyed for himself and his staff an accepted standing in India. As Stilwell allowed me wide latitude of initiative and action, I was free to move about the country and to seek out Indians with whom my Foreign Service colleagues had little or no contact.

Beginning my political explorations, I went to a meeting of the Congress leadership at Allahabad. Uninvited, I intended simply to appear on the scene and ask to be allowed to see and hear as much as permitted. Fortunately, I was in the company of Edgar Snow, who, as a famous liberal journalist, was a presumed partisan of Indian independence and therefore assured of a welcome. In any event, all literate Indians, especially the Congress people, were fascinated by the American newcomers on the Indian scene. It was not simply the novelty of the American presence and personality, it was also, at least during the first half of 1942, an astonishingly widespread assumption that the United States could and might induce Britain to give India back to the Indians. We were expected to identify ourselves with the Indians, for had we not also suffered under the British colonial oppression?

"With the magic password, 'American correspondent,'" I wrote in my diary on May 2, "Ed and I were hustled through the crowd into the council hall. The floor was covered with white canvas on which perhaps 300 people were seated. Ed and I sat on some steps at the side of the hall."

There on the low platform at the end of the small hall were those who only five years later would govern India. Gandhi was absent, but only in the flesh, for although he was at his ashram, in Central India, all of the Working Committee were aware of what he expected of them. Sitting on a chair just off stage was the glamorous super-Brahmin, Nehru. Also on the platform was C. Rajagopalachari, the clever, pragmatic politician from Madras who would in 1948 become Governor General of India. The brilliant, ebullient, poet-politician, Mrs. Naidu, was settled comfortably on the floor with other members of the Working Committee. Maulana Azad, one of Congress's token Muslims, whose membership was pointed to as a refutation of the Muslim accusation that the party was really a Hindu organization and not representative, presided over the meeting, seated on a chair and hunched over a footstool-high table.

The issues before the meeting were conditioned by two recent developments. One was the breakdown of negotiations between Congress and Sir Stafford Cripps, Lord Privy Seal, who had been sent out from London with a qualified offer of independence for India. Each side blamed the other for the failure. The second development was that by bombing some of the east coast towns, the Japanese had suddenly brought home to the Indians the threat of invasion.

Reflecting Gandhi's position, the sense of the meeting was negative and passive—it would be futile to attempt to reopen negotiations with the British; the British would never relinquish control; also, it would be useless to seek to join forces with the Muslim League in approaching the British because the League would not accept a Congress overture. As for the war against Japan, the Congress would not support the British and if the Japanese invaded, they should be met by Gandhian non-violent resistance. Rajagopalachari voiced the only dissent.

"The windows were open," I noted in my journal. "The railroad track lay beyond. An occasional train went past whistling in a piping little voice.

The windows behind the platform were also open, framing in neat symbolism a corner of a small house with a collapsing roof caused by a crumbling wall."

Rajagopalachari was speaking when we came in. A slight, stooped little man swathed in white yards of cotton and wearing a pair of large black glasses. He was speaking in well-chosen English. The atmosphere he created and that created by most of the other speakers was that of a polite debating society. There was obvious relish in the making and receiving of witticisms. The only sense of urgency and crisis was that of having to catch the 11 a.m. train to Madras on which some of the congressmen were returning home.

Rajaji was arguing for his so-called Madras resolution: India was being attacked; Indians had already been killed on Indian soil; it was useless to cry out over the inequities of the present Government; India must unite now; Mr. Jinnah's Muslim League can be brought into a national government. It is a child which wants to sit in the front seat of a car taking a family to the station—if you enter into a discussion with the child on who is to sit up front you miss the train. The principal obstacle to a rational government is the psychological one of Muslim prestige; concede Pakistan in principle and in practice you will find the Muslims cooperating.

Then several other members of the Working Committee spoke. The speeches in native language were sprinkled with English phrases: popular mandate, wishful thinking, subtle brain, child psychology. The members and ladies in the gallery followed the proceedings intently.

Nehru, who had a cold and cough, spoke in opposition to the resolution, of course. He made a very poor case. He did little more than say that the concept of Pakistan was repugnant to him and opposed to the objectives of the Congress. He said that he had sought to bring about a Hindu-Muslim rapprochement, and that if going down on his knees to the Muslims or to the beggars would serve to bring about internal unity, he would gladly do so.

Maulana Azad, who looked and gesticulated rather like a forceful mayor of a small French town, allowed Rajaji a final speech. He [Rajagopalachari] opened with a crack saying that Pandit Nehru, possessing the reputation and personality that he did, had no need to resort to eloquence. He went on to say that time was very short, that the attitude of the Congress might serve in peace time but that in the present crisis the Congress should seize the initiative and seek a solution through compromise with the Muslims. (He did not say here that this was the best revolutionary opportunity before

Indians in many years.) "You have proved your case against the British to the hilt, but what purpose does it serve?" The Congress should take such authority as was offered and use it.

The meeting broke up. The hot, tired young ushers in orange colored saris and soiled chemises ceased their bustling, leaned against the walls and fanned themselves. The young troopers in maroon-colored shorts melted into the sweating, milling crowd out in the sunny street. I saw a banner which at first I thought must be a slogan but which turned out to be an advertisement of a potion designed to induce virility.

"And so with the Burma front collapsed and the enemy of the Indian people on the threshold, Congress adjourns," I wrote, "incapable (for many, many reasons) of adopting toward a threatening dynamic imperialism any more effective program than that employed against a decadent imperialism—non-violent non-cooperation."

In the dreadful heat of the Allahabad mid-day, Ed and I decided that the only course to follow was non-violent non-cooperation with the climate. So we took sweat-drenched naps.

About 4:40 we called on Rajaji, a frail little man with slender hands, the palms of which were dyed lavender. The trouble with Congress is that it has been fighting the British so long that its grievances have become an obsession, observed Rajaji in a cool analytical tone. Congress has the DeValeran mentality; like the Irish it can only object and obstruct. We are presented with the greatest revolutionary opportunity which we have had in many, many years, and we are unable to do anything about it. The purpose of my resolution was to break the stagnant situation in which we find ourselves with an appeal to action. But Congress, again like the Irish, will not accept any considerable compromise (whether with the Muslims or the British) because it talks only in terms of the perfect and complete solution: a united and free India.

Ed asked him if he thought anything could be done, despite Congress's position on non-violent non-cooperation, in Madras to organize the Madrasis to resist any Japanese attack. Rajaji said no. Congress was too strong and he further implied that he would not wish to work outside the Congress framework.

Rajaji declared that the League could not be ignored as Congress sought to imply. While the more enlightened Muslims were allied with Congress, it could not be denied that the League did represent the great mass of the Indian Muslims.

Chiang Kai-shek, he said, had written a letter to Nehru recently in which he complained about the British conduct of the war in Burma, pointing out their many faults. "What good does that do?" Rajaji asked. To my mind this statement, which surprised me, was one of the clearest indications (if sincerely expressed) of a constructive attitude.

The overall attitude of Rajaji was clearly pessimistic. I had the impression that he felt the situation to be beyond repair.

Ed and I rode by tonga [two-wheeled horse cart] to Nehru's elegant residence. Mrs. Naidu, her daughter, several disciples and a young Chinese broadcaster from Singapore were there. Nehru was as aristocratic and spiritual looking as depicted. We sat around eating mango ice cream and listened mostly to Nehru, Mrs. Naidu, and Ed. The stone floors were cool, bowls of flowers were arranged in exquisite taste, everyone looked clean and fresh (save Ed and me). A copy of *Life* was on one of the low tables.

Nehru said that Cripps had done more harm to the British position in India than any one person in a long time. Cripps was a terrible statesman, he hadn't realized how bad a statesman Cripps was, Cripps had no tact and lost his temper. (Mrs. Naidu agreed emphatically.) The failure of the negotiations was not Cripps's fault. He was bound hand and foot by Churchill and [Leopold] Amery [Secretary of State for India]. In reply to a question from Ed, Nehru declared that he had no knowledge in advance of Cripps's arrival of what terms were brought. He had been warned ahead of time that the proposals were "very bad." That was all. Congress had opened negotiations, of course, with the idea of working itself into full power—that was the reason for the initial compromises. But when Cripps fell back to insisting that the Viceroy's powers could not be curtailed, the negotiations collapsed (the Indian nationalists felt that they weren't offered enough to be even a poor Trojan horse). The Churchill-Amery-Linlithgow [Viceroy] combination is the worst India has faced. He quoted with evident satisfaction Amery's defense of the Japanese action in Manchuria in 1931: "You can't blame the Japanese, why they're just doing what we'd do in India."

Corruption in the Government of India is extraordinarily widespread, Nehru maintained. Especially in connection with defense industries.

Nehru and Mrs. Naidu dominated the scene. The other Indians were very quiet and attentive. Ed later told with amusement of Missimo's [Mme. Chiang Kai-shek, who had recently visited India] venture into a sari. La Naidu said, "You know how distinguished and refined looking Mme. C. is in her native Chinese costume. She put on the sari which we gave her and, my dear, she looked so common—those Mongolian features, like a hill girl from Nepal, you know."

Nehru and one of his lieutenants graciously escorted us out to our tonga.

We had no opportunity to say good-bye to the maitre d'hotel of the station restaurant—a rare soul who maintained that life for the white man began to go downhill with the arrival of Lady Curzon, a wealthy American, née Leiter [wife of Lord Curzon, Viceroy at the turn of the century.] Before that the small man had been able to have his three polo ponies, his whiskies and live the life of a God-fearing respectable Englishman. But she spoiled India by bringing in great numbers of her wealthy American friends to show them her Empire and permit them to overpay the natives.

*   *   *

On May 3 I wrote that "the Indian I most wanted to meet was, of course, Gandhi, the Mahatma, the great soul. But he was at his retreat near Wardha in the center of the country. The heat there, some of my Indian friends warned me, became so intense that the countryside catches fire. This further whetted my curiosity."

May 7

The Bombay Mail arrived at Wardha at midnight, six hours late. The obliging station people tell me how to get to the dak bungalow [government rest house], which turned out to be full. So Abdul [a station attendant] gets for me a bench out of the ladies waiting room, I spread my roll on it and go to sleep on the station platform—fortunately no trains unloaded on it during the night.

May 8

At dawn I arise to the interest and delight of a small audience of Indian children who had been impatiently awaiting this event. Abdul gets me a poor breakfast from the Mohammedan food stall and in return gets another extravagant four annas tip.

Passage was arranged for me in what, I was assured, was the most sumptuous tonga in Wardha, painted green, decorated with a painting of Gandhi and lesser prophets and drawn by a runty, indolent white stallion. The driver, with good political sense, wore a white Gandhi cap. He derived great satisfaction from and regularly made use of a particularly cavernous sounding bulb horn.

We left about six. About one third of the way to Gandhiville, I decided to change my clothes—which I did, including underwear, without the driver being aware of the metamorphosis.

We turned off the dusty and already hot road into a straw thatched settlement of one-storied buildings. All exceedingly simple and almost primitive. A young girl in white homespun was rolling up the bedding from five beds set out in front of one of the low thatched houses. Fifty yards away the Mahatma in white dhoti [loin cloth], tucked neatly up his crotch instead of the usual trailing around the ankles, stood with staff in hand talking at length with two small children seated on a hemp bed bare of covering. Around the great man hovered disciples, clean, intelligent, fine looking people, two of whom held black umbrellas over the saintly cranium shielding it from the early morning sun.

I was waiting in front of the office, to which I had been brusquely directed by an occidental woman with, could it have been, a teutonic accent? Two retainers dissuaded me from entering the dark little room in which I could distinguish only a large green safe. I was directed to a bed—they seemed to be everywhere—about 10 yards in front of the office room. Preferring to stand, I watched the Great Soul move by to inspect the room behind the five beds. The train of five or six disciples trailed in the wake of this rustic Friday morning inspection. A gracious Indian appeared to hear my request for a brief talk with Mahatmaji. He directed me to Mr. Desai, the Prophet's secretary. I found him in another thatched house which seemed to be all partitioned inside with wooden bars. But it had a telephone over which people were arranging for train accommodations.

Mr. Desai explained that the Mahatmaji gave interviews only after 4 p.m. When that didn't rout me, I indicating a willingness to wait, he explained that there were no toilet facilities available. Evidently there was a look of incredulity on my face for he finally gave the real reason—the Great Soul was that evening leaving for Bombay and had so much to do before departure. I suggested meeting Mr. G in Bombay. That seemed to strike the secretary as being the solution. Throughout these negotiations Mr. Desai had stood with a fistful of checks—one of which was for 50 pounds made out to Mahatma Gandhi (yes I can read upside down) but I couldn't see who had made it out.

Sitting on a bed in front of this shack was a professorial looking Indian, like Dr. Desai, of refined features. I think he was supposed to be meditating. My presence there obviously distracted him, so his status degenerated into just eavesdropping.

Getting back into my tonga I fell into conversation with three good-looking young Indians perhaps in their late teens or early twenties. They didn't seem to think much of the Congress policy of non-violent non-cooperation, which seemed to me to be blasphemy hardly uttered in that environment.

A few days later I queried a veteran American missionary about Gandhi. He characterized the Mahatma as hypocritical, reactionary, a Hindu partisan and caste biased. He told of attending a rural mass meeting some years earlier at which Gandhi, speaking in the vernacular, whipped the crowds into such a frenzy of anti-British feeling that some of the missionary's Indian friends moved quietly to his side to protect him, lest the crowd mistake his nationality and attack him. The Mahatma followed his harangue with a shorter speech in English on the practice of non-violence. It was the latter exposition which appeared in the press as the text of the Mahatma's address.

Gandhi granted me an interview in May at Bombay. Shortly after the meeting I recorded my impressions of the encounter.

In a quavering old taxi with a Muslim driver, I drove out to Malabar Hill and the pretentious Birla House. A sleekly simple young Hindu took my card. After a few minutes wait in the uncomfortable reception hall, Mahadev Desai came in, his head cocked to one side in greeting.

I was taken onto a verandah skirting the house. We came to a section facing the lawn. The floor was covered with white cotton cloth. I started to take off my shoes but was told it was all right to wear them. Seated on a white quilt and leaning against pillows, propped against the verandah wall was the skinny little saint. Perhaps because of the absence of teeth, he had very little face below a prominent hooked nose and owlish horn-rimmed spectacles. His spotless white homespun was tossed up over a shoulder. In a thin pleasant voice he begging pardon for not rising—"an old man's privilege." I was placed in a chair overlooking him to the left in front of him. On his right were Vallabhbhai Patel (organizational boss), a less sinister looking gentleman and two female acolytes. Desai I lost track of. I explained who I was and that I was an Asiatic of American race. I said that I had come to learn. He cracked back that this was most unusual. "Most Americans come to tell us what to do." His disciples laughed heartily.

As the interview proceeded I became uncomfortable at my elevation. So I said would he mind if I sat on the floor; I had lived a good deal in Japan and found sitting on the floor very comfortable. This seemed to cause some amusement. As I slipped down I noticed Desai, who had apparently been behind me, sly fox. He was hunched over and began edging further behind me trying to conceal what seemed to be notepaper. I later learned that he had taken 45 pages of notes on the conversation. I don't see how it was possible.

As Gandhi expounded in his even thin tone, my mind wandered once or twice and I observed one of the female disciples dozing off. But Mr. G's mind was clicking right along. Nothing fuzzy, excepting, of course, the whole philosophical concept. His mistrust of and obsession with the British was pronounced.

To General Stilwell I reported on May 14 the substance of my conversation with the Mahatma as follows:

> *In opening the conversation with Mr. Gandhi at Birla House, Bombay, I asked him what he thought the United States could do to be helpful to India. He replied, "Persuade the British to withdraw immediately and completely from India." He then went on to discuss the concept underlying this statement, a concept formulated during only the past few weeks.*
>
> *Japan's primary objective in this part of the world, the Mahatma said, is the destruction of British power. Eliminate the British from India and no incentive remains for the Japanese to attack India. The British were not able to withdraw from Malaya and Burma with dignity. They still have time to withdraw from India with dignity. If they leave now it would be best for Britain, best for India and best for the world.*
>
> *I observed that the Chinese had not been saved by a pacific attitude toward Japan from a Japanese invasion, and that Japan's incentives for attacking an independent India would seem to be scarcely less than they had been for attacking an independent China. Mr. Gandhi explained that India is not a neighbor of Japan as is China, and is therefore less likely to be subject to Japanese aggression.*

Mr. Gandhi admitted that a Japanese invasion might nevertheless be possible. In such a case, the Mahatma declared, "Our only weapon is non-violent non-cooperation. We are not a nation of heroes," he said, "I frankly recognize and admit that." He said that he would advocate that the Indian people refuse the Japanese food, water and labor. But he would not want wells poisoned or filled in with earth, because that would be violence. I asked about the application of a policy of scorched earth. He replied that he would oppose such a policy because it would involve violence.

The practice of non-violent non-cooperation against the Japanese, he recognized, would be quite a different matter than against the British. The British imprisoned and sometimes tortured, but they stopped short of killing. With the Japanese it would be for the Indians success or death.

Some of his friends, like Mr. Rajagopalachari, had argued with him that the British were civilized and the Japanese were barbarians, and that therefore Indians should at this juncture cooperate with the British to check the greater evil. His reply, Mr. Gandhi stated, was that India wanted neither British nor Japanese rule, that non-violence was the strongest force in the world and that its impact on the barbarian might be greater than on the civilized man. He said that the Japanese had experienced little contact with the Indian mind, and implied that if Japanese troops were met by non-violent non-cooperation from the Indian masses, they would in effect be defeated.

I alluded to his statement in Harijan that guerrilla warfare "is foreign to the Indian soil" and asked if he meant that to apply to the Muslims and the people of Northwestern India. The Mahatma replied that it was true that the people of the northwest had experience in guerrilla warfare, but it was against the small British garrisons there and would be of little value in fighting the Japanese. He intelligently discussed the exacting nature of guerrilla warfare, its limited value and the careful training and coordination with the regular army required for its success. He observed that training the masses for effective guerrilla warfare was a more difficult task than training regular troops.

In commenting on the futility of cooperating with the British at this juncture, Mr. Gandhi said that the British had been particularly oppressive following the conclusion of the First World War; he expected them, in the event that they were still in India at the conclusion of this conflict, to be even more overbearing than they are at present. He would not admit that the hold of British imperialism on India is relaxing; nor that the United

States might exert its good offices on behalf of India. He stated that American diplomacy was under the control of the British, and that the voice of those Americans in the United States friendly to India was being stifled by the British.

I asked whether in connection with his wish that the British withdraw he also desired that we leave too. "Naturally, yes," he replied.

I inquired of Mr. Gandhi whether he felt that there might not ultimately be general acceptance of Mr. Rajagopalachari's proposal that the Congress concede the principle of Pakistan in order to achieve an understanding with the Muslim League leading to the formation of a National Government. The Mahatma replied in vague terms, seeming to indicate an answer in the negative.

The conflict between the Hindu and Muslim communities Mr. Gandhi attributed to British machinations. Remove British control over India and the differences between the two would "disappear like the miasma that it is." I observed that this interpretation had been given to me by Hindus and by Muslims as well. In as much as both Hindus and Muslims seemed to recognize that they were being used against one another, I found it difficult to understand why they were not able to make common cause to thwart the designs on the communal unity which, as the Mahatma implied, both groups desired. Mr. Gandhi explained that notwithstanding this mutual Hindu and Muslim desire for unity, the British were able to play the communities off one against the other because "it is the British who distribute the loaves and fishes." They favor first one group and then the other, thus fostering communal difference.

Mr. Gandhi remarked that in his five hour conversation with General Chiang Kai-shek and "Madame Shek" he had gone over in detail the same ground which he had covered with me, save for his theory of immediate and complete British withdrawal, which he had only recently evolved. He expressed great sympathy for China, adding that the way for the British and us to help China was to get out of India.

Throughout the interview Mr. Gandhi was very cordial. Although not seeming to do so, he apparently watched my face closely, for he commented with amusement on a smile, which I thought was wholly inward.

In my journal I added: "As the interview was closing he said, 'You can tell whomever you report to that the old man is raving mad.' I must have had a look of bewilderment about me. Once or twice in the conversation I felt somewhat at a loss as to what I should say. There didn't seem to be any logical question to ask or comment to make."

While Gandhi did not make sense in the Anglo-American view of the war against Japan, he was persuasive to the majority of Hindus. He was able to lead them because he not only understood them but also was a concentrated reflection of themselves. He and they knew that the Hindus, at least, lacked confidence in their ability to dispose of the British by force. So for a score of years he had preached satyagraha, non-violent resistance, as the strategy for struggle against the British rule.

For Gandhi, satyagraha was also an expression of the morality that he taught. Non-violent resistance was therefore more than patriotic: it was virtuous. Gandhi was a revolutionary leader, but in the tradition of the Indian ascetic holy man. His pietistic stance and words consequently carried far more weight with many simple people than did the pronouncements of secular politicians. An Indian editor told me that the secret of Gandhi's power over people was that he treated everyone as a child. During the visit of Generalissimo and Madame Chiang Kai-shek to India, they met with Gandhi and, the editor smiled, the Mahatma offered to the imperious Madame Chiang the sanctuary of his ashram where she might "live as my daughter." I did not doubt that Gandhi's treatment of people as children had brought many under his spell. But Madame Chiang—whose troubled psyche caused her to treat everyone as a subject—was hardly one to have been captivated by the Mahatma's playfully audacious soul appeal.

CHAPTER VII

NEHRU AND "THE PROBLEM"

India, I had come to realize, was of concern to the United States not only as a base from which to prosecute the war against Japan but also as a potential entanglement in postwar colonial upheavals. I foresaw dreadful troubles in the final stages of and after the war when the European imperial nations attempted to hold on to or reoccupy their Asian colonies. The United States, following announcement of its intention to grant independence to the Philippines, was in Asian eyes relatively free of the colonial incubus. Indeed, many South Asians thought of Americans as champions of their desire for independence.

The cause of potential entanglement was our alliance with Britain, the Netherlands and the Free French in the war against Japan. These necessary and desirable ties could easily lead us into helping the imperial countries to maintain or reimpose authority over colonial peoples and thus involve us needlessly in alien conflicts contrary to our interests and convictions. With these anxieties in mind, I continued my exploration of India.

*   *   *

About a week after my session with Gandhi, a top Indian official in the Government, Ghulam Mohammed, told me that the Mahatma was preparing to incite some form of mass civil disobedience. I sought out Nehru in New Delhi, hoping to find out what was afoot.

In a two and a half hour visit on May 24, I asked Nehru about the reported plans for civil disobedience. He seemed to be disturbed that the alleged preparations were known. Unconvincingly he pled ignorance; he had been vacationing in the hills. I pointed out the obvious—the damage that disruption in India would do to our efforts to help China. Not only China would suffer, but straining the point in an appeal to his pro-Soviet sympathies, so would the Soviet Union. Nehru expressed, as I reported to Stilwell, "unemphatic agreement and continued to be his charming, dissemblingly sincere self."

Would he support Gandhi in the projected campaign? Nehru was non-committal. Following the advice of two Indian friends who said that "the only way to induce Jawaharlal to reveal what he is thinking is to make him flare up," I asked him if he believed that he should follow the dictates of the Congress Party (that is, Gandhi) even though they were counter to his convictions. He was evasive.

Gandhi had recently said, I went on, that Nehru was virtually his heir, that the Mahatma was not disturbed by Jawaharlal's occasional "apostasy" because he had faithfully carried out the Congress policy defined by Gandhi. Nehru pretended to be unaware that the Mahatma had claimed him as heir and asserted that he had more often won Gandhi over to his point of view than the other way around.

Getting no revelations, I asked why, if statements made to me were correct, was there no published accounting of Gandhi's Harijan Fund, ostensibly for improving the lot of the untouchables. This flustered Nehru, I reported to Stilwell, "Why that's a most unusual question," he exclaimed, "a most unusual question. Why, certainly statements have been published of the use of the fund. Of course, I have nothing to do with the fund. I don't know anything about the administration of the fund."

I was prepared to believe that he had nothing to with the fund. In any event, Nehru launched into a tirade about how badly the outcastes of Dr. Ambedkar's (leader of depressed classes) category abused outcastes of even lower grade. Inevitably, Nehru moved on to a dissertation on the inequities of the British, in historical depth. He then returned to a theme he had earlier expounded to me—how Indians listened regularly to Japanese broadcasts and "gloated" over the British reverses. He now added that the Japanese propaganda was clever. It told the Indians not to be impatient; they would soon be liberated by an Indian army of liberation—composed of prisoners taken in Burma and organized by the Japanese. He implied that the Indian listeners more than half believed what they heard on these broadcasts.

Several days after this conversation, Nehru went to Wardha to get the word from the Mahatma. After his return to his home in Allahabad I flew there on June 2 to find out what I could. Nehru said that he had not tried to present his own views to Gandhi in any detail; that he listened and told the Mahatma that he would go home and think over what he had learned. Nothing definite had been decided, nothing drastic was contemplated and, although the contradiction was not acknowledged, Gandhi demanded the withdrawal of the British even if chaos ensued.

But he and Gandhi were fully aware, I commented to Nehru, that a mass civil disobedience campaign hampering the war effort would alienate American and Chinese sympathies for the Indian nationalists. Furthermore, I failed to see how Gandhi could through such measures persuade the British to quit India. Although Nehru was noncommittal, my impression was that he was in agreement with what I said. But he was obviously not in a happy frame of mind. I felt that he was going through one of his recurring struggles between his intellectual convictions and his loyalty to the Mahatma.

This contradictory, indecisive personality, then, was Gandhi's heir apparent. An upper class Indian by birth and an upper class Englishman by education, Nehru was bicultural, an elegant, intellectual, ornamental aristocrat. Gandhi had overcome the anglicizing influence of his English education and re-Indianized himself. But not Nehru. I wondered if some less diluted Indian would not succeed the Mahatma. And I did not see in Nehru indications of force and command. Curiously, he was perhaps a greater international figure than national figure. Mrs. Naidu had commented that it was unfortunate that in the United States Nehru was regarded as the leader of the Congress Party. He was not. He was the theorist. Patel was the practical man of action.

Ghulam Mohammed told me that he had gone to school with Nehru in England. At the height of the campaign, back in India, to wear homespun and eschew English textiles, G.M. returned one day to the quarters that he shared with Nehru and discovered that Jawaharlal had in the transports of nationalist protest consigned G.M.'s expensive English suits to a bonfire of imperialist fabrics. This annoyed G.M., whose nationalism was not of Nehru's burning kind. Years later, in 1942, Ghulam Mohammed said to me that Nehru was being spoiled by American adulation. G.M. summed up Nehru as "intellectually dishonest and a weakling."

To the Western mind, Rajagopalachari was more comprehensible than Gandhi, and even Nehru. The position that he took at the Allahabad

Congress meeting was characteristic of his practical approach to politics, his willingness to work with what might be possible rather than rejecting any condition that was not, for him, perfect.

Rajagopalachari was cool and matter-of-fact on a subject that was becoming for me a major concern regarding the future—an antagonistic division of the postwar world in two, with the United States and its European allies reestablished in their Asian colonies in one camp and the non-white peoples of the world, opportunistically championed by the Soviet Union in the other. The white peoples, Rajagopalachari said when I saw him on October 20, 1942, cannot afford to continue to antagonize the colored peoples of the world. The colored peoples are going to win their freedom sooner or later. The whites had better grant that freedom sooner rather than later and so avoid the cumulating legacy of hatred.

*   *   *

The Congress Party was under the sway of Gandhi. But the Muslim League was controlled by Mohammed Ali Jinnah. In contrast to Gandhi's ostentatious, loin-clothed simplicity, the lean fine-featured Jinnah was something of a fop in his precisely tailored and sharply pressed suits. After several conversations with him, I commented in January 1943:

> Jinnah, as astute and opportunistic a politician as there is today in India, fulfills the role of fuehrer called for by the circumstances in which the Muslims find themselves (a minority feeling discriminated against by the Hindus.) He has skillfully exploited the apprehensions of his community and has built up the Muslim League as a disciplined organization obedient to his will.
>
> The political credo of the Muslim League, and Mr. Jinnah's battle cry, is Pakistan. Pakistan is a vaguely defined program for a more or less independent Muslim state in the areas where the Muslims are in the majority.

Ghulam Mohammed, whose tailored wardrobe Nehru had patriotically reduced to ashes, was one of those polished, astute Indians who moved urbanely through the two worlds of Asia and Europe. He left what was in effect a sub-cabinet post in the Government of India to become the Finance

Minister of Hyderabad. His final position after the creation of Pakistan was Governor General of the new state within the British Commonwealth.

G.M. was a man with few illusions. Once while in Switzerland, he told me, he had been asked by a European friend (Salvador Dali as I remember it) to describe India. He did so: a great oversized head above and in drifting clouds, a small emaciated body, wizened and ribs showing, then enormous, bloated legs, afflicted with elephantiasis and standing in mire. "That," he said, "is India."

Neither Congress nor the League was a workable political solution for India, Ghulam Mohammed exclaimed to me. The only feasible Indian government, he said, would be one composed of a few politicians—Rajagopalachari and two or three others—some of the more able Indians then serving the British raj, and several of the very competent big business executives.

Like all of the educated Indians with whom I conversed, Ghulam Mohammed was convinced that as the Allies began to win the war the British would be less and less inclined to grant India its independence. Because India was too weak and divided to overthrow British rule, its only immediate hope was that the American newcomers might induce London to grant independence to India. But the Americans, my Indian acquaintances said, were under the British spell. The war against Germany and Japan, they all lamented, would end in another Versailles; as the United States betrayed China at the 1918 peace conference, so it would turn its back on India, in the settlements made by the victors of World War II.

Ghulam Mohammed, like Rajagopalachari and some other Indians whom I drew out on the subject, asserted that American solidarity with Britain at the expense of Indian independence would eventually lead to conflict on the basis of color. Expanding the subject, G.M. said that the Anglo-American bloc had the strength to impose a peace that would be against the desires and will of the peoples of Asia. But that kind of peace would produce fermenting hatred of the whites. It would be a peace only for our time and would end in a war of Asia against the whites.

The president of the racially extremist Hindu Mahasabha was V. D. Savarkar. He lived in a modest house in Bombay's suburbs, where I called on him in May 1942. "A Sikh watchman with a dagger," I wrote at the time, "let me in the gate. I was taken upstairs to one corner of the house where the Hero Advocate of the Hindu people had his small, rather grubby bedroom. Mr. S received while sitting on his bed, clad in a white pajama-like suit and one sock minus its foot. His free toes were agile. Mr. S. was apparently near-sighted—he wore glasses with very thick lenses. Hanging on the walls of the bedroom were four or five pictures of my host, some in color."

The conversation that followed was one-sided. My few questions were answered by harangues: India belonged to the Hindus; the Muslims were foreigners; there must be a Hindu revival, and the establishment of a Hindu raj. Like racial fanaticism elsewhere, Savarkar's message was simplistic, feverish, racially narcissist, and xenophobic. I felt that he did not have the magnetism or the creative intelligence to be a successful leader.

The Mahasabha's vice president, Dr. S. Y. Mockerjee, was a quite different personality. Scholarly and respectable in appearance, he was a former Finance Minister of Bengal. I told him in January 1943 that Jinnah had expressed to me a wish that Rajagopalachari and Mockerjee would approach him with a request that the three of them ask the Viceroy for permission to confer with Gandhi (who had by then been jailed by the British) in search of a solution to the deadlock between the Indian nationalists and the British. Mockerjee displayed great interest in what Jinnah had said and exclaimed that he would get in touch with Rajagopalachari. But on the following day he told me it would be feasible only if Jinnah did not insist on acceptance of the principle of Pakistan. This was an issue on which Jinnah would not compromise. So nothing came of Jinnah's overture.

*　*　*

The 50 million untouchables, outcastes, those belonging to the "depressed classes," were not an organized political force. But they had a politically active champion who had risen from their shared degradation to membership on the Viceroy's Council. He was Dr. Bhimrao Ambedkar, paunchy, bespectacled and prosaic.

Ambedkar wanted independence for India, but only if it meant a better life for the depressed classes. He did not believe in the Congress party's protestations that its enlightened policies already guaranteed fair treatment of the untouchables. The party had failed, he maintained, to work earnestly for the betterment of the outcastes' lot. Furthermore, conservative members of Congress had no wish to remove the disabilities (including indenture of unborn children to lifetime service in payment of a loan) that made the untouchables so useful to upper caste Hindus.

The suggestion that the depressed classes might find an acceptable place in a Congress-League coalition did not appeal to Ambedkar. It would mean, he said, rule by three groups: "the Brahmin, who is a rascal; the Bania (the trading caste to which Gandhi belonged), who is a cheat; and the Muslim, who is a fool." No, he would wait until after the war and then if there was to be a transfer of power, the position of the untouchables should be negotiated with deliberate care among the British and the Indian factions.

This matter-of-fact, unprepossessing, canny politician inspired veneration among the untouchables. On the walls of their rooms his picture hung bedecked with garlands. American missionaries who had seen both Gandhi and Ambedkar amidst their respective followings said that the emotion welling out to Ambedkar was the greater. Untouchables would surge toward him to press their faces to his feet.

A young British officer, six months out of England and assigned to a regiment of untouchables, told me in December 1942, that these soldiers worshiped Ambedkar, actually prayed to him. After our conversation I noted, "During the recent riots they were stationed in Nagpur. The troops seemed to relish shooting Brahmins. In fact, the zeal of three or four of the untouchable soldiers was such that their rifles had to be taken away from them."

Was there friction between the untouchable troops and other Indian units? Yes. Particularly, in his experience, with the Sikhs.

The untouchable soldiers were, to the lieutenant, an interesting contrast to the skeptical Tommies. They had complete faith in their British officers. He felt it rather pathetic that these Indian lads should march down the road singing with great assurance, "And when the German soldiers see the British flag they will all run away." "The poor blokes haven't the slightest idea what it's all about."

Like the untouchables, the princes were not an organized political force. But they had no need of a champion. They did very well on their own, thank you. Financially speaking, they were comfortably off; the Nisam of Hyderabad was reputed to be one of the richest men in the world. And as for being highborn, the Maharajah of Udaipur was a descendant of the moon and had never been to Delhi to pay homage to the British raj because no Maharajah of Udaipur could go to Delhi save as a conqueror.

Going to Delhi, or precisely going to the ball at the Viceroy's House, did have drawbacks for princes. The young playboy Maharajah of Cooch

Behar, who liked Americans, attended a viceregal party in white tie and tails and was enjoying himself dancing with pretty girls when the Viceroy spotted him. Cooch Behar was sent packing, told to change into his satins and jewels and return to sit in ornate display with the other princes below the viceregal throne, which he did.

Another high-spirited young maharajah was Jaipur. Jai was good-looking, engaging and a first-class polo player. In conformity with tradition he had contracted two dynastic marriages—a princess and her niece from the ruling house of Jodhpur. Then asserting his individuality, he sought to take as his third wife Cooch Behar's beauteous, very bright, and emancipated sister, Ayesha. In the ensuing negotiations, Ayesha made her conditions plain—Jai must undertake to remain faithful to her for five (5) years. So alluring she was that Jai capitulated to her demand—an unprecedented humiliation for a maharajah. The princely set was properly scandalized. But Jai survived the traumatic five years and when my wife Patricia (whom I shall introduce later) and I knew them not long thereafter, Ayesha and he seemed to be unscarred by the experience.

As a footnote, Ayesha became active in national politics after India was granted independence. She was a prominent member of the legislature. In 1975 she got into trouble with the executive arm of the government that discovered that she had not turned in all of her treasure.

"Educate a woman and you place a knife in the hand of a monkey." So went an unchivalrous Hindu aphorism. An educated Hindu woman observed to me that among enlightened Indians, the women tended to be (a) more radical and realistic, and (b) less hysterical than the men. Be that as it may, I was impressed by the poise and silken strength of some of the Indian women I met. In mind and mettle they were unsurpassed by any of the men.

In another society supposedly dominated by males—the traditional Chinese—the same was true. In force of character and intelligence Chinese women were easily equal to the men. Again and again in Chinese history women of humble origins worked and intrigued their way into positions of great power. They were simply smarter, tougher and more determined than the men from whom they seized and held power.

*   *   *

Beginning an exploratory tour of southern India in November 1942, I took the Madras Mail from Calcutta southward. At one of the stops I fell into conversation with the train-driver, a toothless Anglo-Indian gaffer. Typical then of these people of mixed British and Indian blood, he welcomed being treated as an equal, for the Anglo-Indians were not fully accepted by either of the societies from which they stemmed. My friend said that he had re-tired some years earlier, but with the war he had been called back. Would I care to ride with him to the next station? Indeed I would.

Just look at this engine, he exclaimed. Patchwork. No new engines for years. The inspector had said that it was a scandal to have such an engine on a mail train. As I wrote in my journal,

> *We started out with some huffing and chuffing dignity—the old man at the controls, the fireman-wallah very business-like. But as we gained speed and the locomotive shuddered and twisted, and as I found myself pitted with ashes, the greater was the crew's nonchalance. At what seemed to me the pitch of the crisis, old ironsides leaned over and croaked, "We're doing 60." I groaned appreciatively. When it was all over and I was marveling that the front of the engine wasn't plastered with sirloins and spare ribs, I asked, "Do you kill many cows?" "Oh yes, and many humans, too. They try to beat you across the track. Now when I was a young engineer in 1908 I killed one, and if it hadn't been for some missionaries who happened to be along, I'd have been in a bad way." I still haven't found out whether it was a sacred cow that he killed or only a human.*

> *In the evening the engineers were changed. The new one too was an Anglo-Indian, but younger. He was worried about an accession to power by Indian nationalists: "We've been having the cream of it in this country and they know it (skim milk masquerading as cream). The British pretend to be worried about the fate of the small democracies after the war—what about us (the Anglo-Indians) whose very existence they are responsible for? I hope they give us Burma if they grant Congress its demands!"*

A wise Swiss doctor, Dr. H. H. Gass, whom I met a few days later, spoke sympathetically of the plight of the Anglo-Indians but they treated the Indi-ans worse than the British did. It was a case of over-compensation and a desire to associate themselves with the master-race.

An English friend had told me that Madras had a seventeenth-century flavor. Indeed, its atmosphere was placid old colonial—low venerable buildings, no concrete and glass cubes, wide quiet streets, shade trees. People wore bright colors and I found them not quite so smoldering, morose or craven as in Calcutta.

I called on C. R. Krishnaswami, Rajagopalachari's son. Dressed in aerated homespun he offered me in greeting a limp, soft hand. Then with his head cocked at one side, he led me into his father's modest little house. The early part of our conversation was interrupted by a little girl of about ten and a boy of about six. I remarked on what attractive children they were. He smiled and said softly, "They dislike foreigners." I thought he should be a little uncomfortable at having said that, so I laughed and said something about not being surprised. "I can say that to you," he remarked, "because you are an American. An Englishman would have been offended and embarrassed. That is a strange trait in the British." I didn't agree with him there, but contented myself with generalizing about most children of any race disliking the foreigner, the strange and grotesque-featured alien. As cases in point, Chinese children, American children. He wouldn't let matters rest though and went on to describe how the British failed to inspire trust and friendship and how even those Indians who professed friendship with Englishmen admitted in private to an active dislike.

The children, incidentally, were not his but his sister's—Gandhi's grandchildren.

Dr. H. H. Gass, who worked among lepers, a stout old Indian merchant and I shared a compartment on the train to Bangalore. In his gauzy white garments, the merchant puffed and ah-ed his way onto the big leather seats, then crossed his bare feet over his thighs in the lotus position. He looked like a *New Masses* caricature of the Indian capitalist bloodsucker. His bearer joined us, squatting on the floor mixing from a hamper various spices, nuts and goos, which he rolled neatly into a damp shiny leaf. This betel nut vegetable cocktail the old man chewed with relish, salivating liberally the while. The result was red-stained mouth and teeth.

The merchant owned jute and sugar mills and 5,000 sewing machines making uniforms. He was on his way to Bangalore to buy a cigarette factory. What to do with one's profits—that was a problem. Put them into goods and the government might confiscate them; put them into land and the Japanese may invade and seize it; put them into gold and silver and you get no returns. Nonetheless, many Indians were hoarding gold and silver, burying them. And then there were so many demands on one's money. He had to give a dowry of five thousand rupees to marry off his daughter.

Although Swiss, Dr. Gass had been born in India, received most of his education in the United States and married an American. He remained calmly quiet during the merchant's stereotypical expositions of the Hindu-Muslim-British relationships and the usual assignment to the United States for liberating India from the British yoke. To me the most striking statement made by the doctor related to the United States and not to India. We had been talking about the numbing poverty prevalent in India. Yes, Dr. Gass observed, but he had seen as acute poverty in Texas and Oklahoma.

Poverty seemed somewhat less oppressive in the highland state of Mysore than in British India and Travannore. Gaunt, pot-bellied children and the diseased and deformed of all ages were less in evidence. This was due in large part, I was told, to the relatively efficient administration retained by the Maharajah of Mysore.

I rattled across Mysore in a charcoal-burning Dodge bus, open at the sides. The country was verdant, rolling and altogether pleasing. The hazards to traffic were cows and apoplectic-faced monkeys. Costumes were gay—magenta, orange, cerise, royal blue. Some of the women wore flowers in their hair; some wore their costumes as sarongs. Further south, in the Cochin countryside, the conservative matrons went about their affairs bare to the waist, while the young women, flouting convention, daringly clothed themselves from ankles to neck.

On the charcoal express a young Indian businessman sat next to me and promptly engaged me in a discussion of The Problem—how to get rid of the British and, he being a Hindu, establish a unitary state. Again it was that Britain was to blame for India's servitude and the United States was somehow or other obligated to put matters aright. Again I held forth no hope that Washington would intervene in this affair.

Were the Indians, in my opinion, capable of democratic self-rule? the young man demanded. Certainly the Indians were capable of self-rule. But he had qualified self-rule with "democratic," a word subject to varied interpretations. My fellow passenger interrupted to rail against the British for not industrializing India enough. He wanted automobile factories. I replied that a well-to-do mass market was a pre-condition for this kind of industry. Commenting on this conversation in my journal, I wrote of a "feverishness and reproachfulness in the Indian mind."

The bus ride ended 7,000 feet up on Ootacamund's tableland, beautiful with wild-flowered downs, eucalyptus groves, streams and a lake. From Ooty I went down to the Malabar Coast by train and along it to Trivandrum by bus, rickshaw, canoe and a night launch in the moonlight motoring through still waterways canopied by palms and abloom with hyacinths and lilies. Most of my time during this journey of 36 hours was occupied by listening to and then, from weariness, merely hearing repeated effusions regarding The Problem—India and the British.

CHAPTER VIII

AN AMERICAN IN INDIA

At Trivandrum I found myself unexpectedly in a reviewing stand seated on the right of the Maharani of Travancore. I had arrived at Trivandrum, the capital of Travancore, that morning and sent a note to the Diwan, or Prime Minister, asking for an interview with him. He had courteously received me, and also arranged for his barrister son, Pattabhi Raman, to show me a solemn religious procession later in the day.

Pattabhi Raman met me at the foot of the canopied reviewing stand, outside of Trivandrum and beside a broad road, freshly covered with white sand, leading to the shores of the Arabian Sea, less than a mile away. Thousands of townspeople and country folk tranquilly lined the road, across from which groves of coconut palms rustled in a light breeze.

Without fuss or fanfare the Maharani and the Princess arrived in a long Cadillac. Pattabhi Raman presented me to the Maharani, an attractive woman in perhaps her mid-forties, and to her daughter, who in her early twenties, was, as princesses are supposed to be, beautiful. The Maharani was the sister of the preceding Maharajah and mother of the reigning one. Her son was now Maharajah not because her brother had died without heirs but because in Travancore succession proceeded from the Maharajah to his sister's son and not to his own. Therefore the spoiled three-year-old son of the beautiful Princess was heir apparent. P.R. said that the young Maharajah was more interested in his nephew than in his own son.

This mode of determining succession seemed to me to have one evident advantage over the familiar passage from father to son. One could be sure

of an unbroken bloodline so long as the women of the ruling house produced both sons and daughters. From the woman's point of view, it ensured feminine dominance without the burdens of authority. What chance
did a maharajah have, boxed in by mother and sister? He owed his princely
legitimacy to his mother, not his father, and eventually would be deprived
by his sister of dynastic immortality through his son.

Her Highness was a lively conversationalist. She told me about a visit
that she had made to Bali and the racial and religious ties between that
island and Hindu India. She worried about how the Japanese might be
treating the Balinese. Somehow we got onto the subject of a room that she
was having done over at the palace and her conviction that "modernistic"
furniture was unlivable. Then a discourse on contemporary Indian painting. Inevitably, we came to the matter of elephants. They have near-human
intelligence, the Maharani declared. One of hers accidentally injured a ma-
hout, whereupon it burst into tears. Travancore, she went on, had a game
sanctuary where no shooting was allowed. This brought to mind the Maharajah of Bikaner: "Poor Bikaner, he is not happy unless he is being photo-
graphed with his foot on the head of some unfortunate animal he shot."

Also in the stand was Dr. J. H. Cousins, an Irishman and archaeologist
retained by Travancore. His wife, unfortunately for him at the time, was
apparently a woman of convictions. In England she had been jailed for
suffragette activities as one of Mrs. Pankhurst's lieutenants, and in India as
a supporter of the Congress. Dr. Cousins's passions however were for the
past and the mystic present. Religion, he said, so imbued the life and manners of the people of Travancore that they had to some extent acquired
occult personalities.

Three non-occult personalities completed the guest list: the exceeding
mild little Assistant British Resident, his compatibly mousy wife, and the
manager of the Imperial Bank. As the afternoon wore on the banker murmured he was missing his afternoon tea. But the Maharani had planned
better. Soon thereafter tomato juice, sandwiches and a wartime rarity—
Scotch whiskey—were served.

The Aarat Procession that we were there to view was led by an enormous elephant caparisoned in crimson with a gold net on his forehead.
Then another elephant, carrying a drummer and two other musicians. Next
came the household cavalry, blue and gold turbans, scarlet sashes and pen-
nants fluttering from lances. There followed mounted officers and a double
line of Travancore infantry stretching to the end of the procession. Between

the infantry lines came men bearing palmyra umbrellas held out to the side of their hips. A group of men bare to the waist, wearing white sarongs reaching to the ankles, crowned with lavender skullcaps, chests and shoulders glittering with golden dust, naked swords, in hand, strode barefoot in front of the young Maharajah.

He was a handsome strong-looking fellow, costumed like the men preceding him, excepting that he wore a green skullcap. Immediately after passing the reviewing stand the Maharajah stopped, turned around and looked in the direction of the Maharani for a few moments, no gestures, no sound. He resumed his march, his sword held before him parallel to his body.

Following the Maharajah and borne above the heads of the participants were three shrines containing the three gods, Sri Padmanabha (He Whose Navel is the World's Lotus), Krishna (the Divine Lover), and Narsinha (the Man-Lion). The gods were being taken to the seashore for a bath of purification. Being fallible, they had sinned. They had taken life, killed. So the Maharajah was escorting them to the ceremony of absolution, from which they would return to the dais from which they had been removed because of their guilt.

Bringing up the rear of the procession were the elephants that would bear the deities on their return trip, people in flowing white garb, musicians on elephants, and finally—an ambulance.

Serenity was the foremost characteristic of the Aarat Procession. Those participating and the spectators were serious but not solemn. There were no manifestations of awe nor the frenzy, groveling or other excesses that accompany some religious rites. As a spectacle, the procession was neither gaudy nor tawdry. The dazzling white sand of the roadway, the stately, swaying palms, the brilliant colors of costumes and caparisons, the harmonious singing of men, gods, and beasts composed a scene of beauty in tranquility.

All of this was far away from the troubles and strife of the world. These I had discussed with the Diwan, Sir C. P. Ramaswami Aiyar. He had received me graciously and without demur, even though my only introduction had been a note requesting an interview, accompanied by my calling card on which I was described simply as "Second Secretary of Embassy of the United States of America attached to the Staff of the Commanding General American Army Forces China-Burma-India." Obviously, I owed this distinguished gentleman an explanation of why I had to go to remotest India to see him. As I noted in my journal:

I explained how we suddenly found ourselves in India, with men, installations and materiel. How we were very much strangers to Indian thought, traditions and institutions; how we wished our relations with India to be intelligent and harmonious as possible, and how in seeking this end we were trying to acquaint ourselves with India. It was within this framework that I was making this introductory tour. Also, we are the allies of the British, we are sticking together. But at the same time we Americans have our own foreign policy and our own ideas with regard to colonial problems.

Sir C. P. roared with laughter and say, "I understand you. Welcome." Which made me feel terribly subversive.

He told me about Travancore. "We have never been conquered. The Dutch tried and we defeated them; the French tried and went away; with the British we contracted an alliance. The theory of our state is that it belongs to the god Sri Padmanabha for whom the Maharajah holds it in trust. His Highness therefore reports every morning at the beginning of his day's work to the shrine of the god for his orders."

Of Travancore's six million inhabitants, Ramaswami Aiyar continued, some two million were Christian, the balance almost all Hindus. Primary education was free and literacy was the highest in India—53%. We then went on to discuss Indian politics and personalities. Sir C. P. concluded that India needed a federated government with strong central executive having tenure of at least four years. On the raj: the British had lost prestige, he said, and were doing nothing to improve their relations with the Indian people. The only moral leadership among the world powers was in the United States. "You must maintain that leadership for the good of the world and you must be on guard at the peace conference against tricks and intrigue." This was a theme that I heard over and over again from Indians.

*   *   *

Returning to New Delhi from Trivandrum, I traveled part way by train with Pattabhi Raman, the Diwan's son, and his wife. I noted at the time that "she was a friendly, plump, pretty young woman with distracting diamonds and pearls on either nostril and hanging from her nose to her mouth. I should think she would run the risk of devouring a pearl with her victuals. Her hair, which reached her hips, hung loose and with her flowing garments she looked like a refined, well-clothed model for Gauguin."

I asked Pattabhi Raman what the British Resident in Travancore did. "Oh, he's the watchdog." Did he pass on the budget, for instance? Certainly not, P. R. replied. Some years earlier he was consulted before the appointment of upper grade functionaries. "But when father became Diwan he soon put a stop to that."

On the subject of the Government of India bureaucracy, P. R. said that it was the most attractive career for young Indians. This, he added, was a sad commentary on the country—an observation that I had heard from other Indians. Yet it was through the bureaucracy that his father and other gifted men—such as Ghulam Mohammed—had risen to constructive and fulfilling positions of power. On the other hand, I wrote in my journal after our conversation, "It's an efficient colonial technique to absorb in the bureaucracy the most promising young men and give them a vested interest in the maintenance of the status quo. Of course, the bureaucracy must be sufficiently hardened and ponderous to resist dangerous innovations by young enthusiasts. In time they break their spirit against the system, but have as compensation material well being which prevents them from being dangerously bitter about it all."

On the subject of the depressed classes, P. R. said that they were no longer an issue. The Congress program for the harijans (outcastes) took care of the situation. He went on to describe the relations between his family and the harijans attached to it. They wanted to know all about the family undertakings, felt free to bring their troubles to members of the family, offered gratuitous advice, and wept when one of the family went off to England. In sum, they identified themselves with the fortunes and failure of the high-caste family. I said that this relationship seemed to me to have much the same quality of benevolent paternalism that had existed between some of the gentler elements of our southern aristocracy and their household slaves. Pattabhi Raman objected to the comparison.

P. R. asked questions about China. Upon my observing that Chiang Kai-shek had a strong strain of Puritanism, that there were Cromwellian traits in him, P. R. said that a present-day leader in Asia—if he is to be a great leader—must have a dominant strain of Puritanism. I agreed.

While at Oxford, P. R. confessed, he had formed a prejudice against Americans, considering them materialistic and without culture. But he had since changed his mind. We had demonstrated (however unpolished we might be) that we had fine instincts and a lively moral sense.

Pattabhi Raman surprised me by showing considerable familiarity with American law. But he thought that our laws did not give enough protection to the privacy of the individual. Contrary to President Roosevelt, he admired the Supreme Court as then constituted, "Now you have a really good one."

Curiously enough, a counterpart of P. R.'s, the forty-year-old son of a retired Diwan of Mysore, had revealed at a meeting that I had with his father at Bangalore several days earlier, that he also was an aficionado of American law. For three years, he said, he had labored on a volume dealing with the commercial clause of the American Constitution. He had sent the first quarter of the typescript to Justice Jackson and had just received a reply from Jackson agreeing to write a foreword.

What the father, Sir M. N. Krishna Rao, had to say was of considerably more interest to me. The former Diwan was a tall, handsome old gentleman with a white moustache and a wine-colored wool shirt, the tails of which hung outside his dhoti. The United States must play a major role in defining the postwar world, he said, because only it is sufficiently detached and principled. The motives of only the Americans are not suspect. Furthermore, the United States must maintain its strength, for only through the possession of it can stability be maintained and principles be upheld. "The natural forces of good," Krishna Rao observed, "moved so gently and slowly."

*   *   *

Gandhi's provocative pacifism led to a showdown with the British raj during the summer of 1942. About a month after I saw him in Bombay he began to call for action that would obstruct the war effort. He advised those whose houses might be requisitioned: "Do not move and take the consequences." The British let that one pass. But when he and his cohorts persisted in their incitement to non-violent obstruction, the British reacted in August by suddenly jailing Gandhi, Nehru and other Congress party members engaged in this agitation.

In a January 1943 survey of the situation in India for General Stilwell, I reported:

> *When the government surprised everyone by suddenly arresting the Congress leaders, the party had no nation-wide plan of action ready to put into effect. Subsequent demonstrations and disturbances throughout the country were for the most part spontaneous outbursts. The Congress was thus proved to have been indifferently organized.*
>
> *If the mind of India during the past spring and summer could have been described as psychopathic—beset with a persecution complex and brooding hatred of the British, often subject to political fantasy and in conflict with its several natures—it has, since the arrest of the Congress leaders and subsequent developments, assumed even more tortured forms. The severe government repression of disturbances, as much or more than the arrests, intensified the persecution complex. These same factors, plus the evident determination of the British not to relinquish within the foreseeable future colonial domination over India, increased the anglophobia and nationalistic feeling.*
>
> *On the other hand, the Congress defeat at the hands of the government initially strengthened the position of the Muslim League and its demands for Muslim autonomy. This was followed in turn by what the Indians believed was a shift of government favor from the League to the Hindu Mahasabha. As a corollary, communal antipathies have grown and are growing.*
>
> *Thus a curious paradox has come to exist. The various Indian communities and factions are drawn toward unity by their common hatred of the British and their desire to be rid of British rule. At the same time, they are increasingly antipathetic to one another because of the British policy of capitalizing on ancient hostilities between the communities and playing them off one against the other. This policy has been repeatedly revealed in one of its simplest forms during the recent and continuing civil disturbances—the exemption of the Muslim community of a village from a collective fine imposed on the village for anti-government activities.*
>
> *The British, of course, protest against any suggestion that they deliberately seek to use any one community or faction against the other. They have played the Indian colonial game so long that, as they acquired their Empire, through fits of absent-mindedness, so now they practice a policy of divide and rule almost unconsciously.*

However decadent British rule in India may be, most of the Indian nationalistic leaders are themselves more decadent and lacking in aggressive vitality. A British official observed to me that he and his colleagues were able to rule India not because they were strong but because the Indians were so weak. The tremendous influence of Gandhi in defining the expression of the Indian revolutionary urge has been a retrogressive one. His philosophy of action began with perhaps over-realistic acceptance, from both religious conviction and tactical considerations, of the fatalism and negativism of the Hindu character. He did not capitalize on the more virile nature of the Muslims (with the result that the Muslims have retrogressed on their part to a program of communalism.) Gandhi's philosophy of action developed into a pseudo-spiritual program of non-violence, non-compliance, non-cooperation, passive resistance and economic primitivism. Such a program activated the masses to indulge in masochism and not to the overthrow of British rule. And Nehru, whose progressive philosophy was in opposition to the Gandhi program had not had the strength to override the Mahatma.

The urge toward revolution in India is therefore frustrated by the relative weakness of the Indians themselves and by the fact that, no matter how incompetent it may be in other respects, the Government of India knows how to use the instruments of control that it has firmly in its hands. To the extent that they have perpetuated an artificial unity in this unnatural situation, the British are right in claiming that they are the one unifying force in India.

It would therefore seem to follow that, in the absence of an intention (whether voluntary or under third party pressure) to effect an orderly transfer of authority to an Indian National Government, the British will be able to extend their control over India into the postwar period. But they will be able to do so only so long as the British raj retains its present vitality and imperialist point of view.

As the system of colonial imperialism throughout the world continues to break up from decay and under the impact of progressive and more rational forces, British imperial rule will be affected. The British raj is not and will not be exempt from the decay nor from the impact of new forces at large in the world.

Therein lies the element of risk. For, if arrangements are not made for an orderly turnover of government to the Indians, the disintegration of the British system of control will release the Indian revolutionary urge into the

*field of action, the artificial unity that now exists will collapse in both
factional and nationalistic conflict and chaos will ensue. Gandhi's influence
will by that time probably have been removed by his dotage, which he is
now entering, or by his death. His successor or successors are likely to be
men with less negative programs.*

*In such a situation lies the potentiality of another great war. For revolu-
tion and internal chaos create a political vacuum into which alien elements
intrude for the purpose of exploiting the confusion to their own advantage.
Rivalries existing outside of the vacuum expand into the vacuum where
they take more acute forms. Such a situation existed in the recent Spanish
revolution. It also existed in modified form in the Balkans in 1914. Perhaps
the most instructive parallel is the case of China.*

In the Indian mind, I stated, we had come by early 1943 to be associated
with the British. That was, in part, because of American silence and inaction
about British imperialism in India, giving the impression that the United
States, at least tacitly, supported it. Projecting this situation into the postwar world, I warned that India in revolt against persisting white imperialism might well attract "the practical interest if not sympathy of the Soviet
Union or China, or both."

This was an ominous prospect—the United States, in a wholly false
position and against its interest, aligned with Britain against a rebellious
India backed by one or both of its giant neighbors.

What could the American government do to avoid such a ramified calamity? While reaffirming solidarity with the United Kingdom, I recommended in January 1943, Washington should at least dissociate itself from
British imperial policy, from the maintenance and reacquisition of British
colonies. This I urged from then on in my advisory capacity, on our propaganda and political warfare people in India, Burma and the South East Asia
Command.

Washington, I said at the beginning of 1943, could go further and try
to induce London to set in train an orderly relinquishment of sovereignty
over India, in favor of an eventual Indian government. Such pressure would
be offensive to the British government, especially Prime Minister Churchill,
who had proclaimed that he had not become the King's first minister to
preside over the liquidation of the British Empire. But American intervention was justified, I believed, because of the heavy postwar risks rising out
of a British attempt to hold India, risks that would strongly affect the

United States because of the close American attachment to the United Kingdom. As I rhetorically put it, "Can we afford . . . to let the British run the risk of losing us the peace?"

Neither the British nor we had fully faced up to Britain's future. Churchill and Roosevelt were determined that Britain should remain a first class power. But Britain could be that only as it possessed its empire. Divested of its colonies it would be, I estimated in 1943, not a first class but a third class power. Yet to cling to its colonies would be to invite a struggle that would in all probability drain Britain. Better, it seemed to me, that it yield early and peacefully than late and bloodily. Which is what, immediately after the war, the British government did—with consummate skill and statesmanship.

With all my concerns over Indian independence, I did not anticipate that liberation from foreign bondage would dramatically improve the lot of the Indian people. On November 20, 1942, I wrote in my journal: "The right to be exploited by their own kind, that's what people wanting independence from foreign rule seek."

CHAPTER IX

WILLKIE, WASHINGTON, AND VINEGAR JOE

My 1942 explorations of India were interspersed with two trips to China and one to the United States. The first trip to Chungking was to assist Lauchlin Currie—and to keep Stilwell informed, so far as I was able, of what Currie was up to.

Currie, as a special adviser to Roosevelt, was sent to China to placate the Chiangs. They were in high dudgeon because China was receiving fewer American supplies than they wanted and because some air support committed to China had been diverted to stem a powerful German offensive threatening Cairo. Madame Chiang and her brother T. V. Soong hinted darkly that China would withdraw from the alliance. The Generalissimo demanded three American divisions, a combat air contingent maintained at a constant level of five hundred planes, and supplies far beyond Washington's ability to deliver. Similar bad tempered bluffing, threats and demands were subsequently made several times during the war by the Chiangs, T. V. Soong and H. H. Kung, the husband of Madame Chiang's oldest sister, Soong Ai-ling.

Currie managed to calm the Generalissimo, who gave him a Pacific Front Plan to take back to the President and the American Joint Chiefs of Staff. This gratified the yearning of both Chiang and Currie to feel needed and important. Actually, the plan was a rewrite of a strategic plan prepared by Stilwell for an American-British-Chinese offensive against Burma, then Thailand and Indochina, involving the commitment, optimistically, of at least one American division.

Chiang gave a banquet for Currie, scattered tables for eight or ten each. I was at one with several cabinet ministers and politicos. In a long white gown the Generalissimo strolled to our table; we all rose to attention; he uttered a pleasantry in his high thin voice; we sat down, stiff upright. No one said a word. The minutes ticked by. Finally Chiang broke the silence to quiz an official sitting next to me. The rest of us remained mute. The Generalissimo rose, returned to his table, and soon thereafter we all said goodnight.

Currie did not take Stilwell or Ambassador Gauss into his confidence. He was fairly open with me, but did not reveal to me what he would recommend to the President. I gathered, however, that he was not favorably impressed by Stilwell. I so informed the General. Stilwell asked me to accompany Currie back to Washington. Maybe I could learn what was afoot regarding CBI. I did not, until after the event. Currie had recommended the recall of Stilwell and Gauss. And he considered himself to be the most suitable replacement for Gauss, a dream that was not to be realized.

Roosevelt, who had been receiving reports of Chinese dissatisfaction with Stilwell, was inclined to follow Currie's advice about the general. The President put great store by getting along with the Generalissimo. His vision of the Big Four gaining victory and dispensing a just peace depended on, he thought, avoiding unpleasantness with Chiang—which the Chinese, so astute in human relations, recognized and exploited. Roosevelt's suggestions to General George C. Marshall that Stilwell be relieved were rebutted by Marshall and Stimson. No one, they insisted, could adequately replace Stilwell.

Shortly after arriving in Washington, I succumbed to a happy conjunction of sentiment, impulse and good sense to contract marriage with a matchless young woman, Patricia Grady. Being conventionally impatient, we flew to Charleston, South Carolina, where instantaneous marriage was legal. I left Patricia in a graveyard near the Court House while I checked out the procedure. We underwent a lackadaisical performance by a seedy-looking functionary, who then held out the marriage certificate. When I reached to take it, he withdrew it and, whether out of suspicion or southern gallantry, I do not know, said firmly, "No, it's for the lady." Because we both felt that a honeymoon was unsuitable in wartime, Patricia returned the next day to her job as a columnist on *The Washington Post* and I to the Department of State, where I was on consultation.

Before leaving Chungking with Currie, infected by his and the Generalissimo's excursions into grand strategy, I composed some expansive thoughts on war and politics. In this and later musings of mine on politico-military matters Stilwell was at least tolerant of my efforts. In my July 31, 1942 paper reappraising CBI, I said that the Chinese Government's objectives were to (a) insure its perpetuation and domestic supremacy and (b) come to the peace table as militarily powerful as possible. China's policy was therefore to conserve its military strength, relying on the United States and (sooner or later) the Soviet Union to defeat Japan. China might take the offensive only if it was persuaded that materiel expended would be immediately replaced with interest. Lend lease to China without any quid pro quo would result in hoarding of the supplies delivered.

As for the British, I continued, they appeared to have no intention of trying to retake Burma in the foreseeable future because, in part, their lost colonies would at the peace conference revert with clear title if they were held by the enemy up to the end of the war. If they were reoccupied with Chinese and American assistance, British title might be compromised. Galvanizing the British into a Burmese counteroffensive might be achieved only if the highest level of the American government pressured London, and also committed a token American force to the enterprise. There were enough British Empire troops in India to do the job.

Here my critical faculties had been marzipanned into wishful thinking. Churchill would not have then yielded to American pressure for action in Burma if for no other reason than that the Germans were still a potent threat to the Middle East. Diverting the Indian army from the country's western defenses would be imprudent. Furthermore, the army might be needed to impose domestic order if Gandhi's agitation provoked insurrection. Finally, the Indian army, on the heels of its demoralizing rout in Burma, was hardly in a condition to take the offensive against the alert, aggressive and tough conquerors of Burma.

Chinese and British generalship having been incompetent and lacking in offensive spirit in the Burma debacle, I wrote, supreme command for a counteroffensive should be American. The main factor limiting American action in CBI was logistic, the 12,000 miles by sea to India, the meager airlift into China, and the self-consuming transportation of aviation and truck fuel to forward bases in East China. The recapture of Rangoon and reopening of the Burma road would ease the problem of supplying China.

I then pointed to the strategic location of China, close in on Japan's flank, the then idle Chinese and British military strength, the possibility of activating these available forces through American bargaining, pressure, and commitment of a token contingent, and ended with excessive optimism that "nowhere else in this war can we do so much with so little."

We could continue limited operation in China, I concluded, supplied by the airlift from India. But if the Allied effort were expanded to the capture of Rangoon and reopening of land routes to China, then the American air offensive from China could be greatly augmented to include long range attacks on industrial Japan and its vital shipping to and from the Southwest Pacific. Or, alternatively, the increased flow of supplies could be designed to support primarily a ground offensive from Burma and China to the South China Sea (Stilwell's plan), severing Japan's land salient to the south. And such an offensive, I added, would tend to deter Japan from attacking the Soviet Union, collaborating with the Germans to knock the Russians out of the war (with disastrous effect on the Allies' position in the West). In raising this consideration I was reflecting what I encountered among Chinese officials in Chungking during the early summer of 1942—an expectation that Tokyo would move to eliminate the Soviet threat from the rear and link up with Germany.

*   *   *

Stilwell summoned me to Chungking a second time, in October. This time it was to help him out with Wendell Willkie, the Republican candidate for the presidency. Willkie was visiting China on a round-the-world junket meant to fabricate an image for himself as a man of vision, an international figure worthy of supplanting Roosevelt. He was a large, hearty fellow and, like so many seeking to thrust their services on the citizenry through elective office, enamored of self, assuming that his unbuttoned personality exuded persuasive allure.

The Chiang establishment was pleased by Willkie's advent. This was a chance to size up and captivate the man who might be the next American president. And even if Willkie did not win the election, as a national figure in the United States he could do much to advance Chiang's interests. So the Chiangs went to work on W. W.

First, they isolated him from Gauss, who had arranged to receive him as a houseguest. Willkie went along with the snub to the Ambassador, which caused Gauss to explode to his staff after a humiliating retreat to his residence, "By God, I would have voted for Willkie last election, but in 1944, I'm voting for that Socialist fellow, Elmer (sic) Thomas." The Chiangs installed Willkie in a luxurious government villa with a retinue of English-speaking officials.

The Generalissimo's role was his usual one with distinguished American visitors: the aloofly gracious soldier-statesman-Methodist-sage of the East. As Chiang did not speak English, and the Republican candidate knew no Chinese, communication between host and guest was under the influence of the interpreter, often the fluent Madame Chiang, sometimes the Minister of Information and factotum for public relations with Americans, Hollington Tong. A graduate of the Missouri School of Journalism, Tong spoke adequate colloquial American.

The Chiangs plied the gullible Willkie with food, wine, flattery and propaganda. Their message to him was: replace Stilwell with Chennault, and give us the ultimate, infallible, all-purpose weapon—air power. The banquets, adulation, and enlightenment persuaded the presidential aspirant of the rightness of the Chinese position. But it was Madame Chiang herself who aroused the susceptible Willkie's passion for China's cause. Madame was a comely matron, who, when she concealed her imperious, calculating nature, could radiate fetching charm. She had enjoyed success in reducing foreigners to infatuation. Early in his acquaintance with her, the hard-bitten Chennault confessed to his diary, "She will always be a princess to me."

So what chance did the impressionable Willkie have when Madame Chiang upped her projection of charm a notch to include coquetry? Costumed in the cloak of an air marshal (after all, it was airplanes the Chiangs were after) at a relief organization tea she opened her heart to reveal she found W. W. a "disturbing influence." The candidate was visibly moved by this coy confession and on the evening of his departure, in the presence of her enigmatic husband, pressed her to fly with him the next day to Washington and he would get her all of the airplanes she wanted.

Willkie did not inform either the Ambassador or Stilwell of his conversations with the Generalissimo. He gave Stilwell a half hour of brush-off conversation, but spent two hours with Chennault. Whenever American newsmen were in the offing, W. W. snubbed his Chinese hosts to cultivate the press. One of the Foreign Office officials attending the statesman presumptive observed that he did not see how anyone as "unstable" as Willkie could have been a successful businessman, much less a serious contender for the presidency.

Willkie could afford to overlook the offense he gave and, had he been aware of it, the contempt behind the smiling and bowing. China and the Chinese were only a stage set for W. W. The reality was his image as seen by the American electorate. With skilled public relations assistants accompanying him and enthusiastic American newsmen reporting on his colorful activities, the candidate could be satisfied with his triumph in Cathay. His image was immortalized in his testament, *One World*, which became an outstanding best seller.

*   *   *

Chennault gave Willkie a letter, dated October 8, 1942, to take back to the President. In it Chennault asserted that if he were provided with 105 fighter aircraft, 30 medium bombers, 12 heavy bombers and their replacements, he could "accomplish the downfall of Japan." He declared that he could do this "probably within six months, within one year at the outside." But—he would need "full authority as the American military commander in China."

That meant, of course, supplanting Stilwell. Then, as a bonus to the quick downfall of Japan, Chennault offered the President an assurance that, "I can make the Chinese lasting friends of the United States."

Chennault's insubordinate bombast was, as General Marshall later described it, "Just nonsense." It slighted two essential considerations. One was logistical, the airlift bottleneck constricting the volume of support that could be given to intensive air operations from East China bases. The tonnage flown across the Hump, the mountain ranges on the Burma-China borderland, had increased spasmodically during 1942 from nothing to about 2,000 tons a month and by mid-1943 would reach 5,000. By the end of 1944, some 40,000 tons would be airlifted. But, in delivering one ton of supplies across the Hump—the airlift terminus in Kunming was still hundreds of mountainous miles from the forward bases—the Air Transport Command burned one ton of fuel. And for every ton of bombs that Chennault dropped on the enemy, he needed about eighteen tons of supplies.

More important, however, was the second consideration, the security of the air bases from which Chennault proposed to launch his stunning air offensive. Stilwell maintained, with War Department backing, that unless the quality of the Chinese forces facing the enemy were greatly improved, the Japanese could, if stung by Chennault's air action, move forward on the ground to take the American-Chinese bases—which is what they later did. Stilwell was not opposed in principle to an air offensive; he strongly favored and planned for it but insisted that the ground forces to protect the bases should first be developed. The dispute, lasting until 1944, between Stilwell and Chennault over strategic priorities, was concretely expressed in disagreement over the allotment of tonnage flown into China: what percentage should be ground force materiel and what percentage supplies for the air contingent. Stilwell prevailed most of the time.

Roosevelt was receptive to Chennault's promise to dispose of Japan in one fell swoop. He wanted a spectacular success to offset the months of defeat and the slogging build-up to counter-attack both Japan and Germany. And he knew that Chiang had set his mind on Chennault's plan, or any other proposal that would rely upon air rather than ground power. So, placating the Generalissimo and trying to give him no excuse for quitting the war were additional reasons for favoring Chennault's nostrum.

*   *   *

Usually I traveled about the vast CBI Theater and to the United States on military orders by the Adjutant General at either the New Delhi or Chungking headquarters. I was known to the staff of both headquarters but not to those of most of the other installations. To them I was outwardly unidentifiable. I ordinarily wore officer's trousers and shirt, but in keeping with my civilian status, went bare-headed and wore no insignia. Very suspect. When MPs stopped me in the street, I explained who I was, showed them my calling card, and left them more mystified than they had been.

Concerned lest I encounter travel complications when without orders from the Adjutant General, I asked Stilwell if he would tell the AG to give me a piece of paper authorizing me to request transportation on my own in case of need. The Old Man dug up a calling card of his, describing him as the theater commander, and printed in his clear neat hand: TO ALL OFFICERS AND AGENCIES OF THE U.S.A. FORCES IN CHINA-BURMA-INDIA: ASSIST AND EXPEDITE TRAVEL OF MR. JOHN DAVIES—Joseph W. Stilwell Lieut. Gen U.S.A. I used this card only once, on a mulish sergeant at an air transport base in Assam, with electrifying effect.

This complex, contradictory man, Stilwell, was rightly called Vinegar Joe. He was often an abusive vulgarian in his speech and writing. And yet—he was also a man who had a discriminating command of the English language and who possessed refined perceptions and tastes. He spent free time during and after the Cairo conference of 1943 zestfully exploring antiquities at Jerusalem, Memphis, Saqqara, and Luxor. "Archeology," he said to me, "is something that could really get to you, especially if you had a few successes."

Stilwell was merciless in his demands on his troops when he believed that the military situation required him to be so. The notorious example of this was his insistence that a small detachment of American infantrymen in the 1944 siege of Myitkyina keep on fighting even though utterly exhausted and incapacitated by tropical diseases. But he was also merciless with himself, driving his sixty-year-old frame beyond the endurance of younger men, going within range of enemy machine gun and mortar fire to hearten his troops, refusing to be flown out to safety in the Burma collapse, remaining instead with those for whom there was no air transport, and leading them out on foot through the tall, tangled wilderness.

Because he was emotionally intense, and on account of repressions pent-up, his dislikes of individuals and nations were magnified into hates. He said to me that he admired a certain officer "because he was a good hater." At the same time he was a warm, considerate human being with an exceptional devotion to his wife and children. His kindness showed in simple ways.

We had come from northern Burma, where Stilwell had been trying to animate an offensive by two Chinese divisions that he had trained and equipped at Ramgarh in India. He had been shaming the division, regiment and battalion commanders by going in the foul monsoon wet right down front to the company commanders and telling them to keep moving into the treacherous, ambushed jungle. Now on our way to New Delhi, we flew in the Old Man's plane, Uncle Joe's Chariot, to one of the Assam bases. It was long after dark and Stilwell was tired and hungry.

Although the mess hall was deserted we roused a cook who, pleased over meeting a military celebrity, prepared chow for the four or five of us. Then the corporal sat down with us to converse. It was about home. Rochester, New York, as I remember it, and how he missed Rochester. Stilwell allowed that his wife came from Syracuse. Sure enough the cook knew some people in Syracuse and he told us all about them, nice things about them.

The meal was over and Stilwell was obviously ready to hit the sack. But the reminiscences had only begun to flow, and we were transported back to Rochester. The theater commander listened sympathetically, suppressed yawns, and occasionally ventured a typically laconic comment meant to qualify the occasion as a conversation rather than a monologue. The homesick cook paused for a thought, and, at last, Stilwell tactfully seized the initiative, thanked the corporal and joined him in looking to the day when the job over here was done and we could all go home.

Scorning ostentation, Stilwell reacted against those who put on airs. The Chungking headquarters staff was to have its picture taken, with the commanding general. As front row seating had not been assigned, the officers who took themselves most seriously quickly competed to occupy chairs close to the center one reserved for the Old Man. I was content, being nondescript, to stand in the rear in the good company of sergeants, corporals, and PFCs. Stilwell strode up to the smiling, expectant array, took in the situation at a glance, spotted me, and made his way through the line of brass to stand with the dogfaces and the cookie-pusher.

Stilwell's unwillingness to dissemble, to conceal his low opinion of pomposity, hypocrisy, and the sacrifice of military considerations to political expediency aroused the resentment of those he held in contempt. Chiang, whom Stilwell in his more tolerant moods referred to as "Peanut," early became aware of the low esteem in which his American chief-of-staff held him. Roosevelt, who was apprised of Stilwell's disrespect toward Chiang and strongly disapproved of it, encountered in 1943 another manifestation of Stilwell's scorn—grim, glum inarticulateness. The President asked him, on a visit to the White House, to state his case regarding Chennault's flight of fancy strategy, which Roosevelt clearly favored. Stilwell's disgust with Chennault's bombastic quackery, the President's facile predilection for the charlatan solution, FDR's dilettante enlightenment of Stilwell that the war against Japan was a piece of pie with Tokyo at the apex, and Roosevelt's anxiously ingratiating attitude toward Chiang caused Stilwell's gorge to rise. But the restraints of decorum before his Commander-in-Chief choked him and explain, I surmise, why he could not speak his piece. Roosevelt wondered if he were sick.

In Stilwell's estimation, most of the British with whom he dealt ranked little if at all above Chiang and his henchmen. His attitude stemmed from the Burma bungle, the negativism that he generally encountered at British general headquarters at New Delhi, and plain, garden-variety anti-British prejudice. Stilwell did not exert himself to hide his opinions of his allies, who were quite aware of his uncomplimentary sentiments.

At the same time, as in the case of the Chinese, he thought well of and even admired some British officers. He spoke with respect of Field Marshal Sir John Dill, representative in Washington of the British chiefs of staff. Revealing his non-Vinegar Joe side, he said that he admired Dill's "human kindness." I also heard him laud General William Slim for his aggressive fighting qualities. Pugnacity was the ultimate quality by which Stilwell measured military men. They could have all the other soldierly attributes, but if they were not fighters, battle-hungry, they were lacking.

When Stilwell, several days after the disastrous session with Roosevelt, met with the one man more responsible than any other for British reluctance to join battle with the enemy in Burma, they got along well. That man was Winston Churchill. Their strategic views with regard to Burma were contradictory, but no one could gainsay Churchill's pugnacity. And that had Stilwell's admiration.

Stilwell's faculty for alienating those with whom he disagreed troubled me. Writing to my wife on February 23, 1943, I said "that the Old Man has about outplayed the role of angry, uncompromising old John Brown, that he can't storm Harper's Ferry, and that he has made far too many enemies." When I had an opportunity, I would talk to him like a Dutch nephew.

For two hours on March 7, 1943 after dinner at his house, where I was staying with Pinky and several other officers, I discussed with the General the intrigues against him in Chungking and Washington, sources of friction between Americans and Chinese and criticism of him that I had heard from various of his officers. I had written in a looseleaf notebook an outline of what I had wanted to say, tearing out the pages as I proceeded. It seem to me that he had to face up to the fact that the Chiangs and Chennault had succeeded in widening the opposition to him beyond Currie and the President to include Harry Hopkins. And now the press, notably *Time*, was becoming critical of him.

Then there was the psychological problem that confronted Americans in dealing with Chinese—specifically the obtuseness of many of his officers in this respect. This imperceptivity seemed to me to be almost insoluble. We had a knack for handling horses and machines, I said, but not other, foreign human beings.

Next I laid before him criticism about himself and some of his senior staff that I had heard from a number of his officers. Reconstructing from what I elliptically wrote after the interview (this was not, everything considered at the time, a conversation to be recorded verbatim and in detail), I told the General that he was considered to be neglecting his larger command responsibilities and spending disproportionate time and effort on lesser combat and administrative activities. It was also felt that his judgment had been faulty in selection of his principal subordinates, particularly his chief of staff. I noted afterward that the only stricture that I could not bring myself to repeat was that he was vindictive.

Shading his eyes from the glare of an acetylene lamp with one hand while doodling lines and triangles with the other, Stilwell took all of this, which lesser men would have regarded, understandably, as impudent insubordination, without a flicker of resentment. Halfway through, he said, "You didn't think I could take it?"

He spoke calmly and quietly in response. In sum, he agreed with regard to the weakness of some of his senior staff, but some had compensating virtues. As for himself, his command was necessarily a one-man show because only he had the weight to deal at all effectively with the Generalissimo, senior Chinese generals and even division commanders. "Things go to pot," I noted, "if the master hand is removed."

Stilwell asked who I thought should be on his next promotion list. I named several, only one of whom was on the list when finally published. He was Frank Merrill, who in 1944 would command the American detachment, popularly called Merrill's Marauders, so sacrificially used by Stilwell at Myitkyina.

*   *   *

In an attempt to counteract the spreading criticism of him in the United States, I suggested to the General that he send me and one of his most vigorous and articulate officers, Colonel Haydon Boatner, who was a China specialist with the Chinese forces being trained in India, to convey informally to influential members of the Washington press Stilwell's view of the war in his theater of operation. Stilwell did not approve of the suggestion. Of the growing opposition to him, he was "disinclined to weigh that risk heavily."

As the Ambassador was due to leave soon for the United States on consultation, I sought to enlist his support for Stilwell and through him that of the higher-ups in the State Department. I gave him a memorandum stating Stilwell's case as I saw it. After explaining what Stilwell's mission was I described the Chinese attitude toward the war. In so doing, I observed that

> *all informed Chinese are keenly aware that of the four principal members of the United Nations [in World War II, "United Nations" meant those allied against the Axis], China has suffered the longest and the greatest in this conflict. Furthermore, like the Russians and the British, the Chinese have a more highly developed political sense than we. Political considerations loom larger in their evaluation of situations (including the military situation) than they do for even the Russians and the British.*
>
> *The Japanese approach the truth when they accuse the Chinese of seeking to make the far [the United States] fight the near [Japan].*
>
> *We have not bled enough for the liking of the Russians, the British or the Chinese. With political considerations looming so large in their calculations they are each fighting not only the common enemies but also, in a negative fashion, their allies.*

In describing Stilwell's problems with the Chinese army, I observed that its

> *officers have no great interest in fighting the Japanese. Even at Ramgarh [the training camp in India] there is some evidence of this. A Chinese-speaking American officer there who has constant contact with Chinese officers expressed surprise that not one of his Chinese colleagues (many of whom had homes occupied by the Japanese) had expressed a desire to get into the field and fight the Japanese. In China, the situation is worse.*
>
> *Venality in the Chinese Army goes along naturally with the apathy. Chinese troops have traditionally had to shift for themselves. Most units have lived off the localities in which they have been stationed. This situation has further deteriorated in most regions bordering Japan—occupied territory. Chinese commanders in these areas have settled down with their wives and families and gone into trade. They control and profit enormously from the contraband traffic across the "fighting" line.*
>
> *For example, a British sabotage unit in Hunan sought to destroy a bridge between the lines and over which the Chinese and Japanese were*

trading. When the Chinese commander heard of the project, he ordered the British out, suggesting that they go fight their own war—everything was peaceful and harmonious there and the British wanted to start trouble. At Hokow on the Yunnan-Indochina border there is lively traffic between Chinese and Japanese-held territory, a certain number of ferries moving across the dividing river between certain hours. The Chinese garrisons draw their rice rations from Japanese territory. One morning late in January the rice ration failed to arrive during the scheduled trips. The Chinese commander became incensed and entered a strongly worded protest. The Japanese, not wishing to disrupt relations, obligingly dispatched the rations by a special ferry after hours.

The Japanese are as corrupt as the Chinese. The difference, however, is that the Japanese can be depended upon to fight when the orders come from the top. Corruption has not yet enervated them.

It would be naïve in the extreme to suggest that all he [Stilwell] has to do to make China an aggressive factor in the war against Japan is to place lend-lease arms in Chinese hands and in consultation with the Generalissimo issue orders for the attack.

All he can do, in fact, is argue, plead and bargain, with lend-lease materiel and the Ramgarh project as the inducement to follow his lead.

It follows that the intemperate eulogies of the Chinese Army which appear in the American press and over the American air (largely inspired by the Chinese pressure groups in the United States and uninformed American sinophiles) only play into the hands of the Chinese factions wishing to obtain lend-lease equipment without restriction to its use (or nonuse). It is scarcely necessary to note that anyone whom the Chinese might suggest as a replacement of General Stilwell could likely be a man whom the group in power in Chungking believe they could use to their own advantage. In feeling this way the Chinese are neither contemptible nor vicious—merely political.

Chinese and Americans have criticized General Stilwell for getting on badly with the Chinese. General Stilwell is not a man who willingly compromises. He has not concealed from the Chinese what he thinks of their incompetence and corruption. Naturally many of them have thereby been offended.

My reaction to this criticism is this. The Chinese army and government are ridden by politics and abuses. Any American military man who attempted to compromise and play Chinese politics would promptly find himself enmeshed and rendered useless for the purpose he was sent out. General Stilwell once said to me that, "My safest course is straight down the road." I am inclined to agree. The Chinese army is not going to be made to fight the Japanese by wheedling and open-handed grants of materiel.

China is badly in need of the Puritan spirit. The Chinese have not produced it themselves excepting, in a modified form, in the Generalissimo. If the Chinese army is to be regenerated, it must be through General Stilwell. What he says sometimes stings the Chinese. But it has not gone wholly unappreciated. More than a score of high-ranking Chinese officers have come to him privately telling him that he was doing China a great service by his forthrightness, that he is needed, and to keep on going straight down the road. And, as has been said, even his political enemies have been impressed by what he has in six months produced at Ramgarh. He may yet perform what has seemed impossible—cause the launching of a Chinese offensive against the Japanese. If it happens it will have been a one-man achievement.

In retrospect this was a gung ho statement of Stilwell's case. I underestimated the strength of Chiang's determined inertia, and even impotence, and how easy it was for the Gimo, with FDR's backing, to frustrate Stilwell's wish to bargain for Chinese action.

After reading my memorandum, Stilwell said that it expressed what he tried to say but that he always became involved in son-of-bitches and bastards in his phraseology. The General then added, "All I want to do after this war is to go walking in the woods with my dog and not see another human being."

The day before I submitted my memorandum urging quid pro quo bargaining with Chiang, the President wrote Marshall asserting that stern bargaining was "exactly the wrong approach in dealing with Generalissimo Chiang." This was because, being a Chinese, the Gimo could not be expected "to use the same methods that we do." The fact of the matter, of course, was that being a Chinese, Chiang was from childhood habituated to bargaining—and maintained himself in such power as he possessed domestically through bargaining.

In his enlightenment of Marshall, the President declared that the Generalissimo had, in effect, unified China under his undisputed leadership and in so doing had created "in a very short time throughout China what it took us a couple of centuries to attain." FDR's disquisitions did not reveal a recognizable Chiang, but they did reveal Roosevelt's fictional view of Chiang and China.

Marshall passed on to Stilwell the gist of the President's communication. On one of the few occasions that he showed me a message from the Chief of Staff, Stilwell handed me the radiogram to read. FDR also criticized Stilwell's "neglect" of air action and called for all out support of Chennault. From my cryptic diary I conclude that the President also wanted to have Stilwell replaced and assigned elsewhere. I assumed at the time that this was the result of machinations by Madame Chiang, who had been a guest at the White House and busily lobbying in Washington. I did not then know that while Madame Chiang continued to be a glamorous success with the public and the Congress, her imperious petulance and bad manners quickly wore out her welcome at the White House. No, it seems more likely that Roosevelt's desire to have Stilwell transferred was due to his conversion to Chennaultism and his belief that he must appease the Generalissimo.

What should Stilwell's response, if any, be to the President's message to the Chief of Staff? I said to the General that he could not debate it. Temporize. I again suggested that he send Boatner and me to Washington. No, he did not want to stoop to politicking.

What happened was that Marshall firmly repeated to Roosevelt the familiar thesis that the creation of ground strength took strategic priority over an air offensive.

*   *   *

Stilwell changed his mind. Ten days after he declined to send me to the United States he told me that I was to go to Washington with the redoubtable Frank Merrill, who would be consulting the War Department. He did not spell out what I should do. He knew what I thought should be done —tell his story. Apparently he was willing to leave it to me how to tell his story.

At about this time Chiang asked Roosevelt to call Chennault, now a major general, to Washington to present to FDR a Chiang-Chennault plan for an air offensive. Whereupon Marshall summoned Stilwell to the capital. My task was simplified by the arrival of Stilwell in Washington.

Because of her access to Eugene Meyer, the publisher of *The Washington Post*, as one of his newswomen and also as a family friend, Patricia persuaded Meyer to invite Stilwell to his house to meet some of Washington's most distinguished journalists. It was more difficult for me to prevail upon Stilwell to accept, but he did. The evening began with a dinner for about eight, after which something like twenty more newsmen joined us. Stilwell spoke and answered questions with characteristic candor. He was articulate, forceful and made an excellent impression—in such contrast to his disastrous interview with Roosevelt. A number of the journalists said that Stilwell had given them their first realistic description of the situation in China.

Patricia and I also arranged for him to meet in our small apartment a number of senators. Again he was a success. And not forgetting the poor orphan of the wartime government, the Department of State, I persuaded Stilwell to meet with Hornbeck and Hull. Who could tell? Something good might come out of it.

Because I recoiled against the Stilwell-Chennault feud—although I was a Stilwell protagonist—I thought that Chennault should be enabled to state his case. Furthermore, I admired him, in contrast to some other airmen, as a serious, fighting flyer. So I arranged for Chennault also to talk to Hornbeck.

After this interview Hornbeck said to me that Stilwell and I were "poor salesmen" and that we should emphasize the positive side rather than the weakness of the Chinese. The situation, however, was that through glib, misleading salesmanship China had been flagrantly oversold to the American people and that the beginning of a positive approach was to face up to, and deal with, China's weaknesses.

Currie asked me how he could make his peace with Stilwell. Marshall had coldly rebuffed his attempts to remove Stilwell. He now wanted to establish friendly relations with the theater commander as part of his effort to entrench himself as the White House man on China. I suggested to Stilwell that he receive Currie, which he did, coolly.

At lunches, over drinks, and in their offices, I met with various Washington correspondents and columnists, briefing them on the CBI Theater. In New York, my fellow China missionary's son, and zealous propagandist for the Chiang establishment, Henry Luce, invited me to lunch and discourse, which changed the mind of neither of us.

After a session with a group of economic warfare bureaucrats I learned that some of my remarks, made in confidence to American officials, had been reported to T.V. Soong and that he was displeased by what he heard. I called on Soong, saying I was sorry that exaggerated reports had been made to him of what I had said. The Chinese Foreign Minister replied, "There are no secrets in Washington. Rest assured, Mr. Davies, that no conference takes place regarding which I do not have accurate and complete information." This boast was not wholly without foundation.

CHAPTER X

AMONG THE NAGA HEADHUNTERS

There were seventeen of us, passengers for a flight over the Hump to China. It was the morning of August 2, 1943, and we were in an American military transport plane, waiting for takeoff from the big Chabua airbase in the northeastern corner of India. A bored supply corporal drove a truck up to the open door of the aircraft and threw parachutes in to us.

Mine and several others were without their survival kits. Sweet-toothed and souvenir hunting GIs were accustomed to taking the emergency rations for the chocolate in them and the jungle knives for the distinction of owning a folding machete. No one seemed to regard this inconsiderate thievery seriously—"Oh, GIs will be GIs, everyone does it."

Eric Sevareid, on his way to Chungking to do a series of radio reports for the Columbia Broadcasting System, William Stanton, a Board of Economic Warfare official, and I were the three civilian passengers. There were also a Chinese colonel and a major, two American junior officers and ten American sergeants and corporals, from Texas to Maine, New York to Montana. Sevareid I had met in Washington. I was also acquainted with one of the American officers, Captain Duncan Lee. Duncan, too, was the son of missionary parents in China. He had been a Rhodes scholar, then one of the bright young lawyers recruited by General "Wild Bill" Donovan for his Office of Strategic Services. Duncan belonged to OSS headquarters in Washington (where I first met him). We had traveled together from Washington via London, Algiers and Cairo, to the CBI Theater where he was now on an inspection tour

The aircraft was a C-46, Curtis Commando, a larger two-engine plane than the reliable workhorse, the C-47. The C-46 was newly developed at that time and, because of the ravenous wartime demand for anything that could fly, it had been put into service before being properly tested out. Not all of its mechanical bugs had been corrected and so it was unduly prone to engine failure.

Nevertheless, we took off with a reassuring roar and as we surged steadily upward and eastward my misgivings subsided. At the rear of the plane I made myself as comfortable as aluminum bucket seats would permit and even dozed a little. An hour or so later, about 9 a.m., after we had cleared the first range of mountains and were over north central Burma heading for the great barrier mountains of the China border, one of the two engines quit.

There was no choice but to head back to base and hope that the remaining engine would hold the altitude necessary to clear the mountains between us and the base. Before long the crew chief, a sergeant came to the rear of the plane and pulled open the door. We were gradually losing altitude and to lighten the aircraft, all baggage was to be thrown overboard. I watched my flight bag go over the side with some regret, for it contained an assortment of presents for Chinese friends and acquaintances, including for Mme. Sun Yat-sen a bottle of fine cognac and a couple of bottles of the brown ink she fancied.

The aircraft continued to lose altitude. I went forward to ask the crew where we were, but the radio operator was preoccupied with emergency communications to the base and the two pilots were staring at their instruments with blanched, silent concentration. I got no reply to my questions as to where we were. It was important that we should know, for the Japanese occupied two narrow salients stretching into northern Burma, and if we were going to have to take our parachutes, leaping into the arms of the enemy might well be proceeding from frying pan to fire. I concluded however, that because the Japanese salients were so thin, the chances were that this would not happen. Assuming that we would soon have to jump, I returned to my seat in the rear of the plane and strapped my only weapon, a kukri, to my dispatch case.

This big curved knife, the kind that the Gurkhas use to lop off heads and the tops of trees, had been given to me the day before by General Haydon Boatner as a plaything or something to hang over a rumpus room mantel. As Haydon had neglected to include a scabbard, I hoped that by tying the kukri to my dispatch case the blade would not draw blood if on landing I tumbled on it. Then I strapped on my parachute, the first time that I had ever donned such a contraption.

Each of us aboard the stricken aircraft was preoccupied with his own little preparations for disaster, his own private terrors. We were a distracted, atomized group; no one took command to pull us together. Word was babbled down from the pilot that we should jump, depart the plane without further ado. Loath to leave the cold aluminum womb of the C-46 and plunge into the steaming primordial jungle some 3,000 feet below, I hesitated to venture forth.

But no one else stepped forward and out the door, and as time was wasting, I decided to get the inevitable over with. In a letter to my wife days later, I wrote, "I stood in the open door of that miserable Commando and declared, 'Well, if nobody else is going to jump, I'll jump. Somebody has to break the ice.'" Clutching my dispatch case and kukri to my chest and with my right hand grasping the parachute release ring, I waddled out into the wild blue yonder.

It was noisy and black, what with the rush of air past my ears and my eyes closed. I had read in novels that parachutists always counted to ten before pulling the ripcord. This I dutifully did and then gave the ring an anxious tug. Nothing happened. I kept falling. So I pulled as hard as I could. Suddenly I was jerked up short, all was quiet, the sky was bright blue with white clouds and above me was the beautiful gleaming parachute. But my dispatch case and kukri were gone. I must have relaxed my hold on them while concentrating on the parachute.

Three other parachutes floated downward several hundred yards away. And there was the wretched C-46 high-tailing it for India. Damnation, I thought, they have unloaded us and now they are light enough to make it back to base. This ungenerous thought was interrupted by a realization that I was swinging like a pendulum as I descended. I had not read of anything like this but recalled that parachutists were supposed to be able to maneuver by selective pulling on the cords. I hauled on a couple of cords, which caused only an alarming spill of air out of the chute. No more experimenting and the chute bellied full again. The final 100 feet or so of the descent seemed to happen in a rush and I hit the side of a hill with a wallop, rolling over, dragged by the parachute. As I was scrambling to my feet, Duncan Lee landed about 100 yards away. Next came a Sergeant Wilder from Texas and finally a Chinese major.

We had fortunately come down on a moderately inclined, treeless mountainside covered with grass and scattered low bushes. The jungle lay below on the lower slopes and in the valley. Although bruised and strained, none of us was seriously hurt. Our problem was not physical but psychological. We had fallen precipitately into a wilderness where we could see no sign of man or his works. What lurked in these lovely, silent mountains and valleys? Tigers, leopards, and wild buffalo, probably. What tribespeople might we encounter—friendly, headhunters, or those who might sell us to the enemy? And where were the Japanese? Our total armament against any attack, from buffalo to the Imperial Army, was Duncan's .45 pistol.

I, at least, was scared fairly stiff. My mouth was dust dry and I was consumed with thirst. Down slope was a stream and in a copse a small pool. There we went to drink and, on knees with hands in the cool clear water, to drink again. Lifting my head from a long draught I saw in the wall of bushes surrounding the pool a parting of the branches and in the opening a face staring at me with intense curiosity. No hostility in the gaze. I smiled and nodded and other faces appeared in the bushes. In no time a half dozen tribesmen joined us along the brim of the pool. They were superb physical specimens in loin cloths and saucer-sized brass disks shielding their genitals, bearing red tasseled spears and carrying long machete-like knives strapped on their backs.

We visitors from the skies were full of apprehensive questions. But how to ask them? The major blurted out in Chinese, "Where are we?" It seemed natural to talk Chinese to the tribesmen for they looked not unlike northern Chinese. No response, not even the appearance of trying to understand. The splendid silent savages simply gazed upon us with utter fascination. I then noticed that a leech had attached itself to my arm. Being without either a burning cigarette or salt with which to dislodge it, I tried to pull it off with my fingers but without success. A tribesman, apparently senior to the young braves who had first come out of the bushes, reached over and with a quick tug detached it. Good—a friendly act.

In a small notebook I penciled a sketch of a locomotive with care and then made the sound "choo-choo, chuff-chuff." The elder and company stared at my pictograph and my puffing face. Blank incomprehension. Deduction: we might be well away from a railroad (all of them in Burma were held by the Japanese). Alternatively, were we close to any of the enemy-held jungle roads? I drew a Japanese flag, but without a red pencil or pen, the result was far from representational art. Tremendous audience interest, but not a flicker of recognition. Were we near a combat zone? Here I undertook to reproduce vocally, but in low key, the sounds of battle as I repeatedly lifted an imaginary rifle to firing position. This was idea number one, quickly followed by idea number two: where was the fighting, if any? I pointed successively to the four quarters of the earth with an intensely inquiring and puzzled look on my face. My performance seemed to be appreciated but the audience gave no hint of an answer to the compound question.

Trying another tack, I attempted to find out how far we were from a British outpost. Again I resorted to the unsatisfactory expedient of drawing a flag, this time a Union Jack. Then, how to get across the idea of distance? How to depict or act out one mile to these bare-bottomed gentlemen? Less difficult, perhaps, it would be to act out distance in terms of elapsed time. So I pointed to the sun, swept my arm down to sunset horizon, whereupon I closed my eyes, laid my cheek on the palm of my hand and gently snored. Then I woke, pointed to the east and brought the sun back to where it was. The reaction was solemn, impassive attention. Quickly now, the key part of the compound question: how many of these diurnal rounds to the sign of the Union Jack? Again trying to look anxiously inquiring (which indeed I was) I raised one finger, two fingers and so on to ten. No dialogue in mime ensued. The show was over.

Shouldn't we move along, the tribesmen gestured. With some misgivings, we assented. Where were we being taken and in what capacity? As we started up a hill a stalwart savage walking beside me pointed up the slope, grinned, and with a slitting motion drew his hand across his throat. While he and his companions had not understood my pantomime, I thought I grasped what he was trying to tell me—a throat was to be cut. But whose?

Thus far the score or more of tribesmen taking us uphill had not demonstrated any hostility toward us. In any event, even with Duncan's .45, we were at their mercy. Our survival and, certainly, any hope of getting back to our kind, depended upon these tribesmen being willing to help us. We had, therefore, to avoid any show of suspicion or mistrust of them or any unfriendly attitude. At the same time, we should not seem to curry their favor. Dignified friendliness, it seemed to me, was the right approach, plus alertness to any signs that we might be transgressing a taboo.

   ✶   ✶   ✶

The path we were following went straight up the side of the mountain, no winding, no seeking out of easy gradient. What can be said for this direct highway engineering is, I suppose, that it is the shortest line between two points. And that it is the least accommodating to an attacker. At the pace the tribesmen initially set, we were panting after 100 yards of climb. They accepted our limitations, slowed down and stopped for rests.

After about half an hour we came to the crest of a ridge and a village whose houses were built on stilts. The ladies of the settlement were out on their verandahs staring down in wonder at what their menfolk had picked up on the lower slopes. They were a diverting sight with their bare bosoms festooned over the balustrades. We were exhorted directly to a long house, which I took to be a combination of town hall and men's club.

From its big verandah the tribesmen, excited, pointed out to us a column of black smoke rising from behind some nearby mountains. The C-46 had not made it back to base. I scribbled a note, cautiously phrased lest it fall into the wrong hands: "Those who bailed out this morning should join the rest of the party at the village. The bearer will lead you. This means you, too, Eric—John and Duncan." By sign language I asked the headman to send the message by one of his men. After much palaver one of the braves set forth, clutching the piece of paper.

Thereafter we stood around in aimless fashion while the tribesmen inspected our clothing and, with particular interest, Duncan's revolver, from which he had prudently removed the cartridges. The atmosphere was relaxed and friendly. While our fears for our immediate safety were quieted, we remained troubled by anxious uncertainties as to where we were and how we would get back to civilization.

The headman appeared to feel this rendezvous should be made into an Occasion. With natural dignity he held forth to me a sword with a silver handle. At a loss as to how to respond correctly, I limited myself to reverent contemplation of the weapon while busily turning over in my mind what sort of ceremonial act I might perform. The most meaningful and least susceptible of misrepresentation, I concluded, was a presentation of gifts. With both arms extended before me and a deferential bow, I handed the skinny old man my parachute. Impassively he accepted the tribute silk.

Next was my wristwatch. Having no trains to catch nor appointments to keep, I reckoned that I could do without a timepiece until I returned—if ever we did—to a way of life ruled by hours and minutes. My first step in the presentation was a brief discourse in sign language on the nature and meaning of a watch. Both the headman and I found this hard going. So I proceeded with solemnity to unstrap the watch and then, as if it were a talisman, strap it on the chief's wrist. His Honor stood stolid, expressionless, leaving me to wonder whether I might just as well have kept my watch.

Meanwhile, preparations were being made for what promised to be a banquet. A big fire had been kindled and jugs of rice beer readied to serve. It was apparently to be a stag affair—all of the men of the village—and rather formal. The headman arranged the seating—or better, squatting—by a protocol with which I was unfamiliar. Anyway, we visitors from the skies were put together.

Then the pièce de resistance was brought in, walking. It was a goat, a live and suspicious goat. It was led over to me. The headman handed me a great long knife and indicated that I was expected to decapitate the goat. So this was the throat my escort down the road had been gesturing about. While it was preferable to be the executioner rather than the executed, the prospect of hacking away at that mean-looking old goat struck me as an honor of which I was not worthy. Sergeant Wilder, as a Texan, seemed to me to be the right man to dispatch this ornery item of livestock. I indicated to the chief that Wilder would represent the Allies in the ceremony. With a visible lack of enthusiasm, the Texan grasped the knife and, as three braves held the uncooperative goat, hacked off the beast's head.

The goat's torso was then passed around the circle and we were invited to drink the blood from the stump of the neck. It tasted rather bland, something like unchilled tomato juice without Worcestershire sauce and lemon. After we had partaken of some sort of fraternity, the carcass was thrown on the fire and an awful stench of burning goat's hair arose.

Several tribesmen on the outskirts of our gathering shouted and pointed up the valley. I could faintly hear the drone of an aircraft. If it were one of ours we should quickly spread out and wave our parachutes. But if it were Japanese, we should not reveal our presence. The noise grew a bit louder, sounding like one of our transports, and then the plane appeared, crossing the valley several miles from us. Yes, it was one of our C-47s. We flung out our parachutes and foolishly shouted and jumped. But he turned away and headed up the valley and out of sight over a ridge. Because he was not flying a straight line but made a sweeping turn, I assumed that he was either a search plane looking for us in response to our C-46's distress signals, or was on a supply dropping mission supporting ground units. In either case, our situation now appeared to have elements of hope.

At last the goat was cooked and we gathered for the banquet. It consisted of unseasoned but pungent goat and vapid rice beer. The feasting was soon over, whereupon the headman took Sergeant Wilder aside and indicated that the Texan should accompany him to some other part of the village. "Be careful about the women," I called ambiguously after Wilder. Duncan, the Chinese major, and I were left among the hoi polloi. We had begun to be bored with the games of charades and animal, vegetable, mineral we had been playing ever since we met our goat-blood brothers. Obviously, it would take a long time to establish even simple verbal communication. Meanwhile what were we going to do, how long would we be welcome, and how could we better signal a plane should one suddenly reappear? Would my note reach Eric and company and would they join us?

Where the devil was Wilder? The sun was now low. Front the edge of the village came a mounting chatter. The messenger to Eric appeared and handed me a note: "Dear John—Eleven men here—two have bad legs—supplies dropped here, plane will return here—rescue party on way—please come here—we are about one mile south of wreck. Eric"

Well, that was clear enough, and encouraging, too. Now the thing to do was to get going immediately while there was still some light. The general excitement over the return of the messenger and the tale that he told of the crash brought forth the headman and Wilder. "What the hell have you been doing all this time, Wilder?" "Oh, him and me, we jest talked." Unlikely story, I thought. But then, conversation between this taciturn Texan and the headman may have proceeded in much the same way as that between a Swedish horse and camel trader I knew from Inner Mongolia and his Mongol business contacts. Ten or fifteen minutes would pass between laconic question or statement and scant response.

After warmly thanking the headman and our other goat blood brothers, we set off with the messenger and an escort of three or four braves. As twilight was descending, the tribesmen wanted to hurry. We were obviously, however, not up to even their normal lope. So they accommodated themselves to our stumbling gait. Just before dark we stopped and the braves bounded into a field of rushes and with flourishes, almost as if in a ballet, whipped their big knives into the rushes, gathering bundles which they deftly bound into torches. One of them collected a tiny pile of tinder, struck a flint and ignited a fire from which he and his companions lit torches.

Off we trudged again, but now in a torchlight parade. Night had fallen and we needed the flickering light because the trail was faint, the going rough and often precipitous. Also, I, at least, found reassurance in the assumption that the swirling fires above our heads would discourage the big cats from preying on us. The torches continued to burn even after a monsoon rain drenched us. On and on we scrambled. I stopped wondering when we would get to our destination; my half awake mind was occupied with the mechanics of keeping a footing and moving forward. After what seemed like four or five hours of this, our guide began to halloo. We came to a low wooden fence, entered a dark village and were taken to the long house. There, most of them asleep around a fire, were our C-46 companions.

*   *   *

Eric was awake. Dripping wet, I greeted him, "Dr. Sevareid, I presume." What had happened since we had parted company? After the Chinese major went out over the side, the next man froze in the open doorway and considerable confusion followed. This accounted for the distance that separated us—jumping did not resume until the aircraft had passed from our view, over a ridge. Everyone survived the crash except the co-pilot, whose parachute seemed to have become entangled in the tail of the plane. The radio operator, who had kept in touch with the base, thereby helping operations locate the aircraft's position, fell into a tree and broke a leg. Eric had landed safely near him and administered first aid. No other serious injuries.

Tribesmen had quickly come upon the scene and appeared to be hospitable. About an hour after the crash a search plane appeared overhead, probably the one that we had seen. It dropped blankets, rations, a radio transmitter (broken on impact), and instructions to stay put. A few hours later a second aircraft circled, dropping a message warning the survivors to remain where they were, instructing them not to enter the village, as the natives might not be friendly, and to stay together. Eric's party signaled a need for medical assistance. Obligingly, late in the afternoon, a third plane arrived overhead and from it blossomed forth a flight surgeon, Lieutenant Colonel Don Flickinger, and two medics, who drifted down on their mission of mercy and reassurance.

By morning the village's hospitality had come under strain. Some of the elders, a conservative element among our hosts, displayed disapproval of our presence in their midst. This was understandable. Twenty-two uninvited intruders, from inner space, occupying the most important house of a small village did constitute at least a nuisance. Fortunately, there were some liberals in the community who came up with a happy alternative to our extermination. That was segregation. With animated, smiling gestures they led us over the fence beyond the pale, to a gently sloping meadow. There in a matter of three or four hours they built us basha houses of boughs. They were open on all four sides, but the eaves sloped widely to within about four feet of the ground.

A supply plane appeared and dropped us instructions to stay where we were until a rescue party from India reached us. We were in an area inhabited by headhunters belonging to an ethnic group called the Nagas. So that we might be able to defend ourselves, bundles of carbines and ammunition were then dropped to us. They fell half a mile down the slope. We dashed down to retrieve the packages, but the Nagas, far fleeter, picked up the armament and presented it to us. Other benefactions rained from the skies—cans of drinking water, American drinking water from the U.S.A. Never mind that it was the monsoon season, that we were camped 100 yards from a sparkling mountain stream, which flowed into a cascading river at the bottom of the valley. I assume that the rescue routine prescribed dumping American water on American boys downed anywhere in the world. We also received on that and subsequent days more practical packages: food, candy, magazines, toilet paper and ink. Important for our relations with the Nagas, the plane dropped sacks of salt, non-existent in this area and so gratefully received by the tribespeople.

The liberals among our headhunting hosts assembled the next day in front of the bashas that they had built for us. With them was a runty bull which they tied to a tree trunk. A ceremony was about to begin, so we all lined up solemnly facing the beast and the tribesmen. The bull was duly slaughtered by one of the Nagas. With some queasiness I waited to see if we would have pressed upon us another libation of fresh blood, but we were spared the wassailing. It seemed appropriate for us to respond in some manner. At, I believe, the suggestion of Eric, we rendered a ragged but loud, "I've Been Working on the Railroad." Now, it would seem that I was pledged to brotherhood with another set of headhunters. I hoped that this did not mean that those of us bound by the goat bond would be caught up in a conflict of allegiances.

*   *   *

Life settled into a rut as we waited for the rescue party to come in over the mountains and through the jungles.

After a peaceful night's sleep on the ground, I would open my eyes, and waiting for me to do just that, there almost within reach was a squatting Naga or two intently watching me gather my wits. From dawn to dusk we were under observation, objects of endless wonderment. The headhunters were particularly interested in our eating. And they prized the discarded C ration cans, pieces of string and cloth. We developed a lively trade in these commodities in exchange for fresh produce.

To minimize the passage of headhunters in and out of our bashas in search of bargains, we set aside a small area in the encampment as an international trade mart. The tribesmen quickly learned that this was the place in which to conduct transactions of a commercial nature. Because I feared that free-for-all bargaining and bartering might lead to misunderstandings and rancor between the Nagas and us, I tried to institute a managed economy. We began with price control—for example, one empty C ration can for two eggs. But then as the savages' demand for these modern conveniences began to be satisfied and as our supply of empty cans piled up from the Air Transport Command's showering us with rations from on high, the bottom fell out of the tin can market. It had all been great fun and the Nagas seemed to enjoy playing store as much as we.

Many of the tribesmen suffered from ulcerated sores. One or two bold fellows let Colonel Dr. Flickinger sprinkle a sulfa powder on their festering afflictions. By the next day it was evident that a healing process had begun. Flick was in business running what amounted to a Headhunter's Memorial Clinic. But only for men, boys, and infants. Even in illness the women were kept away from us.

So, as it turned out, instead of decapitating us, the savages adopted us. I suppose it was because of the manner of our advent into their midst. If we had not come billowing down to them from above, if we had entered

their territory on the ground, across fiercely contested territorial bound-
aries, we would have been ambushed and our skulls added to the village's
collection of trophies. The same might well have happened had we tried to
stay on at the long house after the first night of hospitality.

I worried more about the Japanese than the Nagas. The enemy, I assumed, monitored our radio traffic, therefore knew that a score of us had
come down in the jungle, and was as able as our people to triangulate our
location. In August 1943 the Japanese still had the ability to make strafing
sorties and to send out from their jungle bases patrols and small task forces.
Overestimating Japanese interest in us and our accessibility to them, I advocated slit trenches in and near our camp and guard posts on the perimeter.
My recommendations made no visible impression. Our defensive posture
did not go beyond a couple of our fighting men sitting around a campfire
all night with their carbines leaned against the posts of a basha. We were
an easy, illuminated target for any human enemy. But that same blazing
fire that could betray us to man was our magic protection against the likes
of cobras and tigers.

Fitfully, I jotted segments of a cumulative letter to my wife. On Au-
ugust 9:

> It is afternoon and it is raining, as it does most of the time, for this is
> monsoon season. I am sitting on a piece of a parachute on a blanket on a
> ground sheet on the ground and leaning against a sapling post which forms
> one of the uprights to our palm and weed thatched hut. I can hear the
> stream 100 yards back of me rushing down the steep side of the mountain.
> Across the valley strata of India-silk mist are drifting along the face of the
> opposite slope, whose peaks are lost in the pale gray overcast. Duncan is
> sitting opposite me with one shoe off and one shoe on reflectively scratching
> his leg. Eric lies rolled up in a blanket fast asleep at the other end of our
> nine-man basha.

On August 14 I wrote:

> They dropped us some ink. Funny, I find it hard to write. Eric says the
> same. We do some. No one else does any. I've been down for two days with
> an infection that started from a leech bite, which I got the day I jumped.
> The colonel doctor had had hot compresses on it yesterday and today and
> doped me with sulfadiazine so that I'm pretty woozy. The rescue party gets

here today or tomorrow. I want to be well enough to walk out. It would be humiliating to be carried.

From out of the jungle's green obscurity there strolled into our meadow a young Englishman, blonde, hatless, pale blue polo shirt open at the throat, dark blue flannel shorts, stockings to the knees and heavy brogues. He was unarmed, carrying only a slim bamboo stick and a black Dunhill cigarette holder. This was Phillip Adams and he had come 12 days through mountain jungles to rescue us. He knew how to do so, for he was a civil administrator in the hill country on the Indian-Burmese border and wise in the ways of the Nagas.

With Adams was a task force of some 60 Naga scouts armed with a rare collection of venerable muskets and fowling pieces. Although not uniformed, these Naga warriors had been touched by civilization, for some wore khaki shorts instead of G-strings. An all spit and no polish outfit, the scouts had acted as Adams's bodyguard and would also protect us and carbines on the way back.

This was not Adams's first visit to Pangsha, the village near which we were encamped. He had been here several years earlier, escorted by a detachment of the Assam Rifles, which he had ordered to burn down the village. This was punishment to Pangsha, Adams later told us, for having been excessively active in headhunting.

Adams was quiet-spoken, almost shy, as he outlined to us plans for the march out. I had a feeling that he found us Americans rather overwhelming, the way we swarmed around him, staring at him and pouring out questions. As befitting his station and his prestige in the eyes of the Nagas, he occupied alone a basha a little, but significantly, apart from our bashas. To it he repaired to wash up and change, but, to my disappointment, not dress for dinner. From a jug of rum, his manservant made him a before dinner drink. The servant placed a folding table in front of the basha and set it with white linen and silver. Our pukka sahib sat erectly in his British officer's chair, and was served a proper and, if it was typical Anglo-Indian cuisine, unpalatable dinner. No one was encouraged to approach the table. So the savages and the Americans watched the performance from a respectful distance.

Most of the men of the village were on hand for our breaking-up camp and departure. I was standing near Adams watching them vying among one another for things that we were leaving behind—pieces of rope, cloth, bottles and the like. They were chattering and arguing among themselves apparently amiably enough until several of my headhunting brethren raised their voices in anger and began to jump up and down. Adams immediately tensed and in a low, firm voice said something to several of the scouts at his side. They glided to the area of dissension. Adams himself took one or two of the headhunters by the hair and, together with his trusties, brought the threatened bloodbath under control. It had been a close thing, the admirable Adams explained. When these people begin to jump up and down, their next move is to draw their long knives and lay about them.

The walk out lasted two weeks, over mountain trails and through occasional villages, with our supply planes dropping food and incidentals to us and salt for the villagers. On the way I wrote to my wife:

Most of the time on the trail has been busy—breaking camp, watching the scenery, the porters and the tough savage scouts, engaging in conversation with the rest of the party, wishing to hell the day's hike were over, making camp and shooting the breeze after supper.

It was the toughest trail I've been on. Straight up and straight down so that prospective enemies would find the approaches hard going. And it was beautiful. Six days from our destination we camped at 7,000 feet, whence we could see the great twisting river (the Brahmaputra), which marked our destination. The mists were lovely on the mountains and trailing through the valleys. We stopped by streams and waterfalls to drink cold sweet water and look at Rousseau-like foliage with small bright orchids— moist and vivid pink.

On the last Sunday of our exodus our celestial catering service outdid itself. The boys wafted to us by parachute the kind of Sunday dinner that mom used to cook: hot tomato soup, hot fried chicken, gravy, mashed potatoes, peas, hot biscuits, and for dessert, ice cream with chocolate sauce, coconut cake and coffee. This touching extravaganza represented considerable effort, coordination and skill, and what's more, warmth of spirit.

The appearance of the Nagas and their villages seemed to deteriorate as we approached the end of our journey. The first Nagas whom we encountered were men of magnificent physique, artlessly self-respecting and direct of manner. Those on the frontiers of "civilization" were less healthy looking, less assured and open. It was British policy, Adams said, to protect the

Nagas from outside exploitation. Indian and other traders were not permitted to penetrate into Naga territory, which was treated as a closed anthropological preserve. Fair enough, I thought, so long as the Nagas had a benevolent, effective protector.

I left my headhunting brethren not without a twinge of regret, certainly with appreciation. They had received us with hospitality and consideration. They had been honorable in their dealings with us—they found my dispatch case and kukri and brought them to me, the case badly dented, but all the contents there. And as a spontaneous gift, one of them presented me with a scabbard for my kukri. It was made of two concave slabs of bamboo, bound together with plaited thongs of bamboo and decorated with a line drawing burnt into the slabs: an airplane, below it a parachute, and dangling from the chute, a man.

PART III

PUBLIC AND PERSONAL DIPLOMACY

CHAPTER XI

THE POLITICS OF WAR

The China-Burma-India Theater was a geographical expression created by the Pentagon. In it Stilwell was supreme—but only in command of American forces therein. CBI overlapped with three other theaters: the China Theater, India and South East Asia Command (SEAC).

The China Theater was, of course, under the Generalissimo, with Stilwell nominally his Chief of a non-existent Allied staff. India was under the Commander-in-Chief, India, Field Marshal Sir Archibald Wavell, followed by General Sir Claude Auchinleck when Wavell was made Viceroy. Stilwell had no function in the India command, but maintained one of his two headquarters at New Delhi, the other being at Chungking.

South East Asia Command was headed by Admiral Lord Louis Mountbatten, a dashing, elegant, gutsy, young naval nobleman. He was designated Supreme Allied Commander, South East Asia (SACSEA), contracted to Supremo, to keep pace with the Generalissimo's Gimo. Stilwell was appointed Deputy Supremo. SACSEA's combat domain was mostly water, Ceylon and the enemy-occupied British, Dutch and French colonies, including Burma. When SEAC was created in 1943, I assumed that its function was the amphibious reconquest of the colonies, bypassing Burma and aiming at Singapore. Admiral Mountbatten's headquarters were in an idyllic botanical garden at Kandy, in the mountainous center of Ceylon, about as far as he could be from salt water and the island's few airports.

The crazy quilt of commands as they affected Stilwell were illustrated by his position in the North Burma operations. The bulk of his troops were

Chinese, for which he was responsible to the Gimo. His supporting American Tenth Air Force was based in India, and all of his supply lines passed through India, which made him dependent upon Auchinleck. As the operations were in Burma, he was under Mountbatten. But because SEAC divided the Burma front into sectors, with General Slim commanding the northern one, and because Stilwell insisted on assuming field command in part of the that area, he made himself subordinate to Slim. At the same time, as Deputy Supremo, he was superior to Slim. Fortunately, the two worked sensibly together.

In the CBI Theater structure, Stilwell had command over Merrill's American combat unit in northern Burma, the Tenth and Fourteenth (Chennault) Air Forces, American units training Chinese troops in India and China, and supply, transport, and engineer detachments from Karachi to Kweilin in Southeast China.

Serving him and in some respects under his command were several civilian and quasi-military organizations. The Office of War Information (OWI), in addition to its propaganda to the Chinese and Indian civilian population, provided psychological warfare material, such as leaflets for air drops to the Japanese, and assigned propaganda warfare (PW) specialists to combat areas where, for example, they called in Japanese for surrender.

Another civilian organization was the Board of Economic Warfare (BEW), which purchased strategic materiel for the United States and collected and analyzed enemy economic information. It was on this latter score that it served CBI headquarters. The civilian operations of both BEW and OWI were subject to the supervisory control, in China, of the Ambassador and, in India, of the Personal Representative of the President (as India was not a sovereign state, normal diplomatic relations with exchange of ambassadors was not possible). Insofar as OWI and BEW activities entered the military sphere, the CBI command had at least an interest in, when not authority over such operations.

With his multitudinous military concerns, Stilwell had scant time for these two new civilian agencies. In any event, he did not take seriously whatever they might contribute to fighting the war. His indifference was reflected in the attitude of the senior Army regulars on his staff.

The Office of Strategic Services (OSS), a para-military organization, fared better with Stilwell and his staff. One section of it, Secret Operations, at least engaged in killing the enemy and sabotage. And Secret Intelligence was meant to conduct espionage and get behind the enemy lines. But

Morale Operations, black propaganda, seemed nebulous and Research and Analysis, academic.

The heterogeneous OWI-BEW-OSS expeditionary forces arrived in mounting numbers during late 1942 and early 1943. Stilwell took a direct personal interest in the OSS Secret Operations unit which penetrated into northern Burma for sabotage and guerrilla action. The rest of the civilian and para-military units, perforce, sought contact with and guidance from the theater command through G-2, the intelligence section, of New Delhi and Chungking headquarters. While amiable enough, the theater G-2 was an uninspired mediocrity.

In February and March 1943 I discussed with Stilwell psychological warfare and intelligence by civilian agencies in the theater. Both times he had told me to take charge of these activities. But I had no staff or any desire to head up a desk-bound bureaucracy. At Washington in May, I suggested to Stilwell that he ask for four Foreign Service officers to be detailed to him on the same basis as I. He did so.

Explaining to the Department the reason for Stilwell's move, I wrote on May 29 that "the request arose from the General's realization that he is confronted constantly with complicated political, economic and psychological problems in the prosecution of the war . . . that his staff officers— professional military men—are for the most part not equipped to collect and evaluate information nor advise in these matters; and that he must perforce turn elsewhere for this vital intelligence and advice."

Stilwell, I continued, had orally given me authority to supervise a coordinated OSS-OWI-BEW political, economic, and psychological intelligence and warfare program. As a Foreign Service officer concerned over the encroachment of the new agencies on foreign affairs, I thought that the detail of the additional officers would not only be of assistance to the general, but also provide, under the guidance of the Ambassador and the Personal Representative of the President, political direction to the activities of the personnel of the new agencies and enable us to forestall errors which they might otherwise commit.

The Department detailed to Stilwell three of the Foreign Service officers requested. The fourth was withheld for reasons of health. The three were John K. Emmerson, a Japan specialist, Raymond P. Ludden, a China specialist with whom I had served in Mukden, and John S. Service, a China specialist and my friend since childhood. The transaction detailing these three men went through normal War and State Department channels. The

Far Eastern Division and the Charge d'Affaires at Chungking were aware of the moves. But Ambassador Gauss, who was on vacation, was not. When he found out what had happened, particularly that he had lost Jack Service, his most valued and promising junior officer, he was wroth. And his ire was directed at me as the author of his deprivation.

The Department of State was so slow in issuing orders to my three colleagues, from May until late summer of 1943, that the headquarters went ahead and made arrangements for supervision of psychological warfare and intelligence by military staff members, principally G-2. In the end I was relieved that matters had worked as they did, for it was evident that the four of us would have had little backing from our own Department, and that, had the arrangement I envisaged been put into effect, the four of us would have been burdened with administrative work and entangled in jurisdictional tiffs. We therefore functioned with each agency separately in a consultative and advisory rather than supervisory capacity. As we were of approximately the same rank and I had no wish to act as boss, we operated ecumenically. However, being the one with the longer and wider relations within the theater command, I was treated as senior among equals.

Service and I spent most of our time in political investigating, reporting and interpretation for Stilwell and his headquarters staffs at Chungking, where Jack was initially located, and New Delhi where I had an office and our files. Peggy Durdin, with whom Jack and I had gone to school in Shanghai, who was the wife of the *New York Times* correspondent, Tillman Durdin, and who was a newspaperwoman in her own right, managed our Delhi office with panache. Emmerson was in 1943 and early 1944 occupied primarily with psychological warfare in Burma and study of Japanese prisoners of war in Burma, China and India. Ludden acted as political adviser to the Twentieth Bomber Command, the very long range force that attacked Japan from West China before the Pacific islands closer to Japan were captured and used. We wrote independently of one another, addressing our memoranda to Stilwell, unless the subject was of slight interest to him. As a matter of routine, we sent copies of interest to them to the Embassy or the New Delhi Mission.

*   *   *

One American organization in CBI stubbornly resisted supervision and control by both CBI headquarters and the Embassy. It was headed by

Captain Milton E. Miles, USN, one of the first to denounce me after the war—behind my back. Miles was called Mary only because, as I recall it, his surname had suggested to impressionable midshipmen the movie star Mary Miles Minter. His outfit was the American complement of the Sino-American Technical Cooperation Organization SACO, pronounced by the captain, with grim relish, "Socko!"

Miles had a pennant, he told me, that before the war he flew on his destroyer to bewilder passing Japanese men-of-war. Designed by himself, it exhibited three interrogation marks, three exclamation marks and three asterisks. After I emerged from my parachute jump over Burma I received from Mary a note welcoming me to the Caterpillar Club, and on the paper was rubber-stamped his strange device.

Miles had been sent to China by the Navy Department to establish and operate weather stations, gather intelligence about enemy shipping along the China coast, and lay as much groundwork as possible for eventual landings on the coast. As his was a military assignment in the CBI Theater, he was under Stilwell's authority. He was also initially attached to the Embassy, and therefore answerable to the Ambassador. And for a time early in the war he headed OSS in China. But with all of this, the headquarters and the Embassy knew little of what Miles was up to, and he played with appropriate thin-lipped taciturnity the role of man of mystery. Stilwell asked me to try to find out from Mary what he was doing. So I had several conversations with the Captain.

Most of the activities which the Navy Department wished Miles to conduct were, necessarily, to take place behind enemy lines. Obviously, the Captain would need Chinese cooperation. He found it in the willing—at a price—person of Tai Li, head of Chiang's secret police. SACO resulted. Tai Li headed it, and Miles, who spoke of him as "the boss," was number two.

Tai Li's function was the familiar one of secret police chief in an authoritarian regime threatened by domestic dissent. It was surveillance, spying and repression. His primary concern was internal enemies, not the external foe. "Although efficient by Chinese standards," I noted on November 8, 1943, "the Tai organization suffers from such gangster frailties as venality and leakage to the enemy; hence the recent cracking of the Nanking Tai organization by the Japanese."

The arrangement between Tai and Miles was that Tai would provide intelligence, protection and "guerrillas" to fight the enemy. As I recorded on September 5, 1943, "Miles told me that in return it was necessary for him to trade materiel, which he described as 'wampum.' Tai did not and would not give his information gratis. Furthermore, Tai was not interested in receiving cash payments because, obviously he had all the money that he needed. Nor was Tai willing to provide intelligence in exchange for service, such as the extensive training provided his agents by American military and technical experts sent out to Miles. What Tai wanted was certain specified military materiel—tommy guns and radio equipment."

Mary complained that he was not getting enough wampum. He had lost several thousand tommy guns in a ship sinking and Stilwell was not allowing him enough Hump tonnage. So Tai was withholding intelligence. Miles submitted to Tai's demand for authority to veto the assignment of any American to SACO. The captain declared to me that he did not want Americans who had experience in China. According to Miles, the American component of SACO numbered in late 1943 some two hundred demolition and communication experts, meteorologists, FBI (five, with twenty more due) and Secret Service agents.

His FBI and Secret Service personnel, Miles explained, were to provide to Tai agents scientific police training, which would be used eventually in fifth column activity. Just how this would be done was not made clear. What was clear was that such training was certainly relevant to internal security functions.

Had SACO made use of biological or chemical preparations, I asked Miles on September 5. "We have gotten some good results," he said. I then recorded that

> he explained that by this method one Japanese major general, two brigadier generals, one rear admiral and six colonels had been disposed of. Three of these officers had been dispatched by one female operator. These activities took place . . . in the Hankow-Nanking area. I asked whether the Japanese did not suspect the cause of the deaths of these officers. Miles shook his head. I observed that such operations struck me as being highly dangerous to us. He said that he also had a drug which would be very useful in the event that we desire to capture alive . . . such as air and ground crews at an air base. This drug causes acute diarrhea . . .

I did not doubt that Miles had the drugs and poisons that he spoke of. Whether the poisoning exploits of which he boasted really occurred or were

Tai Li fabrications to impress him, I do not know. Like Mary's claims of demolition and other sabotage, those regarding poisoning were suspect, unless verified by American personnel on the spot. They were not. And I noted in November that the sabotage claimed by Miles was unsubstantiated by CBI headquarters. I assume, however, that the Tai-Miles combination had some successes, more likely in 1944 and 1945.

Tai Li had turned over to him, Miles claimed, three divisions of guerrillas. Tai permitted Mary the privilege of arming them—the tommy guns were primarily for them. From other sources I later heard that at least some of these so-called guerrillas, after having been issued the American weapons, had been enterprising enough to show up for a second helping. Miles also asked Stilwell for ten thousand daggers with which to stab Japanese in Indochina.

In a pretty, luxuriant valley not far out of Chungking, Miles had what he called his farm. This was his bucolic headquarters, occupying several scattered innocent-looking houses. Tai Li agents, sleek young men, were unobtrusively ubiquitous, tending their American charges. On part of the farm that I did not visit, Miles (and more importantly Tai Li) were host to "free" Thai and French groups that Miles claimed to have smuggled across India without British knowledge. He said that he planned to use them for infiltration of Thailand and Indochina.

These political activities Miles conducted without informing the Embassy or headquarters. A young Thai politician who arrived in Chungking sought Embassy aid in going to Washington to organize a free Thai organization, but then disappeared. The Embassy discovered that he had been made a guest of Tai and Miles. Subsequently, Mary received orders from Washington to discuss the matter with the Embassy. Thereafter, while still a guest of Tai-Miles, the Thai suddenly passed away at the ripe old age of twenty-nine.

Gauss objected to the arrangement whereby Miles was attached to the Embassy, and told Washington that Miles "makes no reports to the Ambassador and information regarding the activities of his office is limited to rumor and report from other sources." Gauss was no happier over the Embassy's being associated, because of Miles, with Tai Li's "dreaded secret police . . . and general 'Gestapo' agency." Eventually, in response to the Ambassador's requests, Miles was detached from the Embassy.

Miles was touchy over criticism of him. On September 5, he observed that some Americans in Kweilin had "been making cracks." The captain declared that if this went on that individual might find a knife in his back. He observed that "people disappear in China."

In one of my autumn 1943 conversations with Miles he appeared to be discouraged and wanting to return to sea duty. He gave me the impression that he would rather be evicted by the Theater Commander, which would make him a Navy martyr to Army villainy, than hang on with a failing enterprise. But he would oppose anyone succeeding him. If he had to leave, he would take all of his personnel with him. And if all of this happened, he hoped that what he feared would not occur—that Tai Li would make things difficult for Americans in China.

Miles left none of us who dealt with him in doubt of the powerful support that he had in the Navy Department. His back-up man in Washington was Captain J. C. Metzel, with an office close to that of the Chief of Naval Operations and, Mary claimed, direct access to Admiral King. On one of my visits to Washington I dropped in on Metzel, a somber, wary fellow. We profited one another little.

I filled in Stilwell on what I had leaned from Miles. With all of the major problems engaging his attention—Chiang, Roosevelt, Chennault, and the balky campaign in Burma—the general was not disposed to precipitate a feud with the Navy over what seemed to be a pet project of Admiral King's, and one that did not seriously impede what Stilwell was trying to do. As Miles was in 1943 nominally responsible to the OSS, I thought the organization might appropriately try to lasso Miles and put him in harness.

*   *   *

Major General William J. ("Wild Bill") Donovan, a Wall Street lawyer turned cloak and dagger chieftain, headed OSS. He was a bit of a latter-day Teddy Roosevelt, effervescent and adventurous—a refreshing contrast to the tedious norm of Washington officialdom. He did business with me, about his CBI operations, at dinners in his R Street house and lunches at the F Street Club, where at the bar he announced that J. Edgar Hoover was, of course, a homosexual. This was in those days worse than desecrating the flag and I was surprised that no violence ensued. In any event, emboldened by Donovan's candor, I offered him some months later, on October 6,

1943, a seven-page critique of his operation in CBI. In it I surveyed Miles's activities.

My main criticism to Donovan was political: Mary's dabbling in Free Thai and Free French intrigue and his subservience to Tai Li. "Miles is riding an unprofitable tiger and," I wrote, "involuntarily, the rest of us are riding with him. Very embarrassing . . . I know that you do not want the State Department and the Army to act on this Miles mess so long as there is a chance of OSS itself cleaning it up." Donovan was unable to bring Miles under his control because Mary was both a protégé of Admiral King's and a captive of Tai Li's. The captain could not have functioned in China without the patronage of his "boss."

Donovan went on to build up his own little empire in CBI. It was one of his teams that had the distinction of penetrating Indochina, saving Ho Chi Minh's life and, after the war, entering Hanoi in triumph with Ho.

Gene Markey, a U.S. Naval Reserve Captain, was better known in CBI for having been the husband of, among others, Hedy Lamarr, than for his naval conquests. At his initiative, on my September 1944 trip to Washington, I met Admiral Ross T. McIntire, the Navy's Surgeon General and physician to Roosevelt. The Admiral wanted to know whether I had seen any of his doctors assigned to Miles (who had been promoted to Commodore). I replied that I had not. McIntire exclaimed that he had received no news or reports from them and did not know what they were accomplishing or where they were. I said that we had seen little of any use from SACO but felt that Miles might be, unbeknownst to us, producing for the Navy. "We haven't gotten a thing from Miles either," the Admiral volunteered.

McIntire was worried over Miles's failure to make the large scale coastal preparations expected of him—and time was running short. We were reluctant, I commented, to interfere with an operation seemingly strongly supported by the top Navy command. If it should be cleaned up, that was for the Navy to do. The CBI command did not want to intrude and create friction between the War and Navy Departments. The Admiral, who had recently returned with the President from an Army-Navy meeting in Hawaii, said that he thought that the Miles problem might be solved by Major General Patrick J. Hurley. Stimson and Marshall had chosen Hurley, a former Secretary of War, to be the man whom Roosevelt wanted to send as his personal representative to smooth out the Chiang-Stilwell and other feuds in the CBI. McIntire plainly intimated that one of the reasons Roosevelt was sending Hurley to China was to deal with the Miles farrago.

In the month following my talk with McIntire, Stilwell left China. In November, the next month, Gauss left China. And in January 1945 came my turn to leave China. But Miles stayed on. Rather than being brought to account by Hurley, he became the purveyor of Tai Li's "intelligence" to a receptive Hurley. Stilwell's successor, Lieutenant General Albert C. Wedemeyer, wrung his hands over Miles in a July 5, 1945 message to the War Department: "If the American public ever learned that we poured supplies into a questionable organization such as Tai Li operates, without any accounting, it would be most unfortunate indeed . . . Miles has been Santa Claus out here for a long time." Being Santa Claus did not hold back Mary from promotion, ultimately, to Rear Admiral.

*   *   *

Most American military men think of the war as a soldier's job to be done . . . the administering of a military defeat to the Axis, and no more than that. Most of our officers want the job accomplished as soon as possible, with minimum of fuss over international political and economic issues, which they regard as of secondary importance. Political and economic questions, they feel, can be discussed and decided after the defeat of the Axis.
To our allies the conduct of the war is a function of overall political and economic policy. Military logic is therefore always subordinate to and sometimes violated in favor of political and economic considerations.

I wrote this to Stilwell in September 1943, saying that he was "fully acquainted with this thesis" but that I was examining it anew as a result of conversations that I had had in London during July with the American Ambassador and American military planners who were consulting with their British opposite numbers regarding the war against Japan. The American planners had been told that the British preference was to delay operations in Burma until after a 1945 offensive against Sumatra and Singapore. The Americans were concerned about what a failure to open land communications would do to China. But the British viewed the Chinese as worthless in the war against Japan, and as covetous of Indochina and Thailand.

Ambassador John G. Winant told me that Churchill was willing to see the Chinese collapse.

Winant said something about the Prime Minister that seemed to me to explain a great deal about British policy: that Churchill had been tremendously impressed by the lesson of France. In winning World War I it had been so bled white that it was defeated in 1940. The PM was determined that the same thing not happen to Britain.

On the basis of this and other information, I concluded that the Churchillian policy was (1) Conservation of British manpower—trading time for men in the realization that victory accompanied by exhaustion and decimation is no victory. (2) Repossession and even expansion of empire. (3) Preventing China from becoming a major power. (4) Reducing Russia's strength as a major power by delaying the opening of a second front. "It is not suggested that this picture of British war policy," I added at the time, "—with the exception of the first item—is one which would be drawn by, much less have the support of, the British public and many British officials, including Mr. Anthony Eden," then Foreign Secretary. This policy was Churchill's, I said, and he had the power to enforce it.

Like the British military strategy, I wrote, the Chinese strategy was dictated by political considerations, as Stilwell knew only too well. In sum, Chiang's preoccupation with the growing postwar threat to his regime dictated a strategy of military quiescence, conservation of strength and leaving the defeat of Japan to others.

"Absorbed in their struggle with the Germans and realizing that they cannot depend upon Britain and the United States to defeat the Wehrmacht for them," I wrote,

> the Russian policy appears to have been less political than that of the British and the Chinese. In its singleness of purpose—confined to the defeat of the enemy—it resembled ours.
>
> But while we follow such a policy from choice, the Russians have done so from necessity. A mortal struggle for survival leaves little slack for political picking and choosing. British policy in 1940 and 1941 and Chinese policy before Pearl Harbor had the same attributes of simplicity.
>
> Once the Russians feel, however, that they have won their fight for survival and that they have some leeway for maneuver, it will not be surprising if they begin to make their military strategy subservient to an overall political policy. That point may already have been reached.

There is no reason to cherish optimism regarding a voluntary Soviet contribution to our fight against Japan, whether in the shape of air bases or early opening of a second front in Northeast Asia. The Russians may be expected to move against the Japanese when it suits their pleasure, which may not be until the final phases of the war—and then only in order to be able to participate in dictating terms to the Japanese and to establish new strategic frontiers.

As the Soviet Union's peril diminishes, its need for our aid diminishes. In direct proportion as the Kremlin feels its need of our American assistance lessening, our bargaining position becomes weaker and we are less able to persuade the Russians to act as we desire. We appear to have made little use of our bargaining strength with the Soviet Union because, perhaps, we were not prepared to force through what we wanted and because we would not have been prepared to exploit our advantage even had we done so. Now we find our bargaining strength with the Russians slipping away, as it has been slipping away with the British since Pearl Harbor. Our strong bargaining position vis à vis the Chinese remains. But we have never employed it on any major issue; rather, the Chinese have us on the defensive because of a guilt complex we have with regard to China.

Whatever Soviet policy might otherwise have been, Mr. Churchill's apparent intention to let German dog eat Russian dog can hardly be expected to evoke anything other than a Russian determination to play a role only and strictly in its own interest.

Mr. Churchill's imperialistic policies have already incited the angry suspicion of the Chinese. The Chinese strongly suspect that Britain intends to attempt to reassert its rule over Hong Kong. A responsible and exceptionally well-informed Chinese army officer said to me several weeks ago, "Of course we shall eventually have to fight the Russians, but we shall first have to fight the British."

British determination to bypass Burma cannot be expected to encourage the Generalissimo to adopt a more aggressive attitude toward the Japanese. It is quite evident to informed Chinese that if land communications to China through Burma are not opened, they cannot reasonably be asked to mount any significant offensive against the Japanese.

This particular British policy therefore simply abets the Chinese inclination to sit back and let us fight the war against Japan. It is the practical application of the British thesis that China is worthless as an ally and it carries the implication that the position which we now hold on Japan's western flank is not worth exploiting. If it becomes evident to the Japanese that both the Chinese and their allies consider the China theater to be moribund, the enemy will be free to reduce his garrisons in China and use the surplus troops against us elsewhere.

The British, I continued, had reason for their part to feel less than friendly toward China. The Chinese had occupied territory across the border in Burma and threatened Tibet, which the British traditionally sought to uphold as a buffer for northern India. As for the Soviet Union, Moscow might be expected to intervene to prevent Chiang from eventually attempting what he was determined to do—crush Communism in China. Such intervention, of course, raised the specter of American counter-intervention, and even American-Soviet conflict.

I then touched on Soviet expansionism, and

concern lest the Soviet Union, in seeking to establish its new strategic frontiers, will expand into territories which the other three powers, also for strategic reasons, wish to remain independent or which one of them (China) claims. How far does the Soviet Union intend to penetrate into middle Europe in pursuit of the Germans? What are Soviet intentions in southwestern Asia? What are Russian plans for the use of their Korean division? And if the Chinese Communists are driven to seek Russian aid because of Chungking attacks, does the Kremlin intend to utilize as satellites the Chinese Communists and any territory which they may, with Russian arms, hold or capture? North China and Manchuria, for example.

American policy, I commented in this 1943 paper, seemed to be

more or less committed to certain vague political and economic principles enunciated in the Atlantic Charter and "Four Freedoms." But this policy had never appeared to override the purely military strategy of defeating the Axis. One political policy, however, seemed to have prevailed over military strategy and that was maintenance of Britain as a major power. By its silence the United States had, in the eyes of the rest of the world, acquiesced in Churchill's imperialism.

"The lines of future conflict," I concluded, "are being formed by the course of the present one. We can now be assured of further war and revolution in our time."

Stilwell told me that he thought the President should be exposed to my fifteen-page memorandum even though Roosevelt's practice was not to read anything over a page in length. Currie sent in to the President a copy that I had forwarded to him, with what effect I know not.

My September pessimism over postwar prospects was not new. In March 1943, I had written a jeremiad to my wife lamenting the evil to come and "our incapacity to cope with the problems which will confront us. It's the old, old story of human history. Only, this time, it's going to be of wider scope and greater upheaval. The only course is to do as well as one can and be stoic about what one can't do." Ten days later: "We are going to blunder through to a victory in this war which will be followed by another war well within our time. I don't know which is more important at this juncture—ensuring the victory or planning for what we are going to do with the victory. I am inclined to think the latter is more important."

But the people who were doing this planning—some of whom I had met in Washington—alarmed me. "People with impeccable intentions" but out of touch with reality, theoretical, prone to error.

*   *   *

It probably was some time in 1943 that I was at a dinner given by Stilwell at his house in Chungking for Madame Sun Yat-sen. She was the only appealing one of the Soong siblings, and spoke English with ease and low-keyed, playful wit.

This was the first time that I had seen anyone from outside the small group living with the General dining at his house. He was not a party-giver. Here was this urbane, gentle, great lady, something of a legendary figure in her own right, with six or eight of us American men, a bit in awe of her and striving to make a good impression. The conversation turned to what, when victory was attained, should be done with Japan. I do not recall Stilwell's comments, but some of his officers engaged in what seemed to be a contest over who could propose the most devastating vengeance on Japan. Madame Sun watched the performance with immobile, mute fascination. The suggestion that stays in my memory, perhaps because it has the ruthless tone of a passage out of the Old Testament, was that we sow the fields of Japan with salt.

In 1943 and even 1944, there was no clear definition of American objectives with regard to Japan. Defeat, of course. Roosevelt had announced at Casablanca on January 24, 1943, that we demand unconditional surrender. But what did that mean, beyond ensuring that the fighting would last longer than were the surrender negotiated? (Stalin, incidentally, made substantially this point to FDR with regard to Germany.) Did we intend, after Japan's surrender, to lay waste to the country? Or would Japan be pastoralized, as some in Washington advocated for Germany? Or would we try to avoid creating a power vacuum in that particular quarter of the globe and permit Japan to remain strong enough to serve as a counter in the East Asian balance of power?

I had my doubts about the good sense of war of extermination. On October 20, 1943, in a conversation with a senior British official at New Delhi, I asked whether it was desirable that Japan be totally crushed. Could not Japan be used in the future as a counterweight against the Soviet Union and China? Surprisingly he agreed. Two and a half months later, also in New Delhi, I raised the same question with Major General Wedemeyer, then Mountbatten's American deputy chief of staff. Again, I got agreement. But the Japanese heard nothing out of Washington or London to change their conviction that the Americans and British were implacable, resolved to murder their sacred Emperor, enslave those Japanese whom they did not kill and that consequently to seek conditions for surrender would benefit them nothing.

CHAPTER XII

CAIRO: WITH ROOSEVELT, CHURCHILL, AND CHIANG

Roosevelt, Churchill and Chiang met for the first time at Cairo in November 1943. They were accompanied by their chiefs of staff and other high military officers, including Stilwell, Mountbatten and Chennault. Several Ambassadors were present, but not Gauss. Stilwell took Frank Merrill, Colonel John Liu, who was his Chinese liaison officer, and me. And so I glimpsed the decision making process as practiced by the high and mighty.

The November 20 entry in my diary was:

> We arrived today at Cairo. Yesterday afternoon at the Shatt-Al-Arab Hotel Frank pounded on my door, asked me to come to his room to talk over with him the Old Man's request for ideas as to what he should say to the President. "What should I ask the President for?"
>
> I propped my slippered feet on the bed and said, "Bargaining power." I observed that it was what he needed most, but what Prexy was least likely to be willing to give him.
>
> Frank added American troops. Also four stars, but through the War Department.
>
> The Old Man came in and joined us. Thereby I was brought in on the conference.
>
> We got talking about the QUADRANT (the Anglo-American conference at Quebec) decisions and the main line of attack. Then the question of a

port (on the South China coast). At that point I picked up what I deemed to be a bedbug. I turned it over to Frank, who squashed it between his fingers, and pronounced it indeed to be a bedbug.

We discussed bombing from a certain area and were delighted to conclude that it would support the Navy and just about everyone else. Tentatively I observed that QUADRANT placed a certain place late on the schedule. Couldn't we attack it and step up the timetable by a year or two? With surprising ease they agreed. We began to find an astonishing (to me) number of favorable factors.

The hitch was the water supply line. The Old Man asked, didn't they want to join battle with the Japanese fleet?

I asked the Old Man if he didn't want Hurley as Ambassador at Large. He agreed heartily.

We got back to the main subject. I said that the idea ought to appeal to the Navy. Frank added the Air. That the big talking point was the year or two saved, was what I diffidently emphasized. I was tentative in my suggestions, being in the presence of experts.

Conversation sort of dwindled off. So we went our ways—Frank to get a haircut, and I to take a bath.

After tea with John Liu, I decided to write up a plan because neither Frank nor the Old Man was. So on a sheet of hotel stationery I did so. Frank read it and expressed no great enthusiasm. Later I showed it to the Old Man. Same reaction.

This morning on the plane Frank borrowed my sheet of paper. In about an hour and a half he came back to where I was sitting with the idea presented in War Department style, two and a half pages. I made some changes. We ate fruit, read magazines, talked with the superb Ty [Captain Emmet J. Theisen, the pilot of Uncle Joe's Chariot] and Frank said he would let the Old Man put the thing in his own telling prose style.

November 21. We borrowed typewriter and paper from the Air Force and started work on the plan. Frank telescoped it into one page. The Old Man read it over, said he wouldn't change a word—I suggested several, asking him to bring out coordination with Navy schemes. The Old Man put the paper in his hip pocket and disappeared.

I drafted a paper on the political considerations involved in the China and SEAC Theaters.

The next morning, after typing our paper in final form, Merrill and I sped to Mena House to distribute copies to our acquaintances among the army, navy, and air planners. Mena House, a pleasant hotel near the pyramids, was the site of SEXTANT. That was the name of the conference, which, I thought, in view of its location, might have been better called the Mena Pause.

After delivering our plan, I went to the American Legation to revise my memorandum while Merrill departed to buy an accordion. With my revised memo and Frank's accordion we called on Hurley. He said that he had been summoned by the President. So we pressed upon him our two papers and away he went.

We returned to the comfortable suburban house to which Stilwell and his party had been assigned. Merrill settled down to wring music out of his new acquisition and I sallied forth to spread the word. I dropped off copies of our two papers at the Legation for Winant. Back at our billets, I wrote,

> The Old Man came bouncing in. Pat [Hurley] had told him that the Squire [FDR] was in good spirits and looking for short cuts. I wondered whether Pat gave him the smudgy carbon copy from us.
>
> The heat's apparently on. The planning boys have been told to get to work.
>
> John Liu sort of unburdened. Said that the Chinese had placed themselves completely in our hands. We could have anything we wanted. But not the British.
>
> The Chinese, he said, had no experience in these kinds of conferences. They do not know how to go about the business of a conference. Too many high-ranking officers, not enough colonels for running around, doing contact and spade work. The generals sit around completely uninformed and out of touch. Much of it is a question of face . . . it's a top delegation with the Generalissimo—his best men.

The conference formally opened on November 23 and again I noted that, "the heat is really on. The plan is at the top of the Combined Chiefs of Staff agenda until disposed of." Being of lowly rank, I did not attend the sessions, but was kept informed by Stilwell, Merrill and others.

"The beauty of our little plan," I wrote, "is that it appeals to so many— Ernie [Admiral King], Hap [General Arnold], the Gimo and FDR. Marshall presented the plan as the Gimo's, which General Stilwell had been kind enough to present informally for Combined Chiefs of Staff consideration. At the combined meeting this afternoon King, Arnold, Marshall and Leahy

[Admiral William D., who acted as chairman of the JCS] all spoke in favor of it."

With the passage of years I had forgotten what our little plan precisely was until recently when, in looking over documents relating to the Cairo Conference published by the Department of State in its Foreign Relations of the United States series, I came upon "Memorandum by Generalissimo's Chief of Staff (Stilwell) 22 November 1943, Role of China in Defeat of Japan." It fleshed out the deliberately cryptic and vague entries in my diary.

After reiterating the familiar objectives of opening land communications to China and training the Chinese army, the plan introduced the goal of capturing Canton and Hong Kong, November 1944-May 1945. It also proposed bombing Formosa, the Philippines and Japanese shipping between those islands and China, and "land-based air support of any U.S. Navy activities in those areas." It went on to argue that *"these operations will: (1) Provide greatest aid possible to other theaters, and (2) Cut down Quadrant timetable for final defeat of Japan by one or two years."* The requirements for accomplishing this were the familiar Stilwellian plea for three American divisions, successively in India by March, April, May 1944.

The British chiefs and Mountbatten were taken aback by the plan and objected strongly to it. The proposal that American and Chinese troops retake Hong Kong touched a sensitive nerve. General Sir Alan Brooke, Chief of the Imperial General Staff, sneered at the plan, "Fantastic." He also catechized the Chinese generals, who were present for this session, on the strength and disposition of their forces. The Generalissimo's best men pled ignorance on some factual data and no opinion on broader matters— "as John Liu observed, none of them dare express an opinion without the Gimo's OK." Although Stilwell spoke up on their behalf, it was a humiliating afternoon for the Chinese.

After being briefed by Stilwell, the Chinese generals returned to a military session on the following day where they quizzed their tormentors of the previous afternoon. In response to a Chinese query, the British, I noted, "said blandly that it would take them two hours to figure out how many British army troops they had in India. No, they didn't even have an approximation." This implausible ignorance can be excused by the Anglo-American belief that the Chinese Government, including the military, was insecure, that military secrets divulged to it would find their way to Tokyo.

Our little plan ended up on the cutting room floor, not so much because of British opposition as because of what had always prevented the

China-Burma-India Theater from having a significant role in the war: logistics—the long, long sea, land and air haul to southeastern China. Marshall told Stilwell on November 24 that his objection was logistical. On the following day, General Frank Roberts, an Army planner and old friend from Peking and Burma, said to me that our proposals were premature. And of Colonel Thomas Timberman, another China specialist from operations and plans of the General Staff, I recorded, "Timmy thinks little of our operation in China. We'll be let down [by the Chinese]. Our flanks will be exposed."

Furthermore, the American strategists were coming to the conclusion that the war against Japan would be won by carriers, long-range aircraft operating from the Bonin and Volcano Islands, and naval blockade. No maddening complications from having to deal with allies. As a factor in the defeat of Japan, China was of declining significance. Nevertheless, China was thought to have, however passively, a role in containing the Japanese forces there. For, if Tokyo concluded that Washington had given up on efforts to activate the China front, it would then feel free to shift a significant portion of its armies in China to stiffen its resistance to the American advance in the Central and Western Pacific.

Related to the concern over containing Japanese forces in China was the continuing anxious desire for the upper levels of the American government to keep China in the war. But contributing most to the inflation of China's importance in overall American policy was Roosevelt's persistent determination that China be regarded as a great power, coequal with the United States, Britain and the Soviet Union. Consequently, although China's military significance had diminished, it continued to loom disproportionately large in the American government's calculations.

The conference accordingly considered plans for an offensive to open land communications across northern Burma to China, with the Chinese divisions in India under Stilwell, driving southeastward from Assam to meet with the Chinese forces advancing out of Yunnan toward India. Also examined were Mountbatten's SEAC plans for a limited action over the Indian border into western Burma and an amphibious operation against the Andaman Islands. For security reasons the Chinese were not told the objective of the latter; only that the plan envisaged an operation in the Bay of Bengal.

At Cairo the Generalissimo was his customary self—at once obstinate and shilly-shallying. With the European Theater suffering from a shortage of transport aircraft because of the insatiable demands of the Chinese, the

Generalissimo monotonously pressed for yet more transports and tonnage over the Hump. As for his vacillation, that began on the opening day of the conference when he changed his mind several times about attending the session.

But more disconcerting to everyone involved was his tergiversation over the SEAC plans. He accepted them on November 25. Then that evening Stilwell got a call from Harry Hopkins to come on over, which the general did. To Stilwell's disgust, the assembled Anglo-American upper crust was well into its cups. Accompanying a band, the dignitaries were singing, "There'll be bird shit over / the white cliffs of Dover." In search of a more businesslike atmosphere, Hopkins took Stilwell upstairs to inform him that Chiang had changed his mind about the SEAC plan. The Gimo was against them.

American and British generals talked Chiang into what they thought was agreement, only to have him back off again. And so it went, on again, off again, even to the extent of Mountbatten's pursuing the Generalissimo on Chiang's homeward flight and getting him at a stop in India to say yes. But, of course, once he was in Chungking, the Gimo went back on his assurances to the Supremo.

Chiang simply had no stomach for a Burma campaign. He was defeatist about fighting the Japanese. He had told Stilwell that it took three Chinese divisions to hold against one Japanese, and six to attempt the offensive. Even though he had better than that ratio on the Yunnan-Burma front, he balked at attacking, breaking the enemy blockade and opening a long supply route to India. No, he preferred passively to depend on the Americans to supply him by air until such time as, in routing the Japanese in the Pacific, they opened East China coastal ports for him.

*   *   *

The meeting at Cairo with Roosevelt and Churchill was for Chiang his initiation ceremony into the club of the Big Four. The occasion required him to conceal his basic negativism and to join the bellicose spirit of the brotherhood. This, naturally, created a conflict within him, resulting in his vacillation over course of action. Seeking to shift the blame for his passivity

onto others, the Generalissimo shrewdly made the commitment of his Yunnan forces to a Burma campaign contingent upon SEAC's engaging the
enemy not only in the Bay of Bengal but also in central Burma, well beyond
Mountbatten's proposal of western Burma.

This the British declined to undertake. Then, at the Roosevelt-Churchill-
Stalin meeting at Tehran, on the heels of the consultations with Chiang, the
first step in a deal was taken. Churchill gave in to the Stalin-Roosevelt desire
for cross-channel and Mediterranean assaults on the Germans in France.
Several days later, back in Cairo, Roosevelt took the second step and yielded
to Churchill's insistence that the Bay of Bengal plan be scrubbed. The Prime
Minister's rationale (not accepted by the American Joint Chiefs of Staff) was
that the amphibious equipment assigned to the landings on the Andamans
would be needed for Mediterranean operations. The cancellation of the Bay
of Bengal assault, on top of SEAC's refusal to challenge the enemy with an
airborne seizure of Mandalay, gave the Generalissimo a self-righteous excuse
for doing what he wanted to do: sit tight.

Churchill had no reason to be downcast over the abandonment of the
SEAC plans. The Andaman proposal was premature. And the idea of campaigning in Burma, repugnant. "I hate jungles," he later wrote, "which go
to the winner anyway." The decision against Japan would be reached in the
Pacific. In so far as it was arrived at on the continent of Asia, the decision
would be imposed by the Russians. Stalin had repeated to Roosevelt at Tehran that the Soviet Union would go to war against Japan after the defeat
of Hitler. SEAC's role should then be essentially a mopping up operation,
reoccupying the lost colonial territories. Consequently, Churchill considered
China to be of even less military importance than it had been and the American obsession with Chinese affairs to be that much more futile and tedious.

*   *   *

Roosevelt went to Cairo in large part to achieve a meeting of minds with
Chiang, on whom he relied so much in war and in the fashioning of
conditions for world peace. Yet he took with him no one with knowledge
of the Chinese and their language. Such people existed in the State Department and elsewhere in the United States. Although Roosevelt and
Hopkins knew only a handful of State Department officials, they were

sweeping in their contempt for and suspicion of all but a few of the foreign affairs professionals.

The day before the conference opened I was surprised to encounter at the Legation the dean of the Foreign Service's China specialists, Willys Peck. He spoke Chinese fluently, for years had been acquainted with Chiang, and was the soul of discretion. He was eminently suited to act as interpreter and source of information on China for Roosevelt, and to make a record of the meetings. Had the President brought him? No, Stanley Hornbeck had sent him. Peck said the White House was lukewarm to his coming and agreed only on the condition that he was to be no more than an interpreter. He did not even interpret. He was ignored by FDR. Trying to make him feel not entirely a leper I filled him in as best I could. And the day that the Gimo left Cairo the Old Man gave Peck an account of what happened, for which Willys was grateful. He spoke sadly of the younger men being more sought after—implying that we were more responsive to direction from the top.

Without the inhibiting presence of a knowledgeable American at his side, Roosevelt plunged into cultivation of Chiang and soliciting the Generalissimo's collaboration in building a Rooseveltian world order. Madame Chiang, who at the humiliation of the Chinese on November 23 had reinterpreted the military interpreter, and, bedizened as for a cocktail party, essayed to vamp the Combined Chiefs of Staff, interpreted at the private meeting between FDR and her husband. Hopkins, who also met with the Chiangs, intimated to Stilwell and me that one could not be sure how much she interpolated her own ideas into the translation. This was not a new thought to anyone familiar with Little Sister. So, did the President know what the Generalissimo really said, much less thought? And vice versa?

Roosevelt and Chiang met privately three or four times during the course of the conference. No minutes were kept on the American side. The President's son, Elliott, lent his presence to one of the conversations and perfunctorily recorded for posterity that the two statesmen had discussed Chinese unity—presumably the Communist problem. Continuing his tour of the horizon, Elliott disclosed that Malaya, Burma and India had been topics at an earlier get-together. There was nothing like the careful and accurate chronicling of the Roosevelt-Stalin conversations inscribed by the astute Foreign Service officer who acted as the President's interpreter, Charles E. Bohlen. These records were invaluable in subsequent negotiations with the Soviet government. American officials dealing with Chinese

affairs were without an objective, factual account of the exchange of opinions between Roosevelt and Chiang.

The tripartite Declaration of Cairo, December 1, 1943, made clear, however, that Roosevelt and Chiang had a meeting of minds on what should be
done with Manchuria and Formosa. They should be "restored" to China.
Subsequent presidents have had reason to regret that in the case of Formosa
a decision on the disposition of the island had not been withheld until a
peace conference and determined by a plebiscite.

But FDR believed that a display of generosity, gratuitous offerings of
enemy territory to the Chinese and the Russians, would persuade Chiang
to stay in the war against Japan and Stalin to enter it—when each had every
intention of doing what Roosevelt thought he had to pay them to do. The
President's liberality with other people's real estate was also part of his show
of good faith and noblesse oblige meant to sweeten the Gimo's dislike of
foreign devils and Stalin's Bolshevik prejudices against American imperialists, and so further great power solidarity.

From Bohlen's minutes and later statements by the President we know
that Roosevelt discussed with Chiang and Stalin not only the disposition of
Japan's colonies (Korea to be under an American-Chinese-Soviet trusteeship pending independence), but also a new deal for the Asian possessions
of the British and French. Churchill did not look at all kindly on the latter
exercise. Roosevelt and Chiang agreed that Indochina should not be returned to France but placed under international trusteeship; Stalin was
noncommittal but later concurred. Roosevelt's prescriptions for the future
of India were a revelation of his dilettantism in foreign affairs.

In 1942 he had proposed to Churchill that Britain devise for India an
interim government like that adopted by the former American colonies
under the Articles of Confederation. This, at best, embarrassingly culture-
bound suggestion brought to boil the blood of his good friend the Prime
Minister. Then, at the Tehran conference in one of his tête-à-têtes with
Stalin, FDR said that he was not discussing India with Churchill, but would
lay before Stalin the thought that the best solution for India would be reform from the "bottom," somewhat on the Soviet line. Stalin took this
historically illusioned notion in his stride and explained to the President
that the situation in India was complicated by wide cultural and social
differences and that reform from the bottom meant revolution.

*   *   *

Stilwell took me with him on the day before the conference ended to try to get some enlightenment from Hopkins on White House thinking about CBI. As the President's most influential assistant was ill, he received us in his bedroom—a frail figure under white wool blankets and a pale green counterpane, bright searching eyes, and a surprisingly firm handshake. Hopkins said that the British no more wanted the Chinese strong than they wanted the Japanese strong. But, he continued, they wanted Japan built up after the war. Because Japan would again be our enemy, we must have strong bases in Formosa, the Philippines, and "anywhere we damn please."

We want China to be a major power, said Hopkins. And the Far East will be the most important area in American foreign affairs. "The night before his departure for Tehran," I wrote in my diary, "he had three hours with the Gimo. Chiang and the ubiquitous Madame talked very frankly, violently anti-British and very nervous about the Russians. He said that they were childish in many ways. Wanted Outer Mongolia. He laughed."

Hopkins asserted that the Russians had no territorial ambitions in Asia. And Stalin had only contempt for the Chinese Army. Turning to the Middle East, Hopkins criticized "British lend-lease wrangling" and wanted to repossess all American equipment the moment the war was over. "He apparently was excited over American trade possibilities in the Middle East," I wrote. "Thought it was inexcusable that we had no bank in Cairo."

I raised the problem of policy guidance from Washington to representatives in the field. Again, from my journal:

He recognized the spot our ambassadors are in with lack of direction and duplicating agencies. A small, closely-knit group of men to run the American foreign show is what, he thinks, we need. There needs to be a laying on of hands. He was inclined to dismiss the effectiveness of the Embassy. I told him that there were good men in it . . . Of the State Department— "better leave that unsaid," Hopkins exclaimed.

Hopkins mentioned that he thought we ought to hear from the mouth of the Chief Executive words about our policy. He'd arrange it. He thought secret directives should be issued setting forth overall policy and that they should be distributed to key people abroad.

A couple of hours later, at 12:45 the Old Man and I were scrutinized at the road entry to Villa Kirk by a stalwart Secret Service youth in underwear and field jacket who reluctantly let us by. Then in past the Secret Service men and aides in the hall entry to the drawing room where we sat on an orange divan and watched son Elliott in unpressed o.d. pants pass back and forth. We were shown out on what proved to be a deep porch in the center of which was an effusion of foliage. On a long couch sat the great man. It was, Hello, Joe. He shook hands with a display of warmth.

What followed was a diffused and episodic conversation. It was, I think, the most difficult to record coherently of any I've participated in.

The President began by saying that it—the Bay of Bengal operation— was all off. Looking grim, he said he had fought for it for several days, but the PM wouldn't give in; they were at an impasse. The conference couldn't be broken on this issue. So it was all off. Roosevelt then sought to put a good face on matters. Things weren't so bad—the airlift would be increased, we would work on building up the ninety Chinese divisions and the Fourteenth Air Force (Chennault's). The Generalissimo shouldn't be too dissatisfied. He had asked for a billion dollar loan. The President told him he didn't think he could get it past Congress. But he might let them have fifty million for currency stabilization.

The Old Man very respectfully and gravely asked what our policy toward China should be. I don't recall any incisive answer. The general tenor of his reply was that we want a strong China. Some time ago he told Churchill that 425 million Chinese were not to be overlooked. Churchill exclaimed, "425 million pigtails." The PM says that he will not haul down the flag over any part of the Empire. The President's solution for Hong Kong—let the British raise again their flag, but "the next day as a generous far-reaching gesture let them declare Hong Kong an open port."

Would he please explain, I asked the President, the present and prospective "nobility" of the Russians in Asia? Immediately he said they were like us, had all the territory they needed. I was thinking of security rather than land hunger. So I asked if they would not want for Manchuria a status something like that of Outer Mongolia. Definitely not. He told Stalin that he was sure "Shang," as he called the Gimo, would be willing to make Dairen a free port. Siberian trade with the rest of the world would pass through this ice-free port in bond.

While he did not foresee any Russian land grabbing in Asia, he did remark that he thought Stalin would not stand for "that Eight Army (the Eight Route, designated in the United Front as the Eighteenth Group, Army, was the main Communist military force) being pushed around."

Then, somehow we got onto the subject of colonies. Point blank he asked Shang whether China wanted Indochina. Point blank the Gimo replied "Under no circumstance." And Stalin thought that Indochina should not

revert to France. Trusteeship is apparently the answer. He specifically men-
tioned Korea as unprepared for self-government. What Korea, and pre-
sumably South East Asia, need are international nurture, much along the
lines of our Philippines effort.

I asked what we should do if Chiang's regime collapsed. Without hesita-
tion Mr. President said, "Build up the next man." Then they [FDR and
Hopkins] wanted to know who might be considered next in succession. The
boss and I agreed that there was visible no one person—it would probably
be a group. The Old Man sagely remarked that we wouldn't have to look
for them—they'd search us out.

Hopkins's question about Japan revolved around what attitude we
should take toward the Emperor. I said, in effect, once a tool maybe again
a tool of an equally vicious faction. The President seemed to agree. He
recalled one of his ancestors passing through Japan when the Mikado was
a nonentity, observed that he had been built up in a matter of seventy
years or so.

We heard a good deal about his ancestors. The one who went to China,
made a million, returned home, lost it in a coal mine investment, went
back to China, made another million, went home and put it in railroad
stock which did not pay a dividend until two years after his death. Told
with much laughter.

It was stuff like this and anecdotes about plump Dr. [H. H.] Kung
borrowing fifty million for highway construction (designed to reveal the
shrewd horse-trading instinct of the raconteur), his scheme for going into
the black market with fifty million dollars to buy up the depreciated yuans
("of course I am not a financial expert"), and his plans for postwar avia-
tion from England to Australia via the U.S. which confused and depressed
us. It was part of the politician's brush-off technique. He never directly
came to grips with the real subject at hand—what did he want the General
to say to Chiang about the change in plans, what instructions as to policy
toward China did he have?

Hopkins was present during only the middle part of the conversation.
Pallid with an unhealthy bright pink spot on each cheek, he squinted at us
against the bright sunlight. He asked if I knew Chinese. Yes. Later he said
to Roosevelt, What we need is a tight little group, which will do the job
and keep their mouths shut.

Hopkins announced the Prime Minister. We got up to go. The President
told us to write him personally. He said, "Remember you're both Ambassa-
dors; both Ambassadors." I wondered what Mr. Gauss would think.

In the car on the way back to Mena the Old Man held his head in his hands.

What precisely were the final military decisions of the conference? Nobody seemed definitely to know. Joe went down to the Joint Chiefs. Timmy said the game broke up because somebody grabbed the ball and jumped out of the stadium. After lunch, the Boss went for a last word with the Chief of Staff. Even George Marshall wasn't sure what the score was. And so the Mena Conference ended.

Our final goodbye was to the British soldiers and women's auxiliaries (ATS) who guarded, managed and took care of the house in which we were billeted. It was thoughtfully stocked by His Majesty's Government with a goodly selection of beverages for our solace. We thought it only fair that those charged with our welfare should share in their government's bounty, and so advised them. After all, the war had been far rougher on them than on us. Jack, for example, had been away from home for more than five years—India, Ethiopia, Western Desert, Tunis—and had a five-year-old child he had never seen.

They had thrown three parties in our and General Strat's [George E. Stratemeyer] basements, pathetically simple affairs, excepting for the liquor, for which we were credited by the HMG with having drunk. Little Paddy got sick on beer and gin at the second party. Frank lent them his accordion each time. The soldiers danced with the British ATS girls and one another. The Old Man, Strat, and Frank showed up at one of the parties. John Liu, very red of face, was a great success with a Chinese song.

When I said that the war against Japan was our job, two sergeants protested very seriously, "Oh no, sir, it's ours too." One of them apologetically asked questions about the war. I answered them as best I was able. He said, "Thank you, sir, we couldn't ask the same questions of our own people."

On the morning of our departure, the sergeant major, the batmen and sentries bade us Godspeed and said they were sorry to see us go. Anne, the English ATS girl who was our housemother, had tears in her eyes when we said goodbye.

To satisfy the General's archeological interest, we flew over the Sea of Galilee, Nazareth and Ctesiphon. And so back to India and China.

CHAPTER XIII

THE RESURRECTION OF BRITAIN'S EMPIRE
IN ASIA MAY BE SAID TO LIE OUTSIDE
THE SCOPE OF OUR MISSION

The head of the Political Warfare Executive (PWE) in India was a Mr. John Galvin. PWE was not part of the Government of India. It was an arm of the British Government, engaged in disseminating undercover information, both truthful and fabricated, designed to confuse and mislead the enemy. Galvin, a few British and American propagandists and I discussed on October 30, 1943 at New Delhi our countries' prospects and policies.

Would it be desirable for the United States to become isolationist after the war, I asked Galvin. Emphatically not, he replied. The biggest risk of the United States turning isolationist, I remarked, was perhaps an American feeling that we had been dupes of the British during the war. The American people were willing to sacrifice if they felt that a better world would result. And most Americans, I thought, identified a better world with the abolition of imperialism.

"We cease to be British, we lose our standard of living" if Britain permits the overthrow of imperialism, Galvin responded. He backed one hundred percent Churchill's declaration that he had not become the King's first minister to preside over the dissolution of the empire. I said that it seemed to me that the American Government was committed to the support of the

British Empire because it needed a strong Britain—and Britain could not be powerful without its empire.

At the same time, American forces in South and East Asia, I continued, were in a most compromised situation as far as the American public was concerned. If General Eisenhower was in some quarters referred to as a dupe of the British, how much more vulnerable was Stilwell in his position as deputy to a British commander, Mountbatten. And after American forces joined their allies in retaking Burma and Malaya and those areas reverted to British colonial status, questions might well be asked in the United States why Americans should have been sacrificed to repossess British colonies. Galvin agreed that this was possible.

If Britain did not want the United States to turn isolationist and hoped for postwar American cooperation, I remarked, the British must grant us some freedom in stating the American case in East Asia which, because of the colonial issue, was an area full of more political dynamite than the Mediterranean area. The British should not try to gag us in South and East Asia. Galvin said that he saw the importance of this.

Among other topics, we discussed further power conflicts. Galvin predicted a Soviet-Chinese-Indian-Japanese alignment against Britain, the United States, and the white dominions. And he foresaw, eventually, a war between the two blocs, starting in India.

Galvin's forecast was, of course, similar to apprehensions expressed to Stilwell in my January 1943 survey of the Indian situation. The fundamental difference between Galvin's and my estimates was that I believed that an Indian-Chinese-Soviet collision with Britain and the United States might be avoided if London early granted India its independence, whereas Galvin, unwilling to concede freedom to the colonies, appeared to assume the inevitability of a sweeping East-West war.

In a memorandum recording the conversation with Galvin and others I observed that "imperial rule and interest means association with other people on a basis of subjugation, exploitation, privilege and force. It means a turning by the colonial peoples to any nation or group of nations, which can promise them a change; nations to whom the colonial peoples would not turn were it not for their servitude."

It was not without cause that I said to Galvin that the British should allow us to state the American case to East Asians. American efforts to launch psychological warfare activities in support of American-Chinese military operations in northern Burma met persistent obstruction in 1943 from a General [Walter] Cawthorn, the dour, awkward Director of Military Intelligence, General Headquarters, India. But I did not think that Cawthorn represented a consolidated British point of view any more than Churchill's approach to the colonial problem was shared by all British officials.

The Office of War Information representatives, who were to conduct American psychological warfare, and I encountered British officials who seemed to be cooperative with the American wish to operate independently. Particularly was this so in the case of the British Ministry of Information's Far Eastern Bureau chief, Paul D. Butler, whom I had known and respected as British Consul General in Mukden. Butler had been thwarted and frustrated by Cawthorn and, like many British officials unconnected with colonial administrations, regarded the Government of India as fairly benighted.

But Cawthorn, who was hardly alone in his attitude, was in the position and had the authority at least to hinder the American undertaking. This he effectively did by denying Burmese personnel and printing type (fonts) to the American psychological warfare team. In contrast, the American authorities had provided the British in India the services of ten Japanese-American translators and broadcasters, a 100 KW transmitter, a complete font of Japanese type, and Japanese compositors, and had air-dropped millions of British leaflets over Burma and Thailand. In July and October 1942, I attempted to soften Cawthorn's opposition by reassuring him that we had no intention of issuing propaganda adversely affecting Britain's rule over its subject people or of embarrassing the British.

Nothing happened. On October 30, at New Delhi, before SEAC moved to Ceylon, I gave General Wedemeyer the record of obstruction we had encountered. Wedemeyer passed my report to the Supremo. Three days later I was told that if I got in touch with Cawthorn, the cooperation we sought would be forthcoming. The next day Cawthorn told me that he could not promise assistance until agreement had been reached on integration of Anglo-American propaganda.

The same afternoon at a meeting with General Sir Henry Pownall, the SEAC Chief of Staff, Cawthorn continued his resistance to the American request, but Pownall supported it. On the following day, the British again dealt with the issue, which to the Americans seemed a minor and routine matter, at a high level and with what appeared to be divided opinion. Two OWI psychological warriors and I were met by an army composed of Cawthorn; his colleague, the Director of Military Operations, GHQ, India;

the general in charge of Civil Administration for Burma; and Mountbatten's principal Political Adviser, Maberly Esler Dening, an agreeably decorous Foreign Office type. Again I strove to allay anxieties with assurances that we had no intention of raising such embarrassing subjects as the Four Freedoms. Dening accepted our position but the three East of Suez generals appeared to think that American psychological warfare might prove to be not much different from sedition. The GHQ trio, finally grudgingly, tentatively said that they would loan us six or eight evacuees from Burma as translators and interpreters. Eventually, some Burmese personnel were permitted to work for OWI.

*   *   *

Why was Cawthorn—and so many in the Government of India and the Indian Army—seemingly hypersensitive to the prospect of American propaganda in Burma, and for that matter, to the very presence of Americans in India? I attempted in a November 15, 1943 examination of Anglo-American cooperation in South and East Asia to appraise the British outlook.

The mere existence of American military units in India embarrassed the British because they lessened British prestige, already undermined by Japanese conquests. And prestige, an aura of omnipotence, was the intangible base on which the authority of the British raj largely rested. The American reputation among colonial peoples for sympathy toward self-determination likewise made the British uncomfortable. "While feeling some appreciation for our present silence on the colonial question," I wrote, "the British are, nevertheless, still acutely apprehensive lest there occur some ingenuous American outburst on the subject of liberty for colonial peoples."

The British were also concerned over the possible introduction of American civil administration in parts of Burma which would be occupied by forces under American command. Related to this was a fear that the Chinese would retain or claim whatever section of Burma they recaptured. And in longer and wider perspective, the British were anxious about the American policy of building up China lest an invigorated China aggravate in the Empire the infection of nationalism, or even become expansionist.

For the British, then, the relationship with us in South and East Asia was awkward. "Yet they have to bear with us," I wrote in 1943. They needed us.

The least unsatisfactory escape from their dilemma would seem to be: accept us (for they have no alternative), consolidate us with themselves for efficient cooperation and then, by dominating the integrated partnership, bring us into line with their policy and action.

So there is established the South East Asia Command, in which we and, so far as it can be arranged, the Chinese are to cooperate with the British under a British Supreme Commander. And the Supreme Commander in the person of Lord Louis Mountbatten combines all of the qualities calculated to appeal to most Americans: forthrightness, vigor and glamour. But, alas, we shall never know what confidential orders His Lordship carries from Mr. Churchill designed to inhibit his natural vigor, unless events, perchance, continue to suggest them. Meanwhile, Admiral Mountbatten's British subordinates and Government of India officials emphasize their desire to integrate personnel as well as effort, not only in military affairs but also in matters which have far-reaching political implications.

It did not seem to me that the British were wicked or perverse in all of this. I thought that they were, naturally, acting in what the dominant opinion in London (Churchill) and New Delhi considered to be Britain's national interests.

Fair enough. But in the colonial areas of South and East Asia, Britain's national interests did not everywhere coincide with ours. Insofar as we both sought the defeat of Japan we were in accord. But it seemed to me that "the raising of the Union Jack over Singapore was more important to the British than any victory parade through Tokyo." Whereas, in my opinion, "the resurrection of Britain's Empire in Asia may be said to lie outside the scope of our mission."

In January 1943 I had suggested that Washington should try to induce London to move toward granting India independence. Now, ten months later, I said nothing about independence for Burma and Malaya, but confined myself to the immediate problem raised by our reentry into Burma—how to avoid being compromised in the eyes of Asia by our association with the British in colonial reconquest.

"While highly sensitive to embarrassment by us," I wrote, "the British exhibit a distressing lack of sympathy for the discomfiture to which we are exposed because of our association with them." Were we able to operate independently in Southeast Asia and on our own terms (which would have meant self-determination for those liberated) "we might expect to be welcomed by and have the cooperation of the native population. But because of our identification with the old colonial masters we might expect much the same resistance, hostility and non-cooperation from the native population which will greet the British." Our relations with the free peoples of Asia would also be adversely affected. "The Thais will feel—as many Chinese already do—that we have aligned ourselves with the British in a 'white-ocracy' to reimpose western imperialism on Asia."

However mutually uncomfortable the Anglo-American partnership was,

> we are scarcely more able than the British to extricate ourselves from it. To accomplish our mission, we have as much need of the British as they have of us. The partnership cannot be dissolved. But this does not mean that we should resign ourselves unreservedly to being compromised . . . So long as we retain OWI as an independent American mouthpiece of psychological warfare we can attempt to rationalize our policy to East Asia on our own terms—yet without offending the British. We can hope thereby to mitigate such hostility to us as will develop among colonial peoples and can perhaps even win a larger degree of cooperation than otherwise might be forthcoming. This can be accomplished only if our psychological warfare program preserves a purely American identity.

I closed the November 1943 paper with a recommendation on a related matter—that we remain completely aloof from civil administration of reoccupied colonial territory.

A week later, in Cairo on November 22, I reworked my comments on Anglo-American cooperation. There resulted the memorandum that I distributed to some members of the American delegation at the Mena Conference. Taking into account the fact that Mountbatten's theater of war included not only Burma and Malaya but also the Dutch East Indies and the southern half of French Indochina, I said that participation in SEAC operations would involve us in British, Dutch, and French colonial reconquests.

My theme was that we should concentrate on operations in China, avoiding "the mutual mistrust and recrimination over the colonial question, potentially so inimical to harmonious Anglo-American relations." However, in cooperation with SEAC we needed to open a land route to China through North Burma. "But after the recapture of North Burma there comes a parting of the ways."

"The British will wish to throw their main weight southward for repossession of colonial empire. Our main interest in Asia will lie to the East."

I do not know whether the President saw this memorandum.

*   *   *

"Dickie Mountbatten, impulsive kid," was Roosevelt's characterization to Stilwell and me of the Supreme Commander, South East Asia. The impulsive Admiral undertook at the beginning of 1944 to bring the independent OWI psychological warfare operation in SEAC under his control. Burma was his bailiwick and so he naturally felt that OWI activities in the northern part of that country should be subject to his authority. American and British operations under Eisenhower were integrated. Therefore, why should not they similarly be under him, Mountbatten, as Supreme Commander of his theater.

The reason that they could not, of course, was the difference between the United States and Britain on colonial issues. For Stilwell and his CBI deputy, Major General Dan Sultan, I prepared a statement of our position on integration. "American psychological warfare activities are an expression of the political policy of the United States Government and as such cannot be subject to the control or direction of any foreign authority. The State and War Departments have indicated that they will not accept the principle of Anglo-American propaganda integration in Asia." Instead of integration, we favored an Anglo-American liaison committee to coordinate the two separate psychological warfare efforts.

We made our position known to Lord Louis. The subject was pursued in Anglo-American meetings in Washington in March 1944, when I was there on other business. The British continued to press for integration. We tried to find a formula that would save Mountbatten's face and satisfy the normal military attachment to clear line of command while at the same time preserving an independent American propaganda voice. In April I explained apologetically to General Sultan that I was referring OWI psychological warfare problems to him because some of them were also taking up the time of General Marshall, Admiral Leahy, and the President. "All of this, I think, is highly unfortunate. But our allies will not settle these issues on lower levels, insisting on handling them at top levels in New Delhi, London and Washington."

The Anglo-American Combined Chiefs of Staff issued an ukase calling for the creation of a Combined Liaison Committee to coordinate American and British psychological warfare and related activities in India and SEAC. To make the final arrangements with SEAC for implementing the CCS direction, General Sultan and I flew to Kandy. Lord Louis had moved his headquarters, away from the stifling proximity to the Government of India and GHQ India, to this Ceylonese paradise. SEAC nestled in bowers of boughs in the lush Botanical Gardens at Kandy, well above the head of the coastal plains and the island's only airfield. With winsome British WRENS, the setting luxuriantly presaged the Club Mediterranee—but in military regalia. After all, there is nothing in Clausewitz or Sun Tze that enjoins generals and admirals to seek out squalor and privation amid which to locate their headquarters.

General Sultan was the American commander sent to remedy Stilwell's neglect of administrative matters and, in Stilwell's stead, treat bilelessly with GHQ India and SEAC. He was appreciated and respected by Stilwell and by all of us who dealt with him.

Mountbatten, resplendent in his tropical, white admiral's uniform, received Sultan and me at a Commanders-in-Chief meeting. This was a gathering of his Navy, Army and Air commanders, all of whom were on his list of those who would not be missed, and would before long be replaced. The Supremo was headstrong and used to having his way.

In reporting the meeting to the State Department I said,

> *His Lordship with characteristic charm and impetuosity left no doubt in the minds of his auditors that he did not like the large degree of autonomy that OWI had been given. He allowed himself to be so far carried away as to state that if he were not to have full authority in his theater, he intended to return home. I went over the familiar arguments and after a certain amount of mollifying, Lord Louis conceded that OWI might continue its present operations.*
>
> *After the meeting adjourned, however, he held me over to continue an emotional and confused discussion.*

This was the last rumbling of a mini-storm that had already passed. OWI psychological warfare retained a separate identity. The State Department surprised me by formally commending me for presenting the American point of view with "especial tact and sound judgment."

Not only in propaganda and civil administration did I believe that the American government should function in Asia independently of its European allies. It seemed to me that in activities such as public relations, misunderstandings and misrepresentations would best be avoided if we acted separately. Particularly was this so in the case of a pet project of the Supremo's—a proposed motion picture telling the story of the South East Asia Command. Those charged with its production told me that it was meant to have worldwide distribution, promoted by the British Ministry of Information.

I did not begrudge the gratification that such a film would grant Lord Louis's considerable ego. After all, personal publicity puffs for generals and admirals with elevated self-appreciation were not unknown. What troubled me was that this film would purport to be a documentary and as such should be historically accurate. However, it could not present the balanced truth unless it revealed the dichotomy of the Anglo-American relationship in SEAC. To do that would damage the war effort. Therefore, what would likely emerge would be promotional propaganda masquerading as a reliable documentary record.

While in the United States in the autumn of 1944 I flew to Hollywood to discuss the proposed SEAC film with Frank Capra, then an army colonel. He was in charge of producing the SEAC saga, with expert British assistance. To Capra I described my misgivings about the project. He readily understood the political considerations involved in the "documentary" and urged that I present the issue to the State Department and General Marshall.

Returning to Washington I prepared a memorandum for the Department on the matter, with a copy to the General Staff officers dealing with CBI and SEAC, recommending termination of "joint Anglo-American production of a motion picture depicting the course of the war in Asia." Shortly thereafter I flew to China. I do not know what happened to my recommendation. My concern over the colonial problem was quickly overshadowed by a crisis in the relations between Stilwell and Chiang Kai-shek and by the pressing dilemma of what American policy should be toward the spreading Chinese Communist movement.

CHAPTER XIV

PATRICIA'S PASSAGE TO INDIA;

A SOONG FAMILY FRACAS

Patricia remained in her job as feature writer and columnist at *The Washington Post* after our marriage on August 24, 1942. A year and a day later she received a radio message from me: "Arrived outpost of civilization just in time to send all of my love on our first anniversary." This was the first direct word she had from me following my parachuting into the Burmese jungle. The initial news of the incident came to her when the story broke a week after the jump and an inquiring reporter called her at night to inform her that I had been in a plane that had crashed and, acting on the principle of the people's right to know, asked her to describe her reactions. Following this she learned that I had survived with others and that we were in the jungle amidst headhunters.

Informing me of the reception of my anniversary radiogram, Patricia wrote:

> The whole Washington Post *has been following the story of your adventure with great personal interest. The wire arrived early Wednesday morning . . . and little Martha in our office held a council of war with all present to decide what to do about it. Needless to say, I had not yet arrived at my desk. Finally it was decided that Martha should phone me. Naturally, I asked her to open it and read it to me. Came tearing noises, then ghastly silence, then sobs. Well, what would you think? With the greatest*

self-control I asked her to tell me what was in the message. "It's John," she wept, "It's John." It was several minutes before I could get anything out of her and by that time I had suspected the worst. When I arrived at the office, she apologized for her tears. "I was just so happy," she explained. Omygod.

Wives of military and Foreign Service personnel were not permitted to go from the United States to join their husbands in theaters of war. Exceptions to this ruling were rare. Patricia was ingenious and enterprising enough to have tried a variety of stratagems to get out to India—as a correspondent, as an OWI psychological warrior, as an OSS cloak and dagger girl—but she always ran into, eventually, the disabling fact that she was married to me. If I would get General Stilwell's consent to her coming to CBI, there would be no problem. But to make such a request was out of the question for me.

Patricia was also persistent. After months of maneuvering about and petitioning Ruth Shipley, the autocratic chief of the Passport Division, she extracted a passport from the Department on the condition that she would make her own travel arrangements. So in the autumn of 1943 she began to beat her way out to India by flying commercially to Peru and thence to Argentina and Brazil.

After weeks of waiting at Buenos Aires and then Santos, she obtained passage on a small Swedish freighter, the *Anita*, whose neutrality was proclaimed by large Swedish flags painted on both sides of the hull, amidships, and floodlit by night. Thus illuminated, Patricia crossed the South Atlantic, not so much dodging submarines as the advances of the ship's lecherous captain. She arrived safely at Capetown and from there went by train to Durban. Then by a stroke of great good fortune, she got the first non-priority seat in months on a commercial flight northward. The aircraft was a flying boat that buzzed lazily from water-landing to water-landing, including Lake Victoria, stopping each night for passengers and crew to get mosquitoed sleep ashore.

Patricia's final flying boat stop was on the Nile at Khartoum. Nearby, in desolate badlands, was the big American Air Transport Command (ATC) base on the main line from the United States to CBI. Patricia introduced herself to astonished and appreciative sentries and passenger priority control officers who had not seen a pretty twenty-three-year-old American woman in red slacks since they left the States. What priority did she have?

None. Without an assigned priority it was nearly impossible to travel by an ATC plane.

She did have a copy of a pro forma cable from the Department asking Foreign Service officials to be nice to her. It was signed "Hull," as were all the cables from the Department. The soldiers took this to mean that the Secretary of State had a personal interest in Patricia's welfare. So they put her in a VIP bungalow and posted MPs to protect her.

And they queried the Legation at Cairo—would it request priority travel for Mrs. Davies? The lowest, came back the righteous answer.

It was clear that Patricia's presence was a disruptive influence on the base and that it would not do to keep her in pampered captivity until her number came up—which would be after the end of the war and all the troops had been lifted home. The base must be disembarrassed of her. Imaginatively, she was signed on as a radio operator of a C-47 full of GIs bound for Karachi.

This pleased the legitimate members of the crew, although the regular radioman was taken aback, on boarding the aircraft after Patricia, to find her in his chair staring in bewilderment at a panel of knobs, switches, and bulbs. As they came in to land for fuel at Aden, the pilot showed her how easy it was to handle an airplane. He persuaded Patricia to take his place, covered the windshield with newspapers so that she could not see the runway, told her to listen to the beeps on her headphones, and then cheered her on to a pretty three-point landing on Arabia Felix.

Upon touching down, the pilot tore off the newspapers—and there midway down the runway lay a wrecked bomber. This necessitated a hurried ascension back into the wild blue yonder and a less carefree return to terra firma. I never understood the whole operation, nor inquired deeply into it. I suspect that the co-pilot had something to do with the fortunate outcome.

The wartime flyboys were a breed unto themselves. When in India, I asked a juvenile crew chief, who had taken the place of a bored pilot, why one of the two propellers was stationary. He replied that he had cut its engine to see how the plane would fly on one engine. In a war-weary B-24 bomber, converted to cargo and passengers, the pilot played the game of flying down the Brahmaputra so close to the surface as to raise a wake, even though a week earlier another pilot had torn the bottom off his B-24 and drowned or otherwise killed all aboard by doing just that.

After Aden, Patricia's next stop was Galalah on the desert coast of Muscat and Oman. Then Karachi, where she was billeted with a flock of WACs until she was flown to Delhi. I was then in New Delhi and Patricia's message to me from Karachi was the first word that I had of her since learning that she was marooned at Khartoum. She arrived at New Delhi some three months after leaving Washington. Two days later I left New Delhi for Washington.

The number two man of the American diplomatic mission, George Merrill, whom I had known from Peking, had generously made the guestroom of his spacious bachelor establishment available to me whenever I was in New Delhi. With Patricia's arrival, he took her in with characteristically warm hospitality. She stayed on in the guestroom while I was on my trip to the United States. As George enjoyed entertaining and going to parties, he happily enlisted Patricia as decorative hostess and social partner in the sedate whirl of wartime New Delhi high society. Patricia and I were months later assigned a truncated small house only a hundred yards from Merrill's. We easily continued our relaxed, congenial relationship with George.

Before her initial foray to the Viceregal Lodge, as the Viceroy's mausoleum palace was designated, Patricia was briefed by an anxious George on how to behave in the presence of surrogate royalty. Don't forget to curtsey to the Viceroy—even the Vicereine is supposed to dip and bow to her husband. And don't speak to him unless spoken to.

The Viceroy at this time was Field Marshall Archibald Wavell, who had been replaced in his Middle East command and then, in the first month of the Pacific War, hastily thrown into futile command of the American-British-Dutch-Australian demoralized defense of Southeast Asia. Following the prompt disintegration of ABDA, he was made Commander-in-Chief, India, and finally Viceroy of India. Patricia found herself at this first dinner seated on Wavell's left. His good ear was on the other side. But she was forbidden to start a conversation. And he was noted for his taciturnity.

The slurping of soup unrelieved by light banter, the coldly questioning glances directed at her by the wives of generals and high civil officials, and the prospect of this state of affairs dragging on and on drove her to desperation. She opened her mouth and spoke to the King-Emperor's proxy. It was an inconsequential little comment. The Viceroy responded. Deciding that His Excellency's problem was no more than shyness, Patricia pursued the conversation and drew Wavell out on his experiences in North Africa. In his discourse he confessed that he had been relieved of his Middle East command because of the reverses he suffered in Cyrenaica.

On another occasion at the big house, Noël Coward, who had been performing for the troops, performed for the Viceroy and the top brass. At this gathering he premiered a ditty inspired by his recent encounters with colonels, brigadiers, and generals in India. The lyrics echoed conversations he had heard among pukka senior officers wherever he went in India—reminiscences of former comrades in arms, each concluding with something to the effect of "Whatever happened to old So-and-so? I wonder what happened to him?"

Patricia's laughter drew disapproving glances and the conclusion of that song was followed by scant applause. During an intermission, one of the two generals sitting in front of Patricia, scanning those present nodded in the direction of a young officer in attendance and exclaimed to his neighbor, "By Jove, isn't that old Forsyth's son?" "I say, it does look like him," came the response. "Whatever happened to old Forsyth?" "I wonder what happened to him," added the second general pensively.

When Peggy Durdin returned to being a journalist, I prevailed upon Patricia to "volunteer" her services gratis to the political advisers' office. Although doing so offended her sense of professional worth, she took over secretarial responsibilities without pay until we were able to hire someone. Even after that, she filled in at the office when needed, but not without some murmurs about the injustice of uncompensated indentured service. As a result of my exploiting her, Patricia became well known at the New Delhi headquarters of CBI, on amiable terms with the Deputy Commander of the theater as with desk-bound corporals. One of the officers whom we both found particularly agreeable was a poised, intelligent lieutenant colonel, Dean Rusk. We continued occasional contact to and past his time as Secretary of State.

During my absences from New Delhi, Patricia and George Merrill's sister Ruth visited two of India's princely states. Accompanied by George, they journeyed by train and curtained limousine to the domain of the Sikh Maharajah of Patiala, who had invited them to a lavish house party in his palace high in the mountains northwest of Delhi. The second excursion was to Jaipur for a tiger shoot laid on for Patricia by the Maharajah and Ayesha, the Maharani. They suggested she bring a few friends. So Patricia asked Ruth and several other Americans.

CBI headquarters put a carbine at Patricia's disposal for the occasion. To compensate for the weapon's inadequate throw-weight against tigers, Patricia notched the noses of her bullets—surely contrary to some Geneva Convention. George lent her breeches, a suede shooting jacket, and a hat that looked like a cross between a pork-pie and a jaeger's headgear.

Shortly before she was to climb aboard the elephant, from which she expected to shoot her tiger, an American cavalry colonel whom Patricia had invited, came to her and told her that she should surrender the carbine to him as she was inexperienced in these matters and might accidentally shoot a shooter rather than a tiger. Although deeply mortified, Patricia chose to yield rather than shoot it out with the officious cavalryman.

Herself defenseless against any passing tiger, she and Ruth, with whom she shared an elephant, plodded through the bush in the midst of a procession heavily enough gunned to mow down a battalion of charging tigers. Although one was sighted, he had the good sense to make a fast getaway.

As compensation for being disarmed against tigers, Jai took Patricia shooting crocodiles in a boat lined with blue velvet. She got her crocodile. Then Ayesha had staged for her a fight in a pit between a tiger and a wild boar. The tiger won.

Because it would not have been right for me to take Patricia with me on my travels in CBI, she was dependent on her own resources or invitations from others for trips outside of New Delhi. Major General Raymond A. Wheeler, an army engineer of outstanding competence and discernment who had managed CBI logistics and then been assigned as Mountbatten's administrative officer, invited Patricia to fly in his aircraft to Kandy so that she might join me there. I was with Stilwell during his brief tenure as acting Supremo during Mountbatten's absence in London.

The problem of where Patricia and I might stay at overcrowded Kandy was solved by the courtly Maberly Esler Dening, who turned over to us his bachelor suite in a lakefront hotel. The morning after we moved in I went early to headquarters, leaving Patricia to sleep in. At nine she was awakened by the Ceylonese room attendant who, with obsequious insistence, told her that it was time that she went home.

Although there were cricket grounds at Kandy, SEAC was without an adjacent airfield. The nearest air facilities to this headquarters of a war theater, extending to the South China Seas, were close to Colombo, some 100 twisting kilometers down the mountains and across the coastal plain. On her way back to New Delhi, Patricia went to the airport by narrow gauge railway, sharing a compartment with Dillon Ripley and a mysterious Briton, both assigned to SEAC. Ripley, an engaging ornithologist who eventually became head of the Smithsonian Institution, was high in OSS spookdom. He carried a briefcase of the kind with a grenade in it which would explode were the case tampered with. The Briton, it later developed, was on His Majesty's secret service. And he was similarly accoutered for self-destruction.

It soon became evident to Patricia that Dillon's enthusiasm for birds was shared by his British opposite number. And it was small wonder that they were fairly brimming over with excitement, for Kandy and environs were a bird-watcher's promised land.

In an elated exchange over rare specimens obtained, each spymaster reached impulsively for his briefcase. As Patricia tensed to bolt out the door, they snapped open the infernal containers and drew forth from each, specimens of exotic feathered friends.

*   *   *

Madame Chiang Kai-shek's brother, Foreign Minister T. V. Soong, was a changeful influence on the relationship between Stilwell and the Generalissimo. There was, however, a constant in Soong's shifting approach. It was an overweening and barely concealed ambition to usurp his brother-in-law's position.

After welcoming Stilwell's assignment to China, T. V. turned against the General because the American airlift across the Hump and deliveries of supplies were, in 1942, falling short of Chinese expectations. Soong, who was then in Washington, represented to the Generalissimo that Stilwell was the cause of these deficiencies. With his manifold sources of information in American government and industry, T. V. could hardly have escaped knowing what was common knowledge—that American war production was then insufficient to satisfy American, British, and Russian needs and that, in any event, these took precedence over China's demands. Why, then, did Soong accuse Stilwell?

One explanation might be that T. V. was trying to deflect to the American General likely censure of himself by the suspicious, irascible Generalissimo for failing to extract from the Americans the quantities of aircraft and supplies that Chiang, in his ignorant disregard of war production and logistics, demanded. Alternatively, or additionally, Soong may actually have believed that Stilwell had enough influence with Marshall and Stimson to persuade them, if he had been so disposed, to do him a favor by manipulating the Munitions Control Board allotments so as to give China what Chiang wanted. That Stilwell did not do this was evidence that the American General was not responsive to the Generalissimo's wishes, yet another reason to get rid of Vinegar Joe.

Late in 1942 Soong reversed his tactics. Attempts by the Chiangs, Chennault, Currie and himself to bring about Stilwell's removal had failed, notwithstanding Roosevelt's receptivity to their importunities. The President would not override the opposition of Marshall and Stimson, both men of stern rectitude, who consistently supported Stilwell throughout the General's assignment to CBI. Soong seemingly decided that if he could not lick Stilwell, he would join him.

The Foreign Minister returned to Chungking apparently advising the Generalissimo that if he wanted more American materiel he would have to show signs of serious military intent. Stilwell was astonished and delighted by a suddenly more cooperative attitude in Chungking and told me that T. V. was really getting things done. When he chose to collaborate, Soong was easy for Americans to work with. To a greater degree than his compatriots with American schooling, he was businesslike and efficient in an American style. His Yankeefied drive and impatience, however, grated on conventional Chinese.

Soong's plotting against his brother-in-law soon surfaced. He advised Stilwell to take an interest in two particular generals, both of whom Stilwell thought well of, but whom the Generalissimo mistrusted. Soong also asked the American general to back an arrangement whereby T. V. would acquire wide authority over the Chinese armed forces. Stilwell did not second Soong's nomination of himself.

Playing up to Stilwell did not advance Soong's fortunes. Consequently, in Washington during September 1943, T. V. presented Roosevelt with a scheme whereby two unnamed Chinese generals would be appointed, respectively, Supreme Commander and Chief of Staff in China. This would eliminate both Chiang and Stilwell from command, although the Generalissimo would continue as chief of state. The President passed Soong's brash proposal to Marshall, who buried it.

A few days before Soong laid before Roosevelt his unsubtle prescription for curing China's military debilities, two of his sisters, Madame Chiang and Madame Kung, mystified Stilwell by a sudden display of solicitude for his welfare. They offered to champion the general's case with Chiang, who was more than usually vexed by Stilwell's inconsiderate goadings to action. The General accepted the offer of good offices by the sisters and assumed that their brother had inspired their benevolence.

Indeed he had. But in the sense that they had gotten wind of T. V.'s scheming, felt threatened by it, and immediately sprang into action. They rallied to Stilwell to make him an ally. Madame Chiang felt threatened because her husband was T. V.'s target. And so was Madame Kung's, who was Finance Minister. The sisters wanted to close ranks against their brother, and to that end the rift between the Generalissimo and Stilwell must be patched up.

Mountbatten, then the newly appointed Supreme Commander, South East Asia, was in mid-October about to leave India for Chungking to meet the Generalissimo when Soong appeared from out of the West, also bound for Chungking. Accompanying Mountbatten was Lieutenant General Brehon Somervell, the smoothly proficient chief of the American Army's supply service, whose function was to introduce Supremo to Gimo. Soong advised Somervell, to the General's considerable surprise, that Roosevelt had acceded to the recall of Stilwell, and warned Lord Louis that Stilwell's appointment as deputy Supremo would have "disastrous irrevocable repercussions."

Acting as interpreter between Chiang and Somervell at Chungking, Soong told the American that the Generalissimo demanded Stilwell's recall for having "lost the confidence" of Chinese troops. News of the Chinese demand jarred Stilwell. It also upset Mountbatten. He disliked the prospect, at the outset of his command, of being deprived of the man whom he expected to handle the difficult Chinese, particularly in India and Burma. Lord Louis offered to intercede with Chiang. Stilwell agreed. In advance of his call on the Generalissimo, Mountbatten intimated to Chiang through Somervell that he would not be able to go ahead with plans for the deployment of Chinese troops in SEAC if their commander for nearly two years were removed.

Meanwhile, the sisters had been busy. They enlisted the support of General Ho Ying-chin, War Minister and Chief of Staff, whom Stilwell despised as incompetent, obstructive and conniving. He readily connived, this time on Stilwell's behalf, against Soong. He knew that T. V. was doing all in his power to replace him with General Ch'en Ch'eng, one of Soong's two favorite army commanders. In this topsy-turvy situation, Stilwell, who had also wanted Ho removed and Ch'en made Chief of Staff, now accepted the necessity of a buddy system with the contemptible Ho against T. V.

The dispute, however, was essentially a Soong family fracas. The brother insisted that he could rid Chiang of the intrusive Stilwell and his tactless prodding if only the Generalissimo would press the demand for recall. The sisters argued that because Stilwell enjoyed strong support in the United States, to oust him would provoke severe American curtailment of supplies to China. The high-strung argument raged for a couple of days and culminated on October 18 in temper tantrums by T. V. and his brother-in-law, with the Foreign Minister shouting abuse at the Generalissimo and the soldier-statesman screaming and smashing teacups.

The sisters, Stilwell, and General Ho had won. But on condition that Stilwell perform an act of penance to recover face for the Generalissimo who lost it by backing off from his demand for recall. The busy sisters, acting as impresarios, arranged for Vinegar Joe's performance and coached him on his lines, which he delivered under tight self-control: if he had made mistakes they were due to misunderstanding and were not deliberate. "The Peanut did his best to appear conciliatory," Stilwell wrote after he had "put on the act," read him a short homily on recognizing the proper relationship between commander in chief and chief of staff and on the avoidance of a superiority complex.

Foiled in his scheming, Soong emerged from the fracas a conspicuous loser. Although not stripped of his title as Foreign Minister—that would have given face to Stilwell—T. V. was told by the Generalissimo to stay at home and out of official business. He was not rehabilitated until the summer of 1944. As for General Ch'en Ch'eng, he was relieved of his command and placed in limbo. And General Hsueh Yueh, Soong's other protégé, when putting up a brave fight against a Japanese offensive in 1944, was denied desperately needed resupply of ammunition by order of Chiang, and therefore was badly beaten.

PART IV

THE QUESTION OF CHINA

CHAPTER XV

STILWELL'S WARS

Stilwell's northern Burma campaign aimed to clear the enemy from that area so that a road and an oil pipeline could be built from India to China. Likewise, aircraft would be enabled to fly a safer and more economical route over the Hump. Beginning at Ledo in the northeastern corner of India, American Army engineers, using road-building machinery, slashed through mountain jungles to construct a rudimentary truck route in the wake of the offensive.

It was a prodigious undertaking, begun late in 1942 and completed early in 1945. But the supplies, including fuel, that finally moved along the road and through the pipeline did not nearly equal the volume transported by what ultimately became a greatly augmented airlift. Six months after supply trucks began systematically rolling over the road, the war ended. Imports thereafter entered China through its east coast ports. And the defiant road was reclaimed by the jungle.

Although the road was originally proposed by the Chinese, Stilwell championed it. As a result, he was identified with it and it was represented by some as evidence that Stilwell was both feckless and obstinate. General Wedemeyer, who had been a Pentagon top planner before his assignment to Mountbatten, criticized the road and the northern Burma military operation as thoroughly unsound and probably doomed to failure. Captain Joseph Alsop, a journalist acting as an aide to and spokesman for Chennault, prophesied defeat for Stilwell in Burma. Alsop's denunciations of Stilwell's efforts in northern Burma were contained in his active correspondence with Harry Hopkins and were only one facet of his anti-Stilwell agitation.

Looking back, it may now be said that the road, pipeline and military campaign to gain the ground for them were not worth their cost. In 1942 and 1943, however, when the decision was made, the duration and future course of the war were far from clear. Given Washington's politico-military decision regarding China, attributing exaggerated importance to it in the war against Japan, it followed that all possible ways of getting supplies to China should be tried. It was not enough to rely only on an airlift. This was but one instance of the extravagant expenditure of effort and resources, so characteristic of all-out warfare.

In human terms, the northern Burma campaign and the building of the road and pipeline was epic. It has been often told and so I shall here condense my account.

Elements of one of the three Chinese divisions that Stilwell was training at Ramgarh, India, crossed the Assam border into Burma late in 1943, and soon encountered the enemy. It was a forward post of the proud 18th Division, conqueror of Singapore, and currently occupying North Burma. The Chinese troops, and more so their officers, as a result of years of defeat at the hands of the Japanese, initially lacked self-confidence. Spurred by Stilwell's presence, they won several minor engagements and gained self-assurance.

Three factors, new to the Chinese soldiers, contributed decisively to their improved combat ability. One was that the American supply services made sure that they were adequately fed, clothed and armed and that expended ammunition and equipment was promptly and lavishly replaced. When this sometimes was not the case, it was because of the exigencies of battle or weather and not because of officer graft and hoarding.

Second, the wounded were not abandoned, as so often happened in China. Stilwell insisted on a high level of medical support, backed by a first class American general hospital at Ledo. Air evacuation of the wounded by light planes from jungle airstrips was pioneered in this campaign.

Finally, the American Tenth Air Force controlled the skies over northern Burma. This meant not only freedom from air attacks in the combat area—it also meant that the closely following road and pipeline construction were not harassed by enemy strafing. And, isolated units and those far out on the flanks, moving through roadless jungles, were supplied by air drops.

Stilwell's faith in the good soldierly qualities of the Chinese conscripts was being justified. The failings were not in the privates, corporals and sergeants but in the senior officers. As in the first Burma campaign, ultimate responsibility for timidity, irresolution and inertia lay with the Generalissimo, who continued issuing paralyzing orders behind Stilwell's back to the Chinese commanders in the field.

At the same time, Chiang held back the offensive from Yunnan, meant to drive westward to meet the three Chinese divisions under Stilwell. The Generalissimo had available for this campaign the twelve divisions of the Y-Force, partially trained and equipped by the Americans in the program for reforming and arming first thirty and ultimately a total of ninety divisions. Opposing those twelve divisions was one attenuated Japanese division.

Chiang would not attack for all of the familiar reasons, and some new ones. He did not want to expend the materiel, nor provoke the Japanese, nor risk defeat, even though the manpower odds were overwhelmingly in his favor. Also, the British had not undertaken the major operations in Central Burma and the Bay of Bengal that he had demanded as a condition for moving. In response to Roosevelt's urgings to commit the Y-Force, the Generalissimo added that the Chinese Communists were about to attack his forces, the Russians were behaving in a menacing fashion on the northeastern border, and the Japanese were preparing a big offensive in North-Central China. The last of these three assertions happened to be true. Rather than advancing into Burma, he offered two divisions to be flown to India to join Stilwell's three, and said that he would prepare for the day "when Allied land and naval forces can be dispatched to the China coast."

Washington officialdom, excepting for confirmed sinophiles like Hornbeck, had by now come to share—although not with the same marinated pungency—Stilwell's disgust with Chiang. The Generalissimo's balking at cooperation with those struggling to help him had been topped by his nagging for a billion dollar loan, which Washington declined to grant because it would not solve China's economic problems so long as the Japanese sea and land blockade was not broken. Or, as an alternative, the Generalissimo demanded payment by Washington of expenses incurred on account of the American military presence—particularly construction of B-29 bomber bases—at the artificially high official exchange rate. This would have multiplied the dollar costs by more than six times the real value of the depreciated Chinese currency.

Chiang's financial importunities were accompanied by the customary threat—this time delivered to Gauss by H. H. Kung—that Japan was making offers that just might tempt China to retire from the war. Washington regarded the whole performance as putting a price on the Y-Force's helping to open the way for the road and pipeline. The reaction in Washington went beyond umbrage. The Treasury and War Departments seriously examined the possibility of withdrawing from China. But this could not be, given Roosevelt's commitment to Chiang as an integral part of the Big Four dispensation. So the major financial issues were politely consigned to study and negotiations, where they were slowly suffocated, and the incoming bills were paid through ad hoc haggling.

While Chiang's masterly inactivity was driving Stilwell frantic, SEAC was planning to ignore Burma and prepare for an amphibious advance to Sumatra, Malaya and Hong Kong, as Churchill had always wanted to do. Wedemeyer told me on January 7, 1944, I noted, that, "We shall be unable to join up with MacArthur's and King's drives on Japan if we become tangled in a Burma jungle campaign. Al [Wedemeyer] said that the only way in which we could hope to synchronize ourselves with MacArthur and King would be to go around through Singapore."

SEAC's plan was named AXIOM and Mountbatten sent Wedemeyer, supported by a staff of seventeen, to London and Washington to solicit Combined Chiefs of Staff support. Stilwell learned of the SEAC mission before its departure. He designated his Deputy Chief of Staff, Brigadier General Benjamin Ferris, and me to go to Washington to present his rebuttal to AXIOM. But first we were to report to him at his Burma headquarters.

Ferris stayed close to Stilwell during the hours that we met so that I was unable to speak privately to the general. By saying that I had a personal message for him from his son—as I did—I invited him outside the basha in which Stilwell was conferring on a variety of subjects. I wrote shortly afterward:

Walking slowly in the grass alongside the narrow bamboo corduroy path where the general strolled, I told him that the forthcoming conference was for him the most important yet and that he was sending the weakest delegation he had ever dispatched. I told him that Benny's [Ferris] Anglophobia would not go down with GM [Marshall]. He said that he realized that and had warned Benny to lean over backward on that score.

I said that Benny would be overawed by the people he had to deal with in Washington and would not make a very good presentation of the case. It seemed to me that a positive personality such as General Joe himself, Frank Merrill or Haydon [Brigadier General Haydon Boatner] should go. The Old Man said it was out of the question for him or Frank to go, but that Haydon might be available.

So I started to sell Haydon. I said that he knew from first-hand the history of the Ramgarh experiment, had been through two monsoons on the Assam-Burma border, had directed the operation in the Hukawng Valley and had the dramatic qualities which would appeal to the President if he had the opportunity to see him. . . .

As Wingate [the flamboyant British general commanding the Chindits, Long Range Penetration Groups, operating behind the Japanese lines] made a theatrical presentation for the LRPG, which won over the President, it seemed to me that Haydon could present in dramatic terms the case for advancing and holding territory in Northern Burma.

General Joe agreed to send Boatner.

Ferris, Boatner and I arrived in Washington well before the Wedemeyer mission. Boatner and I promptly went to see Brigadier General Frank Roberts, a China specialist whom I had known in Peking and the first Burma campaign and who was now impressively installed as head of army planners. Boatner stated the Stilwell case. Roberts agreed with it. The only interview in which I joined Ferris was with Stimson. At 11:45 a.m. and seventy-seven years of age, the Secretary of War was in need of a nap, and Ferris's presentation lacked lucidity. It was therefore an inconclusive session.

As I had with Stilwell, I arranged for Boatner to meet a few selected journalists. Boatner spoke plainly, but no more so than had Stilwell the year before, about the lack of cooperation from both Chiang and the British in the northern Burma campaign. What we told the journalists was not a revelation for them, as similar information was circulating in Washington. But the publication of their stories, based on our briefings, provoked Field Marshal Sir John Dill, Washington representative of the British Chiefs of Staff, to protest to Marshall and the President and to upbraid the War and Navy Departments for leaks.

Poor Boatner was called up on the carpet by General Thomas Handy, chief of operations and plans, who, as I wrote at the time, "pointedly wanted to know where the leaks were coming from. Haydon started out by saying he was a soldier and was bound therefore to tell the truth without dissembling to his superior officer. He then asked if Handy wanted to know who was responsible for these embarrassing stories or did he simply want the publicity to cease. Everyone broke out laughing and Handy went on to say that all he wanted was that the publicity cease."

As for me, Timberman told me "that he had explained to Handy that I was under the State Department and sort of on loan to General Stilwell. Haydon remarked a little later that "they" (meaning Handy and company) were just as well pleased that they did not have to assume authority over me." Had not the upper echelons of the Pentagon been so admiring of the indomitable Stilwell in his sea of tribulations—and privately agreeing with what we had said—I suspect that Boatner and I would have been treated much more unsympathetically.

Furthermore, and perhaps having a bearing on Handy's attitude, about a week earlier Boatner was received by the President for a briefing on Burma. Articulate and forceful, he succeeded in doing what, as far as I know, no one else had done—arouse enthusiasm in Roosevelt for Stilwell's Burma campaign. Roosevelt was sufficiently inspired to ask Boatner what he should say in a message to Churchill requesting British assistance to Stilwell.

I took Boatner to a conversation with the newly appointed Under Secretary of State, Edward Stettinius, being groomed to take the place of the invalid Hull. The choice of Stettinius for Secretary of State was revelatory of the contempt with which Roosevelt and Hopkins viewed that office and the professional diplomatic organization. Stettinius was an affable, bustling, photogenic chairman of the board (U.S. Steel) who was chosen, it would seem, not for any acumen in national or international affairs—for he was not thus burdened—but as a greeter and front man for the President and administrator of the State Department, leaving to FDR and Hopkins the real direction of foreign policy.

Stettinius listened to us with lively attention and asked us to tell our story to Joseph Grew, former Ambassador to Japan and due to become Under Secretary when Stettinius took Hull's place. Grew, a professional diplomat, heard us out with more comprehension and asked me to draft a memorandum for Stettinius to send to the White House.

Putting the Stilwell case in broad perspective, I wrote on February 23 that

> our political objectives in Asia are to foster . . . China, which may serve
> with us as a balance should a decadent British-Dutch imperial system and

a dynamic Russia come into conflict. In negative terms we wish to avoid steps committing us to colonial imperialism lest we find ourselves aligned with an anachronistic system in vain opposition to the rising tide of Asiatic nationalism, possibly enjoying Russian support.

The first step in achieving our overall political-military objective is the opening this year of a land route of communications through North Burma into China. This cannot be done unless the British in the Imphal sector and the Chinese in Yunnan, both of whom are inactive, launch offensives in support of the now advancing Chinese-American force in the Ledo sector.

I concluded with a plea that we, meaning the President, press Churchill and Chiang to act in support of Stilwell. I do not know what Grew did with these exhortations. However, an earlier memorandum of mine to Hopkins, arguing American preference for a northern Burma offensive over advance toward Sumatra and Singapore, appears to have passed with approval by Hopkins to the President.

AXIOM, which had Churchill's strong support, but not that of the British Chiefs of Staff, was turned down in Washington. The American Joint Chiefs considered that it would be out of phase. Because the necessary amphibious vessels from Europe could not be assembled until the beginning of 1945, AXIOM would lag well behind the accelerating advances of Nimitz and MacArthur. And the President did not take to AXIOM because of its colonial implications and roundabout route.

*   *   *

Boatner's and my lobbying for pressure on the British to join battle with the enemy in Burma proved to be supererogatory. Early in March the Japanese attacked the rugged Imphal sector, in the middle of the Burma-India border. Three Japanese divisions engaged four British Empire divisions. The enemy objective was to break into the Brahmaputra Valley through which ran the line of communications from the rest of India to Stilwell's forces in the north and in which were situated the big air bases used by the airlift to China.

Having scaled the roadless, jungled range on the border, carrying only limited rations and dependent on capturing British stores for sustenance, the Japanese cut the defenders' supply route from the rear and gave the British a bad time for more than a month. American aircraft were diverted from northern Burma to support the beleaguered forces and Stilwell offered to dispatch a Chinese division as reinforcement, which was declined. Mountbatten asked Churchill and Roosevelt to urge Chiang to open a second front with the Y-Force. The Gimo remained inert.

British counter-attacks, the Japanese failure to capture enough stores to feed themselves, the wispy, precipitous supply line from the Japanese depots in Burma, and the advent of the monsoon—all of these combined to inflict on the invaders grisly punishment by shot, shell, starvation and tropical diseases. With fanatical tenacity the emaciated, decimated Japanese continued fighting until July, when the remnants staggered back down the mountains, littering the sides of the trails with the corpses of those who finally succumbed in retreat.

It was all over these same mountains that Stilwell and his small band clambered in 1942 in escaping the Japanese sweep through Burma. And it was on theses pitiless slopes—so lush, yet so unnourishing—that unnumbered refugees in search of India, also in 1942, perished in starvation and sickness.

At the height of the Imphal battle Chiang was persuaded to order the Y-Force into action. The persuasion took an oblique form to spare Chiang's face. On Marshall's and Stilwell's authority, Major General Thomas Hearn, CBI Chief of Staff, advised Ho Ying-ch'in, Chief of Staff and War Minister, that if the Y-Force did not move the supply of Lend Lease materiel, it would be stopped. This was the kind of quid pro quo bargaining that Stilwell had long advocated and for which Roosevelt had reprimanded him. On April 14, two days after having being told "or else," Ho ordered the Y-Force into action.

It was not until nearly a month later that the Y-Force scrambled down into the gorge of the Salween, crossed the surging river on bamboo rafts and struggled up the western face of the gorge, without being discovered by the Japanese. Pinky Dorn, now a brigadier general, headed the American advisers and liaison officers with the Chinese units. The Y-Force divisions were understrength and neither as well trained nor equipped as the Ramgarh divisions in Burma. And Dorn did not have with this much larger force the authority that Stilwell had across the border.

After a brief initial success, the Chinese offensive degenerated. Dorn's advice was repeatedly ignored; the Chinese generalship was indecisive, misdirected and alternately foolhardy and timid. Manpower was wasted in frontal assaults on enemy strong points and weapons were mishandled. The campaign stagnated as a Japanese force, less than one tenth the strength of the Chinese, refused to be driven out of the bulge in Yunnan west of the Salween, through which ran the old Burma road and toward which Stilwell was driving for a link-up.

March 1944 had been a bad month for Stilwell with his Chinese commanders dragging their heels, Chiang balking at crossing the Salween, and the Japanese on the Imphal front threatening his main line of communications. April seemed a little better, but who could tell for how long? The General decided to make a daring thrust to surprise and capture the airfield at Myitkyina and then reinforce that position by air. Myitkyina, a railhead, was the most important Japanese position in northern Burma.

Stilwell put together a mixed detachment of American and Chinese troops totaling some four thousand. The American element was composed of about one thousand four hundred weary, embittered troops trained for jungle warfare. They were what was left of a detachment of three thousand men, code named GALAHAD. Because Frank Merrill, promoted to brigadier general, commanded the outfit, it was popularly called Merrill's Marauders. The Marauders had entered the Burma campaign in February and fought mobile, grueling actions on the enemy flanks and rear. Combat, disease and psychiatric breakdowns thinned the ranks of the Marauders by more than half during the two months before the advance on Myitkyina.

Guided by indigenous Kachin tribesmen, trained by the OSS, the American-Chinese task force slogged over mountain trails, over what was generally regarded as impassable terrain. After nearly three weeks of this, the exhausted mixed detachment reached its objective, achieved complete surprise and seized the Myitkyina airstrip. By this fact Stilwell also achieved complete surprise over Mountbatten, Wedemeyer, Alsop and others who had prophesied that this could not be done.

No sooner had the airstrip been so brilliantly secured than affairs began to go awry. Merrill had ordered that the first transports should fly in reinforcements and food—some of the Marauders had not eaten for several days. Instead, Stratemeyer's air headquarters sent in an unneeded anti-aircraft unit and engineers. And so it went. In assaulting the town of Myitkyina, held by seven hundred Japanese, two Chinese battalions became confused and engaged in prolonged exchange of fire with one another. For good measure, a larger Chinese force put on a repeat performance the next day. And the Japanese dug in, repulsed all attacks, withstood shelling and bombing, were reinforced to about five thousand, themselves counter-attacked and were determined to resist to the death.

Wasted by three months of unrelieved campaigning, the Marauders expected to be returned to the rear for rest after the capture of the airstrip. Instead, because of the failure to eliminate the enemy garrison in Myitkyina, Stilwell ordered the sick and exhausted Marauders to remain and take part in bloody battle for the town. With G-2 underestimating enemy strength, fighting ground on for two and a half months, bringing glory to no one. At the end, about two hundred Marauders were on their feet at Myitkyina; the rest were dead, hospitalized at Ledo, or convalescent and close to mutiny. And Merrill had been twice stricken by heart attacks; once on the trail, then two days after taking the airstrip.

While each side had the other by the throat at Myitkyina, with the Japanese there refusing to yield as their lives oozed away, the decisive encounter was between the Chinese divisions spearheading the road and the main force of the enemy's depleted 18th Division. The capture of the Myitkyina airfield appeared to release the Chinese division commanders so that they became aggressive and late in June captured Mogaung on the railway. Sharing the honors in this accomplishment were the Chindits, the British raiders created by Wingate to operate behind the enemy lines.

The Chindits had been assigned to Stilwell to disrupt the enemy rear and lines of communication south of the Chinese advance. Wingate was killed in an air crash in March and Stilwell soon developed an acrimonious relationship with his successor, Major General William Lentaigne. Like the Marauders, the Chindits had been hard-driven and were worn from long and harsh campaigning. But Stilwell demanded of them, as he had of the Marauders, performance which they believed to be beyond their strength.

As he was exacting and unsparing of himself, so, in exigencies, he was of his troops. Few, however, were as fearless and consumed by pugnacity and will to overcome as he. There is a limit to which these qualities can be inspired and instilled—a limit reached in World War II sooner among the Americans, Britons and Chinese than among Japanese. More spent than inspired by Stilwell, the Chindits nearly equaled the Marauders in hatred of him.

*   *   *

In mid-April 1944, while the Imphal battle was at its height, shortly before Stilwell decided to order the try for Myitkyina, and just after Chiang reluctantly agreed to send the Y-Force across the Salween, the Japanese launched ICHIGO. This was a major offensive employing more than fifteen divisions. Beginning in North China and sweeping southward, it was meant to seize hitherto unoccupied segments of north-south railroads and capture the southeast China airbases from which Chennault had provoked the Japanese. As Japan's sea communications were increasingly disabled by American submarines and air attacks, one of ICHIGO's end objectives was to open the way for land communications from Manchuria to southernmost China. Another strategic objective was denial to the Americans of air bases in eastern China, from which the 14th Air Force was inflicting considerable losses on Japanese shipping and rail traffic in China. Once these two objectives were attained, western China, where the Chinese armies were reposing, would be cordoned off from direct contact with any American coastal landing.

The Japanese thrust in North China cut with ease through numerically much larger Chinese forces. By early summer the invaders were into Central China. Chennault and Chiang, contrary to their 1942 and 1943 glib assurances to Roosevelt, were now anxious about the security of 14th Air Force bases. Although Chennault had command of the air and the Chinese on the ground greatly outnumbered the enemy, the Japanese kept going—and taking air base after air base. Stilwell and Marshall had been right. Air bases were useful only if protected by ground forces able to defend them.

By late 1944 ICHIGO had virtually completed its mission. One column had pushed westward causing alarm in Chungking and Kunming officialdom. Had it advanced only another forty or fifty miles it would have created panic. It was stopped not by the Chinese army but by winter and having outrun its supplies.

*   *   *

The British put up with a lot from Stilwell. They knew that he nursed an underlying prejudice against them, to which he made exceptions in individual cases, depending on circumstances. Given this basic dis-esteem for the British, Stilwell's intense nature heightened his critical reactions to the unimpressive British performance in Burma, their differences with his strategic and tactical opinions, and the leaden obstruction that he encountered from the Government of India and the Indian Army, hotbed of blimpism.

The Stilwellian anti-British (like his anti-Chiang) vinegar came in three strengths. The weakest was the faintly disguised attitude of curt contempt. He so behaved during his brief tenure as acting Supremo in August 1944, scoring SEAC's overstaffed and over-ranked braid and brass. A stronger fermentation was the oral outburst before members of his own staff: "The goddamn limies won't fight." And although he had initially spoken of Mountbatten as "a good egg" the Supremo became "The Glamour Boy." Naturally, word of slurs came to British ears.

The rawest acetous potion was the angry diary or journal entry. If the day had been a bad one, as so many were, the weary Stilwell vented his pent-up frustrations and blighted hopes on paper. He was not writing for publication but for catharsis and so Lord Louis became "pisspot" and the British in general "bastardly hypocrites."

These, and less elegant expletives, did not then come to the attention of those against whom they were directed. After Stilwell's death in 1946 and the release of his private papers, publicity was given—continuing over the years—to his intemperate vulgarisms. This extra strength Stilwellian fermentation was no more representative of the whole, considered man, than were the denatured memoirs, thick with additives and artificial coloring, of some of his fellow generals.

Although Mountbatten had in the autumn of 1943 helped to dissuade Chiang from demanding Stilwell's recall, by the following spring he was maneuvering to have his deputy removed from SEAC, replaced by Wede-meyer or Sultan, and restricted to China. Stilwell's evident anti-limey preju-dices, his sending Boatner and me to Washington and his abuse of the Chindits had all become just too much. In June Field Marshall Sir Alan Brooke, Chief of Imperial General Staff, asked Marshall to take Stilwell out of SEAC.

*   *   *

Vice President Henry Wallace arrived in Chungking in June intent on smoothing over Chiang's relations with the Chinese Communists and the Kremlin. Roosevelt had sent him on this mission, via Siberia and Soviet Central Asia, not only as an expression of his concern over the Generalissi-mo's worsening relations with the Reds, but also to ease Wallace out of the

United States so that FDR could, without the Vice President's distracting presence, lay the ground for unloading him as running mate at the upcoming Democratic convention.

Wallace was as uncomprehending of the Chinese scene as was Willkie. He did not make a convert out of Chiang. But he did accomplish one important thing, which I had hoped he would. That was to get the Generalissimo's consent to the dispatch by CBI headquarters of an observer group to be stationed in Yenan, the Chinese Communists' "capital." This was a concession that Chiang had long withheld and would later rue.

Wallace's visit marked the reemergence of T. V. Soong in public life. He did the interpreting for the Generalissimo, making clear Chiang's distaste for Stilwell. He also joined forces with Chennault and Alsop in prevailing upon Wallace to send a radiogram to Roosevelt recommending, among other things, the removal of Stilwell from authority in China and suggesting only the name of Wedemeyer as a possible replacement. The Vice President had met neither Stilwell nor Wedemeyer when he made these sweeping command recommendations.

Belatedly, Stilwell had sent Captain Paul Jones, a public relations officer, and me to extend an invitation to Wallace to visit the General at his Burma headquarters. Stilwell was absorbed in the horrors of the Myitkyina siege and the slugging campaign down the Mogaung Valley and could not spare the time to go to China to palaver with one whom he regarded as another meddling blatherskite out of Washington. Once Wallace had concluded his talks with the Generalissimo, I attempted to get to him to deliver Stilwell's invitation. But he had placed himself in the hands of Chennault and Alsop, who politely blocked me off. After I had appealed with some heat to Chennault's and Alsop's higher natures to rise above the Stilwell-Chennault feuding, they arranged for me to be received by Wallace in their presence. Later reporting to Stilwell I said that "Chennault and Co. were very reasonable and decent." I presented Stilwell's invitation and the Vice President sympathetically declined—weather and pressure of time.

What I did not know was that earlier that day, June 26, Wallace had sent his radiogram to Roosevelt recommending Stilwell's removal. Nor did I know that this ostentatious rustic turned strategist had put forward Wedemeyer's name (suggested by Soong and Alsop) only after being persuaded that the War Department would oppose what he thought best—that Chennault should be vested with both military and political authority and empowered to "deal directly with the White House on political questions," thus replacing both Stilwell and Gauss. The outcome of the sly maneuvering at the top of the American Government was that Roosevelt got rid of Wallace before Stilwell—but not before FDR had promoted Stilwell and humiliated the Generalissimo with demands in support of Stilwell.

With Mountbatten and Brooke wanting Stilwell shipped out of Burma and India to China and Chiang-Soong-Chennault wanting him out of China to Burma and India, Marshall pondered the creation of a new role for Stilwell. It was the outgrowth of a concept Stilwell had first broached in 1943—that of Field Chief of Staff exercising considerable authority over the Chinese forces. The wretched showing on the Salween front and, far more, the ineffectual resistance to ICHIGO seemed to indicate that under existing leadership the Chinese could neither check the current enemy offensive nor in the future dispose of the million or so Japanese troops in China, should they continue resistance there after the United States subdued Japan.

After the capitulation of the Japanese home islands, the American people could hardly be expected to sanction a prolongation of the war and the transfer of American troops from the Pacific and Europe to the Asian continent for more fighting and sacrifice. The alternative prospect of the Soviet Army moving into not only Manchuria but the rest of China to extirpate the Japanese was at least as disturbing. If only the Generalissimo would give Stilwell combat command of the Chinese armies and a free hand, maybe the man who had trained and driven the Chinese to victory in Burma could stem ICHIGO and galvanize the Chinese sufficiently to subdue possible Japanese resistance after victory in the Pacific.

Such, seemingly, had been Marshall's thoughts when he on July 1 sounded out Stilwell on possibly undertaking to rehabilitate and direct the forces in China. Somberly Stilwell replied that there was a faint chance of salvaging something in China, but that chance depended on his being given "complete authority over the Army." If the President would send the Generalissimo "a very stiff message . . . the Gimo might be forced to give me a command job." And he saw only one chance to save the situation—a counter-offensive from Shansi in North China, in which the Communists should participate.

Marshall took this glum assessment as agreement by Stilwell to asking the Generalissimo to yield command over his army to an alien soldier whom he detested. The Chief of Staff wasted no time. The Joint Chiefs of Staff rallied to the support of their combative commander, and on July 4 laid before the President a paper harshly critical of the performance of

Chiang and Chennault prior to and during ICHIGO and laudatory of Stilwell as the only man "who had been able to get Chinese forces to fight against the Japanese in an effective way." Because, in part, he had "conducted a brilliant campaign with a force, which he himself made, in spite of continued opposition from within and without and tremendous obstacles of terrain and weather," the JCS requested that Roosevelt promote Stilwell to full general.

Another reason advanced by the JCS for granting Stilwell a fourth star was that he would need the additional prestige for the position they were then recommending: that was command of all Chinese armed forces. This included the Chinese Communist forces. The President accepted the JCS recommendations and promptly radioed the Generalissimo the virtual demands drafted by the War Department. So drastic an approach in so sternly tutorial a tone was a measure of how far Roosevelt had moved from adulation of Chiang.

Marshall and Roosevelt had become justifiably suspicious that Soong was distorting in translation messages from Washington to Chiang and that Madame Chiang had suppressed a radiogram from the President because it might have been unpalatable to the Generalissimo. Consequently, the senior officer at CBI headquarters at Chungking was directed to present personally to Chiang the message from Roosevelt asking the Generalissimo to place Stilwell "directly under you in command of all Chinese and American forces and that you charge him with full responsibility and authority for the coordination and direction of the operations required to stem the tide of the enemy's advance." The senior officer then at Chungking was Ferris and he took with him as interpreter my colleague, Jack Service.

Chiang replied without delay, seeking to evade compliance with Roosevelt's urging. He repeated a request made earlier—the FDR send someone of stature as personal representative to "adjust relations between me and General Stilwell." Chiang wanted someone who would have authority superior to that of Stilwell and Gauss. If he could not be rid of these two unmalleable, ungullible guardians of American interests, then he wanted an American representative through whom he could bypass and overrule them. Chiang continued to spar for time through July and August.

*   *   *

My partisanship for Stilwell had led me at times to overstate Stilwell's case. In a memorandum to the Secretary of State in March 1944, I likened Stilwell to General William S. Graves, who commanded the American force sent to Siberia in 1918. The Secretary of War at that time, Newton D. Baker, wrote "that our allies describe General Graves to President Wilson as "an obstinate, difficult and uncooperative commander." Baker went on to reveal that when he reassured the President "of complete fidelity of General Graves to his policy, in the face of every invitation and inducement of the Allied Commanders, the President replied, 'I suppose it is the old story, Baker, men often get the reputation of being stubborn merely because they are everlastingly right.'"

This was, of course, a bit of exaggeration to offset the vicious criticism of Stilwell by his detractors. Privately, I indicated to him that I thought him a little less than everlastingly right. Perhaps my sharpest comments were two pages of criticism of him dated July 17, 1944. Therein I told him that it was being asked "when you intend to come out of the wood and take over as theater commander." I added, "Stilwell's playing the Burma sourdough contributes to the Washington impression that there is not the leadership in CBI to rate a place in the major league."

The general underlined from "not the leadership" to the end of the sentence and wrote in the margin "Guilty."

Continuing, I said that the suggestion that CBI was slipping from the status of a second class to a third class theater could be countered only if he got out of the tactical and into the strategic realm. Stilwell's marginal comment was "Have we really got a strong argument?"

"Your senior staff officers," I observed of Hearn and Ferris, "are regarded as a garland of millstones around your neck. . . . Your four Gs [heads of staff sections for personnel, intelligence, operations and supply] are looked upon as varying from pleasant mediocrity to senile incompetence." Harris and Ferris, he indicated, "Could be worse." "Right," he jotted regards the Gs, "And we are trying to do something about it."

"Granted that CBI has become the dumping ground for men whom Eisenhower and MacArthur did not ask for, still, that's no reason for the present appalling staff and command situation. There is in this theater enough talent to remedy the situation." The General met my comments with marginal notes on specific individuals and added, "Who else should I fire?" At the bottom of the second page, he wrote: "These memos are always welcome. J.W.S."

For several reasons Stilwell accepted from me what most men in high position would have regarded as impertinence. For one, this paradoxical man had a broad, private streak of humility. And with all of his many prejudices, he was receptively open-minded. But for these traits to show, he had to feel, at least, you were a friend, neither a detractor nor a toady. I got by on this score. He knew that I was sympathetic to him but that I was not seeking favors from him. I was a friendly yet disinterested commentator, and he felt the need of one.

Although I identified myself with Stilwell and felt affection for the gnarled tangle of fierce feeling, I did not cultivate a close association with him. Most of my communication with him was in writing and through normal channels. Perhaps half a dozen times in my two and a half years with him I sought out the General to discuss in person some substantive matter with him. I do not recall having had any wide-ranging military or political conversation with him. While I did not inquire into his communications with the War Department, he several times informed me of messages from Marshall.

Most of my contact with Stilwell was casual—flights with him in Uncle Joe's Chariot, meals with him and those who shared his Chungking billets, and stray encounters of this character. Although I knew that he thought well of me, I had little idea how he evaluated the job I was trying to do for him. So far as I know, he made no efficiency report on me. Because of his multitudinous concerns I had felt that it would have been a selfish imposition to ask him to prepare such a report for the State Department. I reproach myself, however, for not having arranged some sort of efficiency reports to be sent over his signature on my three Foreign Service colleagues.

CHAPTER XVI

THE GENERALISSIMO VERSUS THE GENERAL

In late August 1944, Stilwell again sent me to Washington, this time with Frank Merrill. While Merrill consulted at the Pentagon regarding the proposed new role for Stilwell, I renewed contacts in Washington, the most important of which was a leisurely conversation with Harry Hopkins on September 4. I recorded Hopkins as saying that:

> The Generalissimo's latest messages seem to indicate that he is willing for General Stilwell to assume command of all Allied troops in China, including the Chinese. He [Hopkins] suggested that it was felt that only a foreign commander such as General Stilwell could command both Central Government and Communist troops. I remarked that in view of his experience in the first Burma campaign I found it hard to believe that General Stilwell would not be skeptical of the degree of control which he could exert over Chinese army commanders. I said that I foresaw his authority being undercut at every turn.
>
> This comment apparently came as a surprise to Mr. Hopkins. He declared that General Stilwell had not indicated any doubt of his ability to command effectively Chinese troops. He asked whether or not the American command of Chinese forces in North Burma had not been a success. I replied that it had been but that in India and Burma we had far more control over Chinese units than we have had or will have in China . . . General Stilwell might successfully exert command but that all of the way it would be a hard battle against Chinese recalcitrance, lethargy and indifference, and that I was sure

General Stilwell would be the first to admit this. Nevertheless, full of pitfalls as such an arrangement might be, it seemed to me that the alternative— which was to leave the Chinese to liquidate the Japanese armies in China— was a pretty hopeless solution, and I thought that General Stilwell felt the same way.

Mr. Hopkins stated that General Stilwell would have a great deal of power because the White House would in this arrangement work directly through General Marshall to General Stilwell.

I forwarded the memorandum of this conversation to Stilwell, observing that

I was rather alarmed at the apparent naïve optimism with which Hopkins viewed the message from the Generalissimo . . . It struck me that if Hopkins was so sanguine over the possibility of a foreigner, really in an American sense, commanding Chinese troops, his boss must be laboring under similar rosy illusions. It seemed to me that they were thinking in terms of Chinese Gordon, Frederick Townsend Ward [respectively British and American commanders of mercenary detachments subsidized and used by the impe- rial Manchu government in the mid-Nineteenth Century].

I was afraid that they would expect you to have pretty much the unques- tioning allegiance of whatever forces you might be making use of. And when cases of insubordination, failure to obey orders and other examples of short-circuiting your authority arose that in their romanticism they might be inclined to blame you.

I therefore felt it advisable to give Mr. Hopkins an inoculation.

My doubts regarding effective American command over Chinese troops were not new. I had formulated them explicitly in a February 17, 1943 diary notation:

One of our major mistakes is attempting the impossible—command over the Chinese. We have the weapons, which makes the Chinese willing to string along with us much further than they ordinarily would. We have our ideas of how they should be used and our ideas of command and organization. We want to impose them on the Chinese because we consider the Chinese inefficient and incompetent. We are approaching them with the mentality of Gordon and Ward . . . and it doesn't go down. Chou [homonym for Joe Stilwell] talks about bearing down, discipline . . . and then—he is left hanging in the air.

It is remarkable that Marshall, and much more so Stilwell, thought that Chiang would turn over to anyone, Chinese or foreign, as much control over Chinese troops as Roosevelt asked for. In the first place, as Stilwell well knew, Chiang did not control all of the various armies in China. Those over which he had authority, he controlled by dispersing rather than centralizing command. He trusted no one, scorned the mediocrities he kept as general staff, and dealt directly in any matter of importance with each senior troop commander. All of this being so, Stilwell was undertaking the impossible.

Stilwell did not tell me why he took on this hopeless assignment. Therefore what follows is surmise. The American military of that era shared to a heightened degree the popular national creed that all things are possible provided that you have the guts, grit, gumption and go. To suggest that something was impossible was to be at least a little bit un-American. In particular, Stilwell himself had just proved that by sheer will, drive and stick-to-it-ness what others said would be impossible he had led his forces to achieve—to advance across Burma to take Myitkyina and to build a road through the rain-soaked mountain jungles well on the way to its destination in China.

Now the situation in China was desperate and his superior officer clearly wanted him to attempt the impossible. Like the good soldier that he was, he undertook to do what was expected of him, but asked only that the President would put pressure on the Generalissimo so that "the Gimo might be forced to give me a command job." The idea that the Gimo could be forced to take positive action against which Chiang conceived to be his basic interest was the root fallacy in Stilwell's reasoning. Chiang had been induced to cross the Salween by the threat of withholding lend-lease supplies. But in that showdown the Generalissimo's face was insulated, as the ultimatum was made to Ho. And while moving the Y-Force across the Salween was against Chiang's wishes, it did not really affect his hold on power. The demand that he grant command to Stilwell was, of course, addressed directly to him, it sharply threatened his exercise of authority, and so was both insulting and unacceptable.

*   *   *

Roosevelt was receptive to Chiang's request for a personal representative. He used such appointments with some abandon as a ready device for paying political debts and moving those he thought to be inconvenient to distant parts. As he was at the time, however, preoccupied by conferences with Nimitz and MacArthur, he did not make a choice.

In this vacuum, Stimson mentioned to Marshall in early August that he was looking for some way in which Patrick J. Hurley might be used. Although Marshall was in principle opposed to the appointment of a personal representative through whom Roosevelt might in his disorderly fashion bypass the Joint Chiefs in dealing with Stilwell, he immediately proposed Hurley for the job. This was to forestall nomination of a candidate by Hopkins, whom he rightly believed to be susceptible to influence by Chennault, Soong and Alsop.

Hurley, an Oklahoma lawyer who had waxed wealthy on Mexican oil litigations and other activities and had served as Herbert Hoover's Secretary of War, was acceptable to the President, Stilwell, and, particularly, Stimson. On the basis of my brief meetings with Hurley at New Delhi and Cairo, and in a miscalculation of character, I thought that he would be helpful to Stilwell. The one most pleased with the choice was Hurley himself. He believed, however, that his status as personal representative was worthy of further embellishment and therefore pestered Stettinius to arrange for him to be appointed ambassador. His importunities were not acceded to.

Acting on the principle that one good turn deserves another, Roosevelt designated Donald Nelson as personal representative to Chiang for economic matters. Nelson, a former Sears, Roebuck mogul and deposed head of the War Production Board, had become embroiled in an unsavory row with his successor, causing the President to want him shipped out. In discussing the appointment with me, Hopkins said he was perplexed as to what Nelson might do, but added, "that Nelson would be happy if the Chinese provided him with four or five girls—that would keep him quiet. He [Hopkins] had no doubt that the Chinese would be realistic enough to make such provisions."

My comment on the appointment, in a letter to Patricia, was: "China is apparently to the American political scene what Siberia is to the Russians. Only, Roosevelt's technique is quicker and more humane."

On August 23, shortly after Frank Merrill and I arrived in Washington, I telephoned Hurley to wish him godspeed. He immediately invited me to fly with him and Nelson to Chungking—by way of Moscow. They were due to leave two days later. I regretfully declined: I had work to do. He urged me to hurry back to China.

The Hurley-Nelson routing and Hurley's explanation to the State Department that he wished to fill in Commissar Vyacheslav Molotov on his mission to China and to invite the Commissar's guidance on his approach to Chiang upset the Department. It had been given to understand by Hurley that Roosevelt had approved the visit to the Soviet Commissar for Foreign Affairs. This the President denied, when queried by the Secretary of State. Not surprisingly, Nelson opened the interview with Molotov by stating that he and Hurley were there at the President's behest.

Molotov took the two self-important personal representatives into his confidence—or so it seemed to them. He revealed that the Soviet Union had long supported Chiang and was not connected with those poverty-stricken elements in China who called themselves Communists, but in fact were not real Communists. Speaking on behalf of the Soviet people, Molotov assured those who had gone so far out of their way to seek his guidance that his compatriots would be gladdened by American help to the Chinese and that his Government would make welcome the American Government's taking the lead in China, politically, militarily and economically.

Their self-assurance further inflated by Molotov's encouraging revelations, Hurley and Nelson advised Stilwell at New Delhi that they were going to tell Chiang what to do—unify China (by implication, peacefully) and give Stilwell command. The General liked the sound of this.

The core of Hurley's directive from the President, as he had described it to the State Department, was "to promote harmonious relations between General Chiang and General Stilwell and to facilitate the latter's exercise of command over the Chinese armies placed under his direction." In carrying out these orders, at his first meeting with the Generalissimo on September 7, the personal representative recited to Chiang the reassurance given by Molotov. "Notwithstanding all of this," Hurley reported to Roosevelt, "the Generalissimo still seems skeptical regarding the Communists and stated definitely that any so-called Communist troops serving under General Stilwell would have to submit definitely to the control of the Generalissimo."

*   *   *

Chiang was acutely sensitive to anything that even implied legitimizing the Chinese Communists. Although the Communists' 18th Group Army (GA) was, under the united front agreement, nominally incorporated in the national forces, it did not submit to Chiang's control. The Generalissimo regarded the 18th GA, like the Communist forces not "authorized" by his government, as an enemy. Some 400,000 relatively superior troops considered to be loyal to Chiang blockaded the Communist-held base area in the northwest. The immobilization of this large force in the fighting against the invaders disgusted Stilwell.

He wanted not only those 400,00 inactive Nationalist troops employed against the enemy; he also wished to have the Communist forces committed to the offensive in coordination with non-Communist Chinese forces. In June 1942, I had reported to Stilwell a conversation with Chou En-Lai, then Communist representative in Chungking: "He said half-laughing, half-seriously that if the Generalissimo would permit him, he would take Communist troops under his command for a Burma campaign and 'I would obey General Stilwell's orders!'"

Whether it was on the basis of this statement by Chou or possibly some other about which I am uninformed, Stilwell had told Marshall that the Communists would be willing to serve under his command. Although he had not observed Communist units at first hand, the glowing reports from others on the disciplined soldierly qualities of Communist troops apparently impressed him favorably. Occupying scattered pockets behind and to the side of the Japanese lines in North and Central China, the Communist forces were numerically not insignificant—and they were steadily growing and spreading. They were in all some 450,000 regulars and roughly two million militia.

They were glaringly deficient in equipment of all kinds. Even in the regular units the number of men exceeded the number of rifles, and ammunition was inadequate for any combat beyond skirmishes. The Communist military establishment was, in short, a vast, dispersed guerrilla force inadequately armed with a variety of captured and homemade weapons. Had they been as moderately well equipped as, say the Y-Forces, the Communist regulars would probably have been the most effective military force in China—as indeed they later proved to be—because of their exceptionally strong esprit de corps, élan and support from the populace.

The Generalissimo, who lived an insulated and illusioned life, did not understand all of this. But he did sense that if he acceded to the American wish to activate the Communists against the Japanese, it would follow that the Americans would insist on arming his deadlier enemy. He was therefore adamantly against Stilwell's earlier proposals that the Communists be asked to join in an offensive, and now Washington's demand that Stilwell's command of Chinese troops include the Communists.

For their part, the Communists were cautious. They would accept American command if sanctioned by the Generalissimo—which was a polite way of declining the honor. In any event, the proposal was premature, Chou indicated to Service. The time would be ripe when American troops and supplies were arriving in volume and a counteroffensive was imminent

My interpretation of Yenan's reluctance on this score is that, in the pinched materiel condition of even the 18th Group Army, the Communists simply did not have the firepower to participate in a formal offensive. At such time as the United States occupied a port on the China coast from which they could be directly supplied, the Communists would, with modern American arms and an assured flow of supplies, be ready for a head-on offensive and consideration of American command over a truly allied force composed of Communist, Nationalist and American elements. They did not think that Chiang would permit the Americans to supply them over the then existing line of communications from India.

Related to the issue of command over communist troops was that of control over lend-lease. The authority to differentiate in distribution and to withhold supplies was Stilwell's only bargaining counter with the Generalissimo. He believed that retention of it was essential to the accomplishment of his mission. Chiang and Soong were not oblivious to this and the danger of Stilwell's exerting pressure to arm the Communists. They therefore insisted that control of lend-lease should be transferred to the Generalissimo. Hurley bluntly supported Stilwell in resisting the Chiang-Soong requests.

More crucial to Chiang than the possibility of Stilwell's relations with the Communists and his control over lend-lease was Roosevelt's demand that Stilwell be given command over Chinese troops. Washington had not defined in detail the authority it required Chiang to bestow on Stilwell. Stilwell told Hurley what he reckoned he needed and the President's personal representative presented the requirements to the Generalissimo in mid-September. They were in the form of a commission to be signed by Chiang appointing Stilwell Field Commander of the Chinese ground and air forces and a directive to him to be issued by the Generalissimo.

The commission would have empowered Stilwell to "reward and punish, to appoint and relieve . . . to issue orders for the operations of ground and air forces." In the directive the Generalissimo would have ordered

Stilwell, in preparation for a counteroffensive, to reorganize and relocate ground and air forces. To that end Chiang would authorize him to disband old units, create new ones and shuffle personnel between units. And bespeaking Stilwell's concern for the wretched lot of the ordinary Chinese soldier, he would have the Generalissimo direct him to improve forthwith the livelihood of the troops.

Hurley was heartily in accord with the draft commission and directive that he served on Chiang. After all, such authorizations and orders would not have seemed extraordinary in the United States or any other strong centralized country with a national army. But in Nationalist China they amounted to granting Stilwell license, not simply to reform the Chinese armed forces, but to remake them and incur financial obligations that the rickety Chinese Army could not support. This was a prescription for revolution. It would have meant breaking the rice bowls of those possessing military power. And if they would not let that happen, though it were so ordered by Chiang, how much less would they heed the edicts of a foreign devil intent on putting them out of business?

Again, why did Stilwell attempt the impossible, this time in the extraordinary scope of authority that he sought, including "The Generalissimo must refrain from any interference in operations"? Again, I can only surmise. He had accepted a mission in which the odds were overwhelmingly against success. He could reduce those odds only by drastic action. And so he was asking for the authority to take such unfettered and coercive action. He could hardly have been unaware that the draft commission and directive would be regarded by Chiang as insulting. But after two and a half years of rankling frustration at the hands of the Generalissimo, Stilwell was less than solicitous over the preservation of Chiang's face.

The doomed negotiations dragged on for a fortnight without concession on either side. To the contrary, Stilwell told Soong that if he could not have full authority he would not accept the responsibility. During the sterile restatements of position, the Japanese offensive surged over the Chinese defenses in South China and the Y-Force was stalled on the other side of the Salween. It was then, in mid-September, that Chiang's anxiety over the safety of Kunming and Chungking turned to alarm.

He called in Stilwell and, in effect, announced his intention to pull back the Y-Force across the Salween. This would be to abandon Stilwell's long, anguished efforts to break the ground blockade of China. "The crazy little bastard," wrote Stilwell in a diary explosion against Chiang's "sabotage (of) the whole God-damn project . . . to help China." Forthwith he shot off a radiogram to Marshall reporting the Generalissimo's craven intent and botching interference in the "defense" of South China.

Stilwell's report of the Generalissimo's latest aberrations reached Marshall at the Quebec meeting of Roosevelt, Churchill and the Combined Chiefs of Staff. The tidings out of China arrived on September 16, inauspiciously in the midst of planning purposeful and ambitious advances in Europe and the Pacific. Marshall's staff drafted a message to the Generalissimo from the President, which was signed by Roosevelt. It was a cold and detailed reprimand of Chiang, concluding with "I am certain that the only thing you can do now . . . is to reinforce your Salween armies immediately and press their offensive, while at once placing General Stilwell in unrestricted command of all your forces."

The message was dispatched through military channels to Stilwell for delivery to the Generalissimo and received on September 19. This was routine procedure. But it did by-pass the touchy Hurley. Stilwell, of course, recognized the missive to be as "hot as a firecracker" and was correspondingly gratified. He promptly took the message, with a Chinese translation, to the Generalissimo's residence for personal delivery to Chiang.

Stilwell arrived to find the Generalissimo in conference with Hurley, T.V. Soong and top Chinese military officers. He arranged for Hurley to excuse himself and join him outside the conference room and then showed the personal representative the President's bill of particulars. Feeling that Roosevelt's language was too blunt, Hurley suggested to Stilwell that he, Hurley, convey the substance of the message orally. Under orders to deliver the message directly to the Generalissimo, Stilwell declined, and they proceeded to the conference room where Stilwell handed Chiang what he later described as "this bundle of paprika."

The setting—the Generalissimo being delivered a rebuke by an alien subordinate in the presence of his guileful henchmen—was one in which Chiang would lose maximum face. And Stilwell was not unaware of the grave affront he was committing. The Generalissimo read the Chinese translation in silence, then turned to Stilwell and said "I understand." It having been made clear that the meeting was over, the server of the presidential demands returned to his quarters where in gloating doggerel he celebrated "the blessed pleasure" of having "wrecked the Peanut's face." He gave no indication of realizing that in wrecking Chiang's face he contributed mightily to wrecking his chance of getting anything at all out of the Generalissimo. Following Vinegar Joe's visitation, the Peanut indulged in one of his temper tantrums, which in this instance was a necessary performance in the presence of his retainers to compensate for lost face.

Nearly seven years later in the stimulating heat of a Senate inquiry into American political and military disasters in East Asia, Hurley regaled the solons with a retrospective account of the Stilwell command crisis in which, if only the General had followed his advice, all would have gone swimmingly. The key passage, taken from the records of the hearings, quotes Hurley:

> *Stilwell and I sat on the porch, and he took out and showed to me a cable from the President of the United States. It wasn't addressed to me, as had been agreed to, but it did direct General Stilwell to present it in person.*
>
> *I read it carefully, sitting there by the General. I turned to him and I said, "Joe, you have won the ball game. The Gimo has agreed to everything that the President tells him that he must agree to or else."*
>
> *Stilwell said, "I don't care whether he has agreed to it or not; I am directed by the President to hand it to him."*
>
> *And I said, "Joe, we have had a hard time getting to this place and we are writing your commission now, and I think you better tell the Gimo what's in this, in place of this pretty stiff telegram. He may think it's an ultimatum and that he is being compelled publicly to do what he has already agreed to do. He has agreed to every item of this."*
>
> *He said, "I am directed by the President to present it to him, and I am going to do it."*
>
> *Now, it was a longer conversation than that. I labored with my friend, but he went in and presented it.*

Hurley's portrayal of his consultation with Stilwell is plausible, save for his claim that he had just persuaded the Generalissimo to accede to all of the American requirements for full power to Stilwell. Neither Hurley nor Stilwell mentioned this to me when I returned to Chungking at the conclusion of the command crisis and discussed with each of them what had transpired. Nor was it credible, within the context of Chiang's fixed animosity toward Stilwell—not to mention his nationalist sensitivity—that he would bestow such sweeping authority upon this gadfly American. What would be credible is that Hurley, who was not at all lacking in a capacity for misleading himself, was either in his meeting with the Generalissimo so carried away by his own persuasiveness that he thought Chiang was in agreement with him, or that years later in the exhilaration of testifying before the Senate committee he recalled the distant past in dramatically heightened and wishful terms.

Be that as it may, the Generalissimo took his time in preparing his response to the President. During this interval Stilwell told Marshall that maintaining pressure on Chiang would turn the trick. This was a sanguine expectation; especially as Roosevelt's demands of Chiang were not accompanied by any promises on sanctions for non-compliance. To the contrary, Roosevelt's message mentioned lend-lease, the only American bargaining counter, in terms of an unqualified increase of aid. The conclusion to be drawn, then, was that the President regarded Chiang and China as indispensable and that the only pressure to be expected from Washington was rhetorical.

By September 25, Chiang and Soong had worked out with a shaken and increasingly compliant Hurley the Generalissimo's rejoinder to the President. It was, in short, that Stilwell had been insubordinate; in handing Chiang the message from Roosevelt, Stilwell had made the Generalissimo his subordinate; that Stilwell was unfit for his assignment; and that Chiang insisted upon the recall of Stilwell. The first hint of what the White House reaction might be came to Chungking at the end of September from—so characteristic of Washington—a dinner party conversation reported by Kung. Hopkins had somewhere between martinis and cigars revealed that Roosevelt intended to comply with Chiang's request for Stilwell's recall because of the Generalissimo's sovereign right to demand such a recall.

This hardened Chiang's stand. To a meeting of his political lieutenants he proclaimed that Stilwell must go, that lend-lease must be under his control, and that the Americans were engaged in "a new form of imperialism." Nevertheless, Stilwell and Marshall continued to seek compromise formulas, to no avail. The Generalissimo on October 10 again asked the President to recall Stilwell, pointing out that it was his prerogative as Chief of State to require the removal of an officer. Hurley backed up Chiang, telling the President that "if you sustain Stilwell in this controversy you will lose Chiang Kai-shek and possibly you will lose China with him." The conceit that the United States had Chiang or China to lose was to persist for years in the American mythology about China.

In an October 18 message to the Generalissimo the President gave in to Chiang's demands for the recall of Stilwell. The CBI Theater was divided into the China Theater and the Burma-India Theater. Wedemeyer was appointed commander of American forces in China and authorized "to accept the position of Chief of Staff to the Generalissimo." Sultan was given command of American forces in Burma-India. On October 21 Stilwell left Chungking for the United States.

*   *   *

Following my visit to Washington with Frank Merrill I returned to New Delhi during the latter half of September and prepared to move my base of operations to China. I arrived in Chungking on October 17, two days before Stilwell received orders terminating his CBI command. The atmosphere at headquarters was tensely expectant and Stilwell tight-lipped.

I saw Hurley shortly after Stilwell received his orders. He was visibly upset and said, "I bitched it." That he may have done, but not in any sense that would have altered the outcome one way or another. The forces at work in the Stilwell-Chiang confrontation were far larger and more compelling than he. In a tone of admiration he said that Stilwell took the recall order "like a Roman."

As for Stilwell himself, he said to me, "What the hell, you live only once and you have to live as you believe."

As there was bound to be sensational publicity over his being pulled out, I said to Stilwell that he must provide the press a straightforward account of the situation as he saw it. He agreed, and briefed Brooks Atkinson, *The New York Times* correspondent on leave from Broadway, and Theodore H. White, *Time* Magazine's representative. They were upset over the outcome of the long struggle with Chiang, as both were, like most of the American journalists in CBI, fond of the Old Man.

I was overly disturbed by Stilwell's recall, also influenced by affection for the General. I looked on his removal as a near tragedy for the American effort in China. And like many of those around the General—and in the War Department—I felt that Roosevelt had pusillanimously let Stilwell down.

In principle, Roosevelt had no choice in the Stilwell-Chiang confrontation. Indeed, it was Chiang's prerogative, as Chief of State, to demand the removal of any foreign representative, military or civil, and the obligation of the corresponding foreign Chief of State—in this case, Roosevelt—to accede to the demand. But in practical politics, such situations may sometimes be modified or even reversed if compelling rewards are offered or pressure brought to bear. Lend-lease supplies were the maximum feasible reward that Roosevelt could offer—but they were already being given. As for pressures, the only viable kind available to him was the withholding of lend-lease. However, he had revealed that he would not bargain with it. Therefore all that Chiang had to do was to keep his nerve and remain adamant, whereupon Roosevelt would give in. Which is what happened.

What if Roosevelt had cracked down and terminated aid to China? Chiang had taken into account such a contingency and at the session with his Kuomintang lieutenants early in October explained that "We can get along without them," the Americans. This was probably closer to the truth than the prophecies of collapse used by his wife and brothers-in-law to scare the White House into concessions to the Generalissimo.

Had he to choose starkly between giving (to the extent that he was able) the authority demanded for Stilwell or foregoing American aid, I suspect that he would have chosen the latter. A Stilwell command would have threatened destruction of the intricately balanced structure of military incompetence and mediocrity on which his supremacy depended. A cut-off of American aid would have stopped his accumulation of military hardware but would probably not have affected his power position in China—while he waited out the war in the Pacific.

Usually, however, choices are not starkly either/or. Intermediate options exist. Roosevelt might have been willing to go as far as stopping aid, but held in abeyance acting on his determination while he bargained for Chiang's compliance. And the Generalissimo might have calculated that he could seem to yield to Washington's ultimatum while temporizing, evading and double-crossing Stilwell as he had successfully done for two and a half years. He would not go so far as to give Roosevelt clear reason to cut him off, but push to that limit obstructions to giving Stilwell real authority, and to the extent that he gave it, undermining it.

*   *   *

The Stilwell command crisis was an outgrowth of the broad fundamental difference between Chinese and Americans regarding the war against Japan and the failure of Americans to realize that this difference existed. The roots of the difference extended beyond the two men, Stilwell and Chiang, and the other official personalities involved, to the differing outlook of the Chinese and American peoples. Wearied by decades of warlord fighting, Japanese invasion and bombing, without confidence in their government and army, and fearing the enemy as invincible, in despair the Chinese people looked to the Americans for salvation. The American people, once over the first few months of Pearl Harbor shock, recovered their dauntless disposition and took to the business of war with a vengeance. Because of propaganda and an assumption that others react as one does, Americans mistakenly supposed that the Chinese were of like temper.

The American-Chinese dichotomy was more pronounced between Chiang and the American leadership. The Generalissimo shared the resigned attitude of the Chinese people. His negativism was fortified by preoccupation with the forthcoming war to the finish against the Chinese Communists and the necessity for conserving strength for that decisive conflict. In contrast, the American Government's overwhelming preoccupation was with the prosecution of the current war. It took Roosevelt nearly two years to realize, at the Cairo Conference, that Chiang was perhaps not as spoiling for battle against the common enemy as he. Even after that he did not appear to comprehend the depth of the Generalissimo's dedication to inaction. The President's judgment was, of course, affected by his desire to find common interests with Chiang and enlist his collaboration, along with Churchill's and Stalin's, in building a just post-war world.

Marshall, Stilwell and others of us on the American side who thought that, by bargaining with military and economic aid, Washington might induce Chiang and company to become more aggressive underestimated our ally's genius for passivity. The United States was confronted by a situation in which it was more difficult to generate than to thwart action. And so long as the American Government regarded Chiang and China as indispensable, the impotent were able to bully the powerful.

The concept of the Stilwell mission—an American general equipping, training and leading the motley, raffish Chinese legions on to victory in China, all under the approving eye of the Generalissimo—that expectation was an illusion. Then, to assign an officer who was deemed to be one of the best combat commanders in the American Army to grapple with phantasmagoria, that was dissipation of scarce talent. The tremendous materiel effort—the ships and aircraft hauling war supplies from the United States to Kunming, the North Burma campaign, the building of the India-China road and pipeline, the equipping and training of Chinese armies—all of these were triumphs of American ingenuity, organization, drive, muscle—but not wit.

Looking back on the 1940s, it seems clear that China was not indispensable to the defeat of Japan nor the making of the peace. Furthermore, in view of the prolonged wartime suffering of the Chinese, their dispirited outlook, and the failure of the Chiang regime to win over and inspire the people, I would say that the American Government would have been wise to have accepted that Chiang and his forces have a respite from fighting and that aggressive action was not to be expected from the Chinese. Consequently, a token military effort by the United States in China would have sufficed. That would have meant a modest air detachment sufficient to defend Free China's principal cities, and perhaps, undertake harassing raids, short of provoking Japanese ground offensives. Air transport support over the Hump would have been necessary, but on a much lesser scale than was developed. And the air defense of the Hump route would have been provided by the Tenth Air Force based in India.

For appearance's sake, a prestigious, phlegmatic, superannuated American military figure should have been assigned to maintain ornamental contact between the Joint Chiefs of Staff and the Chinese General Staff. He would have been subordinate to the Ambassador, who, as the President's sole plenipotentiary to the Chinese Chief of State, would have controlled such rare contacts, if any, as might have been necessary between the JCS representative and the Generalissimo. The military representative's function would have been to give the Chinese military establishment face by innocuous briefings and consultation and to request its assistance in American intelligence operations regarding the Japanese.

Thus there would have been no American Chief of Staff to the Generalissimo, or supervisor of lend-lease, or a CBI Theater. No American would have been enjoined to improve the combat efficiency of the Chinese forces, much less to attempt command of them. Without these provocations, face-losing for other Chinese as well as Chiang, relations between Washington and Chungking would have been less strained.

The Generalissimo would, of course, have clamored for supplies far beyond those provided by the commitment of the American air detachment for his defense. Roosevelt's reply would best have been that at such time as Chiang captured a Chinese port from which he could be securely supplied, materiel would be shipped to him (preferably materiel taken from the Japanese in the Pacific). For it should be recalled what actually happened to lend-lease arms and other equipment. Chiang's Nationalists in the Civil War, 1945–1950, used them inefficiently and lost them to the Communists, thereby making the United States eventually quartermaster to the Reds.

Churchill's strategic appraisal of China was correct. After some initial concern over its possible collapse, he took the position that China was not a significant factor in the war against Japan. The "American obsession" with China, as Churchill in his more temperate mood described it, baffled the Prime Minister. Churchill was also right in 1942–44 in opposing the Burma campaigns as a waste of effort and resources. Bypassed, the Japanese in the Burmese salient would eventually have withdrawn or been cut off. If still in Burma when defeat was finally imposed on the home island, they would assumably have surrendered in obedience to the Emperor's command, as did other Japanese forces bypassed by Nimitz and MacArthur.

Likewise, the British attitude toward the situation within China was sounder than that of the American government. London calculated that there was little if anything constructive that Britain could do about the course of domestic events in China. It therefore stood aloof from the power struggle between Chiang's regime and the Communists. Britain maintained its distant, cool composure on through China's civil war, in striking contrast to the distraught, self-destructive behavior not only of the American Government, conspicuously within the Congress, but also of segments of the American public, particularly within the information media.

CHAPTER XVII

MEETING MAO

Stilwell's departure left my status uncertain. The State Department had detailed me from the Embassy to "the China Military Mission headed by . . . Stilwell." Would I be kept on by Stilwell's successor in China, Wedemeyer, his successor in India-Burma, Sultan, or would I revert to the Embassy?

My inclination was to visit Yenan to obtain a first-hand impression of the Chinese Communists. I wanted, following this, a transfer to the embassy in Moscow from which to observe the Soviet entry into the war against Japan, Soviet relations with the Chinese Communists, and Moscow's approach to the Chinese civil war, which I believed would follow on the heels of Japan's defeat. The timetable that I had in mind was flexible; at least several weeks in Yenan and then move to Moscow sometime well before the summer of 1945.

With these aspirations, I asked Stilwell before he left to authorize my going to Yenan, which he did. From there I wrote Wedemeyer on October 12, in expectation of his arrival at Chungking later in the month, offering the services of my colleagues and myself if he wished to have us on the basis that we worked for Stilwell. To put in a bid for a job in the Moscow Embassy, I wrote to Charles E. Bohlen, then handling Soviet affairs at the Department, expressing my wish for a Moscow assignment.

Sultan asked that I be assigned to him. Although I liked and had a high regard for the General, my interest was then less in India and Burma than in the Chinese-Soviet relationship, and so I thanked him and begged off. Settling down at the Chungking Embassy was, on the heels of Stilwell's departure, a fate that I was anxious to avoid. I had several good friends on the exceptionally competent staff and I would have enjoyed working with them. But my relations with Gauss had soured to the degree that I doubted that he would have wanted me and, for my part, I had no wish to put his small store of good humor to a test.

From his cool initial reception of me in 1942, Gauss displayed increasing resentment of me; my peripatetic detail was "ruining the morale" of his staff, I was not performing any useful function, and he was of a mind to ask the Department to cancel my detail and "put you to work." Stilwell told me that Gauss had several times said that he wanted to ask Washington to return me to the Embassy, to which the General retorted on one occasion, "Just try to." Stilwell's detailing me to Currie and the General's taking me to the Cairo conference, to which Gauss was not invited, and my reporting to the Ambassador information gained from those and other contacts, which he rightly felt should have been his, did not endear me to Gauss. But the Department had instructed me to keep the Ambassador appropriately informed; had I not done so, I would have been remiss.

The Ambassador was correct in suspecting that I was behind Stilwell's robbing him of his most prized junior officer—Jack Service. His Excellency also took umbrage at a couple of my actions he considered to be out of channels. But the incident which, I was told, raised his ire to highest pitch involved a letter sent to him by a well-bred, pretty, unspoiled girl who had been serving as a Red Cross hostess, meant to personify to the troops the wholesomeness they were fighting to protect. Well, Frances sought a change in her contribution to the war effort and so became available to the New Delhi office of the political advisers, where Patricia happily handed over secretarial duties to her.

During one of my absences Frances felt called upon to exercise initiative regarding some minor development, the nature of which I have forgotten. On my behalf, unbeknownst to me, she wrote directly to the American Ambassador to China. Now, Ambassadors were in those days addressed by their underlings with deferential ceremony, opening with "The Honorable," saluting him as "Sir," beginning with, "I have the honor to report" or "request" and concluding with a salaam, "Very Respectfully Yours." Being of strong egalitarian inclinations, my practice was to omit the "Very."

Frances omitted everything and wrote "Dear Mr. Gauss" and ended her little note with sincerity but no mention of respect. This was unseemly enough. But what was far worse was the implication that Gauss read into this trivial incident. He assumed, I was later told, that I had impertinently relegated communicating with him to an untutored, cheeky secretary.

In spite of the infelicity of my relations with Gauss, I continue to respect him for his tough-minded integrity. And I felt sympathy for him for the indignities visited upon him by the President. Roosevelt had more than ignored him. Roosevelt had undercut his Ambassador with dabbling and intriguing wiseacres—Currie, Wallace, Hurley and Nelson. Furthermore, Gauss was deeply discouraged over the possibility of the American Government's being able to do anything constructive to the rapidly deteriorating situation in China. Humiliated and disheartened, Gauss resigned on November 1. As a final act of grace and gentility, the White House announced his resignation before receiving his letter tendering it.

*   *   *

Three dominant issues, it seemed to me, confronted the United States in Asia. The most immediate was victory in the war. The second was one that I had explored in India—the proper stance for the United States in the contention between our imperial allies and their Asian colonies. The third was the issue of an American policy, if not beneficial then the least disadvantageous to the United States, with regard to the phenomenal rise of Communism in China.

The Chinese Communist movement was a portentous mystery. Would it sweep over China? What were its connections with Moscow? In the forthcoming Chinese civil war would the Soviet Union intervene on behalf of the Chinese Communists? Would the United States side with Chiang and his Nationalists and in so doing become embroiled in the civil war and with the Soviet Union?

These were not new questions. From the late 1930s it had begun to appear that Chiang was losing his cities and lines of communications to the Japanese and the countryside to the Communists. In June 1943 I surveyed the Chinese-American-Soviet situation in a memorandum for the State Department.

In this survey I recorded an American military estimate that the area then occupied by the Communists had grown to about 120,000 square miles, with a population of some 25 million. The Yenan regime was reported to be remarkably honest and to enjoy strong popular support while Chiang's government was venal, oppressive and without a popular base. Chiang was "a political hostage to the corrupt system which he manipulates," I wrote.

> *The Kuomintang and Chiang Kai-shek recognize that the Communists, with the popular support they enjoy and their reputation for administrative reform and honesty, represent a challenge to the Central Government and its spoils system. The Generalissimo cannot admit the seemingly innocent demands of the Communists that their party be legalized and democratic processes be put into practice. To do so would probably mean the abdication of the Kuomintang and the provincial satraps.*
>
> *The Communists, on the other hand, dare not accept the Central Government's invitation that they disband their armies and be absorbed in the national body politic. To do so would be to invite extinction.*
>
> *This impasse will probably be resolved, American and other foreign observers in Chungking agree, by an attempt by the Central Government to liquidate the Communists. This action may be expected to precipitate a civil war from which one of the two contending factions will emerge dominant.*

In such a civil war, I indicated, Moscow would not allow the meagerly armed Communists to be crushed, and so might be expected to aid them. A Chiang campaign against the Reds would therefore probably "force the Communists into the willing arms of the Russians. The position of the political doctrinaires who have been subservient to Moscow would be strengthened by such an attack. The present trend of the Chinese Communists toward more or less democratic nationalism—confirmed in six years of fighting for the Chinese motherland—would thereby be reversed and they could be expected to retrogress to the position of a Russian satellite." Supported by the Soviet Union, the Chinese Communists would be likely to defeat Chiang. The end result: a Russo-Chinese bloc.

Chiang and company were aware, I continued, of the risks of attacking the Communists. This may have accounted for "reported statements of high officials in Chungking that they must prepare not only for the coming civil war but also for the coming war with Russia." Consequently the Generalissimo would seek foreign aid. "We may anticipate that Chiang Kai-shek will exert every effort and resort to every stratagem to involve us in active support of the Central Government. We will probably be told that if fresh American aid is not forthcoming all of China and eventually all of Asia will be swept by Communism. It will be difficult for us to resist such appeals . . . It is therefore not inconceivable that, should Chiang attempt to liquidate the Communists, we would find ourselves entangled not only in a civil war in China but also drawn into conflict with the Soviet Union."

With the Chinese Communists looming so ominously on the horizon, the American Government was urgently in need of first-hand information about and contact with them. Yet, "no American civil official has visited the Chinese Communist area and no American military observer has traveled in it since 1938." I recommended that a consulate general be established at Yenan and that a military observers' mission be sent to the area.

After six months had passed without creation of an American outpost at Yenan, due to obstruction by Chiang, I wrote on January 15, 1944 another memorandum. I kept this one to a page, to qualify for reading by the President and Marshall. And I sent a copy to Hopkins, hoping he would pass it to Roosevelt. I attached a suggested draft of a message from FDR to Chiang.

In the memorandum I described the American intelligence needs regarding the Japanese, Communists and Russians during and after the war. In the draft message to Chiang, without any mention of the Communists or Russians, I concentrated on the need to prepare for China's recovery of Manchuria and North China. To augment our information of these areas and "survey the possibilities of further operations both ground and air, I consider it to be of the utmost importance that an American observers' mission be immediately dispatched to North Shansi and Shansi Provinces and such other parts of North China as may be necessary." I omitted any request for the establishment of a consulate as being too political and provocative, compromising the possibility of any observers at all.

Hopkins gave the memorandum and draft letter to the President, who instructed Admiral Leahy to consult with Marshall and act. A slightly modified version of my draft letter went out on February 9 to the Generalissimo. Again Chiang stalled. His consent was not gained until Wallace, while visiting Chungking, extracted it from him.

*   *   *

The first contingent of the Observer Group or section (Chiang having objected to the word "mission") arrived in Yenan July 22, 1944. The Group was headed by Colonel David D. Barrett, of Napoleonic physique and genial inclinations. He was a China specialist who rejoiced in the good things of Chinese life and relished conversations in Chinese. Service accompanied him as political observer. Various military intelligence and communications personnel completed the contingent of nine. A second complement, including Ludden, arrived a month later.

"To the skeptical," Service reported a few days after arrival, "the general atmosphere in Yenan can be compared to that of a rather small, sectarian college—or a religious summer conference. There is a bit of the smugness, self-righteousness and conscious fellowship . . ." The American observers also found the Communists to be plain, direct and earnest. The new association seemed to be off to an amicable start.

Mao Tse-tung indicated to Service at the outset that he wanted an American Consulate at Yenan, one that would remain after the conclusion of the war and the departure of the observers. He also told Service that he wished to have a talk with him after Jack had acquainted himself with the Yenan scene. Service needed no urging. He had already begun the first of what would develop into a harvest of detailed and illuminating reports.

One month after Service's arrival, Mao received him—for a conversation lasting eight hours. Not only in length was this an extraordinary dialogue. For here was the dominant Chinese Communist, whose forces within a half dozen years would overthrow Chiang and overrun China, broaching to a junior American diplomat a plea that the American Government collaborate with the Chinese Communists.

In essence, Mao wanted then to avoid a civil war. He wanted Chiang to institute democratic processes in which the Communists would participate. He asked that the American government induce the Kuomintang, that is to say the Chiang regime, to so reform itself. If that regime did not reform itself, then civil war was likely. Chiang's use of American materiel in a civil war worried him. He did not ask that the United States stop all aid to the Kuomintang forces. Rather, Mao thought American aid should go to all forces, including the Communists, which were fighting the Japanese.

Mao said that the Americans must land on the China coast. This would mean American cooperation with both Nationalists and Communists. But the Communists and Nationalists would operate in separate sectors—and the Americans would then see the difference between the two forces: that the Communists had popular support and could fight.

Every American soldier in China, Mao said, should be a walking and talking advertisement for democracy. The Chinese considered Americans to be the ideal of democracy, the Communist boss added. And in a negative sense, the presence of Americans in China could be a good thing, as a restraint on the Chiang regime's oppressiveness. As Service reported the substance of Mao's comments, "Of course we are glad to have the Observer Section here because it will help beat Japan. But there is no use pretending that—up to now at least—the chief importance of your coming is its political effect on the Kuomintang."

Mao did not expect post-war aid from the Soviet Union. The Russians would have their hands full with their own reconstruction. In any event, for the Chinese Communists to seek Soviet help would only make the situation in China worse; there was already enough disunity in China. As for American aid to the Chinese Communists, the Soviet Union would not object to it if it were constructive and democratic in character.

China must industrialize, Mao continued. It could do this only by free enterprise and with help from foreign capital. He said that Chinese and American interests were correlated and similar, that China and the United States can and must work together. The United States would find the Communists would not fear but rather welcome democratic American influence.

Recording the substance of Mao's concluding remarks, Service reported, "America does not need to fear that we will not be cooperative. We must cooperate and we must have American help . . . We cannot risk crossing you—cannot risk any conflict with you."

Service dispatched to CBI Headquarters and the Embassy a full account of Mao's statements to him. The Embassy forwarded a copy of the report to the State Department. Washington did not deign to respond to Mao.

*   *   *

The day after Stilwell left Chungking I flew to Yenan in the headquarter's C-47. Yenan—which we called Dixie since it was rebel territory—was from the air a thoroughly insignificant Northwest China town set in a treeless valley. The eroded, lumpish plateau that rose from the valley floor on either side was, in late October, parched bare and tan. After we turned in the valley, preparing to land, we floated close to the face of cliffs in which were dug caves where the Yenan elite snugly resided, safe from enemy bombing. They waved to us as we passed.

We came down on a dirt landing strip, laid out especially for occasional CBI flights such as this one. The Communists had no aircraft and no other planes came in to Yenan. So our arrival was an exciting occasion. Hundreds of people swarmed to the edge of the strip, staring and smiling.

On opening the plane's door, the air outside was clean, crisp and dry. The sun blazed from a blue cloudless sky. It was all such a contrast to the heavy dank overcast we had left in Chungking. Although men and women dressed monotonously alike in wadded cotton jackets and trousers, the expressions on their faces and their bearing created the impression of a greater individuality, openness and vigor than one got from people in other parts of China.

The welcoming crowd appeared to be a mixture of Yenan society— soldiers, officers, party workers, students and hangers-on. Service was also there and so was Yeh Chien-ying, the Chief of Staff, in brindle, woolen homespun trousers and jacket without insignia. The Communists had mobilized a decrepit truck to transport the American guests to their billets. We were John Emmerson, Teddy White and I, plus maybe a half dozen officers, on a sightseeing tour, who would return to Chungking on the plane the following day.

Our dude ranch, as I called it, sat apart from other buildings in Yenan. It consisted of two newly built structures of stone, brick and adobe. One was eight rooms long without plumbing, but with an outhouse. Heating was by charcoal braziers and lighting by kerosene lamps. Each dirt-floored room had two beds: boards on trestles, straw mattresses, cotton wadded quilts. We ate in the second building, which also served as a stark recreation center. The food was Chinese and good. Chinese orderlies, alert and efficient, kept the quarters shipshape.

On the evening of our arrival, Chou En-lai and Chu Teh, the Communist Commander in Chief, were hosts at a convivial banquet for the foreign visitors and the Observer Group, including the sergeants. Prominent Party and Army figures were also present. Service, Emmerson and I sat at Chou's table, while Barrett and the visiting military brass were at Chu Teh's. The few foreign correspondents, including two representing Tass, the Soviet news agency, occupied a third table. And as if to demonstrate Communist adherence to the united front, the National Government representatives at Yenan, a general and a colonel, had been invited and sat with some unidentified Communists at a separate table.

After the sedate revelry—a temperate indulgence in drinking games without sing song girls—Chou escorted Service, Emmerson and me to his "house" up the side of a cliff. We went through a gate to a small, leveled area like a courtyard onto which faced five or six holes in the face of the cliff. These were the rooms of Chou's residence. We entered one of them, perhaps four by five meters, with a desk, chairs, stacks of books and a pot of white chrysanthemums. Mrs. Chou, a plain, poised, attractive woman in the universal wadded outfit but with a white knitted cap on her head, came in with tea, chatted briefly with Service and me and then left. She was herself a leading revolutionary and survivor of the Long March. In contrast to Mao and Chu, who had either discarded wives or lost them through capture and execution by Chiang's troops, Chou had not before been married. And the Chous' relationship was evidently a good one.

Mao entered the room. I later recorded in my diary:

He is big and plump with a round, bland, almost feminine face. With the direct, friendly manner of the Chinese Communists he strode up to each of us and shook hands. He sat on a little stool to my right; then came Chia-k'ang (Chou's secretary/interpreter); then Chou, JKE (Emmerson), Jack and I completed the circle . . . We talked frankly for two or three hours. Chu Teh came in when we were about half way through.

Those three men sitting around the table, their faces in the half-light of a feeble kerosene lamp, showed up in dramatic contrast. Mao with the slow gestures, the big soft frame and face . . . The incandescence of personality . . . There is an immense, smooth calm and sureness to him.

Chou has a leaner facial architecture . . . His is the personality full of mobility, his anger, his earnestness, and his amusement fully set forth in his face. He is the one of quick, deft gestures. He will make a photogenic foreign minister.

Old Chu is the shambling, slow, shrewd peasant. His face is flat, broad, and homely as a North China mud wall. Yet it has tremendous character. His frame is square and his gait is a rolling waddle, the product of his heavy width and decades of wearing wads and wads of cotton-padded

pants. In repose his face is tough. But it breaks into a wide pervasive laugh
when he is pleased or entertained.

In this meeting I sought to follow up on what Mao had said to Service about the necessity of cooperation between the United States and the Chinese Communists. If American forces landed on a part of the China coast claimed by the Communists, what cooperation could his organization, military and civilian, offer? Mao replied that they would collaborate fully in the event that the American move was large-scale and also involved supplying the Communists. The matter should be further examined. Chu and Yeh, the Chief of Staff, would look into the possibilities with me. But if the United States remained aloof, he was still confident regarding the future for the Communists, because of their steadily increasing strength.

Although I had gained the impression in September at the Pentagon that there was slight interest in a China coast landing, I felt that American cooperation with the Chinese Communists might pre-empt North China, which otherwise the Russians would be tempted to enter when they joined the war in Asia. For this political reason I was eager to see what Chu and Yeh would produce. On Yeh's initiative we went to work the day after the plane returned to Chungking.

The setting was something of a contrast to the Pentagon's anterooms, deep carpets, batteries of telephones, and flags on staves behind solemn men at large polished desks. Yeh and I met in his office, apparently part of his home. The room was maybe four by five meters, earthen floor, simple desk, no telephones, no flags. The fifth participant—really an observer—was Niu Niu, Yeh's fetching three-year-old daughter. She was well padded against the cold and wore a white knitted peaked cap with a red star on the front.

Our discussion in this first meeting was general: the course of the war. I found Yeh to be intelligent, quick witted and straightforward. Some years later, Ludden told me that Marshall, on a post-war mission to China, and after he had dealt with both Nationalist and Communist military men, said that Yeh was the ablest Chinese general he had encountered.

Naturally, I turned to Colonel Barrett for advice and assistance in the consultation with Yeh. We met with Yeh, Chu Teh and Niu Niu. Neither the Commander in Chief nor the three-year-old had much to say. On the following day, October 26, Barrett and I conferred with Yeh and three of the foremost combat commanders, P'eng Teh-huai, Lin Piao and Nieh

Jung-chen. P'eng and Lin were, successively, the commanders of the Chinese "volunteers" in the 1950–53 Korean War. It became apparent that Yeh and his fellow generals were puzzled over how to respond to my broad query. Barrett and I therefore gave them a set of specific assumptions regarding American landings on the China coast.

About a week later Yeh, Chu and Chou, with Mao's concurrence, presented an estimate of what they would do in the event an American force landed near Lienyunkang, coastal terminus of the east-west Lunghai Railway. The objective, I had suggested, would be the creation of airbases in this area within striking distance of Japan, Korea, Manchuria and, of course, all of Japanese-Occupied China. The Communists estimated that two and a half Japanese divisions would be in position to oppose the initial landing attempt. They might be reinforced to five divisions within as short a time as five days. To assure Allied superiority, the Communist estimate called for five American divisions committed to the operation.

The Communist contribution would be, in brief, attacks by 50,000 regulars on the eastern sector of the Lunghai Railway, along which would move reinforcements to the Japanese opposing the landing, and mobilization of the populace within a 200 mile radius of Lienyunkang to provide labor and foodstuff for the Americans. In the rest of North China, Communist troops and militia would engage the enemy and cut his lines of communications. (Chu and Yeh later told me that their total strength was 600,000 regulars and full time guerrillas and two and a half million militia.) The landing and North China offensive, the Communist anticipated, would provoke a strong Japanese counter offensive. Therefore they would need materiel supplied through the captured port. They mentioned, modestly enough, Japanese light arms and ammunition (captured by the Americans in the Pacific).

On November 3, I summarized on two pages the Communist estimate, marked it Top Secret, and addressed copies to Wedemeyer, Stilwell in Washington for old time's sake, and the chief of the China Division at the State Department, John Carter Vincent. I heard nothing in response. The Joint Chiefs of Staff, after all, had decided to bypass China. And rather than thinking in terms of forestalling Soviet action against the Japanese forces on the mainland, the American high command was eager for the Russians to move into at least Manchuria against the Japanese there.

Mao's statements to Service about the Communists' need for post-war American economic aid and investments seemed to me to require further exploration. The Communists had been forthcoming about their military capabilities and limitations. What would they be willing to say about their economic goals?

With Mrs. Chou serving us tea and fruit at their cave, I asked Chou, assuming that they came to power in China, what would be the Communist policy with regard to industry, foreign investments, foreign trade and other economic activities? While they would continue to be faced with landlord-peasant problems and other traditional rural issues, it seemed to me that they would have to prepare for the new economic responsibilities that would suddenly confront them if they came to power nationally, including in urban areas. Chou was evidently interested in the subject, but he did not respond with any significant opinions.

I doubt that Mao had any specific program for American economic assistance in mind when he spoke to Service on the subject. Wanting American aid, capital and trade, I suspect that he invited it without having worked out a blueprint and detailed doctrinal justification. Should the Americans seriously take him up on his overture, the doctrine was flexible enough to permit the expedient adoption of almost any policy that promised benefits.

Therefore, in the absence of a party line on the contingencies that I presented Chou, there was nothing authoritative that he could say. In any event, I hoped that my show of interest might help a bit to keep alive the thought that there perhaps could be an American alternative to war-ravaged, necessitous solidarity with the Soviet Union. The session ended with lunch, Chou quizzing me about American politics, including the role of the Electoral College, followed by ping-pong.

*   *   *

Of the four Foreign Service officers who had been assigned to Stilwell, three of us were now in Communist-controlled territory, Service having returned to Washington for consultation. Before Emmerson and I arrived, Ludden had left on a four-month reconnaissance, on foot and by mule back, of a large Communist area behind the enemy lines in Shansi province. He was the only American Foreign Service officer to observe Communist administration of towns and countryside nominally under Japanese sway. Marching with Communist regulars and guerrillas for weeks on end, and crossing enemy lines with them, he also had a long, close-up look at the Communist military organization. He concluded that the Communists had the support of the populace, that they had effectively organized the peasantry, that their fighting men were exceptionally durable, disciplined and highly motivated, that the leadership was "the most realistic, well-knit, and tough-minded group in China."

The explanation of Communist success with the peasantry was simple. The Chinese peasantry, about 90 percent of the population, was traditionally apolitical. The government and soldiery had been something to be suffered, something to be endured, not something in which one participated. The Japanese invaders would have been received with little or no more resentment than Nationalist or provincial Chinese troops had the Japanese behaved themselves in their relations with the peasantry. But they did not. Their wanton pillaging, destruction, violation of females and slaughter drove the surviving population to furious despair. These people were then receptive to the Communists who came to them and told them not to despair, that with the help of the Communists they must organize, become strong, resist and eventually win out. The party cadres and the military treated the individual peasant with respect, elicited his opinions, urged his participation in decisions and won him over. And the overwhelming emphasis was on nationalism and resistance against the alien invader, not on Communism and revolution.

Emmerson put his knowledge of the Japanese language to use interviewing Japanese prisoners of war and gathering information on Communist techniques in reeducating their POWs. In Burma he had been active in psychological warfare operations, and during the siege of Myitkyina, from just behind the front lines, he had broadcast to the enemy through an improvised public address system. The Japanese were, however, particularly resistant to propaganda. The two hundred or so prisoners taken in North Burma were almost all captured only because they were incapacitated by wounds or disease.

Once taken, though, and because they were humanely treated, the Japanese POWs in northern Burma were remarkably compliant. As they had been indoctrinated to die rather than surrender, no specific rules existed restricting what they might say and do after capture. But that they were alive and prisoners rather than dead and heroes meant that they were indelibly disgraced. At least initially, they declared that they were too ashamed to return to Japan, even if they could. They were beginning a new life and in trying to make the best of a dreadful fate, they sought acceptance by their captors. Emmerson and a small group of thoroughly admirable nisei—from Merrill's Marauders and the OWI psychological warfare teams—understood the mentality of the POWs and dealt with them so persuasively that the prisoners participated in the production of propaganda material directed to their former comrades.

Consequently, Emmerson arrived at Yenan with experience in the matter of POWs. The Communists invited him to inspect their POW operation. It assumed the guise of an educational institution—what they called a workers and peasants school. It was indeed education in the sense that its function was to indoctrinate the POWs. The Communists were going a step beyond the rest of us. They not only interrogated the prisoners for intelligence and consulted them in the preparation of propaganda; they also undertook to convert the captives to Communism, to make them over into revolutionaries.

In charge of this program was a cosmopolitan, mild-looking Japanese known as Okano Susumu, but whose real name was Nosaka Sanzo. He had been the Japanese Communist Party's delegate to the Comintern. Nosaka appeared to have had considerable success in converting his charges, who strolled over unescorted in twos and threes to our dude ranch to answer graciously the questions courteously posed to them by our order of battle intelligence office. In his *The Japanese Thread*, Emmerson recounts his unique adventures with Japanese POWs in India, Burma and Nationalist China and with Nosaka and the boarders at the workers and peasants prep school.

Because of what he had known of Japanese psychology, reinforced by the additional insight that he gained from interviews with POWs, Emmerson looked upon the policy of unconditional surrender as ensuring prolonged Japanese resistance and unnecessary American casualties. In August 1944 he recommended to the State Department that the Japanese should be publicly reassured that, in effect, surrender did not mean extermination and that the Emperor might be retained. Only the Emperor could command, without question, that the Japanese armed forces cease fire and surrender. Emmerson was one of the very few American officials who had the vision and courage to take this position more than a year before the war's end. His recommendation was passed to Hopkins. I do not know whether Roosevelt saw it. In any event, Roosevelt did not modify his unconditional surrender terms and Truman refused to give any assurances regarding the Emperor or even follow up on Japanese peace overtures.

Directed at those who balked at reading any memorandum longer than one page, I wrote in early November three summaries in reply to: how red were the Chinese Communists, what was their attitude toward the great powers, and would they take over China?

My estimate of the redness of the Chinese Communists was affected by my assumption that belief in a creed is susceptible to withering, decay and perversion. The Chinese Communists were backsliders, I said, and would return to revolutionary ardor only if driven to it by domestic and foreign pressure. In this paper I obviously underestimated the commitment of the Chinese Communist ruling party at that time to ideology and the dexterity with which Mao and company manipulated it. At the same time, if I was correct in my supposition that in the oligarchy two latent factions existed—doctrinaires headed by Mao and pragmatic moderates potentially under some of the generals—an American policy of collaboration with the Communists would probably at least have exposed the schism and strengthened the moderate elements. While this is speculative, what did happen is not. The American government behaved as Marxism-Leninism predicted and the doctrinaires triumphed, able to claim the rightness of doctrine.

"Confident in their own strength," I wrote on the subject of Yenan and the great powers, "the Communists no longer feel that their survival or extinction depends upon foreign aid or attack . . . The Communists recognize, of course, that the powers can accelerate or impede their expansion." As for their relations with the Soviet Union, a subject on which I had probed them, they professed to believe that there was no issue over which they would be at odds with Moscow. They claimed that when the Soviet Union entered the war against Japan it would not seek dominance over them and that they expected Moscow to yield Outer Mongolia to them. To both of these assertions I had responded with incredulity.

The Communist attitude toward the British was particularly stereotyped—the traditional imperialistic power that would side with Chiang against them. The United States, I wrote, was their great hope, as Mao had made evident to Service. It was also their greatest fear "because the more aid we give Chiang exclusively the greater the likelihood of his precipitating a civil war and the more protracted and costly will be the Communist unification of China."

Were the Communist goings to take over China? Yes. They had come to control some 850,000 square kilometers with a population of about ninety million. Only if he were "able to enlist foreign intervention on a scale equal to the Japanese invasion of China will Chiang probably be able to crush the Communists." But that seemed unlikely. The Communists were already politically and militarily too strong for him. "The Communists are in China to stay. And China's destiny is not Chiang's but theirs."

CHAPTER XVIII

COMMUNISTS VERSUS NATIONALISTS VERSUS HURLEY

Hurley unexpectedly arrived at Yenan on the headquarters aircraft on November 7, 1944. He was nattily garbed in the uniform of a major general, a costume to which he was much attached. Looking over the welcoming throng, Hurley was moved to give forth with a Choctaw war whoop. The rustic Reds were unacquainted with the customs of American aborigines and so were mystified by the prolonged howl. However, they showed no signs of surprise, probably dismissing the ululation as only another manifestation of outlandish foreign behavior.

The Choctaw war whoop was a part of Hurley's public personality. He exulted in his humble, Oklahoman origins and the dialect, folk wisdom and mannerisms of the frontier. His more flamboyant displays of mesquite, tomahawk and six-shooter culture were reverse snobbism meant to defy and shock effete easterners and Europeans, who he suspected looked down their noses at him. They were also a showman's bid for the attention and applause of paler sorts.

While en route to Yenan I had written to Hurley urging him to come to Dixie to form an independent, first-hand opinion of the Communist leaders. My plea was superfluous. During the time that he was supposed to be harmonizing relations between Chiang and Stilwell, he also interested himself in harmonizing relations between Chiang and the Communists.

The first of these missions of reconciliation was specifically assigned to him by the President. I do not know of any document directing Hurley to essay the second. It would have been in character, however, had Hurley told the President before leaving for Chungking that he would undertake to bring the two sides of China together. And it would have been wholly in the expansive, off-hand Rooseveltian character to tell Hurley orally to go ahead. This would have been not unlike FDR's telling Stilwell and me that we were both Ambassadors—political blather meant to send the auditor on his way feeling good. Unfortunately, those with distended egos, such as Hurley, Nelson and Roosevelt's crass personal representative in India in 1942, Louis Johnson, took advantage of the President's flummery as license to do as they pleased.

Hurley arrived at Yenan thinking that to bring Chiang's Kuomintang and the Communists together was not much different from persuading Republicans and Democrats to accept bipartisanship in a time of national crisis. He brought with him a document defining a basis for agreement between the two sides, drafted by himself with assists from two of Chiang's subordinates. It provided for military unification, Chiang's supremacy in the government, legalization of the Communist Party, and "government of the people, for the people, and by the people."

Feeling that Hurley had his hopes much too high, I warned him shortly after his arrival against expecting the Communists to agree to what was acceptable to Chiang. I told him that they would be hard bargainers. Hurley seemed surprised at what I said and resentful of my cautioning. He indicated that he wished to conduct negotiations with the Communists by himself and that I should return to Chungking on the plane departing the next day. I did so. He also took offense at a similar attempt by Teddy White to prepare him for what he might encounter in his negotiations with the Communists. In a written record of White's attempt to be helpful, Hurley twisted what White had told him and accused the correspondent of being "against the mission with which I am charged."

At his first of three meetings with the top Communists, Hurley was taken aback when Mao explained the depth of differences between the Kuomintang government and the Communists. What he heard was so far from what he fancied the situation in China to be that he explained that Mao's statements were similar to what China's enemies were saying. On the basis of this tactless sally, Hurley turned to his self-imposed mission and complained that "it was asking too much to ask an outsider like him to do all of the work in fixing an agreement." But if Mao would work with him, he later conceded, and they could get Chiang to work with them, then the three of them could unify China.

The Communists accepted Hurley's invitation to put forward their terms. These were, in essence, Communist participation in the central government, in military as well as civil affairs, and a fair distribution of foreign aid. These claims seemed modest enough to Hurley—after all, Henry Stimson, Frank Knox and he himself, all Republicans, were participating wholeheartedly in an administration headed by a Democrat. What he did not understand was that the concept of a loyal opposition did not exist in China and that Chiang's system of balancing off a variety of competing opportunists could not survive the introduction of western democracy with its free-for-all popular participation, particularly when one of the competing forces would be a dynamic, proliferating, disciplined organization determined to destroy that system and seize power.

Eager to contribute to what he hoped would be a magna carta of a new China, Hurley embellished his expropriation from Lincoln. He now pledged the proposed national coalition government to establish freedom of conscience, speech, the press, and assembly, the right of writ of habeas corpus and many other good things, including freedom from fear and want. This inventory of political virtues and platitudes pleased the Reds mightily. Not that they would abide by them in the sense meant by Hurley. Rather, they could endorse them and leave it to an exultant Hurley to deliver the package to Chiang as an agreed Hurley-Communist position. The Generalissimo would, of course, reject the proposal and in so doing appear to be what the Communists always accused him of being—anti-democratic. Meanwhile, smug in their caves and on the side of Hurley's angels, the Communists could entertain themselves with thoughts of Chiang's and Hurley's discomfiture.

And so it was. Returning to Chungking, Hurley sent Soong on November 11 a copy, for the Generalissimo, of the Hurley-Mao Proposal. Hurley had been so pleased with his historic authorship that he had signed the effusion in duplicate, persuaded a willing Mao to do likewise, and assured the Communists that their demands had not only his support but also that of the President of the United States. Soong was appalled by the document and rushed to tell Hurley, at home with a cold, that he had been "sold a bill of good by the Communists" and that the Government would never give the Communists what they asked for.

Two days later, still afflicted with a cold, Hurley filled me in on his activities. He said that the Government wanted the negotiations to be kept secret as the Communists had put it in an embarrassing position. The proposals were fair, he continued, and if the negotiations broke down it would be the Government's fault. Hurley believed that Chiang was willing to make a deal with the Communists but those around him were thwarting his wishes. Soong, whom he called a "crook," was the principal obstructionist, he said. To my surprise Hurley stated that as a condition for the removal of Stilwell, the Generalissimo undertook to come to an agreement with the Communists. I reported the substance of this conversation in a letter to John Carter Vincent.

It took that "crook," T.V. Soong, and the Generalissimo barely more than a week to get Hurley back on the reservation. The trio then concocted a counter proposal to the Hurley-Mao beatitudes. It provided that the Communists hand over to Chiang's government control over all of their forces. When Chou En-lai, then in Chungking, reacted unfavorably to the counter proposal, Hurley enlisted Wedemeyer and Major General Robert B. McClure, Wedemeyer's Chief of Staff, to join him in trying, futilely, to prevail upon Chou to accept the Hurley-Chiang proposition. Thus, in voluntarily enmeshing himself further in the treacherous internal feud between Chiang and the Communists, Hurley improperly and unnecessarily also involved the American military.

Failing to change Chou's mind, Hurley sent Colonel Barrett, who was temporarily at Chungking, back to Yenan on December 8 to argue Mao into acceptance of the Hurley-Chiang position. Mao pointed out the obvious—the Communists would not give up control of their army, their only means of self-defense. He also observed that Hurley had written much of the verbiage of their joint proposal, had urged him, Mao, to join in signing the document, and "much as we would dislike to do this, there may come a time when we feel we should show this document, with signatures, to the Chinese and foreign press." When Barrett reported to Hurley the failure of his efforts, culminating in Mao's threat of publicity, Hurley raged that Mao had tricked him.

Hurley was now, a month after his feckless plunge into personal mediation, thoroughly entangled and exploited by both sides. He was contemptuous of Gauss because the former Ambassador had circumspectly avoided involving himself and the American Government in the machinations of internal Chinese politics. Driven by vanity, ignorance, gullibility and recklessness Hurley would not withdraw to a detached position.

*   *   *

The Generalissimo and Soong were satisfied with Roosevelt's personal representative. To be sure, Hurley had at first championed Stilwell against them and had been beguiled by Molotov and Mao. But Soong, familiar with Americans, had sized up Hurley, recognized his weaknesses—vanity, suspicion and ignorance—and with the Generalissimo won him over in the command crisis regarding Stilwell. The envoy's recommendations to Roosevelt that Stilwell be recalled had so commended Hurley to Chiang and his brother-in-law that they asked the President to assign him on a more permanent basis, adding that "Because of his rare knowledge of human nature, and his approach to the problem, he seems to get on well with the Communist leaders."

Indeed he did, initially. It was a warning to Chiang and Soong how mercurial and impressionable Hurley was. Soong kept close tabs on the envoy and was hostile to any influence on Hurley that might be less than unquestioning in praise of the Chiang regime. He regarded me as in that category, if for no other reason than my association with Stilwell.

"Your intimate knowledge of the situation there," Roosevelt radioed Hurley on November 17, "both from the military and diplomatic standpoints . . . eminently qualifies you" to be Ambassador to China. And so Hurley, agreeing with the President's assessment, accepted the appointment. The Ambassador apparent said to me two days later that he wished to have me on his staff. He proposed to oust from the ambassadorial residence the five Embassy staff members whom Gauss, in Chungking's housing shortage, had generously invited to stay with him. In their place he would install my wife and me—Patricia to be flown from New Delhi to Chungking. This cozy arrangement did not materialize because, with a Japanese offensive westward, Hurley thought it advisable to postpone her arrival.

I did not take seriously Hurley's invitation to join his staff. Wedemeyer had already accepted my three colleagues and me on the same basis that we had served Stilwell. However, other moves were afoot. I had heard informally from Washington that I was to be detached from Wedemeyer and assigned to an unnamed Near Eastern consular post. This rumor originated from a November 8 State Department request that the Army release my colleagues and me for reassignment to regular Foreign Service duty. Wedemeyer acceded in the case of Ludden. As for Service, Emmerson and me, Stimson wrote on November 22 to the Acting Secretary of State, "General Wedemeyer indicates that it is his conviction that unless these three officers are retained, military activities will be hampered."

The report that I was to be sent to a Near Eastern consular post had disturbed me. I envisioned Basra or Aden and assumed that the assignment was a punitive one. I was of a mind to resign from the Foreign Service. In a kindly, avuncular role, Hurley said that I should not resign, that he knew my type, I was a rebel, and that the State Department was "full of pole-sitters" and that my services were needed in the government.

Years later I learned that it was my friend in the State Department, John Carter Vincent, who had instigated the request for my transfer, probably with my best interests at heart, and that the post that he had in mind for me was Colombo. Nothing came of his benevolence because of Wedemeyer's unsparing certification that were Emmerson, Service and I taken from the General, the prosecution of the war against Japan would be adversely affected.

Meanwhile, Hurley told me on several occasions that Soong was urging him to get me out of China. Hurley said to me on November 13 that he was aware that Soong was an intriguer, playing on personalities, attempting to put him off the track "chasing rabbits"—accusations against various American and Chinese officials. Hurley's ready mistrust of others, however, led him at least to half-believe the allegations purveyed to him.

So it was with a whopper that Soong planted with Hurley—that I had confided to Soong—that Wedemeyer was "fascist-minded." Hurley, of course, relayed this choice tidbit to the General and then to me. I went to Wedemeyer to assure him that Soong was engaged in provocation. He said that he had been hurt to think that I might have spoken thus of him. The poison had taken a little, not only with Hurley, also with Wedemeyer.

Hurley put credence in another Soong fabrication—the Foreign Minister had "received intelligence from Yenan" that I had told the Communists that I sent Service to Washington to recommend, in conjunction with Stilwell, American withdrawal of recognition from the National Government and recognition of the Communists. My denial of Soong's story seemed to quiet Hurley's more aggressive suspicions. But after this, again and again, he took at face value Chinese Government "intelligence reports from Yenan." They were for the most part produced by Tai Li's secret police and as such regarded by experienced foreign observers as, at best, suspect.

* * *

Unlike Stilwell, Hurley was not receptive to differing opinion, as I discovered in our encounter at Yenan. Therefore in conversation with him I tried to express in subdued terms my disagreement with his assumptions that he could bring about agreement between the Chiang regime and the Communists. But in my memoranda for Wedemeyer I felt bound to go on record less circumspectly. I sent copies of these memoranda to Hurley.

Shortly after Hurley returned from Yenan, I wrote on November 15 that "We should not now abandon Chiang Kai-shek." However, "we must not indefinitely underwrite a politically bankrupt regime." Hurley was attempting, I continued, to bring Chiang and the Communists together in a coalition government. This was the most desirable solution (certainly preferable to a civil war into which the United States might be drawn). But if the two sides would not be brought together, we would have to choose one or the other.

Meanwhile time was running out, especially if the Soviet Union was going to join the war against Japan. "While being careful to preserve the Generalissimo's 'face,'" we should urgently expand our relations with Yenan and try to "capture politically" the Chinese Communists rather than watching them "go by default wholly to the Russians." We could not expect, of course, to win over the Communists entirely to us should the Russians invade North China and Manchuria, but through wartime and postwar aid we could influence them toward Chinese nationalism and independence from the Soviet Union.

In retrospect, the idea of politically capturing the Chinese Communists was unrealistic. It reflected my underestimation of the Communists' commitment to ideology. Better grounded was the calculation that American aid to the Chinese Communists, who I assumed would take over China in any event, could free them of material dependence on the Soviet Union and thereby reduce the Kremlin's influence on them.

My estimate that a coalition government was preferable to its alternative—civil war—did not lead me to believe that it might be attainable. Early in December I wrote, with a copy to Hurley, that Chiang would not accept the Communist terms for a coalition government, knowing that such a government would sooner or later wrest power from him. As for the Communists, they would not accept less than their own terms. For Chiang and his Kuomintang were in decline. In time the Communists would take over.

On December 12, after Hurley reached an impasse in his endeavors to bring about agreement, I noted that the deadlock—or renewed dragging negotiations—meant that the Generalissimo would continue to deny us exploitation of the strategically advantageous position occupied by the Communists in North China and our activating military collaboration with them. As the war was costing us heavily, we could be justified in telling Chiang that we would work with and supply "whatever Chinese forces we believe can contribute most to the war against Japan." We should also advise the Generalissimo that we should not aid any unit showing an inclination toward starting civil conflict and that, as he was head of the recognized government, we would inform him of supplies we distributed, including those to Communist units.

Because my memoranda were unpalatable to Hurley and also because he rarely asked for advice from those around him, I was surprised on December 13 when he invited me to comment on a message he was drafting to Washington reporting on Mao's rejection of the Hurley-Chiang counterproposal to the Communists. Hurley's draft was matter-of-fact and uncharacteristically cautious—he did not think that further negotiations were impossible. I had little to suggest.

*   *   *

In reply to my October request for a transfer to the Embassy at Moscow, Chip Bohlen radioed me in mid-December from the Department saying that Averell Harriman, then Ambassador to the Soviet Union, was expecting me in Moscow. Although I had thought of moving to the Moscow

Embassy in the late winter or spring, Soong's hostility to me and his influence over Hurley made me wonder whether I could function usefully and whether I should no longer delay joining Harriman's staff. Furthermore, for me the Chinese scene had become rancid, the American Government incapable of constructive action in China, and the course of events foredoomed. The time had come for me to move on.

I informed Hurley of Bohlen's message. He said that I should proceed to Moscow promptly rather than wait until February. That he wished to speed me on my way did not take me aback. I had become accustomed to sudden shifts in his attitude and temper. Only shortly before this he had regaled me with an account of Soong's badgering him to get rid of me and how he told the Foreign Minister that he intended to have my wife and me share his residence, and how he then enjoyed watching "T.V. squirm." Soong's persistent nagging about me nevertheless affected him. And my lack of enthusiasm and optimism over his ventures did not recommend me to him. As he wanted me out of Yenan when he was there, so he now wanted me out of Chungking. Bohlen's message, for his purposes, arrived at a propitious time.

My transfer to Moscow, Hurley said, should be kept secret, as knowledge of it would make Soong unhappy. I assumed that Hurley's concern for Soong's feelings sprang from a futile wish to conceal from the Foreign Minister that I was not being exiled to some obscure post but would be going to an assignment in which I might still be having something to do with Chinese affairs. More significantly, Hurley revealed a psychological weakness in his relationship with Soong, a feeling that he needed to curry favor with the Foreign Minister. He said he would tell Soong that, in accordance with Soong's wishes, I was being returned for transfer. He had recommended Stilwell's departure; he would now counterfeit mine.

Having confided to me his little stratagem for ingratiating himself with the Foreign Minister, Hurley informed me shortly thereafter, on December 15, of certain maneuvers by Soong against me that apparently entertained the Ambassador. The Foreign Minister was pressing him, Hurley said, to have Joseph Alsop transferred from Chennault to the Ambassador. Roaring with laughter, he continued, "T.V. figures that you know too much, he wants to set up his own pipeline to me."

This was the second time that Hurley had treated me to the story about Soong and Alsop—his memory was slipping and so he tended to be repetitious. After we enjoyed the joke anew, the Ambassador received a telephone call from Colonel Barrett, who was to leave that morning for Yenan. I also spoke to Barrett, with Hurley standing close by, and made detailed arrangements for joining him on the drive to the airport. As a third person entered the room at the end of my conversation, I did not for security reasons state explicitly to Hurley that I was flying to Yenan, assuming that he would deduce as much from what I said to Barrett. I soon took my leave, saying I would return in two or three days. The Ambassador made no comment.

I went to Yenan to get a quick last impression of the Communist oligarchy before going to Moscow, and to learn what the Communists might have regarding a rumor of a tacit non-aggression agreement between the Japanese and the Nationalists. It was a routine trip made as a member of Wedemeyer's staff and was unconnected with Hurley's dealing with the Communists. I was cordially received at Yenan, conversed in general terms with Mao, Chou and other dominant Communists, and was again impressed by their intelligence, force and self-confidence. Chou thought that the Japanese and Chiang's regime might have a tacit understanding to refrain from offensive operations, but he had no firm evidence to support this opinion.

On December 18, the day after I returned from Yenan, I called on Hurley, who upbraided me for going there without first consulting him. He said shortly after I left, Soong had telephoned to say that I had gone to Yenan (our movements were closely watched by government agents). Hurley denied that I had left. Thereafter he learned that I had indeed departed for Dixie. Consequently, he fumed to me, he was in an embarrassing position. He had to admit to the Foreign Minister that he had been in error and also try to persuade Soong that he had not been attempting deliberately to deceive him. The Foreign Minister had evidently succeeded in the age-old ploy of putting someone on the defensive through imputing dishonorable motives to an innocent mistake.

In brief, I explained that it had not occurred to me that he did not realize that I was going to Yenan and that, in any event, I went there under standing authority from Wedemeyer. I expressed regret at not having explicitly informed him of my plans. The Ambassador then intimated that I had gone to Yenan to interfere in the Chiang-Communist negotiations. I replied that I had not asked anyone about the negotiations. Hurley seemed to be mollified by what I had said.

On the following day I saw the Ambassador by chance. He declared that Chiang had that morning indicated a wish to reach an understanding with the Communists despite the opposition of such "reactionaries" as Soong. Consequently, Hurley concluded amiably enough in what seemed to me to be a non sequitur, he was the more in favor of my move to Moscow and soon.

It had become abundantly clear that Soong's incitement of Hurley against me and the Ambassador's eager susceptibility to the Foreign Minister's goading meant that my position had become untenable. On December 19 I told Wedemeyer as much. I asked that he release me for transfer to the Embassy in Moscow. My request apparently took Wedemeyer by surprise. As he had been absorbed in a welter of military problems, I had previously refrained from filling him in on Soong's and Hurley's petty intrigues against me. The General said that I should not leave because of Soong and hoped that I would remain with him. Wedemeyer finally agreed to my transfer and wrote to me thanking me for efficient and loyal service.

Unaware that my transfer was in process and that I was only awaiting formal travel orders, Soong continued to excite Hurley against me. After lunch with the Ambassador on December 22, he accused me of having attempted on my last visit to Yenan to wreck the Chiang-Communist negotiations. The Foreign Minister had revealed to him that he, Soong, had received an "intelligence report from Yenan" to the effect that I had advised the top Communists not to take Hurley seriously because he was "an old fool." This piece of provocation was false. But it had a plausible ring because, along with most who had come to know him in China, I regarded Hurley as less than sagacious. Ridicule of the Ambassador was increasing— one American correspondent said to me that he wondered whether Hurley was senile all of the time or only part of the time. On the other hand, neither I nor anyone I knew thought that Hurley need not be taken seriously. We were all acutely aware of his power.

This cleverly planted incitement by Soong was impossible to disprove. An attempt to do so could have led to the ultimate absurdity of an affidavit from Mao denying that I had told the Yenan oligarchs to disregard Hurley, as he was an old fool—and who would believe that? At the same time, even had Soong's allegations been true, it would have also been impossible to prove them unless one began by believing, as Hurley apparently did, that Tai Li's agents had penetrated the inner circle of the Chinese Communist Party. But no one who was familiar with Chinese realities believed that.

After explaining anew the circumstances of my visit to Yenan, I asked what motive could I have for wishing to double-cross him, especially as he had so favored me. This prompted Hurley to catalogue the instances of his goodness to me. And now I had done this to him. He had a good mind to break my back. He had tried to convince the Foreign Minister that he had not purposely misled him. "I got my tits caught in a wringer on that one," the Ambassador reproachfully exclaimed. And it was my fault that he found himself in that predicament. After more patient exposition by me, Hurley remarked that he would take his afternoon nap and to consider the matter closed.

During this interchange I had told Hurley that I considered that Soong was manipulating him. But how could that be that the Ambassador was made the cat's-paw of a man whom he had described to me as a liar, crook and double-crosser, whose lines were so tangled that he regularly met himself coming back? The explanation, it seemed to me, was grounded in Hurley's befuddled entrapment in the alien and deceptive task to which he had committed himself with such incautious flamboyance. As his endeavors to unite the incompatible repeatedly came to naught, he could not bring himself to admit that his discomfiture was caused by his own folly. His vanity demanded an external excuse.

Soong at least sensed and probably understood all of this. With his excellent command of English, his position as Foreign Minister and, in Madame Chiang's absence from Chungking, virtually the sole intermediary between Hurley and the Generalissimo, he was also in a strong position to exploit the Ambassador's vulnerability. And although Hurley mistrusted Soong, he had become deeply dependent upon this clever, forceful man and susceptible to his persistent influence.

Soong deflected from the National Government Hurley's search for the cause of his frustrations and directed it against the Communists and me. But because the Ambassador hesitated to antagonize the Communists, as one of the parties to his hoped for reconciliation, he accepted Soong's imputations that I was the cause of his disappointed expectations. This was the excuse he needed to preserve his conceit—the unification of China by Hurley was being sabotaged by me. Hurley adopted T. V. Soong's fake accusations notwithstanding his belief that the Foreign Minister was perfidious and bent on having me ejected from China because "T.V. figures you know too much."

*   *   *

Among the points made by Hurley in a year-end roundup to the Secretary of State was that his mission was to "sustain" Chiang and "unify all the military forces of China." Civil war, he continued, had been thought inevitable. But since his arrival, "Chiang is now convinced that by agreement with the Communist Party of China he can (1) unite the military forces against Japan and (2) avoid civil strife in China."

The Nationalists and the Communists differed little, if at all, in principles, Hurley went on. "The greatest opposition to the unification of China comes from foreigners." Among them were "some American military and diplomatic officers who believe that the present Chinese Government will eventually collapse and that there can be no military or political unification of China under Chiang Kai-shek." Misrepresenting forewarnings as advocacy, Hurley declared that these Americans believed that the Communists "should" not unite with the Nationalists nor "permit" unification of Communist troops with the Chinese Army. They also believed, he alleged, that the American Government should deal with the Communists but not the National Government.

At a big Christmas party at the Embassy, Hurley lifted a glass to me and boomed, "Here's to you, John." I took this to be a gesture befitting the season. On his departure he said that he was going to stop harassing me. "And you do the same with me." Between his toast and farewell, the Ambassador bound to the back of his head a sprig of evergreen, substituting for a feather and, yelping Choctaw war whoops, led a snake dance around the room.

Before leaving Chungking I estimated on January 4 how the Kremlin might view the situation in China. With "sardonic satisfaction," I thought, watching the Chiang regime decay, the Communists expand and the United States frustrated. If the American refusal of military cooperation with the Communists meant that the nationalistic elements in Yenan lost prestige and "those doctrinaires favoring reliance upon the Soviet Union have been further strengthened, the Kremlin doubtless knows it." It also probably recognized that American cooperation with the Chinese Communists could work to the advantage of the United States. But Moscow might well doubt that Washington would "exploit these conditions so favorable to it" because of American hostility to Communists and attachment to an illusory Chiang. It was

unlikely that American policy can be anything other than a vacillating compromise between realism and wishful thinking ... By our unwillingness and inability to engage in realpolitik . . . the Kremlin may well believe, we stand to lose that what we seek: the quickest possible defeat of Japan and a united, strong and independent China. And the Soviet Union may stand to gain . . . a satellite North China. The Kremlin is not likely to be unaware of what is at stake in this situation—the future balance of power in Asia and the Western Pacific.

My joyless musings went to the Department of State, where, I later learned, John Carter Vincent circulated them upward in the bureaucracy without, so far as I know, comment by him or reactions from others. Aware that my opinions would vex Hurley, I nevertheless as a matter of course, sent a copy of the paper to him. There was no response.

To say goodbye, I called on Wedemeyer and Hurley on the morning of my departure, January 9. In my farewell to the Ambassador I wished him luck in his endeavors. As I recall the occasion, I also said that I hoped that he would not be entrapped by Chinese intrigue in case his negotiations failed. His career had been so distinguished that this would be a deplorable culmination.

Hurley flushed, then turned florid and puffy. He would break my back, His Excellency roared. "You want to pull the plug on Chiang Kai-shek," he shouted over and over again. Indignantly I remonstrated with him. But Hurley was in no mood for reason, the tantrum had to run its course. It did and ended with a civil handshake. I took off for India and, eventually, with Patricia, for Moscow.

Shortly after I left, Hurley professed to have learned for the first time that at the instance of Wedemeyer's Chief of Staff, Major General McClure, Colonel Barrett, and Colonel Willis H. Bird of OSS had discussed at Yenan possible military plans for modest American cooperation with the Communists. He flew into a rage, radioed the President and, in effect, accused McClure, Barrett and Bird of plotting behind his back, wrecking his negotiations and giving the Communists reasons to go around him. An official American investigation disposed of the Ambassador's slander.

January 1945 was a galling month for Hurley. A third incident riled him. Mao and Chou indicated to the ranking American military officer at Yenan that they wished to be received in Washington for an interview with Roosevelt. They asked that Hurley not be informed of their request. The Mao-Chou overture was referred to the theater headquarters where Wedemeyer, quite properly, showed it to the Ambassador. This evoked the predictable outburst and dark suspicions of the luckless officer who had forwarded the Yenan message. Hurley suppressed the Mao-Chou request.

Hurley was now embarked on a course which soon led to his purge of some of the more outspoken Foreign Service officers, domineering even those who remained, and prohibition of reports to Washington in any way critical of the Chiang regime. By spring, Edwin F. Stanton, the senior official in the Department dealing with Chinese affairs, declared that "We can no longer count on receiving factual and objective reports" from the Embassy.

John Paton Davies, Jr.
(JPD) with wet nurse, Fu Ta
Niang, circa 1908.

Omei Shan, circa 1915. The
Reverend John P. Davies,
Sr. (far left) and JPD
(center), along with fellow
missionaries.

Family portrait, circa 1918. From left: JPD, John P. Davies, Sr., Helen MacNeill Davies, and Donald Davies.

At JPD's apartment in Hankow, summer 1938. Left to right: Agnes Smedley, Frank Dorn, F. McCracken Fisher, unidentified Chinese military spokesman (partially hidden), Jack Belden, A. T. Steele (Chicago Daily News), Captain Evans Carlson (USMC), Freda Utley, Chang Han-fu, and JPD.

Vice Consul Asahina and JPD at a Japanese officers rest house in Wucheng, Kiangsi, August 1939.

JPD (holding spear given to him by the Nagas), William T. Stanton, and Eric Sevareid in September 1943 after surviving trek through the Burmese jungle.

Lieutenant General Joseph W. Stilwell with some of his staff. JPD is to Stillwell's left.

JPD in Yennan in October 1944 with, left to right, Chou En-lai, Chu Teh, JPD, Mao Tse-tung, and Yeh Chien-ying.

The American delegation at the Moscow meeting of foreign ministers, December 1945. Front row, left to right: James B. Conant, Benjamin Cohen, James F. Byrnes, W. Averell Harriman. Standing: unidentified colonel, JPD, John Carter Vincent, Edward Page, H. Freeman Mathews, Charles E. Bohlen.

JPD and his wife, Patricia Grady Davies, at their apartment in Moscow in 1946.

JPD in Washington
on November 6,
1954, the day after
being fired by
Secretary of State
John Foster Dulles.

Patricia Davies and
JPD in Lima in 1961
with one of their
Monoprints used in
a British Overseas
Airway Corporation
poster.

JPD in the sunroom of the family's Lima home with some of the more whimsical furniture he crafted behind him.

The Davies family in their Lima living room, 1962. From left: Susan, John, Patricia, Tiki, Sasha. Jennifer is lounging on the rug and JPD is holding Deborah.

JPD and Patricia at their Estilo
s.a. factory in Lima in 1962.

A family portrait taken by
JPD in Lima, 1963. Back
row: Susan, Tiki, John, Sasha.
Front row: Deborah, Patricia
with Megan on her lap, and
Jennifer.

PART V

MOSCOW NIGHTS AND DAYS

CHAPTER XIX

POSTED TO MOSCOW

Coming from India, Patricia and I had traveled by way of sunlit Tehran, Baku brooding shabbily by the Caspian, and devastated skeletal Stalingrad. Now on March 25, 1945, in a Soviet C-47, we came in through the snowy murk for a power landing at Moscow's Vnukova airport. It was like entering a mine—dark, chill, musty and faintly ominous.

This was Patricia's first visit to the Soviet Union. I had traversed the country twice. It was on my second transit of the Soviet Union, in 1937, that on a brief stopover in Moscow I had met, at the American Embassy, George F. Kennan. Now, eight years later, I was back in Moscow. And so was Kennan. He was Minister Counselor, second in command to the Ambassador.

W. Averell Harriman was one of those rare chiefs of mission who not only communicated directly with, but was also taken seriously and listened to by, the White House: Franklin D. Roosevelt and Harry Hopkins. Born to great wealth, Harriman was driven to public service by compulsions of noblesse oblige, ambition and a conclusion that public life is more exciting than making more money. No one in the Embassy was more conscientiously absorbed in his job and worked longer hours than the Ambassador. He occupied himself with unquestioning implementation of Roosevelt's wartime policy toward the Soviet Union, for he was by nature a doer, a man of action rather than an interpretive reporter.

Harriman hospitably took us in at his residence, Spaso House, for several weeks until our assigned quarters were ready. Spaso House was a hive of rooms on two floors encircling a rotunda whose supporting pillars were of lath and plaster, masquerading as marble. Other occupants of Spaso House were the Ambassador's estimable daughter, Kathleen, of about the same age as Patricia, and several bachelor staff members. But the house was more than a residence, for Harriman did most of his work there, either in his bedroom or in a comfortable office on the second floor. He rarely used his office at the chancery where, under Kennan's guidance, the rest of us performed the business of the Embassy.

Among those who worked at the chancery was Patricia. As a wartime measure, Harriman had ruled that only if they accepted a job in the Embassy could Foreign Service wives come to Moscow. As wife of the Minister Counselor, warm, perceptive Annelise Kennan was an exception. Patricia was assigned to secretarial, filing and research tasks in the economic section. It was better than working for me for nothing at New Delhi. But, presumably because of the circumstances of her employment, her wages were set without regard to her qualifications or worth and at a rate barely above that of the menial Soviet hired help.

The advantage that the Government took of her rankled Patricia. A year and a half later I compounded the discrimination when, with the arrival of women clerks at the end of the war, I persuaded her to yield to one of them the research she ably did. She moved to toil in the code room—sheer drudgery—so that no one could say that she was the object of favoritism.

During our stay at Spaso House, Patricia and I rode to work every morning in an Embassy car driven by a Russian chauffeur. It was out the gates, past the Soviet militiaman standing guard, past women in wadded cotton coats, scarves over their heads, and felt boots shoveling snow into dump trucks, and along streets with little traffic, for cars were scarce. On the sidewalks, stooped men and women bundled in cloth overcoats, with fur hats or shawls on their heads, strode stolidly over caked ice and through thick slush. The buildings we passed were old, shabby and nondescript. Then, we saw the tall red walls of the Kremlin, its towers and spires. Into broad Mokhovaya Ulitsa we came. It was more than a boulevard; it was a glacis to the side of the Kremlin, a staging area for a few sections of the great parades through Red Square on the anniversary of the Revolution.

From Spaso House we soon moved to temporary quarters, a small apartment. I wrote to relatives in the United States,

Patricia and I usually go to work in the morning by subway where we rub shoulders with the Muscovites . . . an experience which never lacks interest—

everyone shabbily dressed, no gay faces, most people pasty-faced, no ani-
mated chatter, and always a feeling of primitive force despite malnutrition
and crushing burdens. The women are the amazing people of Russia . . . they
are seemingly as tough and husky as the men. Not big (for neither are the
men) but husky in the sense of amazing endurance. Even the gnarled, wiz-
ened little old women.

The chancery and a dozen or more small apartments for the staff occupied a shoddy seven story building on Mokhovaya Ulitsa facing the Kremlin
and, obliquely, Red Square and St. Basil's. Patricia and I were finally assigned an apartment on the sixth floor with a studio living room two stories
high, a small dining room, a kitchen, an upstairs bedroom and a narrow
balcony. The view from our dining room and bedroom was the Kremlin
and little else. At night the illuminated red star atop the tallest spire dominated our bit of firmament.

On the stair-landing outside our front door stood a bin into which in
the autumn bushels of cabbages and potatoes were dumped. This cache of
staples was meant to last us until late spring. With the wartime ration cards
issued to us by the Soviet authorities, our efficient cook, Maria, brought
supplementary foods from the limited range of the special grocery store
operated by the Soviet authorities for diplomats. A third source of supply
was an Embassy commissary austerely stocked with American canned, bot-
tled and cartoned necessities. Consequently, we fared adequately, although
we missed fresh vegetables and fruit.

In comparison with the Soviet citizenry, of course, we lived fabulously
well. Because of the war—but more fundamentally, also because of the
gross inefficiency of the Soviet economic system, particularly agriculture—
food shortages were appalling. Most of the population lived on black bread
and thin borscht. Meat was a rare luxury.

The difference between the underprivileged and overprivileged in the
Soviet Union was not as flagrant as it was between Calcutta beggars and
maharajahs. In part this was because poverty is not naked and so ulcerously
visible in the sub-arctic as it is in the sub-tropics. And then, the Soviet
upper crust did not practice conspicuous consumption to the extent that
the Indian princes did. Nevertheless, the banquets and receptions given by
the Soviet ruling class, out of the proletariat's sight, were in luxurious contrast to the average citizen's fare.

Official receptions milled around a huge buffet table in the center of a
large salon and beneath the obligatory chandelier. Covering the damask
tablecloth were platters heaped with meats, fish, pastries, caviar and other

luxury victuals. The early arriving guests surveyed and then mentally staked out positions at the table as they conversed perfunctorily and accepted glasses of cloying Soviet champagne. Drink in hand, each guest moved with solemn alacrity to the place at the buffet table closest to his favorite delicacies.

Once in position, it was vital to assume a firm stance—pelvis or abdomen braced against the table, feet planted apart, elbows defensively out. One had to be able to withstand the assaults of successive waves of guests while consuming what one had been able to pile on a plate, replenishing it, quaffing the champagne, and smiling and nodding to acquaintances who had also made it to the table's edge. When replete, it was necessary only to yield to the pressures on both sides to be squeezed out and away from the table.

The dignitary who arrived late could either forgo the hospitality or push, corkscrew and writhe through the heaving pack of Soviet and diplomatic elite to the groaning board. My practice was to have a quiet bite to eat at home and then join the festivities as a bystander. I missed eating all of the smoked salmon that I could devour. But then I did not lose any buttons or have sour cream smeared over my best dark suit.

*   *   *

As the only specialist on East Asia on the Embassy staff, my function initially was to watch and comment on Soviet relations with China and Japan. Some months later I was assigned supervision over all political reporting, including that on internal Soviet developments. Because so much of my work was novel to me and in the nature of unraveling the plot of a whodunit, I enjoyed my labors immensely.

My Moscow assignment was also an exhilarating, educational experience. This was due in a large measure to Kennan, who was not only a highly competent professional diplomat but also an exceptionally illuminative teacher. He had a scholar's knowledge of Russian culture and character. More than that, he possessed an intuitive flair that enriched and enlivened his understanding of the Soviet scene. Kennan's intellectual zest and his subtle insights, penetrating the Soviet phenomenon, found expression in fluent, stylish communication, both in writing and in conversation.

Absorbed with carrying out Roosevelt's policies, Harriman exhibited scant interest in Kennan's commentaries. They were not always explicitly related to winning the war, and their interpretations of Soviet motives, intentions and behavior were not uniformly in accord with the President's view. Kennan had an appreciative audience, however, in his subordinates and some of us served as a hone on which he sharpened his thoughts. As he edited our memoranda and reports, he gave some of us the privilege of going over and suggesting changes in drafts of his dispatches and telegrams. For my part, I found myself in agreement with Kennan's misgivings over Roosevelt's policy toward the Soviet Union. So here I was again, after disagreeing with our policy in China, differing with aspects of FDR's approach to Moscow.

Roosevelt's policy toward the Soviet Union was to help the Russians defeat the Germans and to persuade the Kremlin to help us defeat the Japanese. Defeat of these enemies meant to Roosevelt the imposition of unconditional surrender. This was to be followed promptly by the extirpation of Naziism, Prussian militarism and Japanese militarism. Meanwhile, the Russians were to be persuaded to collaborate with us—and the British and Chinese—in the creation of a world organization for maintaining a just and durable peace.

In Roosevelt's calculations, the fulfillment of this grand design depended on great power solidarity, meaning unity among Roosevelt, Stalin, Churchill and Chiang. For FDR, Stalin was the key personality because of the power that he was and represented and because he was the most standoffish. Roosevelt and Hopkins attributed Stalin's distrusting, unforthcoming attitude (and that of the entire Bolshevik hierarchy) largely to bruised feelings from the Russian Revolution and the formative years of the Soviet Union when the United States and other western powers intervened against the Bolsheviks.

In the White House view, great power solidarity therefore required, as a first step, that Stalin be disabused of his long-standing suspicions and brought to realize that we were sincerely friendly to the Soviet Union. The prescription for this was open-handed generosity in granting aid to the Soviet Union, no bargaining for reciprocal advantages, and support of certain territorial and other claims that Stalin told Roosevelt he wanted fulfilled. If we reposed trust in the Kremlin, the thinking was, that would beget trust of us in Stalin's heart.

Like so many American politicians, Roosevelt had inordinate confidence in the persuasiveness of his personal charm. He brought it to bear on Stalin and said privately that he thought the Soviet dictator was "gett-able." After the 1943 Tehran Conference of the Big Three, where with con-summate bad taste he sought to ingratiate himself with Stalin by joining the Bolshevik tyrant in baiting Churchill, he reported to the American people in a Christmas Eve fireside chat that "I got along fine with Marshal Stalin." Roosevelt went on, "I believe that he is truly representative of the heart and soul of Russia; and I believe that we are going to get along very well with him and the Russian people—very well indeed."

One reason for FDR's satisfaction over his relations with the Maximum Bolshevik may have been Stalin's assurance at Tehran that the Soviet Union intended to join the war against Japan. In the American Government, knowledge of this Kremlin purpose was a deep secret, knowledge of which was quite properly withheld from those who, like me, had no need to know of it. In retrospect, my exclusion was hardly crippling to the performance of my duties. For my evaluation of Soviet intentions continued to be based on assumptions that I had made in China in September 1943:

> There is no reason to cherish optimism regarding a voluntary Soviet contribution to our fight against Japan, whether in the shape of air bases or the early opening of a second front in Northeast Asia. The Russians may be expected to move against the Japanese when it suits their pleasure, which may not be until the final phases of the war—and then only in order to be able to participate in dictating terms to the Japanese and to establish new strategic frontiers.

Anticipating that these new strategic frontiers in the Far East would be to our disadvantage, I did not regard a Soviet entry into the war against Japan as an unalloyed blessing. Although I recognized that Soviet participation in that war would presumably reduce the cost to us of victory, in terms of American casualties, I saw no reason to try to coax or buy the Kremlin into belligerency against Japan. Rather, it seemed to me, that the Soviet Union could not be kept out of the war in East Asia. The only question was when it would act. And the answer to that was, when it wished to do so and no earlier.

Roosevelt, Churchill and Stalin met in February 1945 at Yalta. I was then en route from India to Moscow, and it was not until after the war that I learned what had transpired at the Yalta Conference. One subject dis-cussed there was the entry of the Soviet Union into the war against Japan.

Stalin undertook to do this two or three months after Germany surrendered, provided that certain conditions were met.

Stalin's desiderata, his bill for payment, were not notably modest. They included preservation of the status quo in Outer Mongolia, which was effectively a Soviet satellite, but claimed by China. He also asked for restitution of Russian "rights" lost to Japan in the Russo-Japanese War; return of the southern port of Sakhalin; and at the expense of Chinese pretensions, lease of the Port Arthur naval base; and Soviet preeminence in Dairen, the Chinese Eastern and South Manchurian railways. Revealing an interest in improving the Soviet position as a Pacific Ocean power, Stalin demanded the Kuril Islands.

Roosevelt and Churchill accepted Stalin's desiderata, Churchill perfunctorily as he considered the arrangement to be primarily an American-Soviet deal. The President agreed to Stalin's stipulation that, when advised by Stalin to do so, he would obtain the concurrence of Chiang to the requirements regarding Outer Mongolia and Manchuria. For his part, Stalin expressed a willingness to conclude a pact of friendship and alliance with Chiang.

Thus for what he intended to do anyway, whether paid or not, Stalin received Anglo-American blessings in advance of his real estate expropriations. And with the President accepting the role of bill collector, Stalin was spared the embarrassment (which he would have found supportable) of approaching the Generalissimo directly about Outer Mongolia and Manchuria. All in all it was an adroit performance, but not a strain on the Soviet autocrat's bargaining skills. For Roosevelt was willing to concede a great deal in the belief that by so doing he would accelerate the entry of the Soviet Union into the war against Japan.

The President was eager for this Soviet action largely because of the American Army's estimate of the high cost of subduing Japan. To be sure, the cost would be tremendously reduced if we relied on a prolonged naval blockade and air and naval attrition to force Japan's capitulation. But our Army believed that the American people, with their characteristic impatience for quick victories, would not tolerate such a protracted process. As the atomic bomb was, in early 1945, still an unknown factor, this left assault on Japan itself as the alternative. From excruciating experience, the Army anticipated fanatical resistance to American landings, exacting enormous losses. If, however, the Soviet Union joined the war against Japan before our assault on the main islands, American casualties would be significantly reduced. It was this consideration, assumably, that prompted General Douglas MacArthur, who expected to command the assault on Japan, to urge in February 1945 that Washington secure the commitment of no less than 60 Soviet divisions against the Japanese Army in Manchuria.

As events worked out, the atomic bomb made assault landings on the coast of Japan unnecessary. The bomb may have caused the Kremlin to advance the date for opening hostilities against Japan, but only by a matter of days. Late in July 1945 a representative of the Soviet high command informed his American and British counterparts that the Soviet army would move against Japan during the latter half of August. Hiroshima occurred on August 6. The Soviet Union initiated hostilities against Japan on August 9.

*   *   *

I had been in Moscow less than a month when Hurley arrived, en route from Washington back to Chungking. Roosevelt had died only a few days before this, so we were all in a somber mood and wondering what would happen with a new, little known and untested president. Even Hurley seemed subdued.

He had been rampaging about Washington in March 1945 because, after he had left Chungking, the Embassy staff there had radioed the State Department suggesting a more flexible policy in China—and consultation with Hurley regarding that recommendation. The Ambassador hotly denounced the authors of the message as disloyal to him, demanded their replacement and charged that the State Department career men were in collusion against him. He had descended upon the President, then only a few weeks from death, and apparently got the wasted Roosevelt's assent to a Hurley policy toward China. I say "apparently" because no record was made at the time of the several conversations between the two men, and Hurley's histrionic version rendered six years later before an audience of Senators is less than a wholly dependable historical source.

Memoranda of Hurley conversations in March and April and a Hurley telegram to the new President Truman suggest that the Ambassador had held forth to Roosevelt the prospect that he would be able to produce an accord between Chiang and the Chinese Communists by the end of April, provided that the Embassy's suggestion of qualified cooperation with Yenan is rejected, that exclusive support of Chiang's government be continued, and he go to London and Moscow to line up Churchill and Stalin behind this policy. This, he seemed to think, would induce Yenan to come to terms with Chiang.

Although at this time Roosevelt had also seen Edgar Snow and told him that he was "working with two governments there" (that is, China) and intended to go on doing so "until we can get them together," he permitted Hurley to maintain that the President approved of his policy of sole support of Chiang. The Rooseveltian ambiguity, a distaste for dissension, a desire to postpone a thorny decision, and terminal exhaustion resulted in Hurley's usurpation of control over China policy. The voice of the Chungking Embassy staff was stifled and the murmured warnings of the senior China experts in the Department went unheeded. With the death of Roosevelt, only Hurley could define what the late President's mandate to him had been—and Truman raised no questions on the matter.

But before Roosevelt died, Hurley went to London to line up the British Government behind his China policy. Churchill did him the courtesy of receiving him. Of their meeting on April 6, the Prime Minister recorded that Hurley seemed to wish to converse in civil banalities. Churchill, however, seized the opportunity to impress upon the itinerant envoy, bluntly and forcefully, Britain's unyielding claim to Hong Kong and determination never to give up any British territory. Churchill noted that his visitor voiced no objections. Hurley, in his report to the President and the Secretary of State, represented himself as boldly telling off the Prime Minister regarding the iniquities of imperialism and Britain's obligation to return Hong Kong to China.

Hurley got what he wanted—a British endorsement of his policy: the unification of Chinese armed forces and the creation of a free, united, democratic China. The British approval was an indulgent gesture to the American eccentric compulsion to reform China. In practical terms, of course, what Hurley achieved in London was meaningless.

During his visit to London, Hurley found time to warn the British Government that, according to a Foreign Office memorandum, I was "venomously anti-British." Taking no chances, the Foreign Office tipped off the British Embassy in Moscow. British officials in Moscow, however, were attentively kind to my wife and me.

In preparation for the Stalin-Hurley meeting, in which Harriman would participate, I wrote for the Ambassador a background paper on China. In summary, I said that the prospect for Chinese unity through negotiation was not bright because the goal of a Kuomintang-Communist coalition (which Hurley sought) was probably unattainable—Chiang would not accept a true coalition. Nor could I see Chiang, even with American aid, unifying China by force of arms, accomplishing what the Japanese in nearly eight years had failed to do. Already most of North China was permanently lost to the Communists. To preserve Central and South China for Chiang would require (1) foreign aid on a scale which might well be repudiated by the foreign electorate and (2) reform of Chiang's "venal, inefficient and stale" government, which, however, "like the Bourbons" may well have "learned nothing and forgotten nothing."

In view of the foregoing, the growing nationalism of the Chinese Communists and their possible alienation from Moscow, I raised the question of aid to and cooperation with Yenan, without abandoning Chiang. "If any Communist regime is susceptible to political 'capture' by the United States," I wrote in what is now obviously an overstatement, "it is Yenan." A policy of working with the Chinese Communists, I continued, would "involve competing with Russian drawing-power rather than seeking to block it off," as would be the case were we to continue to back Chiang exclusively.

I do not recall Harriman's reaction, if any, to this memorandum of April 15. He and Hurley met with Stalin the next night and on the seventeenth Harriman left for Washington.

Harriman had invited Hurley to stay at Spaso House. As Patricia and I were still enjoying the Ambassador's hospitality, we saw a good deal of Hurley, who treated me amiably and with whom I avoided talking about China.

On the night of April 16, Harriman took Hurley to a meeting with Stalin and Molotov. Hurley recalled statements earlier made by Stalin that the Chinese Communists were not real Communists and then filled in the Bolsheviks on negotiations between Chungking and Yenan. Stalin obligingly offered to assist the unification of the Chinese armed forces, which Hurley greeted as the best news he had received. Stalin also gladdened Hurley's heart when he "highly approved" of an American desire to train and equip Chinese Communist troops for combination with Nationalist forces under the Generalissimo. Stalin, who had been double-crossed by Chiang in 1927 during the Chinese Nationalist Revolution, described the Generalissimo as "selfless" and a "patriot" and said that the Soviet Union had once "befriended him."

Stalin raised the matter of informing Chiang of the Yalta decisions. Hurley said that was the main purpose of his visit. Although some years later when it was politically fashionable to decry Yalta, Hurley inveighed against the accord, at this meeting and in conversations with Harriman he offered no hint of dissent. The matter was treated as a procedural problem—to avoid Chinese leaks, Chiang was not to be informed of Yalta until Stalin gave a green light.

The next morning when I saw him, Hurley was in high good humor. The communion with the high priests of communism had been a success. And he so informed Washington. Stalin, he radioed, "wished us to know that we would have his complete support in immediate action for the unification of the armed forces of China with the full recognition of the National Government under the leadership of Chiang Kai-shek. In short, Stalin agreed unqualifiedly to America's policy in China as outlined to him during the conversation."

Hurley promptly took off for Chungking and Kennan, who was in charge of the Embassy, as Harriman had left for Washington, settled down to ponder the purport of the Hurley paean. He called me in, and, with incidental comments from me, drafted and sent to Washington a commentary on Hurley's message to the following effect. Stalin could agree with what Hurley said because he could interpret the General's words in his own fashion. Of course, Stalin could approve of unification of Chinese armed forces because he knew that unification was feasible only on conditions acceptable to the Chinese Communists. As for Soviet policy, we believed that it would continue to be fluid, resilient and directed at achieving maximum power with minimum responsibility along its Asian borderlands.

Among the goals of Soviet policy that Kennan listed were "reacquisition in substance if not in form, of all the diplomatic and territorial assets previously possessed on the mainland of Asia by Russia under the Czars." The cautionary message closed with "it would be tragic if our natural anxiety for the support of the Soviet Union at this juncture, coupled with Stalin's use of words which mean all things to all people, and his cautious affability, were to lead us into an undue reliance on Soviet aid or even Soviet acquiescence in the achievement of our long-term objectives in China."

Shortly after arriving back in Chungking, Hurley held a press conference and announced that Washington, London and Moscow were now in agreement on China policy. He expected that this would, in a phrase much favored by him, knock the persimmons off the tree, that the tripartite "agreement" would compel the Chinese Communists to accept the Chiang-Hurley formula and, in effect, capitulate to Chiang. He had held forth this prospect to Roosevelt. But now that he had corralled Churchill and Stalin and proclaimed the accomplishments to an indifferent world, nothing happened. The Chinese Communists were singularly unimpressed.

*   *   *

Jack Service was one of those whom Hurley purged from China in the spring of 1945. Assigned to the Department, Jack continued to maintain contact with the press, as he had done under Stilwell and Wedemeyer. This practice had originated, as in my case, with Stilwell's approval and involved candid background and other briefings of reporters and editors. And so it was that Service briefed Philip Jaffe, editor of *Amerasia*, a small, rather academic magazine concerned with Asia. In so doing, Service lent Jaffe personal copies of several of his descriptive reports on China and orally filled in Jaffe on events there.

Service was unaware that Jaffe had collected at *Amerasia* several hundred copies of official documents from other persons in the government. OSS counter-intelligence discovered this, following which the Federal Bureau of Investigation arrested Jaffe and others, including Service, on June 6. A grand jury unanimously exonerated Service on August 10.

The so-called *Amerasia* case caused a public sensation. Even though Service had been cleared 20–0 by the grand jury, some interpreted as sinister his incautious actions in briefing an editor whom he thought to be responsible and reputable. Meanwhile, I had written on June 27 to my family in the United States, "The news about Jack came as a great shock." I said that I had indicated to senior officials in the Far Eastern Office that "I am quite prepared to come back and do what I can for Jack. And I mean it."

From the Office of Far Eastern Affairs, Joseph Ballantine replied to my offer. There was nothing useful I could do at this stage. The case was under investigation. Raymond Ludden, who was on duty at the Department, wrote to me supplying further information. On July 31 I sent him some of my ideas.

First I would say that if Jack did in one way or the other divulge the contents of official classified material to unauthorized persons (which is the only charge I know to have been made against him) then four issues seem to be involved.

One relates to classification of documents. Who may classify, reclassify and declassify? I do not recollect having seen any instructions on this subject. In my experience classification has been assigned by apparently almost anyone from ambassadors to clerks and from generals to corporals. Similarly, it has been my experience that officers, clerks and enlisted men reclassify either to be a more confidential, a less confidential or unrestricted category. I have seen persons considerably below the rank of Assistant Secretary of State reclassify documents by the simple expedient of drawing a penciled line through the word "secret."

On this subject, a number of questions come to mind. Because a document paraphrasing a newspaper report is marked secret (and I have seen many) may the subject matter of the document not be mentioned excepting to authorized persons? When only a portion of a document is secret and the whole document is classified secret, must the non-confidential portions also be treated as secret even though they are matters of public knowledge? Is a reclassification ever retroactive? Does a classification ever expire? If something which has been classified secret became generally known, must reclassification await the publication some years later of FOREIGN RELATIONS? And so on deep into sophistry.

The second issue seems to me to relate to that even more elastic institution—background information. I first became acquainted with it when early in my career I observed my chief at the time provide American journalists with background information—boldly, intelligently and unquestionably to the national benefit. Since then I have seen the technique employed by quite a variety of government officials and know from newspapermen that it is a widespread practice. As is commonly known, the information given out varies in classification from top secret to unrestricted. My feeling is that, for the most part, the giving of background information is a necessary and wholesome procedure in a democracy such as ours. The resulting public comment may sometimes give aid and comfort to the enemy. But an even greater disservice would be done the American people were background information withheld. Uninformed, a democracy is prey to debilitating doubts and suspicions.

Thirdly, it seems to me that on matters of political policy the public expression of dissenting opinion by government officials should in principle not be prohibited. Such a prohibition affecting policy matters can work so as to deny information to which the people of a democracy has a right. If the "official" position is well founded and the government has been frank with the people, it can afford to permit dissenting opinion from within its ranks. No one suggests that just because dissenting opinions are raised from the Supreme Court that our judicial system is a crumbling edifice.

The immediate objection which will be raised to this principle, I realize, is that international relations are so delicate that granting juniors license to ventilate their immature and impetuous opinions would bring our foreign relations to a pretty pass—witness the necessity of governmental discipline during the period of necessary appeasement of Japan and Spain (now a matter of public record thanks to reclassification of documents). I accept this argument; that is why I said "in principle." But I do feel that the government should be on guard against the natural tendency to adopt a hypochondriac attitude toward international relations and regularly use the excuse of "delicate relations" as a rationalization for muzzling opinion which does not conform to the official line.

So we come to the fourth issue. If Jack, Larsen and Roth did in fact divulge classified information to unauthorized persons, what about all the other officials in Washington and elsewhere who have done the same? The doctrine of atonement, noble and inspiring in theology, is considerably less so in the administration of a bureaucracy. Consistency and equal treatment would seem to be a somewhat sounder principle.

So much for those four issues. If on the other hand it develops that the FBI does not really have anything on Jack, then what? One does not laugh off the label of "spy" with a "Sorry old man, guess we made a mistake, let's call it quits." Maybe a formula could be found for a complete vindication and a quiet face-saving all the way around. I do not know. In any case, that would be a personal decision for Jack to make.

What actually happened was that, after his exoneration by the grand jury, Service was assigned to the political advisory staff of General Mac-Arthur, then the Allies' viceroy in Tokyo. But this was when the Department of State still had some prestige and fortitude.

*   *   *

[Sergei] Vinogradov had been Press Attaché at the Soviet Embassy in Chung-king. As I had known him only slightly and was unaware that he was in Moscow, I was surprised when he got in touch with me—just how I have forgotten—during the first half of June. I do remember that he was casually genial and affected candor. That he sought to establish contact with me was extraordinary because even Soviet diplomats who indulged in social fraternization while abroad in Moscow avoided contact with foreigners or acted with distant reserve if encountered. I assumed therefore that Vinogradov had been ordered or authorized to make the approach either to convey obliquely through me a message to my superiors or, what seemed more likely, to explore the possibility of proselytizing or otherwise recruiting me.

With immense curiosity Patricia and I accepted an invitation from Vinogradov for dinner at his apartment. When I informed Edward Page, a Russian specialist ranking between Kennan and me, of the invitation, he reacted with a start and quickly said that "they" were out to win me over. Harriman was calmly interested in what might develop.

Vinogradov, his wife and mother received us hospitably in their two rooms in one of those hulking, grimy, gray apartment houses. The conversation was in English, which our host spoke easily and, as I recall, his wife did not. The old mother spoke in Russian and then only when addressed by her son.

Vinogradov justifiably prided himself on his command of the American vernacular. He had refined what he had learned at language school in the Soviet Union by studying *Gentlemen Prefer Blondes*. He used Miss Loos's classic as a textbook for vocabulary and syntax. While in the United States, he systematically rode the New York subways as a language laboratory. From Manhattan to the Bronx, Brooklyn and Queens, for hours he listened and perfected his pronunciation and delivery.

My strongest recollection of that evening was neither the younger Russians nor the good food and vodka (with dried orange peel in the bottle), but the taciturn, worn and creased mother. She had refused to leave the apartment when the Nazis neared Moscow and endured the bitter winters without heat and at times without water. When Patricia and I said that we admired the strength and fortitude of the Russian women we had seen, Vinogradov exclaimed, "We were saved by our women."

As Patricia and I prepared to leave, Vinogradov earnestly urged me to read and study, not Loos, but Lenin. His approach was rather like that of a concerned and kindly chaplain opening to a non-believer the way to salvation. It all struck me as a little naïve. How could he think that theoretical Leninism could have appeal when applied Leninism was so manifestly repulsive to, at least, someone conditioned to humanistic beliefs and aware of Soviet realities?

We asked the Vinogradovs to dinner at our apartment. Only he came and seemed ill at ease. I invited him to the Embassy's Fourth of July reception. He did not appear. I saw him perhaps twice later, and then no more. My conclusion was that he did not consider me to be worth more of his time.

*   *   *

It seemed that the very thought of me haunted Hurley—or was it Soong? In a radiogram dated June 19 from the Chungking Embassy and signed Hurley appeared the sentence: "There are also rumors afloat here, that we do not credit, to the effect that John Davies is responsible for news items in the Moscow papers that appear to be adverse to the Chinese Government." The suggestion that I inspired *Pravda* and *Izvestia* provoked, first, Harriman's laughter—for the idea was farcical—and then his angry contempt.

Soong arrived in Moscow on June 30 to negotiate an agreement between China and the Soviet Union, taking into account the deal between Roosevelt and Stalin made at Yalta, to which neither Chiang nor Soong had objected. As part of his reception at the airport, Soong stood to review the march past of the honor guard composed of some two hundred NKVD troops. Conditioning him for his forthcoming huddle with the Soviet chieftains, these superb physical specimens, rifles held high on their shoulders and glaring malevolence at the honored guest, bore down close to the unfortunate Chinese Foreign Minister as they passed by, in perfect cadence swinging their black boots up to a seventy degree angle, then slamming them down stiff-legged with such force that the flesh of their faces quivered.

The thuds of the march past were like rhythmic artillery fire. Soong appeared to be far from happy at this welcome to Moscow.

Soon after Soong's arrival, Harriman told me with embarrassment that the Chinese Foreign Minister had asked that I not be informed of developments in the negotiations and that he, Harriman, felt that he must accede to the request. Knowing Soong, I was less taken aback by this than was Harriman. I considered my exclusion from knowledge of the hapless Chinese squirming in the hands of Stalin to be no great deprivation. And my greater interest was in the broad functioning of Soviet policy.

In an estimate of Soviet policy in East Asia, dated July 10, I said that the Soviet Union might be expected to try to change the situation in that area to its advantage for a variety of reasons. One was security against China, which might "emerge after one or two generations as the greatest single threat to the Soviet Union on the Eurasian continent." Other security considerations were "Korea as a natural corridor for an attack on the Soviet Far East," and the Kurils, Karafuto (southern Sakhalin, then under Japanese sovereignty), Hokkaido and Honshu as potential springboards for attack on the Soviet Union.

"The need for new ports and bases to accommodate an expanded Soviet merchant marine and navy" was another reason for Moscow to seek change in East Asia. The Soviet Union might also be attracted by the opportunities offered by "the internal struggle for power in China" developing at the war's end "into open conflict." The political vacuum in Korea following the end of Japanese rule and anticipated chaos in Japan itself also exerted an attraction on Moscow.

I listed two minimum Soviet objectives in East Asia. One was a security cordon, which Moscow would dominate or win over, composed of Sinkiang, Inner Mongolia, North China, Manchuria, Korea, southern Sakhalin and the Kurils. The other objective related to Japan: a voice in the peace dictate and "an opportunity to exploit politically the postwar situation in Japan."

In seeking to attain its objectives, the Kremlin had three choices: military conquest, political action and a mix of the two. While military conquest would get Moscow what it wanted, "an open display of Soviet power and expansionist ambition would presumably arouse the United States, which the Kremlin prefers not to do. One of the by-products of an aroused United States might well be an Anglo-American denial to the Soviet Union of any real voice in the decision regarding the Japanese islands or access to them." But reliance on political action alone would not be fully effective. Therefore politico-military action was the most likely Soviet course.

Tactically, the Kremlin was likely to maintain a "correct" attitude toward China and Korea, so as to avoid appearing imperialistic to Asians and incurring intensified American suspicion and hostility. It would rely on Yenan to serve the Kremlin's immediate aims in China.

> It is debatable whether Moscow could have counted on Yenan's unques-
> tioning obedience had the American Government last autumn and winter
> (while the Soviet Union was still unprepared to act in Asia) accepted the
> fact of a divided China and realistically and vigorously sought to develop
> the nationalistic tendencies of Communist China. However that may be, it
> is clear that Communist China can now operate only in the Soviet orbit.
> This situation is entirely satisfactory to the Kremlin because it can conduct
> fundamentally meaningless flirtations with Chungking while being fully
> confident that (a) Yenan will resist spontaneously—and probably effec-
> tively—Chiang's attempt to establish Kuomintang authority over North-
> east China and (b) Communist China will become part of the USSR's
> security cordon, because if for no other reason, it will scarcely be accepted
> by any other foreign alignment.

Anesthetization of the United States, I concluded, was a Soviet tactic. "For obvious reasons the Kremlin will be careful in performing its political surgery in Asia to cause during the next two or three years as little shock and pain as possible to the United States. Therefore the present 'correct' attitude and other tactics designed to diffuse the one basic issue of aggres-sive Soviet expansion . . . this anesthetization will be effective in pretty much direct proportion to the degree of ignorance in which the American people are kept with regard to the issues involved."

Some days after submitting this estimate, I commented to Harriman, with the collaboration of Kennan, regarding a radiogram from Hurley, that

> the contention of this message appears to be that if the Soviet Government
> can be persuaded to announce publicly or demonstrate through a treaty its
> support of Chungking (and by inference, its repudiation of Yenan), the
> Chinese Communists will realize that they are without foreign backing and
> will come to terms with Chungking.

We feel that the Soviet Government could quite easily repudiate Yenan publicly without basically altering Yenan's intransigent attitude. We base this view on:

(1) The dual nature of the Soviet system. If Yenan is controlled from Moscow, it is not by the State apparatus—the Government—but by the Party. The State can, when the Kremlin wishes, publicly follow an unexpectedly conciliatory and sedative policy in matters affecting the interests of other powers. At the same time, the Party can do just the opposite, whispering discreetly in the appropriate ears that it's all for show and need not be allowed to affect realities.

(2) Should the Soviet Government publicly repudiate Yenan and the Party pronounce an anathema against the Chinese Communist Party (which is hardly thinkable), it does not necessarily follow that Yenan would capitulate to Chungking's terms. We question even the assumption that if all foreign support were withdrawn from Yenan, it would seek to come to an agreement with Chungking. Readily granting that the Chinese Communists are not as firmly and extensively entrenched as they claim, they are still many times more powerful than during the period 1927–1937 when, with no foreign support save huzzas and poor coaching from the Comintern bleachers, they resisted Chiang with embarrassing persistence. We feel that Soviet influence can sometimes be overestimated. The indigenous strength, vitality and obstinacy of Yenan is a factor not to be ignored and one which, in the last analysis, means that if China is to be unified through negotiations, Chungking is going to have to make the bigger concessions.

CHAPTER XX

HURLEY'S OPENING SALVO

At last the war in Europe came to an end. The Kremlin did not tell its
people of the Nazi capitulation until May 9, two days after the instrument
of surrender had been signed in the West. They were given a holiday on the
tenth. And so it was that some of the Muscovites passing the Embassy on
that morning, instead of striding ahead and staring directly in front of
them, stopped, and looked up at the Mokhavaya building with the American flag flying on it. How it all started I do not know—perhaps someone
of the Embassy staff waved to them from an open window—but soon the
scattered few multiplied to scores, then hundreds smiling, laughing, gesturing and cheering Russians. We gathered at windows to wave and call out in
return.

The two militiamen (policemen) regularly stationed in front of the Embassy could not control the happy, growing crowds. Secret police in black
leather coats rushed in, ordering the throngs, now in the thousands, to
disperse. Incredibly, the multitudes paid the dreaded agents of tyranny no
heed. By mid-morning the huge area to the Kremlin's walls was filled with
jubilant Russians, not only celebrating victory at the end of a long, harrowing war, but also acclaiming Americans as partners sharing their triumph
and joyous deliverance.

When, as arranged by Kennan, a Soviet flag appeared from out an Embassy window beside the Stars and Stripes, everyone applauded and
cheered. Kennan stepped out on the base of a column on the face of the
building and in Russian shouted congratulations on the victory. Surging

roars of approval. It was not until late afternoon that the crowds thinned. Even after dark small groups moved past us, looking up, smiling and waving—and we waved back.

The next morning people walked by the Embassy as if we did not exist, heads down-turned or staring straight ahead. The hours of spontaneous, undisguised Russian friendship with Americans were over. Our partners of yesterday's happy abandon had slumped into regimented submission—no contact with or show of interest in things foreign. The reversion was the sadder for the honesty and warmth of the preceding day's manifestation of American-Russian friendship.

*   *   *

As the Kremlin set about consolidating politically what it had gained militarily in Eastern Europe, it redeployed its forces to join in the kill of Japan. Beset by implacable American pressure and sensing the impending Soviet assault, the Japanese Government put out peace feelers in the summer of 1945. Truman did not respond.

Several of his senior civilian advisers had come to see the desirability of replacing the demand for unconditional surrender with assurances of capitulation that would not involve harm to the sacred person and institution of the Emperor. Their reasoning was that such reassuring conditions would remove a major cause for fanatical Japanese refusal to surrender, for prolonged, suicidal resistance exacting an enormous toll of American lives. And only the Emperor could order surrender. They so advised Truman. This was nearly a year after Emmerson had recommended substantially the same. Truman refused to offer assurances regarding the Emperor.

In the Potsdam Declaration of July 26, the American, British and Chinese Governments reiterated the demand for unconditional surrender. If Tokyo capitulated the Japanese people would be allowed to survive and have a government in accordance with their "freely expressed will." Otherwise—"prompt and utter destruction." No mention was made of the Emperor.

The war against Japan culminated in three bursts of abrupt and towering violence. Two were the American atomic bombings: Hiroshima and Nagasaki. And between the two, the Soviet horde fell upon the Japanese in

Northeast Asia, continuing to attack for days after Tokyo had on August 10 announced a wish to accept the Potsdam demand for surrender.

For the Soviet Union it had been a brief war—declared on August 8, continued through the Japanese August 10 offer of surrender, and not pronounced by Moscow as terminated until August 23. At slight cost, the Soviet Union had revenged its 1905 defeat in the Russo-Japanese War and replaced Japan as the dominant Asian power and, potentially, as the rival to the United States in the Pacific. But the Soviet people, tens of millions of whom had suffered Nazi invasion and occupation and then "liberation," did not react to the end of war in the East, where they were unscathed, with the poignant relief that they greeted the termination of battle in the West.

Directing the war against Japan did not distract Stalin from politically tidying up his relations with Chiang. A despondent Soong, unwilling to accept Soviet terms, had in midsummer left Moscow for Chungking, but returned the day before the Soviet Union declared war on Japan. Stalin told him three days later, as the Soviet Army was overrunning Manchuria, that he, Soong, would be wise to reach an agreement promptly or the Chinese Communists would move into Manchuria.

The Soviet-Chinese Treaty of Friendship and Alliance was signed August 14. It gave the Soviet Union substantially what, at Yalta, Stalin had told Roosevelt he wanted in Manchuria. It also committed Moscow to moral support of and aid to the National Government of China.

In collaboration with Kennan, I commented by radiogram to the Department on September 4 that Moscow did not require the treaty for the "achievement of any of the immediate objectives now being attained by the Red Army advance." The pact's advantage to the Soviet Government was that it lent legality to situations which might otherwise lead to disputes and complaints. Soviet readiness to admit Chinese civil administrators to Manchuria and to withdraw Soviet forces, I continued, reflected mature statesmanship. But the Chinese Communists would be entering Manchuria and the Soviet authorities could be expected to favor Chinese Communist takeover of Manchurian administration after Soviet military withdrawal.

As for broad Soviet assurance of support of the Chinese Government and non-interference in China's internal affairs, I observed, this was a "reaffirmation of a state of affairs which has existed for some years . . . if Kremlin influences Yenan now and in future, it will be through the Party." While Moscow's pledge to Chungking prejudiced Yenan's "ability to bargain on basis of implied Soviet military support," it reduced general suspicions and criticism of Soviet intentions and actions in China.

To its August 10 broadcast announcing readiness to accept the Potsdam demands, the Japanese Government added a condition—the prerogative of the Emperor as sovereign ruler should not be prejudiced. Washington declared on the following day that the Emperor's authority and that of the Japanese Government would be subject to the Supreme Commander for Allied Powers (SCAP). However, the Japanese would eventually be allowed freely to establish their form of government. On August 14 Tokyo accepted the Potsdam terms and announced that the Emperor had issued an Imperial Rescript informing his subjects of the surrender and was prepared to authorize orders to all Japanese forces to cease hostilities.

Following Japanese acceptance of the Potsdam ultimatum, the SCAP, General MacArthur, sent to Tokyo a directive on the procedure for surrender. Imperial General Headquarters passed it to all Japanese forces as an order by direction of the Emperor. As they had obediently gone to war and death for their Emperor, so the Japanese fighting men dutifully bowed to his wish that they capitulate. The Japanese forces in China were ordered to surrender to the Chinese Nationalists, excepting that those in Manchuria were to commit themselves to the mercy of the Soviet Army—which shipped them off to Siberia.

This SCAP procedure was legalistically correct, for Chiang's government was the internationally recognized authority in China. The flaw was that Chiang's government was not everywhere internally the recognized authority. Already, Yenan had ordered its troops to take the surrender of Japanese forces adjacent to their operational areas. In contrast to the Nationalists, who were isolated in the west of the country, the Communists operated in areas behind and between Japanese-held cities and lines of communication in North and Central China. The Japanese, however, faithful to their instructions, refused to yield to Yenan's demands for capitulation and patiently awaited the arrival of Chiang's men. At that stage the Communists were still lightly armed and therefore unable to impose their will on the Japanese.

Clinging to the policy of sustaining Chiang, Washington immediately launched an airlift of Nationalist troops from the backcountry to take the surrender of the Japanese who had so obligingly rebuffed the Communists. Thus at the outset of the civil war, the American government allied itself with the Nationalist side. Rather than disarming the enemy forces in North China and repatriating them, the American-borne Nationalists invited the Japanese to hold the cities and communication lines against the Communists while Chiang's detachments ventured into the countryside against the

Reds. Washington assigned more than 50,000 U.S. Marines to join the Japanese trusties in custodial duties on behalf of the Generalissimo.

Meanwhile, Communist units had begun to move into Manchuria where they picked up arms taken by the Soviet conquerors from the Japanese and their indigenous "puppet" troops. This was the start of Communist offensive capabilities. Chiang, too, ordered troops into Manchuria. They were to take over, as mutually agreed upon, from the occupying Soviet Army. The Pentagon went along with the Generalissimo's foolhardy expedition—fatally over-extending Nationalist strength—by transporting his force to Manchuria by sea.

American involvement in the Chinese civil war had begun with the decision to ignore the Communist claim to take the surrender of adjacent Japanese garrisons. It deepened most evidently with the transport of half a million Nationalist troops by air and sea, the assignment of American Marines to side with the Nationalists against the Communists, and the supply of aircraft, ships, tanks, vehicles and all manner of materiel to the Nationalists.

Why did the American government involve the American people in this alien civil war? The decision—or perhaps, more accurately, absence of decision—grew out of a century of American evangelical, educational, philanthropic and business association with China. There resulted a sentimental, condescending, proprietary love of fictional Chinese, who, Americans fancied, reciprocated with due gratitude, admiration and loyalty. Americans identified these mythic Chinese with the idealized Chiangs. As for the Chinese Communists, they were hardly known to the American people. Insofar as they were, they did not fit the prevailing American mythology about China.

In this subjective environment Washington drifted from backing Chiang's Nationalists against Japan to sustaining them in hostilities against the Communists. With the career officers of the Chungking Embassy muzzled by Hurley, Washington was fed a misleading picture of Nationalist-Communist relative strength. Hurley, Wedemeyer and Tai Li's collaborator, Commodore Miles, during a March visit to Washington, had assured the Joint Chiefs of Staff that with slight American aid Chiang could with relative ease dispose of the Communists. Hurley continued to belittle Communist strength and hold forth hope that the two sides could be reconciled, particularly as he had late in August accompanied Mao to Chungking for negotiations with Chiang, for which he claimed credit and which, predictably, broke down. At the end of August Wedemeyer told the press that he did not consider the Communists to be strong in any part of China and that he did not expect any difficulty in dealing with them.

With the Nationalists and the Communists desperately jostling for position preparatory to all-out civil war, Hurley sounded an alarm to the Department, accusing "imperialists"—the British, Dutch and French—of backing the Communists against the Nationalists, the United States and the Soviet Union. Thus exhausted Europeans, who had more than enough tribulations without seeking them out in China, were lumped with American career diplomats as saboteurs of his mission to unify China. He wanted to return to the United States, Hurley truculently told the State Department, so as to talk to Truman and James F. Byrnes, the Secretary of State, about the "fundamental issue in Asia today." It was "between democracy and imperialism; between free enterprise and monopoly." In his final message from Chungking on September 23 he assured Washington that he was leaving an improving situation in China, with rapprochement apparently taking place between the Kuomintang and the Communists and rumors of civil war fading away.

*   *   *

Once in Washington, Hurley was not at all eager to go back to his post. He pled trouble with his sinuses. But after treatment and conversations with Byrnes and Truman, in early October, he consented to return to China. In response to a request from Chiang and Soong for Hurley's presence in Chungking, Truman on October 20 replied that Byrnes and he reposed confidence in Hurley's judgment and ability and that the Ambassador would resume his duties.

Again, in early November, Hurley changed his mind. He telephoned Byrnes and, according to the Secretary's testimony a month later before the Senate Foreign Relations Committee, "he told me he was in Santa Fe and he saw from the press the news about the situation in China, and that he still did not feel able to return." The Ambassador appeared at the State Department on November 26 to hand the Secretary a letter of resignation. In addition to saying that he was not well, Hurley complained that he was tired of not being supported by some Foreign Service officers, naming Service for a report Jack had written for Stilwell before Hurley had been appointed Ambassador to China, and George Atcheson for a sober suggestion that the changing situation in China warranted reconsideration of some phases of policy. Byrnes coaxed Hurley into agreeing to return to Chungking two days later.

But on the next day, without prior notification to the President or the Secretary, Hurley publicly announced his resignation. He did so in a press release charging that "the professional foreign service men side with the Chinese Communist armed party and the imperialist block . . . continuously advised the Communists that my efforts in preventing the collapse of the National Government did not represent the policy of the United States . . . and openly advised the Communist armed party to decline unification of the Chinese Communist Army with the National Army unless the Chinese Communists were given control." Expanding his accusations, Hurley alleged that "a considerable section of our State Department is endeavoring to support Communism generally as well as specifically in China."

Using the editorial or royal "we," Hurley proclaimed that despite the handicaps hatched by professional diplomats, "we did make progress toward unification of the armed forces of China. We did prevent civil war between the rival factions, at least until after I had left China." But he did not disclose the names of the culprits who had frustrated his salvation of China.

Byrnes was informed of Hurley's broadside immediately after its release. The astonished Secretary thought that the announcement must have been a mistake. He telephoned the Ambassador who confessed that he indeed issued the press release. He complained that he was sick, running a temperature, that people were "shooting at him," and that he had changed his mind because of a speech made the day before by Congressman [Hugh] DeLacy criticizing his performance as Ambassador. Hurley said that he suspected that somebody in the State Department had fed the information to the Congressman. Nevertheless, according to Byrnes, Hurley had concluded with, "Jim, if you say so, I'll go back."

Byrnes informed Truman of the situation. No longer reposing confidence in Hurley, the President accepted the Ambassador's resignation rather than his offer to go back.

Hurley could have retired in dignity from the China scene on a firm plea of ill health. Instead, he chose to foment a national scandal with himself as the central figure victimized by allegedly disloyal underlings. And he dramatized rather than backed away from the immediate objective he had so rashly set for himself: to prevent civil war and to unify China.

All Foreign Service officers, of course, favored the perfectionist goal of preventing civil war and unifying China. The difference between some of us and Hurley was that we thought that his objective was probably then unattainable and that since 1943 the pressing, practical issue was what policy the United States should follow in anticipation of and during a civil conflict from which the Communists would probably emerge victorious. Hurley's insistence on unqualified support of Chiang was, we believed, in error. The time would come when we should choose between the two sides. But meanwhile our recommendation was that, without abandoning Chiang, the United States Government should develop relations with the Communists as allies in the war against Japan and the likely next rulers of China.

Sharp noses in the Congress immediately smelled politics and potential in Hurley's yarns about American officials conspiring with Communists to wreck American policy just as it was about to succeed. The party out of power, the Republicans, scented an issue with which to confound the administration. Senator Kenneth S. Wherry declared that the conduct of those accused by Hurley "skirts the edge of treason" and introduced a resolution for a detailed investigation of the Department. Republican Representatives in the House demanded that the Department "discharge all Communists from the payroll." In accordance with Wherry's resolution, Hurley was invited to divulge all to the Senate Foreign Relations Committee.

In two days of turbulent testimony Hurley repeated his unsubstantiated charges that certain Foreign Service officers had advised the Communists that his policy was not that of the American government and named as saboteurs of his endeavors George Atcheson, Service, two other colleagues (Arthur Ringwalt and Fulton Freeman) and me. He later singled me out as also being "anti-imperialist." With regard to his resignation he told the puzzled Senators, "I decided to fight when I found that the State Department was still trying to destroy me, and I decided I would not be destroyed . . . The attack was on; the same attack that has been going on me by career men all through the thing was opened up anew, and I decided I did not have anyone to defend me except myself, and that I would undertake to do it."

The day after Hurley finished his testimony, December 7, 1945, Byrnes appeared before the committee. The Secretary said that the Service and Atcheson reports, which Hurley had cited to the Senators as evidence of disloyalty, contained nothing to support the accusation. He added: "within proper channels they expressed to those under whom they served certain views which differed to a greater or less degree from the policies of the Government as then defined . . . Whenever an official honestly believes that changed conditions required it, he should not hesitate to express his views to his superior officers."

> *I should be profoundly unhappy to learn that an officer of the Department of State, within or without the Foreign Service, might feel bound to refrain from submitting through proper channels an honest report or recommendation for fear of offending me or anyone else in the Department. If that day should arrive, I will have lost the very essence of the assistance and guidance I require. . . .*
>
> *The other complaint of Ambassador Hurley is that some official or employee did not merely express a different view to his superior officer, but advised someone associated with the Communist forces that the Ambassador did not accurately represent U.S. policy. . . . But Ambassador Hurley had not furnished . . . any specific evidence to prove that any employee was guilty of such conduct. Men who have rendered loyal service to the Government cannot be dismissed and their reputations ought not to be destroyed on the basis of suspicions entertained by any individual.*

*   *   *

After disposing of—for the time being—the agitation stirred up by Hurley, Byrnes went in mid-December to Moscow for a meeting with Molotov and the British Foreign Secretary, Ernest Bevin. The Secretary of State brought with him Benjamin Cohen, the Counselor of the Department, James B. Conant, as adviser on nuclear matters, Bohlen and Vincent. Harriman gave me the responsibility for the delegation's press relations.

In my first encounter with the Secretary's party at the Spaso House gathering I was the butt of friendly joshing about Hurley's accusations. Harriman and the delegation from Washington appeared to think that Hurley had played the buffoon and destroyed his own credibility. The Secretary apparently continued to be tickled by the humor of Hurley's complaints against me, for some days later, at a recess in a meeting of the foreign ministers when light conversation between him and Molotov seemed to be dragging, Byrnes beckoned to me. Upon my joining them, the Secretary turned to the Bolshevik bigwig and confided, "Pat Hurley says he's a Communist, so when he comes knocking at your door, you let him in, hear?" Not a flicker of amusement altered Molotov's mask of frozen formal sociability as Byrne's waggery was translated.

With receipt of the first news of Hurley's accusations against me, my impulse was to resign and rebut him publicly. Patricia and George Kennan dissuaded me, advising silence, letting the preposterous assertions fall of their own weight. In January I received a letter from the Chief of Foreign Service, William E. DeCourcy, suggesting that I might wish to reply to Hurley's charges that I was disloyal to him.

In response I said in part, that I assumed that DeCourcy was not interested in an exposition of "my relations with and view of General Hurley, his disloyalty to Foreign Service officers working for him and his irresponsibility in the discharge of his office . . . I assume that the Department prefers that Foreign Service officers turn their energies to more constructive enterprises." Answering the specific charges relayed by DeCourcy, I said that I did not "communicate to the Chinese Communists information regarding Allied military plans for landings or operations in China," nor advise them that Hurley's "efforts to prevent the collapse of the National Government did not represent the policy of the United States," nor advise them "to decline unification with the Nationalist Army unless the Communists were given control."

During the Byrnes visit to Moscow, John Carter Vincent, who was then the head of Far Eastern Affairs, asked me if I would accept the job of chief of the Division of Chinese Affairs. Surprised and pleased, I nevertheless declined, explaining that I wanted to broaden my experience.

*   *   *

To relatives in the United States I wrote on January 5,

> *Outside the window in the early evening darkness a tall Christmas tree is sparkling in red, orange and green lights. It stands in the center of a little bazaar built in the middle of the great square in front of the Embassy. I have just come back from the bazaar, tiny booths erected on the caked*

snow and selling green oranges, shoddy dolls, vodka, cold buns and copies of the Stalin Constitution. The empty-lived people of Moscow wander around, buy little and listen to the loud speakers mooing Russian folk songs. A few children, bundled so that only their noses show, are hopping about in unsteady dances. It's fundamentally a pretty dreary spectacle.

The other evening Patricia and I listened to 96 recordings of various Russian songs. The overall impression was one of alternate melancholy and vitality. As George Kennan said, "You'd be melancholy, too, if you had to live your life through a cycle of mud and snow with a mostly gray sky overhead and the steppes never-ending all around."

Christmas Eve. . . . I went with the Secretary's party to a dinner given by Stalin in the Kremlin. Up the long, long marble stairs of the Tsars' palace, stairs covered with red carpet, to a large anteroom dominated by an enormous painting of the Tsar Alexander II visiting one of his villages. Then through several corridors past ramrod-stiff NKVD guards at every few yards, through the banquet hall to a gilt and plush reception room where some of the lesser luminaries were waiting. After standing around with our hands in our pockets for about fifteen minutes someone whispered, here he comes. A little gray man in a soldier suit padded through the banquet hall toward us, followed by a retinue of the other big names—Molotov, Beria (head of the NKVD) Malenkov (party boss) and others. He passed down the line of foreigners, a quick shake of the hand, a look in the eye, a pleasant greeting—an Asiatic peasant grandpappy. The rest of the gang shook a few hands then stopped, obviously finding the whole performance rather distasteful and a waste of time.

We went in to a typically Slavic groaning board—caviar to cream puffs. I was, of course, at one of the ends of the table of about fifty and because of my lowly position was able to concentrate on watching. . . .

The men around Stalin are an extraordinary group of human beings. They look as if they have never been exposed to sunlight—pallid and fat. That's the political boys—the marshals are ruddy and fat. Mikoyan, with whom I sampled cordials after dinner, is an exception. He is a swarthy Armenian with a broken hooked nose . . . I rather liked Mikoyan. Like Stalin and Marshal Bulganin, he seemed normal.

After coffee and liqueurs, we went in to view a movie in the palace projection room. A NKVD general stood as guard near Stalin throughout the show. It was a comfortable little movie house with tables in front of the seats. The tables were laden with fruit and champagne. Throughout the show waiters poured coffee and brought around tidbits. It was a documentary film of the USSR's part in the war against Japan. I can safely say that it would be unsuitable for showing to the Marines.

Then we went home, back through the corridors, past the guards in their blue-topped caps, past the enormous painting, under cascade after cascade of chandeliers and down the long, long red-carpeted marble staircase.

We went back to an American Christmas Eve party at Spaso with a loaded buffet and a Soviet dance orchestra made up of unhappy Finns and Czechs who had under a misapprehension fled to this workers' paradise. It was a good party . . . and Patricia looked very pretty with a little red sequined hat on her head.

CHAPTER XXI

POSTWAR MOSCOW

Harriman left Moscow in January 1946 and Kennan in April, after the arrival of Harriman's replacement. The Ambassador had completed his wartime service in the Soviet Union and was ready to move on to what turned out to be three decades of public life in varied positions, among them Secretary of Commerce, Ambassador to the Court of St. James, and Governor of New York. Kennan went to the National War College where, as Deputy Commandant, he instructed future generals, admirals and ambassadors in the enigmas of foreign policy.

Harriman and Kennan were succeeded by Lieutenant General Walter Bedell Smith and Elbridge Durbrow. General Smith came from serving under General Eisenhower as Chief of Staff of the Allied armies in the West. Durbrow was a Foreign Service officer who had been in charge of Eastern European affairs in the Department.

Smith had risen through the ranks from enlisted man to three star general on sheer ability and drive. A thoroughgoing professional soldier, he was surprised when Byrnes offered him the appointment as Ambassador to the Soviet Union. The Secretary explained, as Smith recalled, "A soldier in the Moscow job actually would be an advantage . . . because Generalissimo Stalin had, on a number of occasions, indicated a certain distrust of career diplomats, and had shown some preference for military men." Proceeding from this credulous assumption, Byrnes said that the President and he believed that the Soviet field commanders would have a potent influence on policy, including possible foreign relations. Therefore, Smith's wartime acquaintanceship with some of them was an additional reason for sending him to Moscow—"getting under the Russian skin."

The Foreign Service was (and still is) accustomed to having all manner of persons imposed on it as ambassadors—men and women to whom the President owes political debts (conspicuously, contributors to his campaign expenses), retiring or defeated politicians, cronies of undefeated ones, generals, admirals, men of substance, journalists, academicians, and personages whom the White House would prefer to be abroad in gilded exile rather than in the midst of American political activity. This manifestation of the spoils system proceeded on the premise that diplomacy was a vocation in which the amateur performed as well as, if not better, than the professional. Some political appointees, it is true,—and Harriman was one—performed better than the average professional. The White House, however, usually conceded to career officers embassies that were in unhealthy, hazardous or otherwise unappealing places, or that obviously required an ambassador with professional Foreign Service qualifications and experience.

We on the staff at Moscow had braced ourselves for Smith's arrival. We did not expect him to be the usual political appointee. We knew that by reputation he was an exceptionally able military administrator. But how would he adjust from managing far-reaching armies and air forces at war to commanding a platoon of diplomats engaged in the frustrating intangibles of American relations with a secretive, evasive and implacable Kremlin?

Smith took his role as a diplomat seriously, inquiringly and with good humor. He promptly interested himself in all phases of Embassy operations, particularly in our political and economic reporting on the Soviet Union. He impressed me as brisk, quick-witted and decisive. Only rarely during the year of my acquaintance with him at Moscow did he reveal glimpses of the impatience and hot temper which he repressed to the detriment of his digestive tract.

A week after his arrival Smith was received by Stalin. The Ambassador did not take any member of his staff with him; not even Kennan, who had not yet left for Washington. The odd reason for this, advanced by Smith in his memoirs, was "I thought the meeting might be a stormy one." His real reason, I suspect, was a not unusual one in the case of political appointees at the outset of their new career—false pride, a fear of having a career subordinate witness possible gaffes.

"When is Mrs. Davies going back to America to have her baby?" Soviet employees of the Embassy anxiously asked when Patricia's pregnancy ripened and she showed no sign of preparing to leave. "She isn't going back, she is going to have it here." "But then it will be a Soviet citizen!" "Oh no, it will be an American citizen because the parents are Americans and the father a diplomat." "Ah then," with nodding heads, "that will be all right."

Patricia and I had separately studied Russian with a tutor from shortly after our arrival. Because I was caught up in my regular work and was amply supplied with translation and interpreting facilities, I spent little time on the language and so made slight progress in it. But Patricia did well and, in preparation for hospital confinement on her own, concentrated on obstetrical and maternity Russian.

Writing on June 14 to relatives in the United States I reported: "Night before last Patricia began to have her first pains. . . . She was up all night. . . . At eight I whisked her off to the hospital." It was named after Klara Zetkin, the German Communist, and occupied an old, grubby building. Although she had the necessary document for admittance to this hospital, it took about an hour and a half for Patricia to be received.

Her clothing, bag, watch and even her wedding ring were brought out to me. . . . She was taken into a labor room with five nursing women and about ten women in labor. She was the center, of course, of nurse and doctor attention—all curious and all abounding with primitive Slavic warmth and, I might add, the nichevo *["no worries"] spirit.*

A cylinder of laughing gas was wheeled over for the pangs. After inhaling without effect, and inquiring several times why no effect, she observed that the dial indicated the cylinder to be empty. The Russians don't go much for anesthesia, the cylinder was for psychological effect—so she had her pains in the old fashioned way. After several hours with the nursing mothers and the labor ladies . . . off to the delivery room, another collective establishment where, with two doctors pressing on her midriff and a midwife taking delivery she produced your granddaughter. . . . She said it wasn't bad, but then she is a hardy and buoyant type.

Characteristic of the atmosphere of the place was the old nanny in the labor room who kept saying to Patricia, "You are having such beautiful pains, such beautiful pains." And because Patricia was enduring her labor without outcries, the old nurse exclaimed, "Look," to the wailing Russian women, "what beautiful big pains she is having."

This morning by special arrangement with the little dumpling Professor (Blizayanskaya), who is the autocrat of the hospital and reputedly the best obstetrician in the USSR, I was sneaked in to see Patricia. She had the luxury of a semi-private room which she shares with the wife of a Czech diplomat.

She had not seen the baby, whom we called Sasha, since birth. "The Russians don't bring the infants back to their mothers until the third day and then swaddled like a Chinese baby with only the eyes, mouth and nose showing."

As such matters were within the province of the Interior Ministry, the birth certificate for Sasha was issued by the much unloved NKVD. And at the top of the document was piously emblazoned the summons "Workers of the World Unite!" Establishing a claim for her American citizenship, I arranged for the consular section of the Embassy to go on record at the Department with the customary form reporting a birth to American parents. As a small flourish, I persuaded the Ambassador to sign and seal the document.

*   *   *

Richard C. Hottelet was the Columbia Broadcasting System correspondent in Moscow. He was one of the congenial group of American journalists, including Brooks Atkinson and then Drew Middleton of *The New York Times*, and Walter Cronkite, who at that time worked for the United Press. As we enjoyed their company, Patricia and I saw a good deal of them and their attractive, bright wives.

Hottelet, who had recently arrived in Moscow, dropped in at my office one day in mid-June. Maxim Litvinov, then Deputy Foreign Minister, had agreed to an interview. Dick wanted to talk over with me what questions he might put to the wily old diplomat who had negotiated the establishment of relations between the United States and the Soviet Union, been the first Soviet Ambassador to Washington, and served as Foreign Minister, seeking to mobilize the democracies in opposition to the rise of Nazism and Fascism. He failed, was replaced by Molotov, and demoted to the rank of Deputy Minister.

An intelligent reporter who had been tempered by a Berlin assignment and Gestapo arrest, Dick needed no coaching from me. And with Litvinov he wasted little time in preliminaries. If the West yielded to the claim then being posed by the Kremlin regarding Trieste, the Italian colonies and other issues, would the growing tension between Moscow and Washington be eased? No, the West would shortly be confronted with the next series of demands.

Litvinov's deliberate answer was remarkable in two respects. It refuted a widespread belief in the West at that time that if only Washington would accede to Moscow's demands the Kremlin would be satisfied and that would be the end of East-West friction. The Kremlin, of course, did not want this illusion dashed. Litvinov's doing so was also remarkable in its disregard of the listening devices that Hottelet naturally assumed were planted in the offices by the secret police.

As the interview progressed, the Deputy Foreign Minister seemed to be anxious to unburden himself to the American. Responding readily to Hottelet's questions, Litvinov said that the Kremlin relied on territory to provide security—believing that the more it had the safer it was. Moscow would not depend on collective security because, according to its ideology, conflict between the Communist and capitalist worlds was inevitable. Although the Soviet Union had not yet at that time developed nuclear weapons, the conversation proceeded on the assumption that Moscow would have the bomb. In those circumstances, Litvinov clearly implied, the Kremlin would not be loath to resort to nuclear weapons if thereby it could achieve a quick victory.

Litvinov dismissed the suggestion that in time new men not bound to then current strategic concepts might succeed to power. The young men were being educated intensively in past patterns. As for popular revolt, underground movements and palace revolutions, if attempted, they would in all likelihood be ineffectual.

Hottelet left the Foreign Office excited by having gotten a unique and fateful story, but apprehensive lest secret police eavesdropping be promptly followed by secret police arrest for espionage or conspiracy. Furthermore, he concluded that he could not then broadcast or cable the information he had obtained. If he tried to do so, first the story and then Litvinov would be killed.

From the Foreign Office Hottelet came to the Embassy, where he told me about the interview and his predicament. While he obviously should not make public what Litvinov had revealed, the information was so significant that it should be passed to the American government. I put Hottelet's account of the interview in the form of a cable and classified it top secret to protect Litvinov's identity. Ambassador Smith was greatly interested in the Deputy Minister's extraordinary revelations, signed the message and sped it on its way.

Why Litvinov spoke out so forthrightly puzzled us. If his office was bugged, as we thought it might be, then he was inviting the severest retribution for statements that in Stalin's eyes would be regarded as, at best, grossly indiscreet or, at worst, treasonous—unless the interview was a provocation. To think, however, that the regime would plant a description of itself by a prominent official in terms used by its foreign critics was far-fetched. Even if the office was free of listening devices, Litvinov still took a great risk because one could not be sure on that score. So, why did he, with what must have been desperate courage, expose his opinions of the system he had long served? Our conclusion was that he was disillusioned, knew that he was about to be retired into deep obscurity, and seized Hottelet's request for an interview as the last opportunity to warn the West about the Kremlin.

Shortly after this Litvinov disappeared from public life. Five and a half years later he died and was given a second grade official funeral. It was not until after this that Hottelet, with characteristic decency and honor, wrote for publication the story of his interview with Litvinov.

What Litvinov said made a deep impression on me. It was not that his statements exposed new information and interpretations. It was that these revelations were made by a high official competent to describe Soviet motives and policy. His opinions seemed to me to reinforce my own estimates. In January 1946 I had observed in a survey of Soviet-Chinese relations that the Soviet Union "by revolutionary tradition, by nationalist ambition, and by kinetic nature, was an expansionist force." And the Kremlin was "ideologically convinced that the Soviet system must eventually come into open conflict with the capitalist West and was strategically obsessed with the concept of national defense in great depth."

In a September 1946 letter I wrote,

The other evening we went to a dinner given by VOKS, a Soviet organization for cultivating foreigners, for a visiting American scientist and his wife. He teaches microbiology at the University of Pennsylvania. In his field he is a great man. But in the field of international relations he is perilously close to being a simpleton. Which is true of so many of our visiting firemen. He is so horrified about the atomic Frankenstein he and his fellows have created that he throws the scientific approach overboard in his panicky approach to the problem of maintaining peace with this phenomenal country . . . making an ass of himself in a field about which he is apparently as ignorant as I am of the fundamentals of microbiology.

Still concerned about gullibility and fellow-traveling, I later wrote, "There is a type of American who comes here who is taken in by the caviar and champagne treatment bestowed on him both literally and figuratively, and who thereupon sees nothing but good in the USSR and proceeds like a flagellant to belittle the achievements of his own country. And when he returns to the U.S. he emits a flood of untruths about the USSR, his dabs of whitewash on the mighty sepulcher. When we try in conversation with him to correct the distortions, we are prejudiced and unwilling to see any good in the Great Experiment."

The Soviet cultural functions meant to tantalize visiting intellectuals, scientists and artists from capitalist countries sometimes brought to light interesting Soviet personalities. At one such occasion, a dinner, Patricia had the good fortune to be seated next to Professor Boris Zbarsky. The genial Professor was distinguished for having embalmed Lenin—and for maintaining the cadaver in the pink, in its glass case in Red Square. For these accomplishments he had been awarded a gold medal and a cerise ribbon, which he proudly sported. The man who embalmed Lenin told Patricia that the process by which he preserved Vladimir Ilyich was a secret. She gained the impression, however, that it involved a multiplicity of injections. The Professor indicated that upkeep on the Bolshevik pharaoh was not at all demanding of his time. She concluded that he was waiting around between embalming jobs.

When not prohibited, normal social contacts by Soviet citizens with foreigners were at least frowned upon by the authorities. I thought that this officially imposed ostracism of us should be tested statistically. From time to time over some eight months I selected on each occasion more or less a dozen names of people mentioned in the press as having been active in the arts, journalism, the party, government, education and labor unions. What I wanted were Soviet approximations of the kinds of people we might normally associate with in an open society. I mailed to the selected names at their office addresses (home addresses were not available to us) invitations to drinks at our Mokhavaya apartment. For each of these get-togethers several of our Russian specialists on the Embassy staff were on hand to make our guests feel at home.

Before I lost count and interest we had invited 228 Soviet citizens. Eight came. In response to the r.s.v.p. on our invitations, 57 politely declined. From 163 there was no response. Of those who came, I remember a columnist well known for his anti-American diatribes and a Komsomol, Communist youth, functionary of middle age. They were gratifyingly argumentative.

A woman educator was so obviously frightened that we deduced that she had naïvely come without having been ordered or granted permission to do so. I deeply regretted this incident. It had not occurred to me that, with the pervasive xenophobic warnings issuing from the Kremlin to its subjects, there could exist an innocent who would blunder into what, without higher clearance, was a perilously compromising situation. It was the old story, extending far back into Tsarist times, that well-meant foreign gestures of friendship to Russians could be injurious to those to whom they were extended.

Certain other visitors to the Embassy also ran serious risks. They were persons who claimed to be Americans, who had come to the Soviet Union in the 1920s and 1930s believing it to be a new utopia and, in adopting their new allegiance, renounced their American citizenship.

Paul Robeson's brother, [whose Christian name I do not recall,] walked into the Embassy and asked if we would arrange for his return to the United States. He said that he was employed as a circus performer. He had had enough of life in the Soviet Union and wanted to go home. But as he had rejected his American citizenship and was now a Soviet national we could do nothing for him. As he left he said that when he was interrogated by the police he would state that he had visited the Embassy to read baseball scores in *The New York Times*. Watching from a front window, one of our staff observed Robeson pass the front of the Embassy after which from a passageway there emerged a man in a black coat and cap who fell into step beside Robeson. That was the last that we saw of him.

A gaunt middle-aged, mid-western woman ventured past the two uniformed policemen stationed in front of the Embassy to ask if we could get her out of the Soviet Union. She had with other disillusioned Americans during the years of the Great Depression come to this land of no unemployment. They had been settled on a collective farm north of Moscow. Life was harder than they had believed possible. Then came the war and they were scattered.

She found her way to Alma Ata, not far from the border with China, where she survived most of the war years on black bread and thin tea as a charwoman in a factory clubhouse. She had illegally come by train to Moscow, as some Russians did, without a ticket and the requisite documents. Knowing what the answer would be—for she had repudiated her American nationality for Soviet citizenship—she nevertheless inquired whether we could help her return to the United States. She accepted the "No" stoically and left to live out the rest of the ghastly consequences of an impulsive act born of distant desperation.

We called him the Beekeeper. He was perhaps in his forties, claimed to be still an American and asked to be repatriated. He said that he was from New York, had come to this socialist paradise in the 1920s, had gotten into trouble for anti-Soviet attitudes and then over the years had been shunted along the Gulag archipelago circuit—Karaganda, the Arctic and Kolyma. He had survived, it emerged, by ingratiation, bribery and betrayals. For some years he had lived less dreadfully in Siberian exile and then illegally made his way to Moscow. Here he roamed the streets and slept on railway station benches, in the eerie existence of those without credentials, in the criminal—and political—underworld.

We radioed the Department asking that it initiate an investigation to determine whether the Beekeeper had indeed been an American citizen. Meanwhile, as the Embassy did not as a matter of principle offer asylum— else it would be overwhelmed indefinitely with multitudes of refugees—the Beekeeper had to leave after the interview. We assumed that once he had walked into the street he would be picked up and that if he thereafter returned to inquire what Washington had to say about his citizenship status, he would do so under police control.

This proved to be the case. The Beekeeper came back and said that the secret police had conceded that when he came to the Soviet Union and was disillusioned, the country was weak. But now he must recognize a great change, the Soviet Union was powerful and the future lay with it. He should abandon any idea of leaving Russia. They would insist that he was a Soviet citizen and would not permit him to depart. Therefore back he must go to exile. Which, we assumed, he did. And to cap the matter, the Department radioed that, as I recall it, although the Beekeeper had lived in the United States, he was not an American but a Baltic immigrant who was wanted for robbery.

George and Annelise Kennan took Patricia and me to the Russian Easter midnight service at the Orthodox Cathedral. As George was then Charge d'Affaires, we traveled in the Ambassador's limousine and were accompanied by two or three of the plainclothesmen assigned to the American chief of mission. Like an icebreaker opening a way through packed ice, they took us on foot through the crowd wedged in the cathedral square. We squeezed into the cathedral and a short distance along its wall. Crushed in front of us to the far-off altar stood men and women in drab overcoats facing the fluttering constellation of candles, liturgical trappings and the clergy in glittering vestments. The resplendent music of Easter midnight swelled from two choirs like a surging melodic sea.

The body heat of packed humanity rose to the ceilings and dome of the cathedral and there against the cold stone condensed to fall in droplets on the throng below. In solemn Byzantine splendor the chanting, brocaded clergy circled the center of the cathedral. Above the somber, frayed garments of the dense crowd the pallid wintered faces of Russia were upturned and transfigured by the massed candlelight, ornate ritual and sublime music and mystery of resurrection.

When we left, the square was still filled with a multitude facing the cathedral in reverent silent adoration. Our plainclothesmen in their black leather coats and black caps quietly said, "Give way, comrades, give way." Momentarily and impassively rendering unto Caesar, those in our way opened a passage through which we intruders upon their worship withdrew.

To honor his former comrade in arms, Field Marshal Sir Bernard Montgomery, in Moscow on a visit, Smith gave a dinner at Spaso House. The Ambassador had been unsuccessful in his efforts to establish the personal relationships with Soviet generals, "getting under the Russian skin," that Truman and Byrnes had expected. As a Sultan shuts off his harem from profane and lascivious eyes, so the Kremlin kept its military commanders in purdah shielded from foreign enticement. However, as a special indulgence for the occasion, Marshal [Ivan] Konev was permitted to join Smith and Montgomery for auld lang syne. But the Marshal was chaperoned by several officers, ostensibly of the general staff.

When Patricia and I arrived for the dinner, Smith told her that she would be sitting next to Konev so as to act as interpreter. Alarmed at the prospect, she protested that she couldn't speak Russian well enough. "Tonight you will," the former Chief of Staff said with a brief, authoritative smile.

Seated next to the meaty marshal and his dangling medals, Patricia's sense of survival dictated that she converse in the vocabulary that she knew. At home in the field of parturition and infant care, she advised Konev that she had given birth to a daughter in Moscow. This intelligence seemed to please the Marshal who then proposed a private toast to Sasha. Thereafter from time to time he would lean over, raise his glass and declaim, "To Sasha."

Patricia's ingenuity was taxed by translating three-way reminiscences of martial exploits among Smith, Monty and Konev. With gestures and sound effects she supplemented her basic Russian. Machine gun, for example, she translated with the Russian word for gun accompanied by (a) an extended forefinger pointed at the Marshal's broad belly and (b) a menacing "brrr." And hand grenade was enacted by a fierce bite on an imaginary ring, followed by a quick forward tug of the right hand away from her face and then a lobbing motion across the banquet table. Closely following her translations, Konev nodded his comprehension.

The time came for homage to the heroes present. Smith rose to his feet, glass held high. "To the victor at El Alamein! To the representative of that great Red Army which won the victory at Stalingrad!" Simultaneously Patricia murmured the translation to Konev. The Marshal stiffened in surprise. "But I wasn't at Stalingrad." Patricia repeated that the Ambassador had toasted "the representative"—and she bore down hard on that word—of the great Red Army which won the victory at Stalingrad. Konev shook his shaved-bald head in displeasure, leaned over the table bellowing to the lieutenant general who was his official interpreter, seated below the salt, "*She* says I was at Stalingrad!" The general-interpreter repeated word for word the translation Patricia had given. The Marshal was not mollified. "But I wasn't at Stalingrad," he declared with finality.

*   *   *

By the end of 1946 the question arose where I would be transferred when my tour of duty at Moscow ended in the spring of 1947. In December, responding to feelers on the subject, I indicated a desire not to return to Far Eastern affairs. And I was not interested in an assignment in Latin America, as I wrote my brother, "being too old to learn Spanish." In a

March 1947 letter I wrote that I might be assigned for studies at the National War College in Washington.

Before I left Moscow, another Foreign Ministers' Conference met there. The American delegation, headed by General Marshall, now Secretary of State, was larger than that brought by Byrnes, was nearly self-sufficient and drew on the Embassy for little more than logistic support. The delegation was accompanied by more than a score of correspondents, most of whom were in the Soviet Union for the first time. They wanted to extend their coverage beyond the conference to interpretive reporting on the USSR. With the emphatic approval of the Ambassador I selected an assortment of the Embassy's classified reports on the Soviet Union which we showed to responsible correspondents for their background information.

Even Smith stood in some awe of Marshall. The Secretary of State was an august figure, as no one else that I met had been. In discharging the functions of his office he was aloofly objective, commanding, impersonal and precise. Socially, in the evening over a drink, Marshall was a Virginia gentleman of the old school—urbane, affable and, with the ladies, courtly.

John Foster Dulles was a member of the delegation, appointed as a bipartisan gesture to the Republican Party. Dulles represented himself as the Republicans' expert on foreign relations and the logical choice for Secretary of State in a Republican administration. He too was urbane and affable. But he was a far lesser man than Marshall. He lacked the magisterial presence and aura of integrity that emanated from the soldier-statesman.

I received orders transferring me to the Department. My replacement was my friend Foy Kohler. We had shared apprenticeships at the Windsor Consulate and in-service schooling at the Department. Foy was eventually to crown a successful career with appointment as Ambassador to the Soviet Union.

Patricia, Sasha and I left Moscow on May 2, 1947. It was not without regret, for Patricia and I had formed good friendships within the confined foreign community. But the parting that we most dreaded was Lena's with Sasha.

An ample woman in her fifties, Lena had been Sasha's nurse since shortly after the baby's birth. She lavished grandmotherly love on her "little grand duchess" because, rather tactlessly, "she talks and talks and never says anything." Lena's devotion to my daughter was matched by her belief, after a certain incident, that I was unworthy of fatherhood.

With misgivings, Lena had left Sasha with me while Patricia took her, Maria, the cook, and Hilda, the maid, to see *Swan Lake* at the Bolshoi, a rare treat for the three of them. I took Sashulinka with me downstairs to my office, where misadventure befell her. Crawling from the desktop onto my knees, she fell and raised a lump on her forehead. Knowing that I was in for trouble when the theater party returned, I sought to divert attention from the bruise by printing across the infant's forehead with bold rubber stamps in red ink TOP SECRET and URGENT.

We went back to the apartment to await my fate. When the door opened, the balletomanes' merry conversation was cut short by a collective gasp. The myopic Lena, her worst fears confirmed—her adored Shulkin's forehead apparently bloodied through the negligence of an irresponsible father—rushed forward, snatched the placid infant from my lap and fled with her to the kitchen.

Some months later when the time came for us to leave Moscow, Lena's farewell to Sasha was poignant. For my part, I felt almost apologetic for taking my daughter from the devoted Lena.

During a stopover at Frankfurt we were joined by Valli Teeaar, a cultured young Estonian woman, a refugee who went with us to the United States as an au pair. The four of us sailed from a still bomb-flattened Rotterdam on the *Noordam*.

PART VI

AT WAR AT HOME

CHAPTER XXII

RETURNING TO AMERICA,
AND THE CHINA LOBBY

The satisfying and civilized manner in which to approach New York is on the deck of a ship. None of this being trussed to a seat, hunched and craning to peer through a small window in the sky at a tipping and revolving city-scape. Nor a lurching rush by the rears of factories and tenements only to be suddenly swallowed in the dark nothingness of tunnels. On the deck of a ship a man is free, on his two feet, breathing real air, and may with leisurely dignity review the city, lined up in splendid array, awaiting his inspection. There is even time to engage in conversation with a landmark before it is out of sight.

As the *Noordam* glided into New York harbor on June 9, 1947, Patricia, Sasha, Valli and I were on deck for the traditional viewing of the Statue of Liberty and the skyline. We passed along the parade line, the downtown skyscrapers all drawn up stiffly at attention. It was a stirring sight.

After some years of moving about Asia and Europe in war and its haggard aftermath, Patricia and I had come back to the land of peace and plenty. We would buy a house and, in Foreign Service terms, settle down for maybe four years until we were assigned abroad again. I had a couple of months vacation due me. We would use that time to visit relatives and friends, and look for a house.

Our first destination was Detroit, where we went to see my Aunt Flossie and show her Sasha. The visit also had an unsentimental purpose—the purchase of a car. Although the post-war demand for automobiles still exceeded the supply, Flossie had arranged for my purchase of a dashing Mercury convertible, black with red upholstery. In this conventionally rakish conveyance we proceeded from the epicenter of the motor age to a big drowsy farm in Virginia, near Charlottesville.

The owner of the farm was Patricia's friend Florence Fisher, then a spinster, who preferred a rustic life to the enameled society in which she grew up. For us nothing could have been more relaxing—the buzzing midsummer heat of the Virginia plains, the cool of the high-ceilinged rooms, the undemanding hospitality of our hostess. But I soon began to chafe under the tranquility. And we had to get to work finding a house. So Patricia and I left Sasha and Valli in the Elysian Fields and drove to Washington in search of a house.

Patricia found one in Alexandria, 1707 Duke Street. It was early nineteenth century Georgian, with a neglected big back yard, gingko, black walnut, apple, cherry and peach trees and a profusion of lilac and other shrubs. The location was unfashionable—an unsightly mixture of shoddy residential and commercial structures. But had the property been in a setting befitting its quality, we would not have been able to afford it.

After moving in on September 30, 1947, bursting with the pride and anxieties of a property owner, I wrote, "Went down to the Government Printing Office and bought an armful of booklets on *How to Judge a House, Bricklaying—An Analysis of the Trade, You Can Make it Out of Old Boxes, The Control of Termites, Herbaceous Flowers*, etc." Fortunately, the repairs and alterations of the house were being done by professionals. My reference library, however, did give me a feeling of handyman confidence.

Meanwhile, Patricia and I worked as unskilled laborers in cleaning up the yard, pruning and planting. Gardening was new to me, and although mowing the lawn and weeding were drudgery, most of the rest of it was solidly satisfying. Perhaps this was so because, in contrast to sports, gardening is elemental, an authentic cultivation of life.

*   *   *

My assignment to Washington in 1947 brought me into the midst of developing national neuroses. The relief, gratification and abounding self-assurance of the American people following the victories in World War II soon began to drain. This decline continued into the 1950s.

Disillusion started when it became evident in 1945 that Allied solidarity, particularly between the United States and the Soviet Union, was dissolving. The American Government had raised hopes during the war that the alliance among the United States, Britain, China and the Soviet Union would endure and guarantee lasting world peace. But Soviet expansion into Eastern Europe and Chinese Communist advances against the Nationalists diluted hope for the future.

The American people came to regard the Red Russians and then the Red Chinese as enemies. For even as we had vanquished one set of foes, we were confronted by a new combination of adversaries. And those who became our enemies seemed no less fanatical and malign than those repulsed at such agony and cost.

Especially upsetting to Americans was the violent transformation of China. When the Chiangs and their Nationalists, whom Americans fancied as the true Chinese—our Chinese—were being routed by the suspect, un-Chinese Communists, Americans were loath to recognize that this was caused by Nationalist decadence and Communist vitality. Rather than acknowledging that the transformation of China was being wrought primarily by indigenous forces, most Americans felt that, surely, some fell force outside of China must be responsible for so untoward a turn of events. International Communism masterminded from conspiratorial Moscow was a ready explanation.

North Korea's 1950 invasion of South Korea, American resort to arms in defense of the South, General MacArthur's heedless offensive to China's frontiers, followed by Chinese Communist routing of the American divisions, culminating in a frustrating stalemate rather than a proper American victory—this train of events jolted American self-esteem and self-confidence. It also intensified popular hatred of the Chinese Communists and belief that the United States was imperiled by a monolithic Communism directed by the Kremlin.

The Soviet acquisition of the atomic bomb in 1949 heightened American anxieties. Americans might then for the first time be killed by hundreds of thousands per blast. People wondered how they could escape fragmentation, incineration and radiation. This was in the days even before intercontinental ballistic missiles, when the delivery of nuclear attacks would have been by aircraft, allowing those in the Washington area probably at least an hour or two of warning.

A Washington friend confided that he was buying just the right place away from the city—close enough to get to before the atomic burst, yet far enough so as not to be overrun by refugees less alert and well equipped than he. Another friend had built a commodious, reinforced underground shelter to which there would be controlled admission—his family (no pets), a carpenter, a plumber and their wives and children. My friends were not hysterical survivalists; they were sober, intelligent and well-informed. But they were representative of widespread apprehension, even fear.

*   *   *

The debate over whether to develop a hydrogen bomb, the decision to do so, the awesome tests of thermonuclear weapons only to be followed by Soviet development of such weapons magnified anxieties over nuclear annihilation.

Not only had comrades in arms turned into adversaries and an American monopoly of what was viewed as the ultimate weapon lost to a hostile power, but fear of espionage and subversion also invaded public consciousness. Even before the end of the war, defecting Soviet officials such as Alexander Barmine, Igor Gouzenko, and Victor Kravchenko provided first-hand testimony of the Kremlin's penetration of democratic societies. Then American and other apostate Communists—Whittaker Chambers, Louis F. Budenz, Elizabeth Bentley, Freda Utley, Professor Karl Wittfogel and others—sounded alarms, proclaiming that Soviet-inspired subversion was rife in the American government, academe, journalism and the arts. They named those whom they regarded as agents or dupes of an omniscient, pervasive Soviet conspiracy.

Through congressional hearings and speeches, particularly by Representative Richard M. Nixon and Senators Pat McCarran and Joseph McCarthy, the accusations of the apostates were amplified and given credence. Chambers's charges that Alger Hiss had passed government secrets to him when he, Chambers, was a Soviet agent, caught national attention in hearings starring Representative Nixon. And when these accusations were, in the eyes of the public, in effect confirmed in two court trials, assertions that spies infested the State Department came to be widely accepted.

Dawning doubts that the United States was omnipotent and fears of new enemies, nuclear obliteration and Communist infiltration combined to create a state of mind easily susceptible to exploitation. With varying motives, three categories of persons and institutions preyed upon the national anxieties.

One was the Chinese Nationalists. Striving to extract aid from and involve the United States in their decrepit and doomed struggle against the Communists, the Nationalists recognized that rising American apprehensions provided an opportunity to manipulate the American body politic for their purposes. In addition to lobbying for all-out American support, the Chinese Embassy and other Nationalist agencies in the United States, well connected with the American government and press, fostered attacks on Americans who opposed further futile, entangling involvement with the Nationalists. This calumny was directed particularly against those who suggested realistic recognition that the Communists were going to command China's future.

A second category supported and, in turn, was used by the Chinese Nationalists. It was composed of a mixed, unstructured, freewheeling, variously motivated lot of American publicists, businessmen, military officers, politicians, churchmen and apostate Communists. It was called the China Lobby. The members of this miscellaneous assortment drew their information not only from Nationalist sources but also from collaborating ex-Communists. What the lobbyists had in common was a belief that the United States should sustain the Nationalists and that the American government was, a best, deserting a faithful ally. Most, in their lobbying, attributed this supposed delinquency to alleged pro-Chinese Communist influences in the Department of State, more particularly to some of us who were China specialists.

Prominent in the China Lobby were publishers Henry Luce of *Time* and *Life*, Roy Howard of the Scripps-Howard newspapers and William Loeb of the Manchester *Union Leader*, columnists Joseph Alsop and George Sokolsky, ex-Ambassadors Hurley and William Bullitt, Generals Chennault and Wedemeyer, Clare Boothe Luce and Yale professor David Nelson Rowe. Perhaps the most diligent and evangelical lobbyist was Alfred Kohlberg, a wealthy importer of Chinese laces and embroideries who launched and subsidized a magazine, *Plain Talk*, regarded as the voice of the China Lobby.

The China Lobby members showed no qualms over attacking their government's policy regarding China. Accepting the Nationalists' interpretation of the situation in China, and championing the cause of that foreign government, they maintained, in effect, that what was good for the Chinese Nationalists was good for the United States.

As they assumed identical interests between the Chinese Nationalists and the United States, there appeared to be no question in their minds of a conflict of loyalties. Rather, a suggestion that Nationalist interests might not necessarily be in the interests of the United States raised suspicions of disloyalty to the United States. This was true not only of the China Lobby but also of a China bloc in the Congress.

Usually relying on information supplied by the Chinese Nationalists and the China Lobby, these legislators demanded and voted for increased aid to the Nationalists. And they discovered that accusing the Truman administration of losing China and harboring Reds in the State Department satisfied their sense of patriotic duty and generated compliant publicity that served their political objectives of discrediting the administration and furthering their own political ambition.

Outstanding members of the China bloc in the Senate were William Knowland (for his devotion, nicknamed the Senator from Formosa), Styles Bridges, H. Alexander Smith, all Republicans, and McCarran and James O. Eastland, Democrats. They were, as the betrayal of China theme was expanded, joined at times by senators who appreciated the effectiveness of that issue in their political forays against the Truman administration. These ranged from the reckless barrages of McCarthy to the scattered flak of Robert A. Taft, an influential conservative who otherwise displayed slight interest in East Asia.

In the House of Representatives, Walter Judd, a former medical missionary in China, was the most dogged campaigner for the Nationalists and against the Truman administration. Among those of like kidney were John M. Vorys and Joseph W. Martin. All three were Republicans. Like the senatorial members of the China bloc, they practiced a convenient blending of what they held to be patriotic principle—equating Chinese Nationalist and American interests—and partisan politics.

It was, then, in a national mood of mounting public apprehension, suspicion and anxiety, exacerbated by Chinese agitators, American lobbyists and hostile member of Congress, that we China specialists of the Foreign Service went about our business during the decade following World War II.

CHAPTER XXIII

ASSIGNED TO KENNAN'S POLICY
PLANNING STAFF

In August 1947 I reported for duty on the Policy Planning Staff, of which Kennan had been appointed Director. It was designated by the initials S/P. The S meant that the staff was part of the Secretary of State's immediate office and the P indicated the function, policy planning. As director of the staff, Kennan had ready access and reported directly to the Secretary, General Marshall. The physical location of S/P, next to the Secretary's office, conformed to this relationship with the head of the Department.

S/P, established on May 5, 1947, was General Marshall's creation. He was accustomed, from his years as Army Chief of Staff, to thinking ahead in terms of ongoing campaigns and, in so doing, having at his beck and call echelons of planners. Certainly, as Secretary of State he had no less need of forward planning. S/P was therefore told in a departmental order to formulate long-term foreign policy programs, anticipate upcoming problems, examine broad politico-military issues, evaluate the adequacy of existing policy and coordinate planning with the Department.

The State Department had never had more than occasional ad hoc committees for peering into the future. And there was a real question how something as diffuse and anarchic as foreign affairs could be realistically forecast and programmed. In any event the Department—including the Foreign Service—had always functioned largely by precedent, esoteric knowledge, intuition, extemporization and salvage, and rather liked it that way. So the appearance of S/P was not greeted gladly by the foreign affairs professionals. Only the awesome authority of Marshall and Kennan's professional prestige among his colleagues won for the staff a skeptical acceptance.

In August 1947, S/P was composed of Kennan; Carlton Savage, who had long been associated with Cordell Hull and to whom we listened as the oracle of elemental America; Joseph E. Johnson, a former professor at Williams College; Jacques Reinstein, a State Department economist who had been working on German affairs; and Ware Adams, a Foreign Service officer fresh from Central European assignments. Before the year was out, Johnson had left and others had joined the staff—Henry [Harry] Villard, with experience in the Arab world and Africa, and George Butler, a Latin Americanist. The turnover in staff continued beneficially, on the whole, throughout my four years at S/P.

My advent on the staff had been heralded by some slight advance publicity. John Chamberlain, one of Henry Luce's pundits, in a *Life* article, pretentiously cast as a memorandum to Robert Lovett, had welcomed Lovett's appointment to be Marshall's deputy, as Under Secretary of State, and praised Kennan for being alert to the Soviet menace. But Chamberlain warned Lovett to beware of me. I had been "Stilwell's political officer," Chamberlain said, "Vinegar Joe Stilwell was until his recall the symbolic head of the anti-Chiang, pro-Chinese-Communist movement that later did its best to unseat Pat Hurley as ambassador to Chungking."

Assuming an impartial pose, Chamberlain conceded that I might or might not "support what has become known as the John Carter Vincent Chinese policy": to "merge" Communists in the Chinese government. Chamberlain also denied that Chinese Communism was "different" from Stalinism. And after claiming that both Marshall and Lovett's predecessor, Dean Acheson, was mistaken in his view of Communism, he stopped short of urging Lovett to institute a purge, but did assert that "it is still a fact that the State Department has never had a house-cleaning." While I always felt disturbed by attacks such as this, I do not recall Chamberlain's sniping having created any unpleasantness in my personal relationships.

During the Marshall secretaryship, Kennan was S/P. Without him the staff would have been insignificant. There were two reasons for this. One was the Secretary's reliance on him. The second—the reason for Marshall's confidence in Kennan—was George's grasp of the world scene and his exceptional ability to conceptualize and interpret international relations. The rest of us acted as a sounding board against which he played his ideas, and as critics, contributors and occasionally originators of policy papers which would then be edited, adopted or rejected by the staff as a whole, with Kennan acting as editor-in-chief. Kennan, of course, took final responsibility for papers issued by S/P.

The staff assembled in its conference room whenever there was something to talk about: the draft of a policy paper, a query from the Secretary, an important new international development, or to hear and interrogate someone with something to say, for example, Professor Hans Morgenthau, J. Robert Oppenheimer, Air Marshal Sir John Slessor, the Governor of Puerto Rico (Luis Muñoz Marín) or the Reverend Dr. Reinhold Niebuhr. Staff sessions were conducted informally and with a good deal of spontaneity. Naturally members of the staff freely consulted one another. And because I was acquainted with East Asian specialists in the operating, intelligence and research divisions, I regularly maintained contact with them lest I levitate into ivory towerism.

Having cut its teeth on the Marshall Plan, the staff was, when I joined it, still involved with phases of the European recovery program. The acute crises in Western Europe and in Greece and Turkey continued to be the focus of our attention in the autumn of 1947.

I did, however, react to the draft of a proposed peace treaty for Japan, prepared elsewhere in the Department.

To Kennan, I wrote in part on August 11, that the draft treaty

appears to be preoccupied with drastic disarmament and democratization under continuing international supervision, including the U.S.S.R. But demilitarization is no longer a serious problem in the case of Japan. Even if it so desired, Japan could not in the foreseeable future resurrect itself as a first-class military power. As for democratization, it is questionable whether the presence of the U.S.S.R. on an international supervisory body would contribute to democratic advances. It is likely that the U.S.S.R. in this position would be a disruptive influence in Japan, placing the onus for continued supervision on the U.S. and conspiring to bring about sovietized totalitarianism. The ease with which a coup could be engineered under the proposed treaty is manifest. . . . Occupation forces having been withdrawn, the Japanese government would have at its disposal for the maintenance of security and order only a civil police force equipped with small arms.

Kennan passed the memorandum to the Under Secretary, Mr. Lovett, who replied, "GK: I have sent the 'treaty' back as being wholly inadequate in present form."

My next production had nothing to do with policy planning. It was, uncharacteristically, an effort at literary censorship. General Stilwell had died of cancer in October 1946, and Teddy White, who in disgust quit working "in Mr. Luce's whorehouse," as he called the *Time-Life* publications, wrote to me from New York that Stilwell's widow had turned over to him the General's wartime diaries and other personal papers asking him to arrange for their publication. Apprehensive over unfavorable reaction to Stilwell's private and uninhibited venting of spleen, I told Teddy that I thought that the papers should not be published then. He brought the manuscript—excerpts from Stilwell's papers with his own fluent connective narrative—to Washington.

There it was, what I had feared: raw Vinegar Joe. Teddy omitted most of the scatology, but not the vituperative excesses, the bitter exasperation of a weary, frustrated man unburdening himself to himself. For he was writing in large part for therapy, not for verbatim publication. Stilwell's considered public writings were lean, precise and literate, with a sensitive appreciation of words and meaning.

Teddy returned to New York unpersuaded by me.

In a memo, September 22, I laid the matter before General M. S. (Pat) Carter, the Secretary's personal assistant. I quoted White as saying that Mrs. Stilwell was determined to have the papers published as a vindication of her husband. She could be prohibited from publishing, I continued, but that would probably result in outcries of "suppression" and "persecution." I offered to try to dissuade her by letter, but felt that General Marshall, on the basis of old friendship, would be more effective than I.

My memo was returned with the notation: "Let me see a draft of a possible letter of Mr. Davies to Mrs. Stilwell. G.C.M." I sent a draft in to the Secretary. He suggested a few word changes but emphasized that these were only suggestions and that he did not wish to rewrite my letter.

After a couple of paragraphs easing into the subject, I said to Mrs. Stilwell,

> to those of us who worked for the General, who felt a particular devotion and respect for him, who suffered with him in his tribulations, the matter of his name, his prestige, has been of great importance. We knew he was a

unique and great man in the righteous tradition of an Old Testament prophet, in the tradition of John Brown at Harper's Ferry. We share with you the feeling the Joe Stilwell must not be misunderstood.

At the present time the General's name is held in very high esteem throughout the country. There is some sniping, yes, but that is true of every public figure. And the shots are so few, ineffectual, and far between that I feel they should be ignored. They will be emphasized or magnified by any other course.

I venture to voice two specific misgivings in the matter. One relates to the statement of the General's case as presented in his papers. The other concerns the likelihood that publication will provoke replies from some of those criticized in the papers.

It is a great loss to history that Joe Stilwell died before he could prepare at leisure, in long perspective, and in brisk, lucid Stilwellian prose, a full account of his World War II mission. It would have been a measured and powerful statement of his case before history. What is at hand, however, are fragments—revealing, poignant fragments, most of them written hurriedly when he was harassed and tired. Such papers cannot portray the full stature of the man. And, practically speaking, they are an incomplete and unsatisfactory mosaic of Joe Stilwell's case before the world.

The reopening of bygone issues and the resultant retorts from those criticized may, I think you will agree, have a far-reaching effect on the General's prestige. In publishing these papers Joe Stilwell's last bolt is shot, while others have unlimited opportunity of rebuttal in whatever form they choose. I am sure that you have taken this serious possibility into consideration. My plea is that you again reexamine the whole problem and all that might flow from the publication.

Finally, I ask you to forgive me for intruding into a Stilwell family matter; one which I know is deeply felt. You know that I do so only because I consider myself to be almost one of you and because I therefore partake of your feeling for the General.

On the heels of the letter to Mrs. Stilwell I wrote to Teddy, encapsulating what I had said to her, adding that if they nevertheless felt that they must go ahead with publication, he should get official clearance of the manuscript so that there would be no question of violation of security. I had mentioned this to him earlier because I was concerned lest the War

Department crack down on him for breach of security. Ending on a personal note, I was inspired to offer the future author of *The Making of a President* series a remarkably poor piece of advice—return to being a foreign correspondent and stop trying to report on domestic American affairs as, aside from working on the Stilwell papers, he was doing.

Teddy bore all of my interference with exemplary good will, but argued that the American people "should have the facts now, not as a matter of historical exegesis one hundred years hence." Here I agreed in principle with Teddy. I believed at least as strongly as he that "the facts" should promptly be out. But I feared that "the facts" would be distorted by public reaction, pro or con, to Stilwell's cantankerous presentation of them.

In the end, I received no reply from Mrs. Stilwell, General Marshall agreed that I should drop the matter, *The Stilwell Papers* was published in 1948, the book was a success for Teddy (which greatly pleased me), it proved to each side—pro and anti-Stilwell, pro and anti-Chiang—what each already believed, and the nation continued its slippage into an anxiety neurosis about China, Russia and Communism.

*   *   *

Having acquired materiel surrendered by the Japanese and begun to capture American arms from defeated Nationalist units, the Communists in 1947 went onto an offensive that in two years was to expel Chiang and his legions from the Asian mainland. As Chiang's armies started to fall back, agitation grew in the United States for American intervention on behalf of the Nationalists. I stated in a November 3, 1947 S/P memorandum that while a major extension of Communist control in China would be a serious reversal, it would not be a catastrophe for the United States. As for American assistance to the Nationalists, I said that without political, economic and military reforms in China, large-scale aid would lead to little more than heightened corruption. I doubted that the Nationalists were capable of the necessary reform.

Manchuria, it seemed to me, was a special problem, "a salient pressed deep into the U.S.S.R., strategically outflanking the Soviet Far East . . . an area of vital military and political concern to the U.S.S.R." Furthermore, "the Kremlin probably interpreted the U.S. position at Yalta as indicating

U.S. acceptance of predominant Soviet interest in Manchuria." So long as another power did not intervene in Manchuria and the Nationalist position there continued to deteriorate, Moscow was content that events would go its way. But should the United States "aid the Nationalists to such an extent as to threaten a reversal of this process, the U.S.S.R. would probably take compensatory measures." This might develop into an American-Soviet showdown. I then asked "whether on balance, U.S. security would be served by setting such a train of events in action, and whether, if we must have a showdown with the U.S.S.R., it is desirable that it take place over so limited an object of contention as Manchuria."

I concluded that "there exist strong traditional ties of sentiment between the U.S. and China and a highly vocal body of opinion in this country advocating U.S. aid to the Nationalist Government in the current Chinese civil war. For practical reasons these voices cannot be ignored. Furthermore, a certain amount of aid to China at this time is justified as moral support to the Central Government, the rapid collapse of which would be contrary to our interests."

Consequently, I recommended granting "the minimum aid necessary to satisfy American public opinion and, if possible, to prevent any sudden and total collapse of the Chinese Government. On the other hand, it would be futile to attempt to bring about a complete Government victory in the civil war, including the recovery of all Manchuria. Firstly, that objective is not within the realm of feasibility. Secondly, such an attempt would be regarded by the U.S.S.R. as a repudiation of American commitments and might well lead to a U.S.-Soviet conflict in an area of dubious strategic advantage to the U.S."

The promulgation of the Marshall Plan for Europe prompted demands that a similar program be devised for East Asia. Typical of this advocacy was Governor Thomas Dewey's November 5 accusation that while a great program was being prepared to help Europe, nothing had been proposed concerning China. The Governor, who was already at work to challenge Harry Truman for the presidency in the following year, put this charge in the context of the administration's turning against our wartime Chinese allies, and scuttling China.

"The Far East has, like Europe," I wrote on December 4, 1947,

suffered in varying degrees from the effects of the recent war. But the ills of that area are complicated and intensified by factors which do not generally

*affect Europe. For the Far East is undergoing, in varying degrees and in
varying forms, a profound political, economic, and social revolution. This
revolution is not the product of the war; it is one of long standing and one
which . . . is bound to continue.*

*Thus, an area twice the size of Europe and with a population three times
that of Europe is afflicted with most of the ills of Europe, including ideological conflict, plus those arising from a precipitate and concentrated transition from medievalism to modernism.*

*Politically, the U.S. can play a constructive role in the Far East only
insofar as the Far Eastern people are willing and capable of helping themselves. The U.S. should not, cannot, and will not undertake to dictate the
political future of the Far East. The people of the Far East must, as must
people everywhere, work out their own destiny.*

*An effective rehabilitation of Europe will place a heavy burden on the
American taxpayer. But in assuming this burden, the American people are
able to have some notion of the dimensions of the task to be done in Europe
. . . their contribution is a calculated economic risk. A similar approach to
the Far East as a whole or to China alone, is not possible. They represent
an incalculable economic risk.*

*It is perhaps in the cultural field that the U.S. can play its most construc-
tive role. The greatest contribution which the U.S. has been able to make
to Asia in the past has been in the field of education, science, technology,
and in the presentation of the concept of humanism.*

As the Chinese Communists continued to defeat the Nationalists,
Chiang's partisans in the American Congress and press heightened their
demands that the Truman administration go to the aid of the Nationalists.
The Department of State was the main target of this bombardment which
came also, but less conspicuously, from within the Executive—particularly
from disciples of Chennault, Wedemeyer and Miles in the Pentagon. Characteristically, the State Department was on the defensive and not getting its
reasoning across to the public, much less to its critics.

In August 1948, we examined in the Policy Planning Staff this most
controversial facet of American foreign policy—that in respect of China. I
drafted the first discursive version of a position paper.

Wishing to approach the contentious issues of policy in cooling perspective, I began with an analysis of surging population growth in China.
This fitted in with our concern at that time over worldwide demographic

problems. I considered China's mounting population in relation to its natural resources, which by then available data were thought to be relatively limited.

China's only escape from a Malthusian fate, it seemed, was through industrialization. But it had to be achieved rapidly or China's "relentless fecundity will tend to (a) eat up the initial gains of any industrialization and (b) perpetuate the very instability which so inhibits industrialization." Alternatively, the population pressure might be dealt with by "draconian measures of suppression and coercion against the symptoms of the demographic fever."

Without reference to the Nationalists and Communists, my pessimistic conclusions were that the future for China was chaos or authoritarianism. Authoritarianism might be able to break the vicious population-industrialization circle "by drastic means, such as forcible 'socialization.'" But at best this would be at a heavy, protracted cost to the whole social structure.

China's military significance, again without reference to its political complexion, I assessed in the context of an American-Soviet war. I downgraded the importance of "hordes of raw Chinese soldiery, no matter on which side they were fighting." This was a less than prophetic dictum, two years before Chinese hordes routed Americans in North Korea. And, I continued, "until China develops a modern transportation network in its vast hinterland it will, excepting for its coastal fringe, more closely resemble a strategic morass than a strategic springboard."

Turning to the situation then prevailing in China, I said that the Communists held all of Manchuria, excepting for three urban enclaves. They also controlled most of North China and were threatening Central China, the base of Nationalist power. I listed the foreign assistance received by both sides—the Nationalists far more from us than the Communists from the Russians. On that basis, the more numerous Nationalists, with other overwhelming materiel advantages, should have been winning the civil war hands down. That they were not was because of, in sum, decay, demoralization, atrocious generalship and alienation of the population. The Communists were winning for a variety of reasons, including popular support, skilled political and military leadership, and among the troops, good discipline and high morale.

American policy could not ignore Soviet intentions with regard to China. I indicated that the Kremlin wished to detach certain border areas in Manchuria and Sinkiang, making them separatist regimes controlled by

Moscow, thereby reducing China's power potential and filling out the buffer zone along the Soviet southern frontiers. The other Kremlin concern was "not how the Chinese Communists must be helped . . . to win the civil war—they are doing about as well as could be expected on that score—but how to ensure complete and lasting control over them . . ."

To the proposition that the United States should aid the Nationalists to the extent necessary to reverse the course of the civil war, I said that this would mean overt intervention. "The more openly we intervened . . . the more we would become politically involved, the more the National Government would tend to be regarded in Chinese eyes as a puppet—and thus discreditable, and the more the intervention would cost." It was "a course of action of huge, indefinite and hazardous proportions. The American Government cannot rightly gamble thus with American prestige and resources."

Although I anticipated the disappearance of the Nationalists, when and how it would occur could not be predicted. The situation was so fluid that it would be "misleading at this stage to attempt any detailed charting of a course to be followed for the next several years." American policy toward China should be defined for the immediate future in "the most flexible and elementary terms." These were: continue to recognize the National Government; with its disappearance decide on whom to recognize "in the light of circumstances at the time"; and prevent as far as possible "China's becoming an adjunct of Soviet politico-military power."

Certain principles, I thought, should be taken into account in the conduct of our China policy. We should realize that tremendous indigenous forces were at work in China beyond our power to control. Therefore there were considerable limitations on what we could do to affect the course of events there. To act counter to the basic forces would be to multiply these limitations. To align ourselves with these natural forces would be to multiply our influence.

The Kremlin's ability to utilize and influence China (which was keeping Washington officialdom awake at night) was also severely qualified. "It is impossible that the Kremlin could in the space of the next crucial five years mobilize China's resources and manpower to the extent that they would constitute a serious threat to U.S. security." It remained to be proved whether Moscow could do this over the long run. And if Soviet imperialism did not survive, Chinese Communism would be of minor security concern to us, for it was potentially dangerous for us only if linked with Soviet politico-military power.

Guarding against irrevocable commitment to any one faction or course of action, "we must be willing to cut our losses" in a losing proposition. And "we must place no reliance on the subjective attitude of any Chinese faction or government toward the U.S. Fear and favor always have and still do control fundamentally the attitude of foreign governments toward us, but only if expertly wielded . . . our strength . . . must be exercised in a form which is effective; it must not be dissipated by misapplication."

American military strength cannot be effectively applied in China excepting at prohibitive cost. By avoiding overt intervention and relying on politico-cultural measures, the Kremlin had phenomenal success in riding the ground swell of the Chinese revolution. The most effective application of American strength would be political, cultural and economic.

Echoing the wartime recommendations of quid pro quo bargaining with Chiang, I said, "Economic favor becomes tribute if it continues to be given without exactions. While we must have favors in hand, in the shape of economic aid authorizations, for the post-Chiang situation, they must not be pre-committed. The Executive must have the flexibility to give or withhold."

My draft was refined by the staff and submitted to the Secretary as Policy Planning Staff paper number 39. From the State Department PPS 39 was sent to the National Security Council for consideration. There it was denominated NSC 34.

CHAPTER XXIV

WORKING WITH THE NATIONAL
SECURITY COUNCIL

I was dispatched from the Policy Planning staff several times during October 1948 to the National Security Council office in the old State Department building. There I met in afternoons of solemn communion with a Navy captain and two colonels, one Army, the other Air Force. We were the so-called working level of a recently begun attempt to blend foreign and defense policies. The particular drafting sessions in which I participated had to do with China policy. We made little progress because the military conviction that the American government should expand aid to the Chinese Nationalists and the State Department's position, withdrawal from the Chinese tangle, were irreconcilable.

The captain and colonels were formal and, it seemed to me, somewhat ill at ease. This was not surprising. Many military officers shared a popular suspicion that American diplomats intrigued, bungled and were outsmarted by foreigners, thereby contributing to the causes of war—whereupon the bluff, honest soldiery was called upon to shed its blood to save the country. With the subject under consideration being policy toward China, the captain and colonels had further reason to be suspicious. The State Department was widely considered in the Pentagon to be soft on Chinese Communism and so a dupe, at best, of Moscow. Furthermore, I assumed that my confreres were aware of my identity and how little I was appreciated by Admiral Miles and Generals Wedemeyer, Chennault and Hurley.

*   *   *

Our scant progress caused the Executive Secretary of the National Security Council, from time to time, to open the door enough to poke his head into the room and urge us to redouble our efforts. He was Rear Admiral (retired) Sidney W. Souers, a bustling Missouri businessman turned naval intelligence officer during the war. His assistant, who succeeded him in 1950, was James S. Lay, an electrical engineer who became an Army intelligence officer and then moved nimbly about and upward in the intelligence bureaucracy. Both were unassuming, a rare personality trait in Washington.

My military collaborators and I were unable to produce an agreed paper. I do not recall what happened to the failed effort. Logically, the subject would have been referred to the senior policy officials at State and Defense for resolution.

The practice of combined planning grew out of World War II. Prior to that, foreign policy was formulated in the White House and the State Department with occasional ad hoc consultation with the Navy and War Departments when military considerations had to be taken into account. The nature of World War II and Roosevelt's method of governing changed this. The war was politically surcharged: Fascism, Nazism, Communism, Democracy, Imperialism, Colonialism and Nationalism. There were also the mundane rivalries and frictions among allies. Consequently, multiform political factors entered into military planning and operations. And so American officers, who prided themselves on being apart from, if not above, sordid politics, found themselves taking account of political considerations and eventually accustomed to indulging in political judgments.

Roosevelt's manner of governing reinforced the military's trend toward participation in formulating foreign policy. The President was very much his own Secretary of State. He slighted the State Department and during the war the Joint Chiefs of Staff was probably closer to the White House on major foreign policy matters than was the State Department. Their guidance often came from the White House through military channels, bypassing the State Department.

With demobilization following the end of the war, some of the abler military reserve officers transferred to the State Department and the Foreign Service. They not only smartened up the creaking administrative structure of the department, they also introduced a greater awareness of military factors in international affairs.

Of broader significance were certain basic organizational changes. Waging World War II had taught the Executive and the Congress that the government needed to be better coordinated and, in the case of the armed services, consolidated—however reluctantly. The National Security Act of 1947 therefore provided for, among other things, the subordination of the three military departments to a Department of Defense, the creation of a Central Intelligence Agency and the establishment of a National Security Council.

The composition of the Council changed during its first years—and thereafter. But the core of the NSC was the President, the Vice President and the Secretaries of State and Defense. Truman regarded the Council as a body whose other members served as advisers to him in important questions of foreign and related military affairs. Decisions, however, rested solely with the President. And a decision had no validity unless it was recorded in writing and signed by the President. This was a procedure that Winston Churchill, when Prime Minister, had imposed on his cabinet to discourage any tendency to misquote oral statements, whether from faulty memory or less forgivable reasons.

In its infancy the staff of the National Security Council, later so bursting with derring do, was suitably wee, limited in reach and dependent on others. In addition to Souers and Lay, there were a junior assistant or two with supporting secretaries. My impression was that this was a remarkably unobtrusive arm of government. The NSC grew during the Truman administration, but not nearly to the proportions to which it later swelled.

Mercifully, there was no such straddling mandarin as a National Security Advisor to the President. The Secretaries of State and Defense were deemed to be sufficient for advice in national security matters. When stubborn differences occurred between the two, they were resolved by the boss of both—the President. It is difficult to imagine George C. Marshall as Secretary of Defense and Dean Acheson as Secretary of State feeling the need of or tolerating a referring factotum between them and, even more, between them and the President. As for Truman, he insisted that the head of the NSC staff be no more than an executive secretary whose authority was limited to moving papers and recording decisions; certainly not to intrude into policy-making and operations. He was expected to spend his evenings and Sundays contentedly at his desk or home, not luxuriating in TV talk shows, pontificating at variance with the Secretary of State, broadcasting cacophony in the American government.

Admiral Souer's anxious urging of my three military confreres and me to produce an agreed paper was meant to spare the members of the NSC, especially the President, the exertion of thinking through the problem and coming to a coherent decision. Exhortations to concurrence are constructive when differences are not basic. Pressure to produce unanimity in the face of fundamental disagreement, however, risks producing platitudes. These are an evasion of the Government's responsibility to choose consciously among conflicting courses of action—and so to govern.

*   *   *

Acheson believed that only major issues should be brought to the NSC for decision by the President. To encourage frank discussion he thought that sessions of the NSC should be limited to members of the Council meeting without assistants. This assumed that the Secretaries of State and Defense were informed on the issues under consideration and that the President was willing, alert and intellectually capable of engaging in what Acheson called "the anguish of decision." Truman was such a president.

A scant three years before my sessions at the NSC office, General Wedemeyer, Commodore Miles and Ambassador Hurley (whose expertise presumably derived from having been Hoover's Secretary of War and from his rank as Honorary Major General in the Reserves) met on March 27, 1945 with the Joint Chiefs of Staff. The triumvirate from China assured the JCS that the Communists could be suppressed if comparatively little aid was provided to the Nationalists. And Wedemeyer declared at a press conference on August 30, 1945, "I do not believe that the Communists are strong either in number or effort anywhere in China. . . . Regardless of their number or equipment I do not anticipate any difficulty with the Communists."

Then the Secretary of War, Robert Patterson, on November 20, 1945 dismissed the significance of the Communists, asserting that the 60,000 United States marines then in China could walk from one end of China to the other without serious hindrance for, after all, hostilities between the Nationalists and the Communists were no more than comic opera fighting. As the civil war spread to involve a cast of more than two and a half million Nationalist troops and more than one and a half million Communists, and as the Nationalists suffered crushing defeat after defeat notwithstanding

American aid, the Pentagon came to the conclusion that the Chinese conflict was not a musical comedy.

Miscalculations of Chinese Communist military capabilities were characteristic of the initial underestimation of Asians who had been and were to become our adversaries: Filipino insurrectionists, the Japanese, the Chinese and the Vietnamese.

From belittling the Communist armies, the Pentagon swung in 1947–1948 to viewing them with alarm. They were regarded as willing and loyally subject to the Kremlin's orders. Should they win the civil war, they might be expected to join with the Soviet forces to form a juggernaut which would overrun Southeast Asia in pursuit of the Kremlin's terrifying objective of world domination. To most of the American military it was as simple as that.

The conventional Pentagon wisdom was that the only counter to the red onrush, short of massive, last resort American military intervention, was the Chinese Nationalists. But their performance had been so hesitant and bungling that, if they were to be at all effective, they would have to be bolstered by American materiel and "advisors."

This was a prescription for more of the same, despite experience and current evidence. Advisors had been and were, with scant effect, counseling and supplying the Generalissimo and his commanders. The flow of benevolence began in 1941 with a mission headed by Brigadier General John Magruder. Then came Stilwell with his extensive advisory, training and supply structure, followed by Wedemeyer and, finally, Major General David G. Barr heading an advisory group of 1,300. As for materiel, Barr testified that during his time in China, at the height of the civil war, the Nationalists had never lost a battle for lack of arms and ammunition.

Nevertheless, responding to the fervent Secretary of Defense, James V. Forrestal, the Joint Chiefs of Staff recommended on August 5, 1948 "well-supervised assistance to the Chinese National Government, with safeguards against misuse of such assistance and with inclusion of military equipment assistance." This seemingly virile call to action, characteristic of too many planning papers, contained qualifications emasculating the recommendations.

Two qualifications: "well-supervised" and "with safeguards," rendered the recommendations practically meaningless. For supervision of assistance to be effective meant going beyond making sure that bills of lading, invoices and receipts were tidy. It meant making sure that the aid was not hoarded (which so disgusted Stilwell), sold on the black market or yielded to the Communists (which so offended Barr), but put to the use for which it was given. Once the assistance was turned over to the Nationalists there were virtually no safeguards against misuse short of inserting an American chain of command from Chiang's general staff to company level with authority over the use of aid. This was manifestly out of the question, as demonstrated when Stilwell sought something of the sort, resulting in Chiang's demanding and getting Vinegar Joe's recall.

Therefore the JCS recommendation was sophistry.

The State Department's opinion that the United States government should militarily disentangle itself from the Chinese civil war provoked Forrestal to declare that the government had no policy toward China. This was in accord with the popular assumption that policy meant action. Don't just stand there. Do something! In reality, of course, policy also includes passages of inaction, watchful waiting or calculated aloofness.

Shortly after Acheson became Secretary of State and was delving into China policy he quizzed four or five of us with experience in China. When my turn came, I said that China was like a house whose roof and walls were collapsing and that before we could decide what, if anything, might be sensibly done, we had to wait for the dust to settle. Acheson later in one or two public statements advocated waiting in China until the dust had settled. This stimulated, from China Lobby types, furious accusations of no policy, defeatism and softness on Communism. Acheson was not cowed by the outcry. But letting the dust settle was not adopted as a foreign policy slogan.

CHAPTER XXV

REVISITING ASIA IN 1948

With stopovers at Frankfurt, London, Paris, Brussels and Delhi I went in mid-1948 to Bangkok for a Foreign Service conference on the situation in Southeast Asia. My three or four days at Delhi were spent with Patricia's parents. Henry Grady was then Ambassador to India.

Dramatic changes had taken place on the subcontinent since I had been there three years earlier. Britain had liquidated its Indian Empire, yielding sovereignty to two new states, India and Pakistan. Gandhi had been assassinated by a Hindu fanatic. Nehru, no longer a leader of subversion, and out of jail, was Prime Minister of India. Mountbatten had moved from being Supreme Allied Commander, South East Asia, to being the last Viceroy of India, and then the ceremonial Governor General of an independent India within the Commonwealth. And Jinnah was his opposite number in Pakistan.

The Gradys took me to a reception at the Gymkhana Club given by the Foreign Minister. "It was a different scene from what we knew," I wrote Patricia, "no uniforms, a diplomatic corps, few familiar faces among the throng of Indians. Nehru was there, beautiful, all in white—thinking other things when with the Ambassador and me; attentive and animated with Mrs. Grady." She had a faculty for empathizing, had joined the Gandhi funeral procession on foot. "There is no question that your mama is a smash hit with the Indians." The Ambassador had in his dealings with Delhi officials "spoken a few homely truths to them, which he worries over having done. I tell him not to fret—no American Ambassador can be universally liked, he represents too much power."

I saw Nehru twice again—at a Grady reception and a farewell function for the Mountbattens at the megalithic edifice which had been the Viceroy's "house." Both times his thoughts were veiled by charm. As for Lord Louis, he had been under great strain for more than a year, managing the division of India and the transfer of authority to the two new governments, accompanied by the migration of millions of Hindus and Muslims and the murder of hundreds of thousands in communal rioting. Now in a few days he would return to Britain. In a white dinner jacket he moved about in the crowd repeating pleasantries. I congratulated him and wished him well and he was conventionally gracious.

The Bangkok conference was attended by representatives from most Foreign Service posts in Southeast Asia and from China and India. The center of concern was the problem which had so occupied me during the war years—the colonial issue. Although it had been disposed of in India, colonialism had now become further complicated elsewhere in the region by the growth of Communism. I drew on the proceedings at the conference for a subsequent S/P paper on Southeast Asia.

From Bangkok I went to Java. There I saw my brother, sister-in-law, Martha Anne, and my parents, who were on their way from China to the United States. Donald was serving as Vice Consul at Batavia, now Jakarta.

Indonesia in late June 1948 was an inflamed and festering example of the colonial problem. This stemmed from the resistance of Indonesian nationalists to Dutch attempts to reimpose Netherland sovereignty over the archipelago following Japan's surrender. As negotiations alternated with fighting, the nationalist attitude hardened and became more radical. I summed up the situation in a memorandum written on the day before my departure, saying of the Dutch, "Their pride, their stubbornness, their folly in attempting to recreate a lost past in the Netherland East Indies are proving to be their undoing."

At Singapore, the American naval liaison officer took me to meet the Sultan of Johore. His Highness had several palaces, as I wrote to Patricia.

But he doesn't live in them. He lives in a quite modest country house with one sentry at the gate and one doorman. He met us at the door, six feet, big, paunchy, rotund Malay features, gray hair. He is, I think, 74 and his

Rumanian wife (No. 3) is in her thirties. He was dressed in khaki shorts, khaki ventilated shirt open at the throat and a reddish brown cotton jacket. We went into his overstuffed drawing room, displaying the shoddiest aspects of Malay and Rumanian taste, festooned with portraits of himself and Her Highness. Commander Smith and I had stengahs [Scotch & soda] and HH a Coca Cola because his second wife was Scotch and ran away with someone else. He was in an agitated frame of mind because of the Chinese Commie terrorists now on the rampage in Malaya—not for his safety but because of an economic disruption . . . I didn't get to meet Her Lupescu Highness; she was off playing golf, having been at an All Malay Sultans' Ball until 4:30 am.

Commander Smith then drove me to Bukit Serene.

Bukit means hill. And Serene means serene. It was built by the Sultan for the faithless Scotswoman. He abandoned it along with whiskey when deserted. It is now the residence of Malcolm MacDonald, Commissioner General for the U.K. in Southeast Asia. The place looks as if it had come out of Snow White and the Seven Dwarfs and made of butterscotch and rock candy. But it is very big, very comfortable and the great reception room and verandah command one of the most irenic vistas in the world—down a verdant slope to a panorama of estuaries, inlets, bays and low, distant, gently undulating hills stretching to infinity. It was sunset and the scene was visibly changing every second. I found it difficult to concentrate on conversation with the charming, unpretentious and intelligent Mr. MacD.

In India, where independence had been granted, the dominant problems were economic development and still smoldering animosity between Hindus and Muslims. In Indonesia, the issue was independence. In Malaya it was, most pressingly, Communist insurgency. As it agitated the Sultan of Johore, it was the main topic of conversation that evening at Bukit Serene. The Communists, principally ethnic Chinese, were operating from jungle bases. The British troops found this jungle guerrilla warfare frustrating.

MacDonald questioned an Englishman, also a guest, who had been in Borneo for many years, asking him for suggestions as how to deal with the guerrillas. The old Borneo-hand recommended the recruitment of Dayaks from the Borneo bush. British soldiers were handicapped in jungle warfare by boots and gear. Barefoot Dayaks could slip through the rain forests, more than a match for the insurgents. MacDonald's reaction was open-minded interest. But the Communists were not destined to be suppressed by wild men from Borneo. Years later they were reduced to the dimensions of a nuisance by less romantic means, by a continuation of military, political and economic measures isolating and decimating them. They were, however, not eradicated.

"The dawn departure from Singapore by this flying boat took us," I wrote Patricia on July 3,

along a stretch of the swampy Malay coast. It was the beginning of the world, the dawn of creation—the diffused pale gray light, the thin drifting mists like Benaras silk across the face of swamp and sea, vapors and algae. On our way to Batavia we were so high and the late morning sun was so forthright that the scene had sharp definition. But this time we were in the midst of trailing wispy mist and close to the globular jungle, so moist, so lush as to look like dark green mold—the beginning of living matter.

Next we were over cobalt waters indenting deeply and with manifold convolutions the coastline of Indochina. We have passed over handsome Camranh Bay. The hills are mouse brown-gray, the muddy rivers are flanked by green rice and there are long stretches of bright tawny beach. Squat little islands rise abruptly from the sea like turtles with their backs out of water.

I am impressed by the persistent fecundity and vitality of the Chinese. No city teems like Hong Kong. Calcutta may be as thickly crowded as this, but so many of the human organisms there are limp or inert. Along the waterfront the sampan people are loading or unloading, going ashore or going aboard. On the streets they're going somewhere or coming from somewhere. I did see one scene of real placidity—eight babies and toddlers with mothers, sitting, crawling or dozing on the sidewalk. Babies are everywhere, in the shops, on the sidewalks and on the streets—and, of course, at all hours, and all being coddled, petted and cooed at.

Inexplicably I was invited to the Filipino Consul's reception on the anniversary of Philippine independence.

He was a nice little man in dress costume, which consisted of pale beach pants, a white cotton shirt, suspenders and over it all a transparent embroidered shirt. There was a covey of nervous little Filipino women in their fluffy outfits and I drank successively beer, gimlets and champagne. The Governor arrived; the Consul made a stirring but inaudible speech about freedom and toasted the King. H.E. then spoke about how pleased the older nations were to have the Philippines (pronounced as a conifer) now one of them and toasted the President of the Philip-Pines. A Filipino band, composite of cabaret orchestras, then went to town for dancing and everyone— especially the Filipinos—relaxed and had a good time.

July Fourth was celebrated by the American Consul General on July 5. At his reception, with the honor-bound glass of champagne in my hand ready for a toast to Harry S. Truman, I was given a cable from Washington that Patricia had given birth to Patricia Florence Davies. Born on July 4th in George Washington's hometown, our little firecracker could hardly have been a more certified American. Harry Truman could wait. I had my own private toast to sip.

*   *   *

What should American policy be toward Southeast Asia? This was the question to which I sought an answer after my return from that area.

About the area as a whole I made some generalizations. Among them were that, militarily "its indigenous offensive strength is insignificant, but its native defensive capabilities are great in terms of guerrilla warfare. Politically, democratic governments are far in the future of Southeast Asia. If SEA countries are to attain stability, they must for the foreseeable future be governed despotically, whether benevolently or otherwise. While the demands of native leaders for freedom from foreign domination are in part motivated by nationalist aspirations, they are also inspired by a desire themselves to dominate and exploit their own people."

On the issue of whether to grant a colonial country independence before it is ready for self-government, I wrote, "the question of whether a colonial country is fit to govern itself, however, has little validity in practical politics. The real issue would seem to be whether the colonial country has the capability of making continued foreign rule a losing proposition for the metropolitan power. If it does, then the colonial country is ready for self-government—whatever its state of political maturity."

"The six million Chinese in SEA constitute a minority problem afflict-ing the entire region," resisting assimilation, outdoing the natives as busi-nessmen and financiers, remitting wealth back to China and are generally feared as a potential fifth column. The overseas Chinese provided the Chi-nese Communists with ready access to Southeast Asia. Moscow seemed to have allowed the Chinese Communists to take the lead in developing Southeast Asian Communism because the region "has been heretofore of minor strategic importance to the USSR."

> *However, this is no longer the case. The Soviet horizon has expanded and the CCP has waxed alarmingly in strength. For the same reason that Mos-cow lashed out against Titoism, it may entertain long-range misgivings over the very nationalist feelings which Communism aggravated and ex-ploited in colonial countries. For the same reason that Moscow opposed a Balkan federation, it must disapprove CCP hegemony over SEA Communism.*
>
> *Finally, a word of warning . . . about winning SEA to our side in the struggle against the USSR . . . it must be remembered that anti-white sentiments are profound and widespread in SEA. Fundamentally, the peo-ple of SEA have at this stage little interest in the struggle between the US and the USSR. It is to them a remote conflict between two white titans. They would resist obvious Russian imperialism as vigorously as they have fought and continue to fight Western democratic domination. They will tend naturally to gravitate toward the power which benefits them more and shows the greater strength, provided that it does not menace what they consider to be their vital interests.*

The two alarmingly problematic countries were Indonesia and Indo-china. The two emaciated imperial governments, the Dutch in Indonesia and the French in Indochina, had failed in purblind efforts to reimpose themselves on these former colonies. In mid-1948 they were maneuvering clumsily, militarily and politically, to retain as much authority as they could.

In the case of Indonesia, my estimate was that "if the Dutch resort to force, whether in collaboration with their puppets or independently, they will involve themselves in long guerrilla warfare which will be economically ruinous and politically damaging to them, and which will give encourage-ment to extremists and Communist elements who are likely thereupon to replace the present relatively moderate republican leadership." Therefore the United States should favor negotiations then in progress whereby the Dutch would promise to transfer authority to a sovereign Indonesia which would voluntarily join in the creation of a Netherlands-Indonesian Union. "If no solution can be promptly reached through negotiations, the US should take under serious consideration recognition of the [Indonesian] Republic."

The American government had been and was more concerned over policy toward Indochina than toward Indonesia. Roosevelt had opposed the resumption of French sovereignty over Indochina, but shortly before his death seemed to have weakened in this resolve. The State Department was split on the issue. Those dealing with Southeast Asia tended to favor recognition of indigenous nationalist aspirations. The European-oriented officials, who were not only in the majority but also in the senior positions, leaned toward support of French imperial ambition. They did so because France was our ally and needed to get back its colonies to regain its self-esteem and sense of glory so caponized in 1940. Under Truman, the American position was that the United States would not stand in the way of French efforts to reestablish French authority in Indochina.

As Washington had ignored overtures from Mao and Chou En-lai, so it made no response to 1945 pleas from Ho Chi Minh for opening relations with the Communist front organization he led, the Viet Minh.

My 1948 analysis was that

the Indochina situation is in an advanced stage of deterioration. The Communists have captured control of the nationalist movement . . . they are using nationalism to oppose the French in a well-organized, disciplined and militant manner. The French have been defeated at every turn in their attempts through both military and political means to reimpose their rule over Indochina.

Being unwilling to negotiate with the Viet Minh regime under its Communist leader, Ho Chi Minh, the French are currently attempting to establish an Indochinese regime composed of native collaborators . . . Even if the French achieve apparent success, this is likely to be short-lived. Only a prompt grant of real sovereignty can have any prospect of success against a regime so dynamic and well-organized as the Viet Minh.

If instead of seeking a real solution the French are niggardly and dilatory, there is every prospect that the Viet Minh regime will continue to

control the situation making the French position even more untenable than
it is at present.

Committed as the American government was to France and, by extension, to its self-destructive attempt to prove its national virility, there was
little that I could practically recommend as American policy. Recognition
of the Viet Minh, as recognition of the Chinese Communists, would have
made *realpolitik* sense, including the creation of an Asian balance of power
advantageous to the United States. But in 1948 this was in both cases not
feasible for domestic political reasons in the United States. Nor was Washington, aquiver with activist compulsion, a sense of mission and gnawing
anxieties over monolithic Communism, able to adopt a quiet, neutral position. Therefore my recommendation was pap:

> *The US should continue to press the French to make a prompt and gener-*
> *ous offer of sovereignty to the Yuan-Bao Dai regime [collaborating with*
> *the French]. The US, however, should remain strictly aloof from negotia-*
> *tions between the two parties. If the collaborationist regime is established,*
> *the US should grant it recognition only when it is evident that a majority*
> *of the independent states of Asia will do so. If the Yuan-Bao Dai regime*
> *collapses and there is no prospect of the establishment of a truly nationalist*
> *regime through unaided French efforts, the US should take such steps as*
> *appear to be practicable at that time.*

I do not recall what effect if any my views in this Southeast Asia paper
had on the Department. I do remember that the contest between those
dealing with Western Europe and the embattled few arguing for an understanding of the Southeast Asian case—outstandingly Abbot Moffat and
Charlton Ogburn—continued as the Dutch finally came to an agreement
with the Indonesians and the French embroiled themselves even more disastrously in Indochina. As for Washington, ignoring the alternatives of
realpolitik and neutrality, it drifted and lurched toward miasmal involvement of the American people in Indochina.

CHAPTER XXVI

"THE MOST NEFARIOUS CAMPAIGN OF HALF-TRUTHS AND UNTRUTH IN THE HISTORY OF THE REPUBLIC"

With her command of Estonian, Russian, German, French and English, Valli found a position in the Library of Congress. We maintained contact with her then and after she married John Shannon, becoming thereby a Foreign Service wife, living in unexpected places, winning friends wherever she went and finally retiring tastily in Tennessee on Apple Pie Farm.

John Grady Davies was born on January 3, 1950. After sizing up his robust frame and nature, his mother and I concluded that we needed help. So we turned to the priest, the batushka, of the Russian Orthodox Church in Washington, but not for solace and spiritual guidance. Rather, knowing that he tended not only the religious but also the temporal needs of his flock, Patricia inquired whether, perchance, he knew of any displaced person willing to accept domestic employment.

And so it was that Vladimir Maliev, coming from across the Potomac in Washington, arrived for an interview. As he knew no English, the batushka had placed him in a taxi with instructions to the driver to deliver him to our house in Alexandria.

Vladimir had no sooner introduced himself to Patricia than the taxi driver came to the door with a brown paper bag that his passenger had forgotten. Vladimir explained to Patricia, "Hleb na dorogu"—bread for the road—and opened the bag revealing a loaf of bread. But of course, starting off on a journey of unknown distance and duration, the prudent traveler over steppe and tundra provisions himself with emergency victuals.

Vladimir was a Cossack, fortyish and trim of figure. His outstanding features were his spreading moustache and his aplomb. Yes, he and his wife, Anushka, would accept employment. She was to help care for the children and he, rather vaguely, was to help around the house.

To get away from the house, Vladimir would wheel young John, then three months old, in a perambulator up and down Duke Street. As he did so he addressed the infant in parade tones:

> Ivan Ivanoushka,
> Ruski Tsarevich,
> Romanov Cossack!

We soon became a station on an underground railroad for several of Vladimir's Russian refugee friends, this time escaping servitude on American farms. They claimed that they had been exploited by the American who had sponsored their entry into the United States. Unhappily, there seemed to have been some truth in their complaints. We sped these bewildered displaced persons on their way to whom else but the batushka.

Life as a domestic was not for Vladimir. His unfettered spirit yearned for free enterprise on his own spread. Through the incomprehensible brotherhood of Russian displaced persons he learned of and negotiated the acquisition of a strawberry patch on the banks of the Potomac near Mount Vernon. Our cautionary advice was disregarded. Vladimir and Anushka, after two months with us, left without ceremony for their strawberry homestead on what, perhaps, was once a part of General Washington's plantations.

Again the batushka came to what might be described as our rescue. This time it was with Pavel and Agrafina Yakovlev. Pavel was a stolid Latvian in, probably, his sixties, who had been an imperial guardsman at St. Petersburg in the days of the Tsar. This couple lasted stodgily with us into 1951. Then their daughter was taken in marriage by a rich, they said, Balt who had made good in New England. He had advertised for an unspoiled Baltic maiden without pretensions. The daughter apparently met specifications. Naturally, Pavel and Agrafina promptly took leave of us to move in with the newly-weds.

*   *   *

Of the various shocks to the American people during the five postwar years, three direful developments occurred in the short span of four months. The Soviet Union unexpectedly exploded a nuclear device, signaling the start of a race in weapons of mass destruction. The American government then raised the rivalry to another dimension by a decision to produce thermonuclear weapons. Second, the Chinese Nationalists fled to Formosa and the Communists established a new Government of China. Third, Alger Hiss, the very model of the privileged, trusted bureaucrat, was convicted of perjury for having denied that he had passed secret documents to Whittaker Chambers for transmittal to a Communist espionage ring, whereupon the Secretary of State, Dean Acheson, in an unguarded outburst of Christian compassion (Matthew 25: 34–46) declared at a press conference that he would not turn his back on Alger Hiss.

The setting was consequently laid for ever more accusations of betrayal. The popular and respected *Saturday Evening Post*, in its issue of January 7, 1950 featured two articles. One was the first of a series of three articles by Joseph Alsop entitled "Why We Lost China." (The other, incidentally and also in the mood of the time, was "How You Can Survive an Atomic Blast.") While serving as aide to General Chennault, Alsop had been a passionate protagonist of the Air Corps General in the Chennault-Stilwell feud. He was also an ardent admirer of T. V. Soong, whom he classified as one of the "modern" Chinese who were the country's only hope against a Communist takeover.

Before publication of the series, Alsop pressed me to read and comment on the manuscript. Not wishing to entangle myself futilely in what I expected to be a slashing attack on Stilwell and me, I declined his invitation.

In the lead article, Alsop opened with a broadside. "Throughout the fateful years in China, the American representatives there actively favored the Chinese communists. They also contributed to the weakness, both political and military, of the National Government. And in the end they came close to offering China up to the communists, like a trussed bird on a platter, over four years before the eventual communist triumph. . . .

"The present study is the story of the American complicity in China's political decay, and that of the American attempt to bring the communists to power."

The burden of Alsop's article was that Stilwell's hatred of and insubordination toward Chiang, his working with reactionary Nationalist elements, together with his and his political advisers' disregard of the "Modernists" and partiality toward the Communists, combined to bring the Communists to power. He asserted that if the "Modernists" had received "reasonable American support [they] would have defeated the communists in the end." Parenthetically, because I have not commented elsewhere on this Alsopian thesis, I might say at this juncture that it never seemed plausible to me. Alsop's "Modernists" were few, disparate, unorganized and politically no match for either the old guard surrounding Chiang or the Communists, even had the "Modernists" coalesced and received extensive American support.

Stilwell, I and probably Service and Ludden, according to Alsop, concocted a scheme whereby Chiang was to be pressed to form a coalition with the Communists. Second, American diplomatic relations, in effect, were to be established with the Communists by dispatching an observers mission to Yenan. Third, supreme command over all Chinese armies, including the Communist, was to be sought for Stilwell. Finally, Stilwell was to be authorized to apportion American aid between the Nationalists and the Communists.

Alsop's reconstruction of past positions was faulty. Preoccupied with military matters, Stilwell gave little thought to the uncertain theory of coalition. I do not recall ever having heard him discuss the subject. I favored a coalition to the extent that it seemed preferable to a ravaging civil war. But I doubted that a coalition could be realized because the two sides were irreconcilable. And I assumed that the Communists would win, whether by takeover from within a coalition or by force in a civil war.

Stilwell looked benevolently on the establishment of the Observer Group at Yenan, but played no active part in its creation. And it was little more than an observation post. Overtures to the American government by Mao and Chou and forwarded to Washington by Service and me while with the Group did not elicit the slightest reaction. This was a long way from diplomatic relations between Washington and Yenan.

As for seeking supreme command for Stilwell over all Chinese armies, I had always doubted that Stilwell, or any foreigner, could exercise command over Chinese forces in China.

I opposed open-handed granting of aid to China—and the Soviet Union. My recommendations were that aid should be used to bargain for concessions that we sought. And the distribution of assistance belonged with the American commander in China who, by his position, was best qualified to determine whether the aid was being used for the purpose for which it had been granted—prosecution of the war against Japan—or was being horded or expended in factional strife. Aid should be given, I said, to whatever forces—Government, provincial or Communist—which contributed most to the war against Japan; but we would not supply any element that showed an inclination toward precipitating civil conflict. In this context, I thought that Stilwell should have the authority to apportion aid between the Government and the Communists—or to withhold it from both.

After Stilwell's recall in October 1944, according to Alsop, the political advisors persisted in advocating that China be treated like Yugoslavia, that the American government abandon Chiang as the Allies had Mikhailovich and support the Chinese Communists as the Allies had backed Tito. Alsop charged that implementation of this policy would have brought the Communists to power some four years before their eventual triumph. This formulation of at least my position was premature. While I anticipated an imminent need to establish working relations with the Communists, I wrote shortly before leaving China on transfer to Moscow that "We should not now abandon Chiang Kai-shek."

However, Alsop continued, our "emotional bias," presumably against Chiang and company and in favor of the Communists, was indefensible. This, together with the Stilwell-Chiang feud, "prevented any serious exploitation of our opportunity to glue together a workable Chinese government." And the emotional bias, Alsop asserted, was maintained at the State Department nearly to the time of the Nationalist collapse.

Having helped to launch in the mid-1940s the calumnies against certain of us in the China service, Alsop began in 1950—as evident in the *Saturday Evening Post* series—to qualify his attack. Perhaps because of the excesses of the China Lobby and the China bloc in Congress he shifted after the first two *Saturday Evening Post* articles from rhetorical assault to defense of me. In his syndicated column on January 23, he referred to "the attempt, now going on in the Congress and the radio, to prove that there was some sort of pro-Communist plot in the State Department. There was no such plot." Alsop then said that I "astutely foresaw the possibility of Titoism when no Russian expert believed it possible." My "policy was simply to promote Titoism in China . . . a perfectly respectable policy."

Others were less discriminating. Ivan Peterman, in the January 11 *Philadelphia Inquirer*, described me as "Stilwell's pro-Red advisor" and as a "tool of the Chinese Commies."

Freda Utley, she of combative ideological oscillations, who in 1937 at Hankow championed the Chinese Communists as like nineteenth-century English radicals, now in 1950 agitated fiercely against them in her role as a leading activist of the China Lobby. In *The China Story*, advancing the theory of the pro-Communist conspiracy in the State Department, she charged that the "Davies-Service clique" had almost complete control over military and civilian reports from China to Washington. We also exercised, according to Miss Utley, a quasi-monopoly in the formation of United States policy.

＊　＊　＊

A relatively obscure Senator on February 9, 1950, at Wheeling, West Virginia, proclaimed that "While I cannot take the time to name all the men in the State Department who have been named as members of the Communist Party and members of a spy ring, I have here in my hand a list of 205 that were known to the Secretary of State as being members of the Communist Party and who, nevertheless, are still working and shaping policy in the State Department." This was Joseph P. McCarthy, heedless of the truth, in eager search of a theme that would bring him into the national limelight and win him votes back in Wisconsin.

Press reaction on the following day was scant. But for a week McCarthy repeated, revised and embellished his accusations and taunted Acheson and Truman. The press found the Senator's effrontery to be irresistible. His lies and distortions became front-page news and he a celebrity, precisely what he wanted.

McCarthy's reckless, relentless demagoguery angered the Democrats, who at first underestimated the Senator and then came to fear him. Most Republican politicians initially were wary of their junior Senator from Wisconsin because they recognized him as a mountebank and thought that he would be exposed as such. But then, as they observed McCarthy's brash sensationalism featured in the press and radio, winning public support and putting the Democrats on the defensive, they aligned themselves, with few exceptions, with the fearsome McCarthy, even as they sometimes murmured tut-tut at his tactics.

The bureaucracy reacted variously. Some bureaucrats become McCarthy's fellow travelers, from apologists to collaborators. Many, however, were uncomfortable with or disapproving of the Senator's roving fusillades. And those of us who were his targets were apprehensive, listening to the radio, scanning the headlines at newsstands for reports that McCarthy had again stigmatized one or all of us as disloyal and, by implication, traitorous.

Reacting to McCarthy's denunciations a fortnight after the Wheeling speech, Senate Democrats initiated the creation of a Foreign Relations subcommittee, headed by Senator Millard Tydings, to investigate "whether persons who are disloyal to the United States, are, or have been, employed by the Department of State." The hearings lasted four months and served McCarthy as an amplifier of his flummery.

Owen Lattimore was McCarthy's principal prey on this occasion. A professor at Johns Hopkins University, Lattimore was the outstanding western scholar on Mongolia, Manchuria and Central Asia. During the war he had been a deputy director of the Office of War Information. My connection with him was slight. I had first met him in Peking when I was a language attaché at the legation. I later encountered him two or three times in Washington and Chungking. In the 1930s I plodded through two of his scholarly works, one on Manchuria, the other on Mongolia.

In testimony before the Tydings subcommittee, McCarthy accused Lattimore of being the top Russian spy in the United States and the key man in a Soviet espionage ring. The Senator then declared that a passage from my memoranda, published in the White Paper, expressed a point of view akin to Lattimore's as revealed in his wartime writing. Thus I was linked to an alleged Soviet spy ring.

With little background knowledge of Communism, the Soviet Union and China, McCarthy derived his opinions from reformed Communists and other zealous Red-hunters. His inspiration for tying me in with Lattimore appears to have come from that ideological quick-change artist, Freda Utley. Miss Utley testified before the Tydings subcommittee that I would not acknowledge that the Chinese Communists were under Moscow's orders, that my published reports and those of Service resembled the writings of Lattimore and that we therefore belonged to "the Lattimore school."

She did not agree with McCarthy that the professor was a spymaster. Rather, she asserted, that he was more important than a spy—he was a master molder of opinion. General Marshall, she charged, had been dependent upon the State Department's China specialists in formulating and conducting a disastrous postwar China policy. But the advice that he purportedly received from us had been concocted, she insisted, by Lattimore. To McCarthy and his tutor, I was in one fashion or another a part of a conspiratorial pro-Communist cabal.

This attribution of conspiracy dominated the offensive by the China Lobby and the China bloc in Congress against certain of us in the Foreign Service. Some educators and journalists were also branded as involved in the alleged conspiracy. Among the former was, as we have seen, Lattimore and, later, John K. Fairbank of Harvard. And Utley told the Tydings subcommittee that Theodore White was one of the "pro-Communist" journalists.

Thus because various Americans in varying degrees concluded that Chiang's Kuomintang was decadent and that the Chinese Communists were a virile, rising force, the China Lobbyists and their confederates charged those Americans with disloyal collusion. The accusations were, in effect, that what we independently reported and predicted was what we willed and plotted to bring about. Hurley had presaged this perversion when Teddy White and I had separately warned him that the Communists would not readily acquiesce to the Chinese Government's terms for national unification. Hurley reacted to our attempts to help him by charging us with working against his self-appointed mission.

McCarthy and his supporting witnesses failed to prove disloyalty in the State Department. In the subcommittee's final report, the Democratic majority concluded that McCarthy's charges were "a fraud and a hoax" representing "perhaps the most nefarious campaign of half-truths and untruth in the history of the Republic." The report also asserted that "For the first time in our history, we have seen the totalitarian technique of the 'big lie' employed on a sustained basis."

Condemnation did not faze McCarthy. Nor, more importantly, was the American public disabused of its suspicions of the State Department and its China specialists.

*   *   *

In his red hunt before the Tydings subcommittee, McCarthy did not fail to tally-ho Jack Service. The Senator's charge was the by then familiar one that

Service had in 1945 passed classified documents to the editor of *Amerasia*, a monthly magazine dealing primarily with Asian affairs. A grand jury had unanimously, 20–0, exonerated Service. But McCarthy insisted that Jack's incautious briefing of a journalist, whom he took to be reputable, was espionage.

Following McCarthy's testimony, and in the third month of the subcommittee's investigation, Service was summoned to a hearing before the State Department's Loyalty Security Board. On the second day of the proceedings, May 26, I appeared as a witness on Jack's behalf. The chairman of the three-man board was Conrad E. Snow, a highly respected New Hampshire lawyer who had served in both world wars, attaining the rank of brigadier general. The two other members of the board were a conservative, judicious Foreign Service officer, Theodore C. Achilles, and Arthur G. Stevens, a State Department official with broad experience in the government. The hearing, held in a plain small room in the Department, was businesslike, to the point and free of legal histrionics and chicanery.

The Board probed persistently Service's and my briefing of the press. The genesis of the practice, I explained, was Stilwell's recognition that "in a democratic society . . . public opinion is necessary for the support of the war effort . . . He felt that the American people were being misled about many of the realities in China. He felt that this made his job more difficult . . . He indicated very clearly to me that he wished me to brief the press, and, subsequently, that other members of the State Department who were detailed to his staff should do likewise." Stilwell's instructions to me were oral. Later in my testimony I indicated that I had transmitted orally to Service the General's wishes in this regard.

In response to a question from the chairman regarding our relations with the press I referred to the restraints we imposed upon ourselves in filling in newsmen. We exercised our individual judgments as to what might properly be revealed. Such matters as directives and policy guidance from the State and War Departments should not be divulged. But "the material which was reportorial about the local situations, political, social, economic—those we felt were the grist for the press mill to provide an enlightened American public . . ."

Answering further questions, I made a distinction between two types of briefing. One was information provided for background, not attributable to the briefing official or the government. A second was for attribution, in which the releasing source might be revealed. (This latter type included communiqués and official press releases issued by military press officers.) "Such information as we did give," I testified, was in all instances "given for background."

This led to the matter of classification. Some documents were classified confidential or secret only to protect the source, not the content. The chairman asked whether I might have felt free to give such information. I indicated that I might have, "Provided the source was not compromised." (A prime example of classification to protect a source was my designation of top secret to the Moscow Embassy's telegrams reporting indiscreet comments by Maxim Litvinov.)

There was I observed, "a tendency to grossly overclassify." I, too, overclassified . . . "It was epidemic." The chairman asked if, after I had classified one of my reports confidential or secret, I would later feel free to reveal of the information so classified. I answered, "That would depend entirely on my judgment of the circumstance."

Q. You wouldn't in every case didactically refer to the classification on the paper, but use your judgment as to what you reveal or not reveal?
A. Precisely, and I believe that is very much the procedure now in Washington.

The Board wished to know whether my briefing of the press for Stilwell deviated from the procedure I followed at Foreign Service posts. I described how at Mukden, under the guidance of my Consul General, I had made selected classified reports available to certain American newsmen. As at Mukden, where our confiding to the press was designed to counter the propaganda of the Japanese Army's puppet regime, so at Moscow as "operation prophylaxis for the American public on the internal situation in the Soviet Union" I permitted, under the direction of Ambassador Walter Bedell Smith, reputable American newsmen to read and take notes on assorted classified reports.

During the three weeks following this appearance before the Board, I was twice requested to return for further testimony. What were the views of the political advisers, I was asked, regarding wartime American policy in China? They were set forth in the State Department's White Paper, I replied. I then went on to quote from my wartime memoranda to the effect that in a Chinese civil war in which we supported the Nationalists, the Communists would win control of China and, forced into dependence on the Soviet Union, they would of necessity become a satellite of the Soviet Union. This would create an alignment of power in Asia unfavorable to the United States. Did Service and I agree on this interpretation? My answer was yes.

Hurley had charged that Service and other Foreign Service officers were pro-Communist, Stevens said. Did I ever hear Service say anything that would support Hurley's accusation? Foreign Service officers are pro-American, I replied, and Service evaluated the Chinese situation in terms of what was best for American interests.

Continuing, Stevens stated that Bishop Paul Yu Pin (a Chinese Catholic and busy supporter of the Nationalists) had asserted that Service had "hammered" at Stilwell to force him to make demands on Chiang to arm the Communist forces. How close was Service to Stilwell? The General had few intimates, I said, and although he was friendly to Service, Jack was not close to Stilwell. Stevens brought out through questioning me that at the time Service was alleged to have been "hammering" Stilwell, the General was, I observed, "down in the mud in Burma," while Jack was in Yenan. The bishop's charges I said were "ridiculous."

In volume, my testimony was a small fraction of that presented to the Board. What effect it may have had on the Board's findings, I do not know. Anyway, Jack was cleared. He had stood up admirably under the dual ordeals of senatorial and State Department interrogations.

John Paton Davies, Jr., was a dedicated and exemplary public servant. He was a highly experienced, learned, aware, and deeply observant Foreign Service officer—as the reader can see from this memoir, which contributes so much to our knowledge of the history of U.S. foreign relations in the 1930s and 1940s. For specialists it fills in important details and gaps in our knowledge of the period, and gives a consistently realist, hard-nosed analysis of policies toward China, India, the Soviet Union, and World War II more generally, especially in the China-Burma-India theater. For generalists it sheds much light on history and on a man whose name exemplifies the lost opportunities of the McCarthy era.

Davies clearly was one of the very best Foreign Service officers this country has produced. That his political biography should have been written by a discredited demagogue, a disgrace to the U.S. Senate, is one of the many lasting tragedies of the McCarthy era. Paradoxically, though, Senator Joseph McCarthy's ignominious attacks may have the result of drawing readers to this book.

Davies had a full life before the 1950s, with truly exciting experiences in countries few Americans had ever visited, let alone studied, yielding a wealth of unusual experience and memorable anecdotes. Any number of famous figures from the 1930s and 1940s appear in these pages, with finely honed impressions of them by the author. Franklin Delano Roosevelt is the most prominent, and Davies clearly thought him little more than a politician, if a highly accomplished one, and a naïf about world affairs—but then FDR always ignored the State Department and Foreign Service. This is the opposite of a stuffy diplomat's memoir—Davies is a fine writer, and manages to do what others would like to do: tell the truth about their superiors, like Ambassadors Clarence Gauss or Hurley, or the priggish Stanley Horn-beck, with wit and aplomb and a certain dry, indirect style that is most effective. Even the memoranda that he prepared for the State Department, ordinarily not the stuff of riveting reading, come to life as we see Davies cull them and comment on them in hindsight.

Davies worked on this autobiography, off and on, for twenty years. It was left unfinished at his death, with only the last chapter capturing the opening moments of McCarthy and McCarthyism. The reader longs to hear him comment on his experience in the 1950s. He had many axes to grind, but the only one he hones in this book is reserved for Patrick Hurley, his ambassador and nemesis—and everything he says about Hurley strikes me as accurate. Hurley was an oil man from Oklahoma who knew nothing about China; Secretary of State Dean Acheson once said that "trouble moved with him like a cloud of flies around a steer."[1] For historians Davies's omission of the early 1950s is unfortunate; it would be fascinating to see his fine mind turned to one of the darkest periods in American history. When George Kennan returned to Washington in 1947 from Moscow to be the head of policy planning in the State Department, the first person he asked to join him was Davies. In 1948 Secretary of State General George C. Marshall awarded the Medal of Freedom to him, then aged forty, for his service in China and India during the war. For four years Davies was near the top of an office central to the development of postwar American foreign policy, in perhaps the most critical period in the country's history as communism spread over half the globe and the Soviets acquired the atomic bomb.

On June 27, 1951, however, Davies was handed a long letter detailing what the author, General Conrad E. Snow, chairman of the State Department's Loyalty Security Board, thought was evidence of Davies's disloyalty to his country. Included in "Charge No. 1: . . . you were bitterly anti-Chiang Kai-shek and Nationalist Government. . . ." Chiang's backers in the United States had finally succeeded in getting even with the man who correctly foretold the Nationalist loss of the civil war. It is not irrelevant that the Nationalists spread huge amounts of money around Washington during this period—to journalists, magazines, and all too many politicians. Kennan said at the time that the Nationalist government had "intrigued in this country in a manner scarcely less disgraceful to it than to ourselves."[2] When Davies asked for the names of those who had made accusations against him and for a forum in which he could personally confront them, he was denied.

"Charge No. 11" linked the Foreign Service with academe and with alleged communists, accusing Davies of having "close and habitual association" with, among others, Anna Louise Strong, Agnes Smedley, and John King Fairbank (that is, two radical feminists and a professor at Harvard). The reader already knows the nature of Davies's association with Smedley and Strong, the former an early and archetypal radical woman who first distinguished herself politically in the Seattle General Strike of 1919, the latter a classic "fellow traveler" who looked and acted the part, and the last the father of the field of modern Chinese history in the United States. This is pure guilt by association in the slender confines of the "American community" in China, which in the places Davies served could often be numbered on the fingers of one hand. Get a few Americans together at the Consulate in Hankow, and an eclectic group of adventurers are likely to show up. Professor Fairbank encouraged dissent from U.S. policy toward East Asia in the 1960s and always had an open mind about his students' work, but he was anything but a radical and had been badly singed by McCarthyism (he was reduced to assuring his inquisitors that he believed in free enterprise capitalism), which in turn intimidated much of the East Asian field in the United States for a generation and longer.

Here was the flimsy evidential basis for eight security investigations Davies suffered, including an abrupt reassignment in 1953 from Germany to Lima, Peru, as a Counselor to the Embassy. Still no evidence of disloyalty to his country could be found—and so the ninth inquiry looked into his "judgment, discretion and reliability." In November 1954, Secretary of State Dulles seized on this first negative finding, in the ninth investigation, and in a true profile in cowardice (widely recognized as such at the time) he terminated Davies's State Department career—while offering to write a recommendation for him for future employment. Davies had refused to resign, or to retire with his pension, and now needed a job (the one thing Dulles got right).

It is this other part of Davies's life—the years that followed his dismissal from the Foreign Service—that the reader also longs to know about. Davies went back to Lima and spent the better part of the following year exploring options for employment—journalism, international business, soup factory (yes, a soup factory), lumber exporting, but finally settled on making furniture. Although a novice to this trade, he quickly gained expertise, winning international design awards for his furniture crafted from exotic tropical woods found in the Amazon. His custom furniture company, Estilo s.a.

("Style") expanded, creating monoprints inspired by Pre-Columbian designs. These prints and wall hangings were sold to private collectors and hotels, but the earnings from the business were "feast or famine" as Davies later reported to one of his daughters.

While visiting friends in Mexico in 1955, Patricia suffered a terrible car accident that hurled her through the vehicle's windshield. Although her injuries were serious and required extensive recuperation, both she and Davies approached what had happened with the same steadfastness they had demonstrated in their prior struggles with McCarthy.

Deciding that his children needed to experience the culture and community of the United States, and finding that the union situation in Peru was undermining any chance of Estilo being successful, Davies and his wife moved their large family, including their dachshund, to Washington, D.C., in 1964. At this time he had been writing a Sunday column for *La Prensa*, the liberal Peruvian newspaper owned and run by his good friend, former prime minister of Peru Pedro Beltrán. George Brockway, publisher of W.W. Norton, approached him about writing a series of essays about world affairs, which was then published as *Foreign and Other Affairs*.

Five years later, in 1969, amid the failure in Vietnam and the falling out among foreign policy elites over what to do about it, he finally succeeded, at the age of sixty, in getting his security clearance restored—but not his job, and very little of his pension. (The story of the Democratic administration's rather pusillanimous clearing of him—just for security reasons, not reinstating him—is recounted by John Finney in the August 31, 1969, *New York Times Magazine*.)

With money tight, Davies and his wife decided to move once again, this time pulling up stakes and venturing to Málaga, Spain. While there he published his second book, *Dragon by the Tail: American, British, Japanese and Russian Encounters with China and One Another*. He also during this period wrote several articles for the Sunday *New York Times Magazine*, including an analysis of the political situtation in Portugal. During the summers in Spain, the family would become gypsies, traveling to different European capitals.

After a sojourn in Paris and rural England, the family moved to Asheville, North Carolina, in 1979, where Davies worked on this memoir. He died on December 23, 1999. Five months later, Patricia, who had developed oral cancer in 1983, with a number of reoccurrences over the subsequent seventeen years, died on May 28, 2000. She had always said, once John died, her job was done. Part of that job included a legacy in the form of 7 children and 12 grandchildren.

*   *   *

Few would know that John Paton Davies, Jr., had an artillery battery's worth of ammunition to defend himself against McCarthy's inquisition in memos he wrote for the State Department in 1949–1950, memos that clearly place him on the conservative side of U.S. foreign policy toward East Asia. Among the more mystifying episodes in this period is the rise of Republican critiques of President Harry Truman's Cold War policy of containment, which was denounced as passive when it wasn't called appeasement. The alternative for much of the right wing, including General Douglas MacArthur and Dulles, was "liberation" or "rollback": moving toward "positive action" against world communism, as Dulles always put it. And in a twist of historical irony, one of the first rollback documents surfaced within the State Department in the late summer of 1949, and penned by none other than John Paton Davies, Jr.

This is a much harder phenomenon to explain, because it does not begin to fit the labels and symbols with which Americans thought about their politics. The rollback strategy emerged within the government not just among people who can be labeled "rightists." This policy of liberation had its only significant application during the Korean War, when Truman and his secretary of state, Dean Acheson, decided to invade North Korea in the fall of 1950, trying to roll back communism and topple the North Korean regime. John Foster Dulles, with whom most historians associate the term rollback, was in fact a centrist seeking to channel and constrain raucous rollback constituencies in the Republican Party. (He was an advocate of the march into the North, but when it turned into a catastrophe in December 1950, he secretly told many people, including Richard Nixon, that rolling back existing communist regimes was out of the question, and might well lead to World War III.)

Rollback emerged as a real policy option in the course of interdepartmental deliberations leading up to NSC 48, the most important Asian policy document before the Korean War (Truman signed it at the end of 1949). An August 16, 1949, paper, one of the first in the NSC 48 series and titled

"A Survey of the Strategic Importance of Asia to the US" (top secret but unsigned and with no department of origin), inaugurated basic themes that would continue down to the final approval of the document. It dilated frequently on the necessity to take the offensive, used the term "rollback," and sought to include Taiwan in the American defense line.[3] Shortly thereafter Davies wrote to Kennan that the United States could no longer afford "to follow indefinitely a policy of avoiding risks of conflict with [the Soviets] at whatever cost to us." He thought the initiative now rested in the "reckless hands" of the communists, but that the United States could reverse that through the use of covert means, "coercion by punitive action," "coercion through a selective use of air power" (including limited airstrikes on Manchuria), and the like. Airpower, he thought, provided a better means than the outmoded gunboat diplomacy and small-scale expeditionary forces of the imperial era. He added the interesting observation that the United States "could not embark on such a course [intervention], even on a limited scale, until the Communists have so acted as to justify our retribution along the lines of this paper." Kennan so trusted Davies that in 1948 he attached him to a super-secret, tiny group charged with giving policy guidance to the CIA's new operational covert arm, the Office of Policy Coordination. This office became involved in dirty tricks and black arts, including psychological warfare operations against China in 1949.[4]

In late August 1949 a State Department review committee had produced the phrase that would later be embodied in NSC 48 (and NSC 68, the most famous document of the period) and that would symbolize the conjoining of containment and rollback. An unsigned paper on East Asia policy said the overall objective of the United States should be to establish "free and independent governments," but "the objective of the immediate policy of the United States was to *check and roll back* in the [Asian] area the threat of Soviet Communism" (emphasi added). The Communists had seized the initiative, and Washington should get it back. But this was to be liberal rollback, Kennedy-style Cold War interventionism. The United States should support Asian nationalist aspirations, help correct "social and economic disadvantages," urge states in the area "to join in a reaffirmation of the traditional policy of the 'Open Door,'" and seek multilateral instead of unilateral approaches. On China, the United States should seek every opportunity "to drive a wedge between China and the Soviet Union"; in Indochina, "steady pressure" should be brought to bear on the French "to interpret liberally" their rule.[5]

Around the same time John Davies weighed in with another rollback scheme. It called for holding offshore island points "from Hokkaido to Sumatra," but also looking beyond containment to "vigorous measures of political warfare to reduce" communism in Korea, China, and Southeast Asia, as well as building "an apparatus which will enable us to employ our and Japan's economy as an instrument of political warfare." He also began thinking about and even recommending under certain conditions a "preventive war" against the Soviet Union.[6] So Davies was thinking along the very same lines as his McCarthyite adversaries. More important, though, was the prescient way in which he anticipated strategies that Richard Nixon and Henry Kissinger would revive two decades later: As John Finney put it in his *New York Times Magazine* profile, "Davies's difficulty was that he was foresighted to the point of being prophetic. As he was to explain to [his State Department inquisitors]: 'If in our struggle with the Soviet world we are to win out without resort to war, a split in the Soviet-Chinese bloc would seem to be an essential prerequisite. Short of the overthrow of the Soviet regime, the most devastating political defeat that the U.S.S.R. could suffer would be Peking's defection from Moscow's camp.' "

That, of course, did not help him keep his security clearances within the State Department. After the Republicans came into office in 1953, it was just a matter of time until Dulles hauled him onto the carpet. In addition to the State Department's loyalty inquiries, perhaps Dulles had also read Justice Department investigations of Davies developed in 1953. It is doubtful, though, that he knew that this august Department worked with Charles Willoughby (MacArthur's intelligence chief) and Chiang Ching-guo (Chiang Kai-shek's son, with long experience in the KMT secret police) on the cases of John Davies and Owen Lattimore. Perhaps most shocking (a scandal then and now), it is now clear that the information in several of these cases was faked. (Even MacArthur did not trust Chinese Nationalist intelligence, which almost always scripted its estimates to please the Generalissimo.)[7]

The political waters darken even more when we begin to understand the extraordinary conflicts that went on at the time within the government—the FBI hated the CIA, MacArthur wanted to keep both out of his bailiwick, McCarthy thought the CIA harbored more Reds and liberals than any other agency, the CIA saw itself as an island of reason amid the bedlam of anti-communist witch hunts—and the witch hunters themselves said Davies was a Red for public consumption, but actually believed he was a

CIA agent. Bonner Fellers, part of the MacArthur entourage, frequently called for rollback policies in the 1950s, and thought the CIA harbored "a group of Marxist-Socialist pro-Communists," including Davies—whom he alleged to be on the CIA payroll even during his forced exile in Lima.[8]

McCarthyism appeared to die with the man himself in 1957, but it has had an extraordinary and lasting influence on our foreign policy.[9] Foreign Service officers reacted to the inquisition of the China hands with a cringing silence, leaving Averell Harriman (who always defended Davies and was subject to red-baiting himself)[10] to find "a disaster area filled with human wreckage" when he became head of the Bureau of Far Eastern Affairs in 1961.

The United States is still a provincial country, in spite of all its power, and it is still true that Foreign Service officers who come to know the language and culture of another country will be perceived as internal foreigners in their own land. And so the military carries out most of the tasks of empire, yielding the inane result that there are more people in the Pentagon's marching bands than in all the Foreign Service.

All fair-minded readers will come away from this book thinking, what a fine man of such remarkable experience, and what a tragic waste—what a wound to this country—to dismiss him at the height of his powers. We read this memoir and become aware of our losses.

Notes

1. Quoted in Bob Rackmales, "'Grace Under Pressure': John Paton Davies," *Foreign Service Journal* (July–August 2008): 48. The reader might also want to consult John W. Finney's useful article in the *New York Times Magazine*, "The Long Trial of John Paton Davies" (August 31, 1969). For a general account of Davies and others tarred by McCarthyism, see E. J. Kahn, *The China Hands: America's Foreign Service Officers and What Befell Them* (New York: Viking, 1975).

2. George F. Kennan Papers, box 24, memorandum on Kennan's differences with the State Department, September 1951. On Chiang's money in Washington and elsewhere—a subject still distinctly under-researched—see Bruce Cumings, *The Origins of the Korean War*, vol. 2, (Princeton, N.J.: Princeton University Press, 1990), 106–10.

3. See this document and many others in Cumings, *Origins*, vol. 2, chap. 5.

4. Davies to Kennan, Aug. 24, 1949, State Department Policy Planning Staff files, box 13. Davies's involvement with the Office of Policy Coordination is discussed in an undated memorandum from his papers at the Truman Library, provided to me by Tiki Davies. See also Finney, "The Long Trial of John Paton Davies."

5. State Department, 795.00 file, box 4267, "Tentative Findings on US Policy in the Far East," September 2, 1949.

6. Quoted in Michael Schaller, *The American Occupation of Japan: The Origins of the Cold War in Asia* (New York: Oxford University Press, 1985), 157. Davies discusses his views on preventive war in a letter to his wife, dated December 2, 1954. I am indebted to Tiki Davies for sharing this and other personal letters with me. See also Finney, "The Long Trial of John Paton Davies."

7. On the 1953 episode see Charles Willoughby Papers, box 23, John W. Jackson letters, written on Justice Department stationery to Willoughby and to Ho Shih-lai, both dated Oct. 16, 1953. The faked files are discussed in Robert P. Newman, "Clandestine Chinese Nationalist Efforts to Punish Their American Detractors," *Diplomatic History* 7, 3 (Summer 1983): 205–22.

8. See correspondence between former president Herbert Hoover and Bonner Fellers in Hoover Presidential Library, Post-Presidential File, box 328, Fellers memorandum of Jan. 1, 1953; Fellers to Hoover, Nov. 8, 1955.

9. We still live in a political milieu where anyone who can be labeled a leftist or "revisionist," or who just harbors controversial or nonmainstream views, has little or no chance of making an impact in Washington, or being hired by any Republican or Democratic administration. When I was a new graduate student in East Asian Studies at Columbia University in 1968, one of my advisers told me point blank that my antiwar activities, if they continued, would obviate any possibility of a job in Washington; he then told me that his deepest fear was a revival by the right wing of the witch hunts of the 1950s. The whole field of modern China studies was shaped by McCarthyism, and still is if we speak of specialists whose fondest desire is to advise presidents. The result is a remarkably constricted foreign policy debate inside the Beltway; people seem to arrive at their foreign policy positions along partisan lines, or with an eye to a future government position. Or they filter information and policy through presuppositions and rules of thumb that are mostly beyond examination—especially their own. Exceptions exist, of course, preeminently George Kennan, who became a prominent critic of U.S. foreign policy after he left Washington, yet continued to advise presidents. But he had the political insulation of having been the father of containment, and it is difficult to think of contemporary examples. Our country is the worse for it.

10. It is still astonishing that this son of one of America's wealthiest men was suspected by James Angleton of being a Soviet mole. Angleton, head of counter-intelligence in the CIA, thus launched "Operation Dinosaur" to smoke Harriman out.

INDEX

ACKNOWLEDGMENTS

My siblings, Sasha, John, Susan, Jennifer, Deborah, and Megan, and I would like to acknowledge the encouragement of our many friends and express our gratitude to Todd S. Purdum, Dr. Bruce Cumings, and the staff of the University of Pennsylvania Press—especially Bill Finan. And a heart-felt thank you to Michael M. Kaiser for his support and assistance throughout.

Tiki Davies